Teaching Representations of the First World War

Edited by

Debra Rae Cohen and Douglas Higbee

The Modern Language Association of America
New York 2017

Printed in the United States of America

Library of Congress Cataloging-in-Publication Data is available for this title.

Names: Cohen, Debra Rae, editor. | Higbee, Douglas, 1970- editor.
Title: Teaching representations of the First World War / edited by Debra Rae Cohen and Douglas Higbee.
Description: New York : The Modern Language Association of America, 2017. | Series: Options for teaching series ; 41 | Includes bibliographical references and index.
Identifiers: LCCN 2017016895 (print) | LCCN 2017026320 (ebook) | ISBN 9781603293068 (EPub) | ISBN 9781603293075 (Kindle) | ISBN 9781603293044 (cloth : alk. paper) | ISBN 9781603293051 (pbk. : alk. paper)
Subjects: LCSH: World War, 1914-1918--Literature and the war. | World War, 1914-1918--Study and teaching. | War in literature--Study and teaching. | War and literature--Study and teaching. | Literature, Modern--20th century--History and criticism.
Classification: LCC PN56.W66 (ebook) | LCC PN56.W66 T43 2017 (print) | DDC 809/.93358403--dc23
LC record available at https://lccn.loc.gov/201701689

Options for Teaching
ISSN 1079-2562

Cover illustration of the paperback and electronic editions: Frederick Varley, *Gas Chamber at Seaford*, oil on canvas, 1918. Beaverbrook Collection of War Art, Canadian War Museum, CWM 19710261-0772.

Published by The Modern Language Association of America
85 Broad Street, suite 500, New York, New York 10004-2434
www.mla.org

Contents

Introduction 1
Debra Rae Cohen and Douglas Higbee

Part I: Critical Paradigms

What Is War? 17
Anne E. Fernald

The "World" in World War I: Learning to Think Globally 28
Claire Buck

What Is the Relation of the First World War to Modernism? 40
Vincent Sherry

Rupture or Continuity? The Myth(s) of the War 51
Patrick Deer

Part II: Global Narratives

Code Switching and Representations of the Great War 65
Margaret R. Higonnet

World War I Regenders America 74
Pearl James

The Impact of the First World War on Pan-Africanism: The Transcendence of National and Imperial Boundaries 85
Richard Smith

For King and/or Country: British Dominions and the Literary Interplay between Imperial and National Identities 93
Stephen Cloutier

Beyond *All Quiet on the Western Front*: Representations of the First World War in Germany 102
Wolfgang Natter

Challenges and Contradictions in Teaching French Great War Literature 110
Nancy Sloan Goldberg

Teaching Representations: The Jewish Experience in Eastern Europe during the First World War 118
Glenda Abramson

South Asian Literature of the First World War 125
Santanu Das

The Great War in the Middle East: Two Perspectives
T. E. Lawrence's Lessons 138
Stephen E. Tabachnick

Fictional Representations of the War and of Its Consequences 144
Amaya Martin

Part III: Cultural Motifs

Shell Shock as a Narrative Paradigm in Great War Psychiatry and Fiction 153
Wyatt Bonikowski

Resisting the Call to Serve: Mutiny, Pacifism, and Conscientious Objection in the First World War 161
Meg Albrinck

The Ties That Bind: Modernist Cultures and the Rise of Fascism 169
Bonnie Roos

Inside and Outside Sexual Identity: Queerness, History, and the First World War 177
Laura Doan

Thinking about Space: Mapping and Perception in World War I Literature 185
Eve Sorum

Teaching the 1918 Influenza Pandemic as Part of a World War I Curriculum 193
Jane Elizabeth Fisher

The First World War in Consumer Culture 201
Celia Marshik

Part IV: Genres

Mud, Machines, and Madness: Teaching the Art of the First World War 213
Marguerite Helmers

A "School of Arms": Teaching Children's Book Culture of the First World War 221
Elizabeth A. Galway

Staging the First World War 228
Andrew Maunder

Life and Death at the Front: Life Writing, Literature, and the Language of War 235
Carol Acton

Representations of Time: Film and Great War Writing 242
David Williams

Memorials as Text: Debating the War's Meaning through Monuments 249
Deborah D. Buffton

In Their Time: Teaching First World War Short Stories and the Case of Richard Harding Davis's "The Man Who Had Everything" 257
Scott D. Emmert and Steven Trout

The New Great War Novels: Revisiting the War's Myths through Contemporary Fictions 265
Marlene A. Briggs

Graphic Novels and the First World War 277
Jan Baetens and Hugo Frey

From Brel to Black Metal: The First World War in Popular Music and Music Videos 284
Peter Grant

Part V: Places and Pedagogies

From the Global Archive: Teaching World War I with Digital Tools 293
Jeffrey Drouin

Teaching the First World War through Community-Based Learning 302
Elizabeth Outka

Bild und Text im Ersten Weltkrieg: A Genre-Based Approach to the First World War for Intermediate-Advanced Students of German 308
Laura McLary

World War I Landscapes at the United States Naval Academy 316
Mark D. Larabee

Part VI: Web Resources

First World War–Related Web Sites: A Bibliography 325
Douglas Higbee

Notes on Contributors 335
Works Cited 341
Index 369

Debra Rae Cohen and Douglas Higbee

Introduction

Why is it that we can never quite escape the First World War? Even as the last veterans of the conflict passed away a few years ago, an adaptation of Michael Morpugo's *War Horse* drew crowds in London's West End, on Broadway, and later on screen. And if the veterans' deaths seemed officially to close a chapter of the past, their commemoration, paradoxically, underscored the impossibility of any real closure. Even the mention of the soldiers' experiences, or of the phrase "Great War," conjured the same array of evocative images—trenches, gas, mud—as marked Morpugo's sentimental tale, attesting not only to the war's central position in our cultural consciousness but also to the codification of its representation.

Indeed, a large part of the story of the war, and why its study and teaching remain vital to us today, involves the tracing, and the cultural uses, of such codification. The First World War was an epochal *event* in its unprecedented casualties and global scope; it served as a key *catalyst* for historical cultural developments from the rise of fascism, the decline of empires, and the proliferation of new communications technologies to daylight savings time, pub closing hours, and the Burberry. But in some respects the war's own *myth* represented its most salient shaping of the century that followed—and thus necessitates our urgent attention as teachers. In the First

World War's representations and memory and their effect on national and global cultures, we can find profound lessons for our own day and insight into how our own day came about.

When war broke out in Europe in August 1914, few thought it would last more than a few months. But by the time the war ended in November 1918, dozens of countries had been drawn into the conflict. Modern weapons—high explosive artillery, machine guns, poison gas, airplanes, tanks—wedded to often outdated tactics produced an unprecedented number of casualties: ten million soldiers were dead and twenty million wounded. Great Britain, France, Russia, Italy, Serbia, and the United States battled Germany, Austria-Hungary, and Turkey in Western and Eastern Europe, the Balkans and the Gallipoli peninsula, the Middle East, Africa, the Atlantic, and the North Sea. Troops from India, the British Dominions, the Caribbean, Africa, and Asia fought alongside Europeans in these various theaters, underscoring and challenging the relationships of empire.

But the depredations of this first "total war"—by definition—extended to noncombatant populations. The Germans occupied parts of France and Belgium and sent zeppelins to raid British cities; the Austrian army committed systematic atrocities in the Balkans; and the Turks pursued genocide against the Armenians. Life on the home front—a term itself newly employed during the conflict—was systematically and often radically altered. Women worked outside the home in unprecedented numbers as nurses, in munitions factories, and in other jobs vacated by fighting men, and government's reach extended more deeply into people's lives in the form of rationing, conscription, propaganda, and the curtailment of civil liberties—all changes that continue to affect us today.

And, more broadly, the war initiated, or at least hastened, key facets of our social, political, and cultural inheritance: the war made it impossible to ignore the enormous capacity—and capacity for destruction—of modern industrial technology; it precipitated the demise of three European empires and sparked the rise of several illiberal regimes; and the war's initial reinforcement of traditional gender roles—men at the front, women at home—was a victim of its own success.

From the beginning, representation was an integral part of the war's processes. Propaganda imagery helped shape attitudes toward the enemy, toward enlistment, toward the responsibilities on the home front. Film footage, real and staged, brought the war home in new and profound ways, revealing, even as it obscured and sanitized, the experience of the trenches.

Diverse literary treatments in poetry, fiction, drama, and such nonfiction genres as diaries and memoirs sought to come to terms, during and after the conflict, with a war that seemed to escape comprehension.

But as such chroniclers as Samuel Hynes have detailed, dominant narratives soon asserted themselves, first among them the myth that portrayed the war as a futile slaughter, initiating a modernity of disillusionment. Henri Barbusse's *Le feu* (1916) was the first major European work of fiction that challenged the predominant early optimism in public discourse with a picture of soldiers' lives as obscene degradation. Postwar works such as Erich Maria Remarque's *All Quiet on the Western Front* (1928), Robert Graves's *Good-bye to All That* (1929), and Ernest Hemingway's *A Farewell to Arms* (1929) extended and elaborated Barbusse's themes, rendering waterlogged trenches, barbed-wired and cratered battlefields, and the haunted visages of soldiers the indelible images of the war.

These novels and memoirs, and especially the work of celebrated soldier-poets, diagnosed a significant division between combatants and noncombatants—one that lies at the heart of Wilfred Owen's famous lines from "Dulce et Decorum Est":

> If in some smothering dreams you too could pace
> Behind the wagon that we flung him in,
> And watch the white eyes writhing in his face,
> His hanging face, like a devil's sick of sin;
> If you could hear, at every jolt, the blood
> Come gargling from the froth-corrupted lungs,
> Obscene as cancer, bitter as the cud
> Of vile, incurable sores on innocent tongues,—
> My friend, you would not tell with such high zest
> To children ardent for some desperate glory,
> The old Lie: Dulce et decorum est
> Pro patria mori.

Owen's sense of an ontological chasm created by the war—that there are those who understand the truth of war and those who do not, an attitude James Campbell has termed "combat gnosticism"—was substantiated by events of the postwar era. Politicians and commentators fretted over the reintegration of soldiers into peacetime society and often made promises to veterans that were impossible to keep: British Prime Minister David Lloyd-George's vow "to make Britain a fit country for heroes to live in" is perhaps the most memorable (Gosling). British poet Ivor Gurney, a veteran of

Passchendaele struggling with shell shock, in “Strange Hells” (1922) best articulated the disappointment many veterans felt:

> Where are they now, on state-doles, or showing shop patterns
> Or walking town to town sore in borrowed tatterns
> Or begged. Some civic routine one never learns.
> The heart burns—but has to keep out of face how heart burns.

Yet the cultural representations of the war in the decades that followed often presented veterans not as singularly marked by experience but as emblematic of society as a whole. Singing in the film *Gold Diggers of 1933*, itself partly inspired by a veterans’ march on Washington in May 1932, Joan Blondell evoked a “forgotten man” whose plight is both explicitly a veteran’s (“You put a rifle in his hand / You sent him far away / You shouted ‘Hip hooray!’ / But look at him today”) and universal, generalizable to herself and her Depression-era audience.

Elite as well as popular arts promoted this equivalence: the rough syntax and psychological inwardness of Gurney’s poem bear a family resemblance to the fragmentary works of writers such as T. S. Eliot and Virginia Woolf, who would make the soldier-writers’ version of the war into a paradigm of modern alienation. Indeed, this myth of generalized disillusion—most influentially propounded by Paul Fussell in *The Great War and Modern Memory* (1975)—so poetically appealing, politically useful, and pedagogically manageable, still often serves as the master narrative for our teaching of the war.

Yet this narrative is only part of the wider story—the global story—of the war. And scholarship over the last few decades has worked to recover the diversity of war experience, to stress the multiplicity of total war rather than its universality. These expansions and remappings of the field, drawing on postcolonial perspectives, revisionist historiography, feminist rediscovery, media theory, and new understandings of modernism and modernity—along with a wealth of newly developed material and virtual resources for study—have only rendered more complex the task of teaching a dauntingly enormous subject. First World War representation is, of course, multinational, emanating from dozens of belligerent and colonial languages, literatures, and cultures. It is also multigeneric, comprising poetry, fiction, memoir, drama, film, and official and popular propaganda. It is taught in courses from surveys to seminars, for all levels and types of students—sometimes taught piecemeal, sometimes as the focus of a class. Yet never have course options been so vast and course design so difficult.

Now, at a time when the centennial of the war promises both to provoke renewed interest in its representations and to incite a new consolidation of myth, it is deeply important to offer methodological maps for negotiating this ever more complex pedagogical terrain.

This volume attempts to provide those maps, charting both problems and opportunities of a global and increasingly interdisciplinary field of Great War studies. We've arranged its thirty-five essays under five rubrics: Critical Paradigms, Global Narratives, Cultural Motifs, Genres, and Places and Pedagogies; we also include an annotated list of digital resources. All readers will find the Critical Paradigms section useful, as it frames the key questions and issues associated with teaching First World War representations. Beyond that first section, readers will be able to make use of individual chapters that most closely fit their teaching needs.

The word *representations* in our title not only gestures toward the range of artistic and popular work available for use in the classroom, especially in the burgeoning fields of visual and periodical studies—it also signals the intricate relations between individual artistic productions and the developing conceptions of the war itself. Thus our Critical Paradigms section is organized around four major questions that have persisted over the last several decades as scholars have grappled with the unpacking of First World War myth. Each of these initial essays takes up a set of pedagogical challenges that face those attempting to teach the Great War, locating specific texts and making suggestions for teaching in the context of these critical discussions.

Thinking beyond the Battlefield

Anne Fernald's essay takes up the broad question, "What is war?" To ask this question of a class is generally to receive a stunned and quizzical response. Even today, as guerilla warfare, suicide bombers, and the "war on terror" stress the term, for American students, at least, "war" is still largely what soldiers do. The assumptions of "combat gnosticism"—that only combatant representations can deal adequately with war experience—continue to dominate student expectations, despite those assumptions' inadequacy to reflect the spectrum of total war. And this highlights our first decisions as educators: How do we ourselves delimit the study of war, of this war? What bounds do we place on war representation? How can contemporary war theory help us frame this issue? Can we avoid valorizing the scene of combat?

And if we still maintain that the battlefield represents the central event, how far should we trace its ripples? Vera Brittain's *Testament of Youth* (1933), for instance, was quickly assimilated to Great War curricula after its reissuance in the late 1970s—in part because, though grounded in noncombatant experience, it is also conformable to the standard myth narrative, including Brittain's VAD service in France and Malta as part of a recognizable arc of disillusion. Clara Viebeg's *Töchter der Hekuba* (1917), though set far from the battlefield, usefully depicts the material conditions of home front life for a range of German women. But what of, say, Colette's *Mitsou, ou comment l'esprit vient aux filles* (1919)? For Agnès Cardinal, the novel is central to French Great War literature, a deliberately oblique representation of a relationship doomed by the gendered strictures of a divisive and violent society.

Feminist scholarship on the war has done more than extend the wartime canon to include works by or about women; it suggests that war itself must be defined and taught differently once one factors in the experience of women—counteracting the longstanding cultural practice of defining war by gendered boundaries, with the combat zone, in the American political scientist Cynthia Enloe's terms, "wherever 'women' are not" (15). Thus it has let us look differently, too, at the assumptions of combat gnosticism and the notion of the incommensurable gap between combatant and noncombatant. Though audible, for instance, in the violent resentments of Siegfried Sassoon's quatrains and visible even in the windowpane that separates marching soldiers and female supporters in the propaganda poster "Women of Britain say GO!," this trope itself forms part of the changing pattern of the war's cultural mythology, more recent analyses have argued, and must be interrogated as such. Much recent critical work has been involved in tracing the discursive processes by which such gaps were defined—as in Beatriz Pichel's discussion of the gendered photographic practices French officials used to represent the wartime dead. Even during the war itself such processes were discernible and often exposed: Rebecca West's *The Return of the Soldier*, by means of its unreliable narration, both portrays such a gap and undermines its exceptionalism, representing it as congruent with the mechanisms of class distinction.

In the classroom, tracking the way gender is deployed, for example, in the discourses of mobilization can help students denaturalize easy oppositions between combatant and noncombatant by highlighting national differences. Both British and American propaganda posters often deployed women and children as goads, shaming those who failed to enlist; in Russia, as Karen Petrone has shown, posters tended to tout the heroic masculinity of soldiers in relation to an effeminized enemy and to depict the Imperial Russian Army as an idealized patriarchal family. In these discourses, and in those that followed the war—as Klaus Theweleit memorably showed in his study of the representation of gendered bodies—masculinity was intimately bound up with ideas of nationhood.

Fernald's essay thus engages with issues taken up throughout the volume; Pearl James's essay, in the "Global Narratives" section, probes the pedagogies appropriate to the gendered particularities of national war myth, while in the "Cultural Motifs" section essays by Wyatt Bonikowski, Laura Doan, and Eve Sorum examine particular embodied modes of experience and their representation—shell shock, same-sex desire, spatiality. The bodily specificity that, paradoxically, a broader definition of war brings into focus—a consciousness of classed, racialized, gendered bodies and their political positionalities—is reflected, too, in the volume's consciousness of classroom demographics, as in the "Places and Pedagogies" essay by Elizabeth Outka.

Learning to Think Globally

For those teaching in English-language classrooms, capturing for students the cultural range of a global war may prove most daunting. Claire Buck's essay, which takes up the question of what we mean by "world" war, examines these challenges in both practical and theoretical terms, tracing the resonances of words such as "global," "imperial," "colonial," "postcolonial." Certainly recent critical developments in the humanities, such as the growing recognition of transnational networks of cultural production, have underscored the necessity for parsing these terms. In Great War studies, military historians have increasingly sought to recapture aspects of the battlefield beyond the Western Front trench experience, and cultural historians have argued that a comparative context is necessary to understand the experience and meaning of the war and that focusing on single nations risks reflecting the nationalism that helped bring the war about.

Alan Kramer's recent *Dynamic of Destruction* includes in its cultural comparativist sweep not only Germany, France, and Britain but also Austria-Hungary, Serbia, Italy, Russia, Belgium, and the Ottoman Empire in order to document a modern "logic of annihilation" that has roots in "modern culture" (27). Kramer explicitly disassociates himself from the notion that the war can be collapsed into a single narrative, stating that "[i]t is simply not the case . . . [that] there was a common 'myth of the war experience' that was valid everywhere. Beyond certain similarities in the cultural and mental responses to war one cannot extrapolate from the German war experience to draw conclusions for other nations at war" (210).

The case of Erich Maria Remarque's *Im Westen nichts Neues* (1929) demonstrates Kramer's point and the need for comparative national contextualization in the classroom. Its translation, *All Quiet on the Western Front*, has often served as the sole syllabus representative of the nonanglophone literature of the war—not least because its plot is easily assimilable to the narrative of disillusion. But, as scholars like Wilhelm Schwarz and Margot Norris have discussed, Remarque's novel was far from characteristic of the German response, even into the 1920s, which often read the war as an occasion for the purgation of cultural malaise. Thus the popularity of *Im Westen nichts Neues* needs to be understood in terms of the deeply divided political and literary post-Versailles scene of its publication and in relation to more militaristic writers like Ernst Jünger, whose works are far less often taught or, until recently, even available in translation.

Similarly, Jean Renoir's *La grande illusion* (1937) has been often shown in classrooms since it was first released on video. Its universalist antiwar elements are easily transferrable to the post-Vietnam era even as they are clearly warning, in the film's own moment, of the Second World War to come. Yet its treatment of class as perhaps the most persistent of categories—cutting across national lines even in wartime—is best understood through the long-suppressed history of French wartime mutinies and through similar sentiments in earlier works like Barbusse's *Le feu*, the memorable opening passages of which cast both sides' soldiers as "slaves" whose eventual alliance will transform the world.

Such national grounding needs to be balanced by transnational understanding, as Kramer emphasizes. So, too, do literary scholars such as Santanu Das, whose collection *Race, Empire, and First World War Writing* (2011) seeks not simply to "extend" our understanding of the war "beyond" the Western Front but also to decenter this center/periphery model. Das's collection reaches across both national and disciplinary lines to understand the imperial basis of the war in terms of networks of exchange. He acknowledges that Eurocentrism is not the only reason for the disproportionate critical focus on the Western Front, for instance citing Gail Braybon's assertion that "the war poets have written more words about the conflict than all the non-white troops put together" (7). And indeed in Das's collection the voices of Asian and African workers and soldiers in the British, French, and German armies are heard primarily by way of "intimate accounts" rather than literary production (8).

These disparities raise important questions for the teacher seeking to pursue global approaches in the classroom, as issues of literary hierarchy may further complicate the already formidable task of forging a truly global curriculum. What happens in the literature classroom if the bulk of the conventionally literary works are European? Further, does a comparativist, side-by-side approach demand a level of contextualization that may not be possible in all classroom settings? Does simply assigning, say, Mulk Raj Anand's *Across the Black Waters* combat a Eurocentric perspective, especially when institutional markers for course and coverage (if it is assigned, for example, in a class called Modern British Novel) may reinscribe it? Are certain genres—as Tim Kendall claims of war poetry (*Modern English War Poetry*)—less amenable to comparativist approaches because poets are encouraged by war to engage with their own national literary traditions? And what limitations are imposed by the availability or suitability of translations?

The practical and theoretical questions Buck raises in her essay are addressed variously throughout our section on global narratives and the volume as a whole: Margaret Higonnet explores a variety of pedagogies of translation, while Stephen Tabachnick and Amaya Martin offer competing visions of teaching the Middle Eastern war. Other essays frame approaches to transnationalism bounded by the colonial (Stephen Cloutier), the pan-African (Richard Smith), and even the global network of contagion (Jane E. Fisher), while still others augment our understanding of individual national literatures.

Yet in assembling this volume, too, we have confronted choices and dilemmas similar to those we outline above. Even in a volume of this breadth, it has been impossible to cover every nation, every group, affected by the war; perhaps no single volume can do so. And given the likelihood that the readership for this volume will be an English-language one, we have aimed as much at including various modes of diversity—a range of pedagogical *philosophies*, pedagogical *objects*, and pedagogical *techniques*—as at global range. While we consider the volume to endorse a global pedagogy of the war, we have not expected each individual essay to be equally global in its focus or to approach its pedagogic function in the same way.

Rethinking Modernism, Thinking about Myth

Because representations of the war are so often taught in survey courses that locate them in the modernist period, the vexed question of the relation between modernism and the war remains a pressing one, as Vincent Sherry explores in his essay in the "Critical Paradigms" section. And here too issues of boundary and network, and of literary hierarchy, complicate classroom decision making. In the past, textual choice for courses on the Great War was often dictated by an emphasis on modernism, as part of a teleological narrative of artistic fragmentation that valorizes the elite and the avant-garde. In the classroom, however, this could often lead to an underemphasis on, for example, the sentimental, the patriotic, and the pastoral. Even the feminist rediscovery of nurse's narratives from the conflict has tended to favor those, like Mary Borden's *The Forbidden Zone* (1929), that employ formal elements one can identify as modernist.

But recent study of what might be termed middlebrow modernism—or, in Kristin Bluemel's formulation, "intermodernism"—shows us how to emphasize certain continuities with a culture of realism that at the same time need not represent the nostalgic embrace of past forms. This scholarship sees modernist experimentation as just one part of a complex network of representation and marketing. Mark Wollaeger's *Modernism, Media, and Propaganda* (2006), for instance, finds surprising links between the modernist writer and the propagandist, both of whom specialize in controlled information flow; both emerged not from "cataclysmic discontinuity," he argues, but from a media ecology "already undergoing rapid change under the pressure of new media and increasing flows of information" (xvii).

Wollaeger's insights are suggestive for the classroom; in a sense they invite us to reverse figure and ground, making use of propaganda materials, whether pamphlet, editorial, or poster, not simply as context for artistic works but as part of ongoing debates over the dissemination of information. The inclusion of nonelite modernisms; popular fiction; "nonliterary" novels; light verse, such as that included in Vivien Noakes's *Voices of Silence: The Alternative Book of First World War Poetry* (2006); civilian periodicals; and soldier-produced papers like the *Wipers Times*, *Stars and Stripes*, and the *Liller Kriegszeitung*, produces a very different narrative from one that involves elite materials alone. Several of our essays—notably Celia Marshik's on consumer culture, Elizabeth A. Galway's on children's books, and Marguerite Helmers's on fine and popular art—suggest productive ways of broadening the World War I curriculum in the interests of a more nuanced version of modernity.

None of the issues we've discussed here are, of course, separable from one another. For in teaching the war so many of our decisions come back to one basic question: Does the war entail rupture or continuity? Do developments on various home fronts decisively change the position of women? Do representations of the war serve as culmination or as radical break?

What role does nostalgia play during and after the war—and nostalgia for what? How do we explain the simultaneous postwar diffusion of modernist elements through mass culture and the selective embrace of older tropes and motifs? Do we dwell, in the classroom, on the fracturing of literary forms or the building of nations? Patrick Deer, in our final "Critical Paradigms" essay, "Rupture or Continuity?," examines these questions and the implications for our teaching of both the myth of the war as radical rupture and its more recent correctives. For the historian Jay Winter to see the war, Europe-wide, as a "counterrevolutionary moment" in culture, for instance, reflects not only his reading of "world" as Europe but also his determination to privilege a meaning of "culture" articulated in terms of "ordinary people" (*Legacy* 170). Cynthia Enloe's argument about women's experience of war as an ideological, economic, and psychological struggle uncontained by the temporal markers of treaties opens up the possibilities of teaching the "post" *as* war. Sherry in *The Great War and the Language of Modernism* (2003) locates the central disruption of the British war not in the trenches but on the home front, in "the disestablishment of a rationalistic attitude and practice" (14) in liberal language that the war entailed, and thus recuperates not only the centrality of modernism but also the idea of the watershed event.

Here too, then, thinking comparatively is key. The very concept of postwar national myth means something very different in, say, Canada than it does in the countries east of the Rhine, where war merged into revolution, civil war, or prolonged political instability. And both the key moments for myth and the mode of their deployment differ from country to country. In France, as Leonard V. Smith has argued, a dominant narrative of soldier as victim silenced other versions of the "embattled self." In Australia, the centering of Australian nationhood in the myth of the heroic Anzac has been complicated by recent research exploring the contribution of aboriginal soldiers. And scholars are currently recovering the contributions of Indians, Africans, and African Americans, weaving these soldiers' experiences into their nations' struggles with colonialism and racism. All these offer different possibilities for organizing classroom experience.

For teachers in a variety of disciplines, a useful organizing focus for tracing the multiple threads of wartime and postwar culture can be the grammar and vocabulary of memorialization. The unique positioning of material and literary memorial discourses that face both past and future makes them a key site for the molding of national identities and the crafting of myth, as Charlotte Mew's poem "The Cenotaph" (1919) early on recognized and as Deborah D. Buffton explores in her essay here, "Memorials as Text." Yet—and this is the challenge of tracing the myth in the classroom—the meaning of Great War memory, overdetermined by definition, cannot be reduced to the tropes of any single memorial or explained away in a single set of formal gestures.

Questions of rupture and continuity necessarily bear on how one presents the progression of "modern memory"—whether, as the continuing spate of Great War–centered novels and films would suggest, the war remains, in Ted Hughes's term, the "ghost" by which certain national cultures remain haunted. Several of our essays here—including some concerned with unconventional genres—take up this issue. David Williams discusses ways of teaching filmic modes of war memory; Peter Grant argues for the use of World War I–inspired popular music as a pedagogical tool; Marlene Briggs discusses how the ongoing myth of the Great War continues to serve as a vehicle for expressing the concerns of today's novelists, as in the works of Pat Barker and Sebastian Japrisot; while Jan Baetens and Hugo Frey trace such contemporary reimaginings in the genre of the graphic novel.

Thinking about Engagement

New technologies for museum and archive, shifting as they do our mode of interaction with an already mediated past, throw into relief the very meaning of words like *experience* and *testimony* even as they make an exciting new kind of "witnessing" accessible to the classroom. Not only do digital collections make possible student exploration of nontraditional materials—such as those treated here by Fisher, Marshik, and others—but they also both enable and demand new forms of classroom engagement. Jeffrey Drouin, in our "Places and Pedagogies" section, examines such challenges and opportunities, emphasizing digital possibilities and pedagogies, while our appendix offers an annotated bibliography of online resources. Other forms of classroom engagement, though, remain equally viable and immediate: Andrew Maunder discusses restaging drama in the classroom as a mode of recapturing "hidden voices," and Elizabeth Outka offers methods for teaching the war through community-based learning.

Essays like Mark Larabee's, on teaching at the United States Naval Academy, and Laura McLary's, on teaching the war in the foreign-language classroom, describe the challenges of specific institutional settings yet also remind us about the need to focus on the particularities of our own classroom demographics. Indeed, this volume, in its very heft, diversity, and range, serves as a reminder of the multiplicity of the war both in its moment and in its possible classroom manifestations; instead of replacing one grand narrative with another, it will, we hope, help teachers allow the war's many stories to emerge.

Assembling a volume like this is a prolonged and often arduous process—and so we'd like to thank the contributors to this collection for their enthusiasm and diligence, and James Hatch and Michael Kandel at the MLA for seeing us through it. We'd like to thank, too, those many teachers who offered up proposals that could not be accommodated even in a volume as capacious as this one. Doug owes particular thanks to Suzanne Ozment, former executive vice-chancellor at the University of South Carolina, Aiken, for a course-release grant to get this project rolling, and the Office of the Vice President for Research at the University of South Carolina for a RISE grant, which helped see it completed.

Part I

Critical Paradigms

Anne E. Fernald

What Is War?

War is politics by other means, as the Prussian strategist Carl Clausewitz (1780–1831) once explained. It is the attempt to resolve a political conflict by violence. Clausewitz's euphemism for that violence, the elegantly vague "other means," ensures the memorability of his phrase. More recently, both Michel Foucault and Hannah Arendt have emphasized the obverse: showing how often politics is war by other means.[1] If war is state-sponsored, large-scale violence, the state, at its worst, understands and deploys politics to control its citizenry as totally as in wartime. To understand war, then, we need to understand it in relation to politics and violence. We also need to consider how we define war's opposite. Since Saint Augustine questioned the justice of the Pax Romana (27 BCE–180 CE), thinkers have debated the question, What is the opposite of war?[2]

The decision to wage war is one of the most consequential moral choices we make. The struggle to achieve and maintain a just peace is one of the most challenging and abstract human goals. We can come to a better understanding of the human experience of peace and war through artistic representations: "If literature cannot avoid representing violence . . . it is also, in some essential way, haunted, stained, and defaced by that very reliance" (Cole, *At the Violet Hour* 19). Whatever we see as war's opposite, it is not literature. The violence of war at once unites and divides us: patriotism, hatred of a common enemy, and propaganda may bind citizens together; differing attitudes to the conduct and continuance of war, protest, and unevenly distributed sacrifice separate us. Clausewitz analogizes war to dueling on a large scale, but scale is one of the main challenges to imagining, representing, and teaching war.[3] To understand war, its scope and scale, we need to draw upon a pedagogy of variety. Variety means more than a list; it means developing a rich archive, curated to demonstrate the complexity of war, using the time line and the map to trace the war's uneven effects. Only when we begin to imagine war's reach, forward and back through time, at work, at home, and around the globe, can we begin to comprehend the extent of war's grip on our imaginations. At that point, we can begin to inquire into the nature of war and help our students come to their own conclusions about whether and when armed conflict might be justified and whether and how it might be contained. This essay suggests some strategies for teaching representations of war that help students reach those conclusions.

Teaching representations of war in the undergraduate classroom demands that we devise lessons and choose texts that help students grasp the scope and scale of the conflict. One historian laments that "an average British school pupil's impression of a four-and-a-half-year conflict that stretched across the globe [World War I] is that it took place on July 1, 1916, in a trench in France, seen through the eyes of a man called Wilfred Owen" (Pennell 13). Limited as this may be, American students are even less well informed. While most British students can offer a quick if shallow response, American students are unlikely to have any associations at all with the war (Neiberg, "What"). The United States's involvement in the war was brief, but, as Michael Neiberg notes, "its impacts on the home front were dramatic," particularly with respect to race relations: booming northern factories set the Great Migration in motion, at once increasing racial violence and making possible great cultural flowerings, including the Harlem Renaissance. For the historians Catronia Pennell and Neiberg, literary representations of the war can be a source of distortion. These cautions from historians can be a useful corrective for those of us who teach the war through artistic representations.

For a course on representations of war to help students imagine the conflict, not only historians but also thinkers from many disciplines play a powerful role in setting the context. The approach must be interdisciplinary, and a course must focus on war's intensity and its importance in human experience without glamorizing violence. Such an approach demands attention to time, space, and the relationship between violence and fear. One reason for studying war and representations of war is the desire to learn from the mistakes of past conflicts to prevent future wars. After a cataclysmic event, people often look back for clues: What could we have known?

Thus the time line of war does not begin when war is declared but in the events leading up to war. Understanding war entails studying the cultural, political, and historical conditions of a society before a war breaks out. For example, popular fiction in England before World War I suggests that some writers of that time sought to understand the social changes under way. Both invasion stories and detective novels were popular; the one genre spoke to the insecurity of an island nation while the other spoke to the hope that an intelligent person could sift through the clues to solve a problem. Still, sifting through the clues can be a daunting task: "Between what matters and what seems to matter, how should the world we know judge wisely?" (Bentley 5). This, the first line of *Trent's Last Case*, a popular 1913 detective novel, presents an intriguing snapshot of one prewar sentiment.

Only in retrospect can we see clues to what came next. Paul Saint-Amour's recent work on the pretraumatization of Europe in the interwar years (1919 to 1939) suggests new ways to read the moments before a war, demanding that a pedagogy of war begin before the war's declaration: "The disaster that arrives and the disaster that might arrive have equal powers to engender a 'collective psychosis' " (6). Europe before World War I may not have been pretraumatized, but neither did the war emerge out of a vacuum. Sticking to the example of World War I, before the war we will find expressions of vague foreboding (as in invasion literature like Erskine Childers's *The Riddle of the Sands* [1903]), hopes that just the right clues will yield an answer (detective fiction), a desire for the hygiene of violence, assertions that a large war is almost impossible (the thesis of Norman Angell's bestselling 1909 book *The Great Illusion*), explorations of the psychology of war, particularly the glamour it holds for young men (William James's "The Moral Equivalent of War"), and the war plans of Count Alfred von Schlieffen, which called for a brutal, decisive victory. We may dismiss Angell in the light of Schlieffen and James, but in the years before the war it was not at all obvious who was right. Barbara Tuchman's 1962 *The Guns of August* remains one of the most important and influential books on World War I precisely because of her account of the diplomatic and military maneuverings in the few weeks between the assassination of Archduke Franz Ferdinand and the beginning of the war. A recent work, one of many published at the centenary of 1914, is titled *The Sleepwalkers* for its thesis that political leaders drifted almost passively into a war of unimaginable horror (C. Clark).

To take another example, in 1912 the Spanish painter Pablo Picasso (1881–1973), then working in France, painted *The Scallop Shell*, a medium-sized oval canvas mostly in the grayish brown tones of cubism but featuring two scallop shells and, to the right, the French tricolor flag with a fragment of the phrase "Notre avenir est dans l'air" ("Our future is in the air"), an advertising slogan from the Michelin Tire Company and part of a campaign to support French aviation. The development of airpower during the war meant that "[w]ar had become three dimensional" (Neiberg, *Military Atlas* 152), and while England suffered more air casualties from German bombing raids than France,[4] a March 1915 bombardment of Paris killed twenty-three people. Neither Picasso nor Michelin could have known how the slogan would resonate in the future, yet both knew enough to deploy it.

The prelude to war is important, but it is unlikely to be any course's sole focus. Literature published during the war can capture the immediacy, authenticity, and disorientation of conflict. In modern times, the outbreak of war marks a change: an atmosphere of foreboding becomes the lethal atmosphere of poison gas. Anyone trying to understand war through its representations needs to be alert to that change and to a representation's contexts of composition. The Gettysburg Address and Lincoln's Second Inaugural Address draw their power at least in part from the tension between Lincoln's will toward a Northern victory and the uncertainty of the outcome. Tennyson's outrage would not have had as much force if "The Charge of the Light Brigade" referred to some distant conflict. Rebecca West's *The Return of the Soldier* (1918) gains poignancy in part because the eponymous soldier returns to an ongoing conflict. Many of the most powerful lyrics of World War I, too, were written in the trenches. Tim Cross's anthology *The Lost Voices of World War I* (1988) includes only works of writers who died in the conflict. With contributions by more than sixty writers from across Europe, in the original language as well as English, the anthology represents an impressive international range, from the well-known (Edward Thomas, Guillaume Apollinaire, and Charles Péguy) to the nearly forgotten. Even so, the focus on time and combat drastically limits the spaces depicted: there is not a single woman writer in the collection.

Furthermore, no wartime literature can offer knowledge about the war's outcome.

Wartime prose, moreover, is often written in support of the war (Buck, "British Women's Writing" 100), a perspective that, for all its historical interest, might not be the best primary focus for a course (or unit within a course) on war. Other views are unlikely to get a hearing and may even be unthinkable in the atmosphere of a nation at peril. Furthermore, focusing only on literature published during a conflict risks perpetuating the "pervasive . . . belief in a standard trajectory from naïve enthusiasm to ironic disillusion, despite contrary evidence that both criticism and support for war coexisted from 1914 onwards" (88). The restrictions imposed by wartime censorship (such as the Defence of the Realm Act [DORA] in England) limited what could be published during the war. Debra Rae Cohen describes how in *Zeppelin Nights* (1915), Violet Hunt and Ford Madox Hueffer signaled their debt to the German writer E. T. A. Hoffmann while being sensitive to DORA rules and to the increased anti-German sentiment after the sinking of the *Lusitania* (16–21). The pacifist novella *Aleta Day* (1919) expressed too risky a sentiment for readers in Canada immediately after the war; its author, Francis Marion Beynon, was forced to emigrate to the United States, and the book, now republished, has yet to reach a wide audience.

Thus an exclusive focus on the literature of wartime leaves much out. Longer works—novels, plays, epic poems—may not be much written in wartime, and a course on representations of war should balance works written during a conflict with those that benefit from historical perspective. After all, Homer's *Iliad* tells the story of a war that occurred four centuries before. *War and Peace* (1869) takes place during the Napoleonic Wars (1799–1815) but was published a half century later. Although there's a particular immediacy to contemporary accounts of war, perspective adds new resonances and makes different stories possible. The passage of time made it possible for Sébastien Japrisot to revisit the brutal treatment of French desertion in his 1991 novel *Un long dimanche de fiancailles* (*A Very Long Engagement*).[5] Peter Weir's exploration of the intersecting identities in *Gallipoli* (1981)—Australian, Irish, Aborigine, Egyptian, and English men and women of a range of classes and castes—shows the fateful battle through a distinctively late-twentieth-century anti-imperial, antiracist lens.

To Neiberg's point about the centrality of the war to the Great Migration, African American literature offers a range of options. The immediate postwar novels of the Harlem Renaissance touch on the racism experienced by African American soldiers: Claude McKay's *Home to Harlem* (1928) has a disaffected deserter as its central character, while the final chapters of Jessie Fauset's *There Is Confusion* (1924) are set in the war. However, neither novel is primarily about war. We get a much different picture of war's toll if we later include the shell-shocked Shadrack, central to Toni Morrison's *Sula* (1973), and a still different image in the recuperative, heroic graphic novel *The Harlem Hellfighters* (2014). In fact, expanding our time line far beyond the war's end makes it possible to include new stories, stories that could not have been told earlier. Historians and literary critics are now paying greater attention to the many contributions of imperial soldiers as well as Native Americans and African Americans. Santanu Das reckons the number of "non-white men, combatants and non-combatants, mobilized into the European and American Armies . . . to well over four million" (*Race* 4). Recent work by Das and others sheds light on those contributions and the historical traces left by soldiers, laborers, volunteers, and noncombatants. Das's *Race, Empire, and First World War Writing* includes documents from Vietnamese and Senegalese participants. In this regard, historians are leading artists. Joe Lunn presents the oral history of Demba Mboup, a Senegalese griot or storyteller who served in World War I and was interviewed in 1982 and 1983 about his experiences ("France's Legacy"). His story and that of the 140,000 other West Africans who served in the war await their literary retelling.

As the story of the millions of imperial volunteers and forced laborers emphasizes, we must also consider war's spaces no less than the times of war, both its proximities and its distances. One of the many ironies detailed by Paul Fussell in *The Great War and Modern Memory* is the proximity of the Western Front to home for some. Many English soldiers spent months in trenches only seventy miles from the English shore. This meant that soldiers received not only mail but also tarts and fresh eggs from back home, that an officer might breakfast in the trench and dine at his club in London (64). The proximity of the Western Front to England was reciprocal: it meant that English people in the southern counties could hear—quite distinctly—the battles in France, just another way modern warfare blurs war front and home front. Of course, what was ironic proximity for the English soldier—and "over there" for the American, as the popular song of 1917 had it—was home to the French and Belgians, whose villages became the Western Front.

Home front itself is a term from World War I, coined not to contrast it and the war front as much as to legitimize home, where workers were manufacturing the munitions and other goods necessary to mobilize on a grand scale. While propaganda posters such as "Women of Britain Say—'GO!'" or "Je suis une brave poule de guerre"[6] suggest that the home front was war's opposite, in fact during World War I the home front was soon understood as another space in which to conduct war. The *OED*'s first attestation of the term suggests as much, quoting the *Times*, in April 1917: "The unity of the fighting front and the home front [in Germany] ought to be still more thoroughly understood" ("Home Front"). From the beginning, the home front was integral to the war effort, not only as contrast, as the thing soldiers fought for, but also as the site of training, manufacturing, convalescence and recovery, propaganda and censorship, and even as a military target.

Disorienting as proximity can be, equally strange is the powerfully long reach of a war across continents and oceans. In *The Odyssey*, Ulysses's journey home from the Trojan War takes him throughout the known world of the Mediterranean. In the eighteenth century, revolutions in Haiti and the North American colonies reverberated across the Atlantic. When an Atlantic crossing still took weeks, poets, painters, and writers on both sides of the ocean documented the effects of these wars. We find responses to the reach of the World War I by women from as far as New Zealand and West Virginia. In 1915, Katherine Mansfield had an affair with the writer Francis Carco, the logistics of which became a source for her story "An Indiscreet Journey"; both Mansfield and Carco were originally from the South Pacific (New Zealand and New Caledonia, respectively). In 1919, two African American sisters in West Virginia, Ada and Ethel Peters (ages eighteen and seventeen) published *War Poems*, a book detailing the bravery and struggles faced by African American soldiers in the war. Cecily Hamilton offers a partial entrée into the global effects of World War I in her 1919 novel *William: An Englishman*. Stationed in France, the protagonist finds that "after a week or two he no longer turned his head at the sight of a gang of Annamite labourers" (from the Annamite Valley in what is now Vietnam) and that "the sight of a turbaned brown trooper bargaining in the marketplace with a swift-spoken bare-headed French woman was an oddity and nothing more" (201). Nonetheless, if we want to truly investigate the experience of colonial participants in war, we have to look more deeply and, often, beyond the chronological confines of the war and immediate postwar years.

The reach of war is global, and the spaces of war are not confined to the battlefield alone. As we think about the spaces of war, it is important not to reinscribe a hierarchy based on proximity. We need to remain alert to the detailed descriptions of wartime life in the trenches, in a munitions factory, on a transport ship, in a hospital, marching for peace, or fishing on the Big Two-Hearted River without seeing one space as more real than another. Thinking about spaces away from the battle, we need to disaggregate spaces of power—cabinet offices, military command centers, propaganda ministries—from spaces of affect—the village left behind, the graveyard, the grieving mother's room. When war seems safely elsewhere, the state can demonize the enemy, while civilians, far from the front, can feel "the abstract blood-thirstiness" that contrasts with the thinking and experience of soldiers (Elshtain, "Reflections" 50). As Jean Bethke Elshtain cautions, "Because it is now possible for us to destroy the enemy without ever seeing him or her, abstract hatreds are less likely to rub against concrete friction" (*Just War* 271).

Technological advances involve people in faraway wars; these same advances bring war very close to home, imbuing all spaces with an atmosphere of dread. Moreover, we need to think about the complex intersection of power and affect in spaces where civilians carry on war work: the computer console that monitors and carries out drone attacks, the munitions factory, the field hospital, the shop that prints the posters announcing the next rationing scheme. In these spaces, women and men of different nations and ranks mix, as well as the motives of power and affect. As fear penetrates spaces away from the traditional battlefield, security becomes an increasingly complex issue. Fear and the administration of fear, to use Paul Virilio's terms, become preoccupations of the state. Virilio takes his term from Graham Greene's depiction of England during the blitz of World II, when Nazis were "fighting a merciless war against the British *from the inside*" (13), and he writes of his own boyhood in that war in France, when "the ones who were bombarding and killing us were in fact our allies" (16–17). All these are spaces of war.

Trying to grasp the scale of the conflict, in both space and time, leads us to ask, Does war break with the world of the past, or is it a manifestation of processes that were already under way? What is the relationship between war and other cultural changes? Such questions accrue around any major conflict, not least World War I. Changes in women's roles that were well under way before 1914 were initially threatened and then accelerated by the exigencies of war. Christa Hämmerle cautions, however, that "soldierly masculinities were valued far more than women's partially expanded roles" (4), while Laura Doan details the uneven recognition of gay women's participation at a time when many did not know that women could be lesbian or queer.

The year 1914 is a convenient date, but it obscures as much as it illuminates. Virginia Woolf, a lifelong pacifist, demoted military dates in favor of cultural ones. She suggests the peacetime date of 1910 as central to the development of the modern world, instead of 1914 or 1919. Her assertion, "On or about 1910, human character changed" (*Essays* 3: 421), reminded people that major cultural changes were taking place before the beginning of the war. Less well known but in a similar vein, she intervenes in *Mrs. Dalloway*, having Peter Walsh reflect on what he has missed living and working in India: "Those five years—1918 to 1923—had been, he suspected, somehow very important" (71). Five years during which millions died in the influenza epidemic, the Treaty of Versailles was signed, and wartime rationing was gradually eliminated. The return to so-called normalcy was long and painful, marked by a society that had to adjust to loss.[7] By 1922, a full year before Peter returns to London, T. S. Eliot had published *The Waste Land*. His view of the war as a tragedy with cataclysmic effects on both the individual psyche and the very foundation of civilization had begun to take hold. Peter Walsh has missed a lot. And he only dimly perceives what Woolf's novel vividly portrays: that in spite of Clarissa's declaration that the war "was over; thank Heaven—over" (5), the war is not yet over.

Considering both space and time as we construct our syllabi, we both orient and disorient our students to what war is. We question the time of war, looking at how war is imagined before, during, and after battle. We extend the spaces of war, finding stories of war far beyond the trenches, seeing the distant people whom war touches and the many contexts, near and far, in which we see war's effect. Only then can we return to the question of scale and the difficulties of imagining any scale that is not human. As Virilio notes:

> Proportions are essential. . . . Being human takes place between 1.5 and 2 meters, not 18 meters, which would be the world of sycamores and sequoias. Looking at a computer chip, the scale is down to half millimeters. The pollution of "life size," the pollution of proportions is nothing more than the pollution of the relationship of being in the world. (73–74)

The prominence of the bayonet in World War I literature registers this attempt to return war to a human scale, or so Sarah Cole hypothesizes (*At the Violet Hour* 29–30). Just at the moment when the machine gun and aerial bombardment make killing efficient and abstract, poets return to an image of personal violence as a reminder of a human-sized weapon.

Recent thinkers on war and its origins have added weight to Sigmund Freud's hypotheses about the human relation to violence and the way a legacy of violence reverberates through generations. Work by Elaine Scarry, Judith Butler, Susan Sontag, and Cole highlight the impact of violence, the vulnerability of the violated body, and the difficulties of communicating the experience of pain. Our sense of the origins of war varies with our perspective: Cole writes, "Nothing is older than the story of violence" (3), while John Horgan compares the origin of war, about six thousand years ago (31), to the much earlier origin of Homo sapiens. Unfortunately, "once an invention is known and accepted, men do not easily relinquish it" (Mead 404), and in the six thousand years since we have invented war, writing, and civilization as we know it, war has been a part of the human experience. During the early days of World War II, both Margaret Mead and Woolf wondered how to supplant war with something else: "For this, two conditions . . . are necessary. The people must recognise the defects of the old invention, and someone must make a new one" (Mead 405). Or, as Woolf put it, "We must compensate the man for the loss of his gun" (*Essays* 6: 244).

As we think about the times and places of war, we must include in our thinking these legacies of trauma and fear. The Schlieffen Plan to conquer France by way of Belgium is of interest not only to military strategists. It exemplifies the importance of considering the human costs of such strategies. War story after war story testifies to such costs. Proportions matter, as Virilio says, and they need to come into account before we begin to weigh whether or not a conflict is just.

In his field-defining book, *Just and Unjust Wars*, Michael Walzer offers a taxonomy of reasons we go to war, summarizing centuries of just war theory. His work provides some structure for the largest questions of all: What is the value of sovereignty and territorial integrity to the men and women who live in a particular state's territory? How much killing is systematic killing? If a war is justified, who should fight it? Does anyone have the right, a duty, to fight? If a state or group of states (or the United Nations) decides to intervene, how should the intervention be conducted? What kind of peace should the invading forces seek? Instructors and contexts will change the extent to which we entertain these core questions in our classrooms, but our answers will be much richer if we have first explored the full range of times and spaces of war.

Notes

1. In *Discipline and Punish* Foucault writes, "'[P]olitics' has been conceived as a continuation, if not exactly and directly of war, at least of the military model as a fundamental means of preventing civil disorder" (168). Arendt writes, "If we turn to the literature on the phenomenon of power, we soon find out that there exists an agreement among political theorists from Left to Right that violence is nothing more than the most flagrant manifestation of power. 'All politics is a struggle for power; the ultimate kind of power is violence,' said C. Wright Mills, echoing, as it were, Max Weber's definition of the state as the 'rule of men over men, based on the means of legitimate, i.e. allegedly legitimate, violence.'"

2. See, for example, Elshtain: "[I]n chapter 19 of *The City of God*, Augustine presents a vision of earthly justice, order, and peace and a definition of a commonwealth that goes much beyond notions of self-interest. . . . Importantly, Augustine extols *justice*, not *peace* as the highest value, the most noble good. Peace may, in fact, be an *unjust* order—the peace of the *Pax Romana*, for example, for it was a *pax-ordo* of compulsion. Just war must be understood within a larger frame of justice" (*Just War* 4). See also Paul Ramsey's essay on Augustine in the same volume.

3. See the introduction to book 1, chapter 1: "War is nothing but a duel on an extensive scale."

4. In 1916, Zeppelin raids on England killed nearly three hundred people and injured seven hundred more (Neiberg, *Military Atlas* 154).

5. There is also a 2004 film of the same name. Stanley Kubrick's 1957 film *Paths of Glory* touches on similar material.

6. Full caption: "Soignons la basse-cour. Je suis une brave poule de guerre, je mange peu et produis beaucoup" 'Let's take care of the poultry. I am a fine war hen. I eat little and produce a lot' (Douanne).

7. For a popular history of the immediate postwar period in England, see Nicolson.

Claire Buck

The "World" in World War I: Learning to Think Globally

We routinely use the First World War's global nature to mark its difference from previous wars, yet the teaching of its literature remains grounded in the history out of which it was born, that of imperialism, colonialism, and the nation-state. Scholars over the last three decades have successfully challenged an overly narrow definition of war writing as rooted in eyewitness, frontline experience. An emphasis on a single theater of war, the Western Front, and on the perspective of European and North American writers has been less easy to dislodge. This is despite the increasing number of studies by historians and a handful of literary scholars seeking to "embed the experience and memory of the First World War in a more multiracial and international framework" (Das, *Race* 1). The student of First World War literature and culture has increasing access to studies of war theaters beyond the Western Front and to analyses of the home fronts in India, Ireland, Senegal, Australia, and more. More and more research is available on the experiences and perspectives of over four million nonwhite combatants and noncombatants recruited from Europe's subject peoples and from other ethnic and racial groups, such as African Americans, Maoris, and Chinese.[1] Yet the literature classroom is still centered on European and North American war writing. Why little has changed is both pragmatic, to do with the availability of resources, and methodological, a matter of the reading practices we bring to war writing. So why should we reframe our teaching?

The most obvious answer is that the First World War was a global conflict, even though the term *global* was not widely used until later in the twentieth century. The war was primarily fought in Europe, Africa, and the Middle East, but its reach extended far wider. Belligerent states included the United States, Japan, China, and Central American nations in the political orbit of the United States (Forty 363–64). The postwar treaties redrew the map of Eastern Europe, dissolving the Austro-Hungarian Empire into ethnic states, creating British- and French-controlled mandates out of the former Ottoman Empire in the Middle East, and consolidating Japanese control of Chinese and South Pacific territories (Morrow 304–14). The postwar settlement also parceled out Germany's African colonies to the European allies as mandates. What matters here is not so much the war's global extension as its relation to globalization in the twentieth century and the associated shifts from the nation-state to global capitalism and from colonialism to neocolonialism.

Such recognitions entail the question of whose version of the global we are talking about when addressing the *world* in World War One. The "who" can be outlined in statistical terms.[2] All the European belligerent nations and Turkey relied heavily on their empires for manpower and resources. Britain's settler colonies, the dominions of Australia, New Zealand, Canada, South Africa, and Newfoundland, contributed 1.3 million soldiers (Das, *Race* 4). Women served overseas and at home as nurses in, for example, the Australian Army Nursing Service, the Canadian Army Medical Corps, and the New Zealand Expeditionary Force. The soldiers were mainly but not exclusively men of European origin. Of the approximately 100,000 men from New Zealand, for example, more than 2,200 were Maori and 460 were Pacific Islanders, while some 500 Aboriginal and Torres Strait Islanders were among the 400,000 men of the Australian Imperial Force (Shoebridge; Das, *Race* 13). Despite deep political divisions, around 210,000 Irishmen from both nationalist and unionist communities served in the British army (Jeffery 6).

The European powers drew heavily on the nonwhite subject peoples of their colonies. In August 1914, faced with a huge shortage of men on the Western Front, Britain turned to its standing army in India, and for the first time Indian soldiers fought against white Europeans in Europe. By December 1919, around 1.4 million men from the Indian subcontinent had also been recruited as combatants and noncombatant labor. While

India contributed the largest number of men, Britain mobilized its colonial subjects from across the empire, including West Africa and the British West Indies. The French armed forces, which already had 90,000 *troupes indigènes*, mobilized an additional 500,000 colonial troops from Algeria, Tunisia, Morocco, French West Africa, Madagascar, and Indochina (Das, *Race* 4). Both Italy and Germany used African soldiers, from Libya, Eritrea, Somalia, Togo, Cameroon, Burundi, Rwanda, and their other colonies, in combat in African theaters of war (Koller 114).

War personnel came as well from outside the European and Ottoman empires. Most famously, the United States entered the war in 1917, although many Americans, men and women, participated as soldiers, doctors, nurses, and administrators from the war's outset. By the war's end four million American men had served, half of them overseas. Of this total around 400,000 were African American and 17,000 Native American (Mjagkij xx–xxi). Less well known is the number of non-European, nonwhite combatants and noncombatants that the French and British employed from outside the colonies across the war zones. For example, 140,000 Chinese were employed in labor battalions on the Western Front and in Mesopotamia, while Germany, France, and Britain all drew troops and support from what Christian Koller calls their "semi-colonial regions" (113), as in the example of the 200,000 Egyptians mobilized by Britain into the Egyptian Labour Corps and Camel Transport Corps (*First World War*). The fact and scale of their participation make a compelling case for changing the way we teach war writing. But statistics alone don't show us how to do it, and as with any venture into world literature the seeming impossibility of adding new content to already stuffed courses, and the limits of our expertise—linguistic, cultural, and historical—can easily feel overwhelming. This essay identifies recently uncovered writing by and about the non-Europeans at the core of First World War history and suggests ways to broaden our teaching of who and what made up the war.

Access to resources alone is a significant challenge to the reinvention of our teaching. As with many of the major shifts in the literary canon, curricular change depends on the entwined processes of primary research and the creation of new editions, translations, and anthologies. Editions and anthologies are available in their original languages and in translation, often widely so, for French, German, British, Canadian, Australian, New Zealand, Irish, and American war writers, although it has taken a long time for women's writing to gain prominence in the anthologies. Resources present a far bigger challenge once we move outside Europe, the United States, and the former British dominions. This is only in part a matter of what kinds of war writing are in print or available in digital and online formats.

Almost twenty years ago in 1999, David Omissi, in *Indian Voices of the Great War*, made available a substantial selection from a larger archive of letters written home by Indian soldiers serving on the Western Front and in Mesopotamia or recuperating in hospitals on the south coast of England. These letters were translated, excerpted, and transcribed as part of the British government's censorship of Indian troops in Europe. The same year, Joe Lunn published *Memoirs of the Maelstrom: A Senegalese Oral History of the First World War*, based on interviews with Senegalese veterans and other witnesses of the war. Another important work, *Across the Black Waters* (1940), by Mulk Raj Anand, one of India's most prominent Indo-Anglian writers, had been reprinted in 1978 by Vision Press in Delhi. Anand's postwar novel represents the story of sepoys serving on the Western Front as an episode in the history of India's anticolonial movements. Each of these three texts puts the voices of soldiers from the European colonies in conversation with canonical war writers from Britain and France. The fact that Anand's Indian war novel has become increasingly canonical in British and American war writing while the letters and oral histories remain more peripheral speaks to methodological obstacles to change. The practices of reading enshrined in the literature classroom mean that Anand's novel, with its possibility of study next to other novels, can be subsumed into comparative studies. That these works are not studied on their own terms, as artifacts of cultures outside the West, is one danger of adding them to the curriculum. But the imperialist impulse of literary studies also means that the comfortable genres, the easily assimilable texts by non-European writers, are the ones absorbed. Such is not the case with "nonliterary" texts by troops and laborers from the former colonies and other non-European regions. The relation of literary studies to the archive is ambivalent at least.

The work of Santanu Das is illustrative here of the entanglement between how we read and the availability of materials. Das has probably done more than any other literary studies scholar to put First World War writing in a global context. He has published many articles on Indian experience of the war in Europe and Mesopotamia and on the Indian home front. Just as important is his edited collection *Race, Empire, and First World War Writing*, which aims to make visible the field's scope and foster interdisciplinary and comparative work. In the context of the 2014 centenary he has become a spokesperson in the British media for a multiracial and international perspective on the war and is a collaborator on a range of online and museum projects.[3] His research archive on India and Indians is remarkably diverse. He uses traditional literary sources by educated elite and middle class Indians, such as the diaries of Major Amar Singh; poems by the female nationalist leader Sarojini Naidu; the letters of Captain Doctor Kalyan Kumar Mukherji, who was a doctor with the Indian Medical Corps in Mesopotamia; and the memoir of Sisir Prasad Sarbadhikari, who records his experiences as a medical orderly and in a POW camp (*Race* 73–81). Singh's diaries and Naidu's poems were written in English and are in print, but Mukherji and Sarbadhikari's writings were privately printed in India in Bengali and have yet to be reprinted or translated. Access is thus doubly complicated by availability and by language expertise. Das's research, like that of historians such as Lunn and Omissi, aims to represent the war experiences, perspectives, and memories of men and women from nonliterate or preliterate, preindustrial backgrounds (Lunn, "France's Legacy" 108–09). He uses Punjabi folksongs, soldiers' letters, photographs, family memorabilia, and sound recordings made by the Prussian Phonographic Commission of Indian prisoners of war in Germany, which includes 250 languages and examples of traditional music. Even a signature, written by a sepoy in English, Urdu, and Gurmukhi on a page of an Australian soldier's diary is part of the new archive. These sources chart the history of war from below as well as from an elite perspective, attend to India as a home front, and push back against the tendency to characterize Indian war experience as uniform. They are, however, far more familiar to the historian than to the literary scholar. We find that Das, a literary critic, is unusual: it is historians who are largely responsible for researching and making available the primary sources used in the literature classroom.[4]

The British Library's vast archive of letters from Indian soldiers, easily available to students through Omissi's selection, is a good example of the disciplinary conundrums we face. Literary scholars are not new to questions about reading diaries and letters, but these materials are often relegated to a supporting role in discussions of war memoirs, fiction, and poetry. As Omissi, Das, Claude Markowits, and others have cautioned, these letters cannot be treated at face value. Their relation to the sender of the letter has gone, as Omissi terms it, through "layers of filtration" (*Indian Voices* 4). While some of the letters were written by the men themselves, most were written by scribes, probably other Indian soldiers and possibly the Indian officers who were also acting as censors. Letters were subject to regimental censorship by officers and censored at the Indian Base Post Office. Censorship reports to the India Office and other government departments in London included extracts from the letters, translated from Gurmukhi, Hindi, Marhartti, Garhwali, Gurkhali, and Bengali (6). Neither should the letters be assumed to be a medium for private communication even aside from military and colonial surveillance. The sender would expect them to be read aloud to family and a wider community. Omissi frames these questions as a historian concerned with "evidence" and the identification of "distortions" (4), but as texts in the literature classroom the letters offer rich opportunities to consider colonialism as well as war as a context for questions of authorship, reading, translation, and interpretation. Das, following Jay Winter's example, invokes Pierre Nora's concept of *lieux de mémoire* ("sites of memory") as an approach to reading the letters and other textual artifacts (*Race* 22). As palimpsests, the letters bear traces of numerous writings and overwritings, including the peasant Indian soldier encountering European combatants and noncombatants in Europe. A remarkable example of overwriting uncovered by Das is Rudyard Kipling's access to the censorship reports—he plagiarized these letters word for word in *Eyes of Asia*, a series of four fictional works largely aimed at Americans that are either in the form of a letter by an Indian soldier or concern the act of letter writing or its reception in India ("Writing" 38). Put in dialogue with the actual letters, Kipling's war propaganda suggests new lines of literary transmission between the colonized subject and the metropolitan center.[5]

New configurations of texts such as these offer rich possibilities for the classroom as well as the literary scholar, bringing the war and colonialism together in order to investigate the degree to which they are entangled in war writing and in colonial and postcolonial literature. But can the letters, oral histories, folksongs, and sound recordings be more than supplementary historical documents that complicate and amplify our understandings of the traditional canon of war writing? This question is certainly not particular to literary studies of the First World War, involving as it does debates about the politics of aesthetics and what kinds of texts belong in the literature classroom. Specific to First World War studies, however, is the degree to which the field has become interdisciplinary as it has moved out of the purview of military history. A global approach to the war depends heavily on a multidisciplinary lens. Yet the traditional armory of the literary scholar rather than the historian can enrich readings of texts such as the Indian soldiers' letters. Das, for example, analyzes narrative structure as a neglected facet of the letters (*Race* 82). His point reframes the place letters have in the literature classroom, not by turning them into literary texts but by insisting that our methodologies can contribute to a richer, more nuanced, and more accurate understanding of the First World War's global nature. The result may lead to collaborations among teachers from disciplines such as literary studies, linguistics, art history, history, archaeology, and media studies.

The call for multidisciplinary approaches to the world in the First World War has been accompanied by a renewed push for comparative approaches. Investigations of war writing across national borders has focused largely on the European belligerent powers, particularly France, Germany, and Britain, and the Western Front. And despite its availability, war literature from the former dominions has not been brought into conversation with British war writing, not least because writers such as Frederic Manning and Katherine Mansfield were subsumed into the category of British literature.[6] In 1976 Holger Klein edited a collection of essays, *The First World War in Fiction*, which also included essays on American writers such as John Dos Passos and E. E. Cummings. Other work followed, ranging from Tim Cross's ambitious international anthology of First World War writing, *The Lost Voices of World War One* (1988), which included Slavic and East European writing, to critical collections and studies, such as Frank Field's *British and French Writers of the First World War: Comparative Studies in Cultural History*, Elizabeth Marsland's *The Nation's Cause: French, English, and German Poetry of the First World War* (1991), and Jay Winter's *Sites of Memory, Sites of Mourning: The Great War in European Cultural History* (1995), which contains two comparative chapters on European war literature. As Harro Grabolle points out in his own comparative study, such work by literary scholars tended to take genre as a starting point for the study of Western Front experience and attitude across national borders (14). By contrast Winter, as a cultural historian, although focused on Europe, opened the way for wider comparative studies of war memory.

The feminist critical challenge to the conflation of war writing with the male combatant also emerged in a comparative frame with *Behind the Lines: Gender and the Two World Wars* (1988; Higonnet et al.), leading to two important anthologies of war writing: *Lines of Fire: Women Writers of World War One*, edited by Margaret Higonnet (1999), and *Women's Writing on the First World War*, edited by Agnès Cardinal, Dorothy Goldman, and Judith Hattaway (2002). Both anthologies significantly internationalize war writing, with Higonnet's anthology extending coverage to India, Armenia, Hungary, and the former Cameroons. Nonwhite, non-European women were and remain, however, virtually invisible in First World War studies. The formidable task of recovering the experience and histories of male combatants and noncombatants from non-European societies is magnified in respect to women, with a few exceptions. These include, for example, the experiences of elite and highly educated women, such as the Begum of Bhopal and the Indian nationalist leader Sarojini Naidu, or rare glimpses offered in an interview with Abitisindo, a Malawi woman who worked as a courier in Manda (Das, "Ardour," 349, 355–56 and "Indian Sisters!" 25–35; Higonnet, *Lines* 324).

Comparative treatments of war writing don't in and of themselves necessarily revise the meanings of the global in war writing. As the editors of *The World in World Wars* point out, the geography of the war, its "units of research," and its conceptual frameworks have been defined according to a European and North American view (Liebau et al. 1). Grabolle presents the most extreme version of European exceptionalism when he adapts, as a justification for his study's Western Front focus on British and German war writers, a comment by Bernard Bergonzi that "it was here [the Western Front] that the major crisis of English civilization was centred, and where most of the writers who responded underwent the experiences that subsequently matured into autobiography or fiction" (qtd. in Grabolle 14). Transnational and postcolonial approaches orient comparative studies toward a critical reexamination of the who, when, and where of war literature.

In "Male Identity and Martial Codes of Honor: A Comparison of the War Memoirs of Robert Graves, Ernst Jünger, and Kande Kamara," Lunn offers an alternative model. His discussion of *Goodbye to All That*, *In Stahlgewittern* ("The Storm of Steel"), and Kamara's oral war memories establishes significant continuities among three elite British, German, and Senegalese Western Front combatants. Despite radically different cultural origins, each enters the war voluntarily in accordance with the standards of honor, duty, and military service instilled by his family and elite status. Lunn demonstrates how these memoirists' interpretation of their war experience and its relationship to their postwar societies diverge. Graves, embittered by the war yet on the side of the victors, participates in and contributes to "the myth of war experience" and to the concept of the "lost generation" sacrificed to false ideas. Jünger, on the side of the defeated, contributes to a German version of war experience that seeks to "give meaning to the nation's blood sacrifice" through the resurrection of the nation (734). For the "exploited" subject of the colonial world, war service demonstrates "African dignity" through "martial equality," so that Kamara's oral memoir interprets the sacrifices of the Senegalese Tirailleurs as the "avant garde" of the anticolonial independence movement (734–35). Lunn complicates our understanding of the war's aftereffects on formations of elite masculinity and their relation to family and nation by introducing an equivalent set of values in a colonial African society with a markedly different relationship to the organizing categories of class and nation. By adding his oral interviews with Kamara to a canonical First World War genre, Lunn also revises our understanding of both memoir and war writing as literature. It is hard to imagine a class of students who wouldn't enjoy and be enriched by this encounter, which will be further augmented by the completion of Lunn's *African Voices from the Great War: An Anthology of Senegalese Soldiers' Life Histories.*

Lunn's reading is illustrative of what First World War literary studies can gain from a comparative approach in a postcolonial frame. There is however no template for such readings, because the reconceptualization of war in global terms implies multiple sites of inquiry and a plurality of perspectives rather than the casting of the war as "an episode in the history of globalization" from a North Atlantic perspective (Liebau et al. 5). Bewildering as these multiple possibilities may seem, we can also see new constellations of war texts in the curriculum. The studies of marginalized war histories, such as Lunn's recuperation of Senegalese war experience and memory through oral testimony, Dina Rizk Khoury's research on Iraqi war memoirs and poetry, Abdallah Hanna's interviews with rural Arab and Kurdish veterans about their forced recruitment into the Ottoman armies, and Das's compilation and analysis of Indian voices, can enhance a range of courses in different world literatures. They also offer new perspectives in colonial and postcolonial literature courses. As multiple scholars have noted, service in a European imperial war has been seen in largely negative terms by nationalist and anticolonial movements outside the former dominions. A nuanced and less uniform picture is now emerging. We have already touched on the different value war service might have for colonized subjects, whether for elite or peasant Senegalese under French rule, for one of the approximately 1,130 Jamaicans who died in the war (R. Smith, "'Heaven'" 265), or for working-class migrant Irish women in British munitions factories (Culleton 39–41, 43–45). The war occasioned a massive "transcontinental military migration" that created cross-racial and cross-cultural encounters in Europe and other war zones (Koller 114). Such encounters might be between African American troops and white French civilians, Chinese laborers and North Africans in France, or between white Australian nurses and Arab Egyptians in Alexandria or Cairo. The potential for new identities, transnational or transcultural, brings new considerations of the war's role in postwar independence and anticolonial movements and the histories of postindependence societies. In the context of world literature and postcolonial literature classes, study of the war and the experience of the subject peoples of the European and Ottoman powers unfolds outside Europe's and North America's war stories.

The question remains as to what these hitherto marginalized voices can bring to the teaching of war literature in the traditional literature curriculum in English, American studies, or European languages departments. Once again, there is no single answer, but perhaps the most significant theme to emerge is that of the new encounters and proximities that resulted from the large-scale wartime movement of both European and non-European combatants and noncombatants. Those encounters that are presently receiving the most attention concern contact across race and color lines, and sometimes, but by no means always, between colonizers and colonized. For many African American soldiers, encounters with white French civilians contrasted starkly with their experience of racism at home and in the United States Army. In the postwar New Negro Renaissance, no-man's-land becomes a charged site of racial encounter, imagined as a space "the very deathliness" of which "configures it as an egalitarian space" (Whalan 74). No-man's-land allowed African American writers such as Jessie Fauset and Victor Daly to explore new forms of masculinity, dramatize cross-racial intimacies, and highlight the embodiment of the white man (69–78). The POW camp is another site of historical inquiry that, as Das and Heather Jones argue, reveals sympathies arising from shared experience of colonization or racial identity. British and German assertions of racial superiority over, for example, Turks and Indians gave grounds for identification between these groups. While a British rank-and-file soldier, such as P. W. Long, might portray the Turks as cruel Orientals and empathize with Indian POWs, those same Indian captives formed sympathies with their Turkish guards across enemy lines (Das, *Race* 80–81).

If no-man's-land is "a space of revelation and truth" (Whalan 293) in African American war writing, the military hospital is a charged site where white women physically care for non-European men. Alison Fell, a scholar of Frenchwomen's war writing and the international women's movement, examines memoirs and letters by white French and British nurses for encounters with Indian, African, and West Indian soldiers as patients. In these texts, the absolutism of racialized and cultural otherness is challenged, negotiated, or simply reinforced. For one British nurse in France, Edla Wortabet, the myth of the African savage is confirmed by a Senegalese soldier who tells her that "in his country they kill their enemies and eat them" (166).

Other nurses write as amateur ethnographers fascinated with physical and cultural otherness. On the other hand, a nurse such as Thérèse Soulacroix wishes to refute "the many things [that] are said" about Africans—for example, that "they have bags filled with horrors . . . and they are dangerous for young and pretty women" (169).

In canonical European, North American, and Australasian war writing there are many glimpses of "proximities" in the war zones and on the home front (Das, *Race* 17). By attending to these often fleeting moments in the text, literature scholars and teachers center questions about the relation of war writing to imperial frameworks and colonialism. In his memoir *Undertones of War* (1928), Edmund Blunden places Chinese laborers as a backdrop to the ruins of a French convent (Buck, *Conceiving* 78). The hero of Siegfried Sassoon's *Memoirs of George Sherston* (1936) encounters Indian cavalry in France and serves in both Palestine and Ireland. Enid Bagnold, famous for *National Velvet*, includes an encounter with a single African soldier and with a home population of "Lascars, Chinese, children, Jews, niggers from the docks" in *Diary without Dates* (1918), her memoir of Voluntary Aid Detachment work at the Royal Herbert in London (61). When we read canonical war texts together with the voices, textual and oral, of such peripheral figures—Chinese, Indian, and African—war writing becomes another contact zone, representing new encounters and possibilities of relationship across racial, cultural, and national divides, in the classroom today as well as for the wartime and postwar reader. To do them justice, we need to recognize that the world of the First World War for Europeans and North Americans was conceived within imperial and racial paradigms. We also need to center the "other" stories these works invoke.

Notes

1. The 2014 centenary has seen a massive increase in the volume of digital and print resources.

2. Precise numbers for the range of combatants and noncombatants discussed in this essay are difficult to establish. For example, the total of 210,000 Irish volunteers doesn't include Irishmen who enlisted in units in Britain, the dominions, or the United States. See Das, *Race* 27n7; Jeffery 6; and Koller for useful commentary.

3. For the range of these collaborations, see the Web site *Cultural Exchange in a Time of Global Conflict: Colonials, Neutrals, and Belligerents during the First World War* (www.cegcproject.eu).

4. The war diary of the Mexican American José de la Luz Sáenz, an invaluable new resource for the literature classroom, is another example of a work edited by a historian, Emilio Zamora, rather than by a literature scholar.

5. Another instance would be E. M. Forster's memoir of his wartime relationship in Alexandria with Mohammed El-Adl. By including a selection of El-Adl's letters in the memoir, Forster turns his writing into a site of memory for the colonial subject as war subject (Buck, *Conceiving* 93–112).

6. Outside the purview of this essay but worth signaling here is the impact of new approaches to Scottish and Welsh war writing that consider the regions as part of an archipelago rather than a unified nation.

Vincent Sherry

What Is the Relation of the First World War to Modernism?

The literary and political history of the First World War accounts for the special interests and particular difficulties in teaching the modernist literature of this event. To begin with, we should understand *modernism* in the root sense, that is, as the "ism" of the "modern," where the suffix adds the special intensive of a self-conscious belief in the modern as the establishing circumstance of art. Given this understanding, the war that defines the crisis of the modern age should be represented most indicatively by the literature we denominate as modernist, where the watershed event of the war, which is the term most historians apply to the differences it signals in European and world history, clearly stakes the moment of modernist consciousness. However, the actual literary history of the event complicates this nominal logic. There is a literature that is nonmodernist in the sense that it is perceptibly traditional in its poetic devices and narrative strategies and not at all intentionally or even noticeably experimental, and for a long time this literature owned a pride of place in the canon of war writing. There were obvious and even powerful reasons for this preference. This writing was done by combatant poets and novelists and memoirists, where the urgency of the experiential circumstance simply overrode any interest in technical invention for its own sake. This kind of writing was established early on (by the end of the 1920s) as the literature of major record; it was endowed with the authority of witness to a conflict that represented the profoundest disruption to European culture since the Reformation. Alternatively, most of the writing of the war years that we identify as modernist was produced (with several signal exceptions) by civilians, under the conditions of a cosmopolitan culture constituted by the antimatter of the combatants' ordeals. Added to the difficulties this difference signals, there is the perception (often warranted) that, beyond its distance from the signifying events of history, the modernist literature of the war years is notably and even willfully difficult, obscure, hermetic. The First World War has thus produced or reinforced the opposition between a perceptibly elite modernism and an assignably populist traditionalism. While this antithesis can be overridden by any number of intellectual maneuvers, it had a longstanding effect in our understanding of literary modernism's relation to the war, so that the gradual entry of modernist literature into the canon of war writing reveals issues in teaching this literature in the context of a historical event to which it was for a long time only questionably attached.

The chief orienting point in the history of the literary criticism of the war is Paul Fussell's 1975 classic, *The Great War and Modern Memory*, which, besides reinforcing a relatively small canon of white junior-officer-class writers as the reliable authors of the event, presented the importance of this literature in ways that excluded most of the major literary modernists. Fussell argues that the contrast the actual conduct of the war afforded to current (Edwardian and Georgian) expectations helped establish irony as the primary, defining mode of modern literary awareness. In its intensest demonstrations, he reserves this modern sensibility to writers who report from the combat zone. The vanguard of history, the brink of those outmoded conventions, lies on the firing line. Civilians such as "Joyce, Eliot, Lawrence, Pound, Yeats were not present at the front," Fussell calls the roll, "to induct them into the new idioms" (174).[1] To *induct*: the verb preserves associations of military conscription and the processing of mass armies, even while it intimates a rite of passage into some exceptional understanding—the awareness shared by a literary clerisy baptized by fire. A kind of "combat gnosticism" underlies Fussell's consideration of war literature as its intensifying, but limiting, condition (J. Campbell).

Fussell acknowledges that this critical restriction leaves a problem intrinsic to the question of war's relation to modernist literature. The "roster of major innovative talents who were not involved with the war is long and impressive," he concedes, including "Yeats, Woolf, Pound, Eliot, Lawrence, and Joyce—that is, the masters of the modern movement" (313). By contrast, the writers who were moved "to recall in literary form the war they had *actually experienced*" were "lesser talents–always *more traditional* and *technically prudent.*" Memoirists and poets such as "Sassoon, Graves, and Blunden are clearly *writers of the second rank*" (314; emphases added). If "their compulsion to render the unprecedented actualities they had experienced brought them to grips with the modern theme which we recognize as the essence of [the] ironic mode," their actual writing—the "traditional" forms, the "prudent" style—did not alter in answer to that world-changing event (313–14). Conversely, in this account, the main event of Fussell's modernity remains unengaged by those "masters of the modern movement," who, presumably, will have developed the methods and sensibility of literary modernism somehow and somewhere to the side of their modernity's formative event. The picture that emerges from this version of literary history witnesses an unexpected, reverse allocation of timely and anachronistic temperaments, majority and minority statuses.

This problem constitutes the circumstance in which some of the most important critical work of the last twenty-five or so years has taken on the task of relating the war to modernist literature and, more broadly, cultural modernism. In *The Rites of Spring: The Great War and the Birth of the Modern Age* (1989), Modris Eksteins expands the mainly literary frame of reference in Fussell's account into a broader canvas of cultural history, where the peripheral force of avant-garde movements before the war was at once relocated and recognized as the energy of technical modernity that eventuated in the war itself. This is the energy, in Eksteins's understanding, with which modernism conspires in its most radical elaborations, and while this understanding is ratified through some aspects of German cultural history, it remains cogent only for a relatively small number of authors who have survived as writers of lasting interest in the subsequent history. Alternatively, in *A War Imagined: The First World War and English Culture* (1990), Samuel Hynes works in the specific and local sphere of English literary history, where he proposes that the myth of the war—as the watershed event of modern history—was in place mainly or only after the war, where it established awareness of a modernist literature that is decidedly postwar and, so, of potentially secondary intensity. These two approaches witness the difficulty of relating modernist literature to the event of the war in its own historical present: Eksteins's modernists are ahead of time, while Hynes's modernists are behind the times. This legacy leaves the immediate historicity of the modernist literature of the war as the most compelling element in the question of the connection between the two approaches. What follows here is one way of understanding the historical consciousness of the war's modernist literature in its own moment, even as this imaginative awareness lasts into writing the major record, which was done into the late 1920s.

In this undertaking, we need to recover the values and practices that were brought into the cultural production of the war by its three main national protagonists—France, Germany (and Austria), and Great Britain (England, Ireland, Scotland, Wales).[2] This is, in a word, liberalism. The term refers not only to a partisan interest (when *Liberal* is capitalized) but also to an attitudinal frame of mind; it locates the point of defining reference in the cultural history of post-Reformation, Enlightenment Europe. Its root meanings deal with ideas and feelings of liberation, and this radical semantic shows in the experiences of deliverance into that zone of emancipated possibilities chronicled—ironically or not, and the irony is an important part of the longer story—across the public cultures and major literatures of the war's opening moments. The significance of this early moment in the war for both modernist and nonmodernist literatures may be seen in a frame of lengthened historical reference.

This perspective includes the origins, outcomes, and implications of the European revolutions of the late-eighteenth and mid-nineteenth centuries, most obviously in France in 1789 (and again in 1848), then in protonational Germany in 1848. In England, there was the residual but persistent and increasing pressure of an ever-deferred revolution, which, already by 1930, George Dangerfield saw (in *The Strange Death of Liberal England: 1910–1914*) as the threat that the war effort's centralization of national energies again helped deflect. The promise of emancipation through these revolutions (or near revolutions) gave the content and depth of intimately known expectation to the namesake value of liberation in *liberalism*. By 1914, however, this value imaginary had engendered a system of mercantile capitalism whose failure to satisfy the expanded masses of a European population was more than manifest. Unrealized, the dream of freedom in those European revolutions had led to the profounder restlessness in the populations it purported to serve. The extraordinary release of war feeling in the summer of 1914 expresses the climacteric, at once the failure and the apotheosis, of a long European history of liberalism.

One advantage in teaching the modernist literature of the war is that the recovery of this lengthened historical memory joins the writing done in the intellectual capitals during the war with the novels and poems and memoirs written out of combat experience. This opening moment's not so slowly evolving reversal features imprisonment in the trench system as the proof by refutation of the dominant idea of liberation, which has ground down into the awful inversion of stalemate and stasis in a war that has lost command strategy as well as local tactic. Again and again in combat literature, the physical prepossession and emotional intensity of being closed in may be read as the representation of the negative space of liberal freedom's positive concept and mythology, which brought the nations there to begin with. In the civilian circumstances from which the modernists will respond to their war experience, there is of course a different and specific protocol of political liberalism in the capitals of each national protagonist. For the sake of coherence in the space allotted here, we may take the case of Britain as a representative type, beginning with the political predicament in which the governing Liberal Party found itself, since this internal crisis in partisan politics opened out into a public culture that would provide one of the most demonstrable responses for the modernists residing in wartime London: Ezra Pound, T. S. Eliot, and Virginia Woolf. For these modernists registered the crisis in that majority dialect and took it as the opportunity to create a new literary idiom, one whose import may be equal to that of the tradition whose breakdown occasions these innovations.

In the history specific to the formation of the political difficulty in England, rival factions in the Liberal Party were already formed before 1914 on the issue—in principle—of war. To one side, liberal tradition maintained that armed force required an informed act of moral reasoning; a choice for war would need to be reasoned freely (the namesake value of liberalism provided the muse) in public and in accord with the loftiest ethical values. To the other side, however, Liberal imperialists considered the British military as an instrument of practical security; they had parlayed its powers strategically and tactically, aligning themselves with other European nations for the sake of mutual security but exposing themselves to conflicts that could not appeal to the loftier moral reason. While Liberal imperialists held the most powerful positions in the government, the logic of foreign policy was still controlled in its public discussions by moralist protocols. Accordingly, the chief ministers needed to keep private their alliance building with France and Russia, but officially they continued to deny the existence of these "secret agreements" (dubbed as such by an already suspicious public). The divisions in this partisan system moved to an inevitable crisis in early August 1914, when the network of European connections was being activated.[3] The moral cause of the war might be doubted, indeed profoundly doubted, but the rationale of the partisan case was asserted in a language of moral rationalism all the more strenuously and, apparently, unabashedly. There was a kind of travesty rationalism in the language of the liberal war in England: the logical compromises and moral hypocrisies of this public language would provide the most powerful provocation for the modernist response. There is a mimic wit and savage caricature in their parody of rationality, which, for all the somber comedy of its performance, should not lose its profound importance. For this antic reason presents an animadversion of the majority value in the mainstream culture of European Enlightenment modernity. It takes the attitudes and practices of public reason, which John Rawls has rightly understood as the sealing principle in post-Reformation Europe's liberalism, and turned them on their head—at the very moment in which these values were invoked and practiced in order to explain and make acceptable the greatest duress that Europe had undergone in centuries.

This timely accent may be heard even—or especially—in the words of a poet of Roman antiquity, as recast in the major enterprise Pound undertook through the second half of the war: "Homage to Sextus Propertius" (1919), a creative translation that features this Roman poet as the signal voice of Pound's own modernist moment. The poet sounds the modernist difference to his classical original in the note he dubs into it, a note that echoes the political idiolect of his own day already in the first verse paragraph: "Out-weariers of Apollo will, as we know, continue their Martian generalities, / We have kept our erasers in order" (205). Here, as Pound recasts his Latin original in an extensive interpolation that retains the guise of a poet's invocation of his Roman muse, he acknowledges the deity reigning over the discourses of the current war: Apollo, the god of logic as well as of music and poetry, is also a liberal divinity, but he has been suborned to the work of current verse, worn out not by generals but by the "generalities" of war, by political abstraction, by ideological argument, by the speech of reason-seemingness. Accordingly, the verbal art special to "Propertius" features an interplay between an archly rationalist syntax and a wittily impenetrable vocabulary. This passage is representative:

> For Orpheus tamed the wild beasts—and held up the Threician river;
> And Cithaeron shook up the rocks by Thebes and danced them into
>   a bulwark at his pleasure,
> And you, O Polyphemus? Did harsh Galatea almost
> Turn to your dripping horses, because of a tune, under Aetna?
> We must look into the matter. (206)

On one side, Pound's speaker builds a progression of apparently factual statements as logical, commonsense propositions of obvious knowledge. On the other side, however, his reader confronts allusions to chronicle legend and literary fable that are fetched from the depths of Mediterranean antiquity and featured, it seems, for their very unfathomability. Who, most of us must ask, was Galatea? And how close did she get when she "almost" turned to the horses of Polyphemus? That specifying adverb is Pound's interpolation,[4] whose blank space in the Latin original reveals the hollowness of Pound's (carefully) concocted knowledgeability. There is a particularly pseudological quality to this tone, as indicated by another interpolated word, the first "For." This conjunction establishes the expectation of cause-and-effect sequence, the impression that some logical proposition is in process. It builds some presentiment of commonsense meanings, one that Pound complements with those reassuring words of common speech. He steadily undercuts this promise, however, by enforcing the awareness that we do not know these mythological personages very well, if at all. His conceit echoes to the background sound of these times. This is the darker matter, the tragic backdrop to the hijinks of the poem's verbal surface, its performative foreground, so that, all in all, in a sort of tonal chiaroscuro, the rising rhythm of Pound's verbalist humor includes the dying fall of a recognition that recalls a language that has produced the worst catastrophe of historical record.

The same circumstances underlie the poetry of his conational and modernist companion, as we can see in a signal instance of Eliot's war verse: "Gerontion." This poem was finished in the summer of 1919, in the same month the Versailles Treaty was finalized, when Eliot was working in Lloyds Bank in London. His presence in the Colonial and Foreign Department at Lloyds keyed him into the schemes and implications of the Versailles agreement, and a profound dispiritedness echoes through this poetic product. The "little old man" of the title speaks an extended monologue, which presents a character in voice of contemporary liberalism in its senescence. This generation has authored in words a war its old men have not fought in body, reflecting the opposition between youth and age that shows so extensively in other war literature. Eliot's title personage speaks indeed for that older generation in the opening lines:

> I was neither at the hot gates
> Nor fought in the warm rain
> Nor knee deep in the salt marsh, heaving a cutlass,
> Bitten by flies, fought. (29)

The speaker admits his inactivity in the recent war and offers an apologia through a verbal ritual, at once well rehearsed and ill performed. The clausal construction of these opening lines presents the progressive discriminations of verbal reason—"neither / Nor / Nor"—but in contorted sequence. The ambitious program and plan of a thrice suspended period turns into the wreckage its phrasal sequence makes of it in the end. The rhetorical fiction challenges and reverses the liberal notion of history's proceeding gradually and rationally to improved futures; that notion has devolved into the unlovely muddle of the final line. This is the same history that, in the well-known meditation in the central section of this poem, presents a maze of "cunning passages" (30). This figure provides a trope not only for the confusions of experience in historical time, nor an image alone of the map of trenches that had been etched into the spatial imaginary of every European, but also and most of all a metaphor for the many passages in which the warrant of this liberal war was writ. This is the idiolect that the modernist poetry of the war represents at once in a heckling echo and creative counterrhythm.

The "little old man" of Eliot's poem is a personage Virginia Woolf might have actually known. He would be the junior contemporary of her father, Sir Leslie Stephen, a dean in the clerisy of Victorian liberalism, who put its core values of "reason in all things" into the extreme form of his own intellectual personality. It is the echoing of the words of the father that constitutes the sounds history was making for Woolf, and in her most significant work she speaks this language back against its source in a literary riposte of imaginative depth and moral consequence. She is a most readable and teachable author, and the students' appreciation of her work is informed by an understanding of the historical context that makes hers the most representative of modernist responses.

Consider the extraordinary provocation, in 1922 (the year of the publication of *Jacob's Room*), of this single-sentence paragraph: "And then, here is Versailles." The sentence comes in the midst of a prewar Continental tour that is taken by the eponymous Jacob (128). Yet the full historical import and meaning for this allusion to Versailles dwells in a history that has not yet happened: the war that will officially conclude in the Great Hall of Mirrors at Versailles has not even begun. As a name and place, nonetheless, "Versailles" cannot help but stir an immense range of associations for the reader, in 1922 and after. Also, as a nominal monument to the first age of reason, Versailles stands as an emblematic site, one that recalls in particular the fate a rationalistic language will have suffered in prosecuting the war that is (only) formally concluded there. Measured and reasoned speech cannot comprehend the range of meanings and feelings its words have picked up from the history they failed to regulate. For a sensibility formed in accordance with the liberal belief in the speakable reason of things, the most expressive record of the war's meaning lies in this shortfall of language, and this significance resonates in the silence around this highly charged counter.

The unspeakable is the most expressive dimension of Woolf's representation of the war in the famous middle section of her third novel of the 1920s, *To the Lighthouse* (1927): "[A shell exploded. Twenty or thirty young men were blown up in France, among them Andrew Ramsay, whose death, mercifully, was instantaneous]" (133). The bracketing action "Time Passes" performs on this character's death reenacts the strategy evidenced in this central section's framing of the novel, where, in effect, the war is parenthesized, contained as an interlude: the life of the Ramsay family goes on, in the domestic circumstance of their summer house on the Isle of Skye, in the first and third parts of the novel. Far from diminishing the import of the war, however, this section presents the conflict invisibly but unmistakably, displacing the turmoil into scenes of natural upheaval and leaving the unsaid all the more powerful in being resistant to direct linguistic formulation.

The war finds its voice most indicatively in the great novel of the middle of the decade, *Mrs. Dalloway*—or, rather, several voices. There is Mrs. Dalloway, reassuring herself at the beginning of the novel that the war is ended, even as the memory lengthens and intensifies through the course of her story. There is the unfortunate Doris Kilman, that Anglo-German relict of pan-European conflict. There is Septimus Warren Smith, the psychologically tortured veteran, who speaks the delirium of his living memory of the war in internal monologues. There is also Dr. (Sir) William Bradshaw, a knighted man of science, a figure laying claim to high and representative importance in the broadest compass of cultural politics, who aims his professional attention, in the early postwar moment of the novel's historical fiction, at rehabilitating veterans with combat trauma. A spiritual colleague of Leslie Stephen, Bradshaw performs a role in the rhetorical fiction of the novel, framing the thematic protagonist of its historical story as a particularly liberal motto and refrain: "Proportion," where the sense of balance, or, more exactly, scale or ration, goes to the root meaning of rationality. The manifest failure of the curative function of Bradshaw's word sounds not only through the melancholy consequence of Septimus's suicide. Proportion, involving larger and smaller, more and less important, is the theme word of power in prewar England, and while it organizes main and subordinate clauses in Bradshaw's exemplary paean, it is the measure against which the internal monologues of Woolf's own prose rebel—with the particularly insubordinate clauses of Clarissa's representative speech here, which features her sorting, shopping:

> And as she began to go with Miss Pym from jar to jar, choosing, nonsense, nonsense, she said to herself, more and more gently, as if this beauty, this scent, this colour, and Miss Pym liking her, trusting her, were a wave which she let flow over her and surmount that hatred, that monster, surmount it all; and it lifted her up and up when—oh! a pistol shot in the street outside! (13)

The veteran Septimus, it turns out, registers simultaneously the motor car explosion this closing phrase invokes. For him, the noise echoes to the background sound of his trench experience. The holocaust Smith's response embodies as a physical memory consummates the logic of liberal reason in history. The sentence presents the disheveled remnant of that degraded, disproved, inconclusive rationalism, to which it sounds its own triumphant antiphon. The specifically modernist idiom that Woolf typifies thus recovers a resonant memory of the history occasioning it.

This is a memory more specialized than the one Fussell has restored to the mainstream literature of the war, but its recovery allows us to read and to teach an essential part of the war's literary history in these major modernist authors.

Notes

1. Other attempts to situate the work of literary modernism in relation to the Great War are Trudi Tate, *Modernism, History and the First World War* (Manchester UP, 1998); Allyson Booth, *Postcards from the Trenches: Negotiating the Space between Modernism and the First World War* (Oxford UP, 1996); Sarah Cole, *Modernism, Male Friendship, and the First World War* (Cambridge UP, 2003); and Vincent Sherry, *The Great War and the Language of Modernism* (Oxford UP, 2003).

2. One of the most important developments in the criticism of the literary and cultural history of the war has been the attention paid to the involvement of countries outside the European zone of a conflict that is, after all, fittingly dubbed the First *World* War. Recent work on the experience of the war by the colonial populations of Britain, France, and Germany includes Santanu Das's *Race, Empire, and First World War Writing*, and it has been followed by Das's ongoing work on the cultural production of the war on the Indian subcontinent. Further work in this non-European frame of reference represents one of the most significant growing points in the scholarship of the Great War.

3. These secret agreements and the influence they exert on British policy and action were revealed in the major exposé by the founding director of the Union of Democratic Control (of foreign policy), E. D. Morel (see esp. 35–41, 273–300).

4. The relevant texts of Propertius's Latin and a standard prose translation are provided helpfully by Ruthven.

Patrick Deer

Rupture or Continuity? The Myth(s) of the War

The First World War continues to exercise a potent, often mythic hold on the modern imagination as the historical event that marked a radical rupture with everything that went before. Even after a century the Great War remains a crucible for modern myths, as the conflict in which the dreams of modernity collided with patriotic nationalism, imperial ambitions, mass culture and communications, and technologies of violence forged by a century of capitalist modernization. In the centenary year of 2014 in Britain, for example, World War I was at the center of an ideological battle over the teaching of history in the national curriculum, with an education minister trading barbs with long dead poets, revisionist military historians, and indignant cast members of a television comedy set in the trenches, *Blackadder Goes Forth*. In the United States, by contrast, critics drew parallels between an emerging canon of Iraq and Afghanistan war fiction, written mainly by veterans from an all-volunteer military, and the literary generation of World War I. There can be no escape from the mythic, it seems, only the attempt to guide students through the mythmaking that emerged from those bloody and decisive years of total warfare, 1914 to 1918. Fortunately the war's literature provides us with rich and ironic guides, not only to "the pity of war," as Wilfred Owen put it, but also to its heroism, sacrifices both civilian and military, to its horrors, seductions, mystifications, and historic aftermath.

The great challenge of encountering First World War literature, even a hundred years on, is to balance the desire to demystify with a critical exploration of the war's various myths. I focus here on several: the myth of the war's immediacy; of the Western Front as opposed to global war; literary myths of modernist rupture, irony, and pity; history written by the victors and by the defeated; gendered, class, and racial mythologies; the battle over military history; and the still ongoing postwar mythmaking. Read in this light, the literature of the Great War is best approached as a mix of rupture and continuity, crisis and reconstruction, fragmentation and consolidation.

Remarkably for a war whose centenary has recently been celebrated, the greatest challenge to teaching the literature of the First World War may be its shocking immediacy. The "troglodyte world" of the Western Front's trenches, mud, and no-man's-land seems to define modern industrialized warfare, offering a gritty corrective to the distant, seemingly virtualized war zones of contemporary conflicts like Iraq, Afghanistan, and beyond. It looked that way to many soldiers and civilians during World War II: as the British war poet Keith Douglas wrote in 1943, thinking of one of the greatest World War I poets, "Rosenberg I only repeat what you were saying." Yet this was the first mass-mediated war, even if press photographs were censored, the taking of photographs by soldiers was banned by military law, and the conflict belonged to the silent film era. Students may not have heard of Isaac Rosenberg or Keith Douglas, but they may well be familiar with clips from the propaganda film *The Battle of the Somme*; the official war art of Paul Nash; propaganda posters declaring, "Your Country Needs You," "Women of Britain Say Go!," and "What Did You Do in the War Daddy?;" or Lewis Milestone's haunting film adaptation of Erich Maria Remarque's *All Quiet on the Western Front*. The visual culture of World War I is an ideal place to start complicating students' conceptions about the war.

Beyond the mythic Western Front a whole world waged war. The sheer power of representations of trench warfare in northern Europe can obscure the truly global nature of World War I, whose other fronts included eastern Europe, Italy, the Balkans and the Dardanelles, the Middle East, and Africa and involved troops from every continent. The focus of Great War literature on the European experience also helped downplay the vast contribution and casualties of colonial troops, like those from Ireland, Africa, or from the Asian subcontinent (Das, *Race*). The conflict saw a vast mobilization of colonial troops: 827,000 Indian troops served, for example, of whom over 64,000 were killed; and approximately 210,000 Irish troops, both Protestant and Catholic, served in the British army, of whom at least 35,000 were killed. The theaters of war extended over western Europe, Italy, the Balkans, Russia, the Middle East, Africa, Asia, and Australasia. Excavating this larger context, especially of subaltern subjects at war, requires that students move beyond literary discourse into other kinds of archival and documentary resources. Recent critical accounts of the Great War show a welcome tendency to reframe the poetry, novels, memoirs, art, and film within this larger interdisciplinary and transnational context.

Reading the war through modernism can also distort our view. World War I's global scale and diversity of perspectives has often been obscured by the tendency of European and Anglo-American writers and critics to see the war as a modernist rupture that sanctioned rebellion, revolutionary innovation, and an oedipal overthrow of traditional authority. World War I was indeed followed by widespread anticolonial and nationalist uprisings in what historians have called the "crisis of empire" of 1918 to 1922, yet the European empires regained their hold by deploying violent force, reinforcing colonial political authority, promoting imperial propaganda at home, and modernizing their war machines, most notably through imperial air power and the bombing of civilian populations. Once again, the colonies provided laboratories for experimentation. This logic of imperial consolidation and the modernization of state and military power would have profound consequences domestically and internationally in World War II and beyond.

The war's dominant myths were shaped along national and imperial lines by the victorious Allied powers. But the mythologies of defeat in Germany and Italy, as critics like George Mosse have powerfully argued, shaped the interwar period and the rise of fascism just as decisively (see also Theweleit). When they encounter the literature of the First World War, readers are confronting not merely the myths of 1914 through 1918: students may need reminding that they are also participating in nearly a century of postwar arguments about military strategy, memorialization, and appropriation of the war's memory and meaning. This is in part because of the staggering death toll of the war and its global reach, which left war memorials in most villages and cities in Europe, across the United States, as well as in the colonies of these warring empires.

Students can be asked to consider why it is that despite the vaster scale of suffering in World War II, the trenches of the Western Front loom with such mythic and iconic power in modern memory. The answer must lie partly in the remarkable juxtaposition of myth and reality in the popular memory of the First World War. Although it is now over a century behind us, the war also brought into high relief many of the defining features of modernity that industrialization, imperialism, and modernization unleashed in the previous century.

Ironically, given these contested national mythologies, it was an American literary critic and World War II veteran, Paul Fussell, who set the terms for much of the ongoing debate about the ways that Great War literature has shaped the historical and popular memory of the conflict. For Fussell in *The Great War and Modern Memory*, World War I was a shattering descent into irony, disenchantment, and satire in which the shared literary education of the officer class, the theatricality of the conflict, and the "ridiculous proximity" of the home front and Western Front all played a crucial part (64; see 64–69). Fussell was in many ways, as Samuel Hynes has influentially argued, extrapolating from a contemporary myth of the war that emerged from about 1916 onward in the work of a wide variety of writers, especially poets like Owen, Siegfried Sassoon, and Rosenberg; novelists like Rebecca West and Virginia Woolf; or memoirists like Robert Graves and Edmund Blunden. This mythic version of World War I was then crystallized and solidified in the boom of war writing in the 1920s and 1930s, which produced such remarkable works as Virginia Woolf's *Mrs. Dalloway*; Robert Graves's *Goodbye to All That*; Edmund Blunden's *Undertones of War*; Remarque's *All Quiet on the Western Front*; Ernest Hemingway's *In Our Time* and *A Farewell to Arms*; David Jones's blend of experimental poetry and prose, *In Parenthesis*; Ford Madox Ford's *Parade's End* novel sequence; and Vera Brittain's pacifist memoir *Testament of Youth*.

What of the defeated? This British and American ironic literary vision of the war rapidly captured the imagination and persists as a dominant myth of the conflict, much to the irritation of military historians. But it is important to remember that readers of German and Italian would encounter a less ironic vision after 1918, which also built on nineteenth-century traditions of memorialization, religious and romantic symbolism but to different ends (Mosse). As Mosse has observed, this was a rival mythologization born out of national defeat, which helped feed the imaginary of fascism:

> The myth of War Experience was designed to mask war and to legitimize the war experience; it was meant to displace the reality of war. The memory of the war was refashioned into a sacred experience which provided the nation with a new depth of religious feeling, putting at its disposal ever-present saints and martyrs, places of worship, and a heritage to emulate. (7)

This dissonant vision can be found in texts like Ernst Jünger's *Storm of Steel* or the protofascist Freikorps archives explored in Klaus Theweleit's *Male Fantasies.*

The sheer diversity of the postwar literary boom is a reminder that First World War literature also challenges our conventional critical definitions of *literature.* As Samuel Beckett wrote of Joyce's *Work in Progress,* "the danger is in the neatness of identifications" (3). Though we might not consider it among World War I literature, the first section of *Finnegans Wake*, for example, contains a lively satire of a military museum in which Finnegan's resting place is located "behind Hill 60" near Ypres, an "all hallowed hill" on a World War I battlefield: "beyind Ill Sixty, ollollowed ill!" (7). As the inclusion of Joyce—an Irish noncombatant writer who spent the war in neutral Zurich—suggests, war writing disturbs national boundaries, as well as those between realism and modernism, combatants and civilian writers, conforming to tradition and the urge to make it new. Forced to improvise in the face of censorship, surveillance, and propaganda and secrecy, writers in wartime frequently have to camouflage their literary strategies and draw on multiple genres and techniques as they struggle to make their own perspectives and voices heard.

Critics like Fussell, Hynes, and Mosse continue to draw the ire of military and social historians, who blame them for fostering a mythic version of the Great War as a futile war fought by a heroic, disillusioned, and suffering soldiery commanded by incompetent general staff, "lions led by donkeys." Some British revisionist military historians—and politicians—have recently argued, for example, that World War I should be commemorated as a "war of national survival" (Sheffield, "Once" 7), even a national victory. They cite drastic improvements in leadership, strategy, and tactics that allowed for the development of more mobile forms of modern all-arms warfare and military success in 1918. Yet by seeking to redeem the conflict as a national victory, they may risk replacing one ideological narrative with another. Nevertheless, revisionist historians have crucially and irrevocably shifted the terms of the debate by stressing both ruptures and continuities in the war's historiography. As the cultural historian Jay Winter influentially argued in *Sites of Memory, Sites of Mourning* (1995), for example, when people grieved for those killed in World War I, they drew on traditions of mourning and memorialization, including classical, Romantic, and Christian sources that long predated the war.

Given this wide array of mythmaking, students may find it liberating to be reminded that their task is not to demystify the texts that they are reading. They must leave behind the safety of assuming that World War I literature primarily documents the illusions—and disillusionment—of patriotic societies who rushed naively to slaughter and were manipulated into waging war by fiendishly effective official propaganda. Reading First World War literature through the various possible meanings and uses of myth, or through the lens of ideology, may help students foster a more complex approach. Myths can be usefully discussed in at least three different ways: descriptively, in an anthropological sense as the founding narratives by which societies understand themselves; as the mystifying beliefs, or false consciousness, held by people about their ways of life and behavior; and, most usefully for teachers and students of literary texts, as enabling fictions by which people use narratives they know to be partly true and partly false in order to make sense of and shape the world.

One of the earliest post-1918 myths held that modern states and their propaganda apparatuses were all-powerful in their production of false consciousness and war fever. In fact, historians have discovered that wartime propaganda was far less effective than either governments or their citizens believed. Ironically, this failure likely spurred the Nazi propagandists or the ministry of information to perfect techniques of media spectacle, advertising, and propaganda in preparation for the next total war (Wollaeger; Ferguson).

Why, then, did people keep fighting? Many didn't. The 1914 Christmas Truce famously suspended hostilities on the Western Front for a day or two, allowing for fraternization and a now fabled game of football/soccer in no-man's-land. In Ireland, the 1916 Easter Rising challenged British colonial rule during the height of the Great War. The 1917 Bolshevik Revolution pulled the Russian Empire out of the war. And historians have documented a much higher level of mutiny and desertion during the conflict than strict censorship and harsh military law had people believe (Hochschild). Rather than the Hobbesian desire for violence that revisionist historians like Niall Ferguson have argued was a motivation for World War I, against the liberal tradition of protesting "the pity of war," or contrary to the willing capacity for violence by both men and women in arms explored in Joanna Bourke's *An Intimate History of Killing*, the answer seems to have been a more prosaic combination of popular stoicism, group loyalties, war weariness, and the desire to see it through. This, combined with improvements in military tactics and technology, as well as censorship, official secrecy, surveillance, and old-fashioned coercion by wartime states, protracted the conflict and produced the eventual Allied victory (Sheffield, "'Oh!'"; Bond; Travers).

Perhaps the best way to encourage students to explore the complex, often contradictory mythologizations of the war is to have them read canonical texts alongside lesser known but readily available work of women writers, writers from non-European or international traditions, or popular culture. It is worth reminding students of the powerful ambivalence of writers like Owen, Sassoon, and Hemingway toward patriotism and propaganda, even though their realism and outrage seems so distant from Rupert Brooke's patriotic melancholy. Even Sassoon's letter of protest, "Finished with the War: A Soldier's Declaration," read out in the House of Commons and published in *The Times* in July 1917, is a strikingly unstable document. That Brooke's "The Soldier," Owen's "Strange Meeting," or Elinor Jenkins's "Dulce et Decorum?" can be read for their complex play of sympathy, outrage, belief, and doubt suggests both the richness of First World War literature and its continuing relevance. More canonical poetry also needs to be counterpointed against the diverse perspectives to be found in international anthologies of World War I poetry: perspectives of American writers like Archibald Macleish, Carl Sandburg, Mina Loy, and E. E. Cummings; German poets like Georg Trakl, Wilhelm Klemm, and August Stramm; Russian writers like Anna Akhmatova, Osip Mandelstam, and Marina Tsvetayeva; or international modernist writers like Guillaume Apollinaire, T. S. Eliot, and Ezra Pound, the Dadaists Tristan Tzara and Hugo Ball, or the futurist Filippo Marinetti (see, for example, Silkin).

Even before war poets began documenting the horrors and pity of war, the warring nations produced a flood of propaganda, overt and covert. The British government dispatched painters, both traditional academicians like Muirhead Bone and experimental artists like Paul Nash, to the front under the official war artists scheme. The results of this extraordinary collaboration between art and propaganda are readily available on the Imperial War Museum's Web site, making for wonderful juxtapositions of text and image.

As digital natives immersed in visual culture, students can be superb analysts of the rhetoric of the image of World War I propaganda.

Though war reporting and war photography were severely censored, the war did make it onto cinema screens in official propaganda films like *The Battle of the Somme* (1916). Millions of cinemagoers witnessed this silent film of battle, with piano accompaniment, convinced that they were seeing glimpses of actual death and destruction. Clips of the film, such as the famous staged attack sequence thirty minutes in, will give students a very different sense of the spectacle of war than that afforded by *YouTube* clips from Iraq and Afghanistan, war movies like *Saving Private Ryan*, or video games like *Call of Duty*. After World War I, filmmakers were very much aware of the competing claims of war as spectacle, realism, and romance. The panoramic vistas of a film like King Vidor's *The Big Parade* (1925), for example, which offered spectators commanding visions over the battlefield, can be strongly contrasted with the harrowing realism of claustrophobic trench warfare depicted in G. W. Pabst's *Westfront 1918* (1928) or the classic closing sequence of Milestone's *All Quiet on the Western Front* (1930). The medical response to the war also produced the remarkable and disturbing documentary *War Neuroses*, of shell-shocked soldiers from Netley Hospital in 1917, available on the Wellcome Trust's Web site.

If the dominant rhetorical mode of World War I is to group elements in ironic dichotomies, in what Fussell memorably described as "adversarial proceedings" (79), then students may be better served by assignments that call attention to that binaristic tendency and resist it. It is instructive to have students select, from the anthology they are using, small clusters of texts that speak across the great divides of the conflict. In the case of the United States literature of World War I, for example, Hemingway's much anthologized short story of a veteran's iconic and ironic return to small-town life, "Soldier's Home," from *In Our Time*, can be powerfully counterpointed with the war writing of Willa Cather or John Dos Passos, or with W. E. B. Du Bois's "Returning Soldiers." In this short essay published in *The Crisis* (May 1919), Du Bois captures the mix of patriotic pride, outrage, and betrayal experienced by African American soldiers of the 369th Harlem Hellfighters regiment as they returned from Europe, where their regimental band had introduced jazz to Paris, to the unemployment, lynchings, and race riots of the "Red Summer" of 1919 at home (Sammons and Morrow).

This makes the choice of an anthology of World War I poetry or writing a crucial question for both teachers and students, since it is only in recent decades that poetry collections have included substantial contributions by women writers, writers of color, the trench poetry and marching songs of soldiers, popular songs of the period, or a comparative, transnational selection of writings that cuts across national boundaries. Women's civilian war poetry is now readily available in major anthologies, like Catherine Reilly's groundbreaking *The Virago Book of Women's War Poetry and Verse*, allowing for a far more diverse and usefully uneven sense of home front writing. The decidedly unliterary, satirical, and sometimes obscene trench poetry and soldiers' songs are available in collections like Roy Palmer's *"What a Lovely War!": British Soldiers' Songs* (1990) and on Oxford's *The First World War Poetry Digital Archive*. Like the poetry of women on the home front, they provide an invaluable counterpoint to canonical Great War poetry, allowing for a fuller range of voices. Ironically, however, postcolonial writers from this "imperial war" remain strikingly underrepresented. Fortunately, there are some excellent guides available in Tim Kendall's invaluable recent *The Oxford Handbook of British and Irish War Poetry* and Santanu Das's *Race, Empire, and First World War Writing*.

Teaching World War I literature thus presents an ideal opportunity to draw students' attention to the principles of selection, inclusion, and exclusion, as well as to the questions of value and taste that go into the construction of a canon of texts. Students may be surprised to learn that W. B. Yeats, as editor of the *Oxford Book of Modern Verse* (1936), deliberately "rejected" much of the best-known Great War poetry on the grounds that "passive suffering is not a theme for poetry" (xv). His introduction is a fascinating document that allows a rare glimpse of literary history or myth in the making. As Yeats admits, "I have a distaste for certain poems written in the midst of the great war; they are in all the anthologies" (xv). This is especially striking given that Yeats, an Anglo-Irish Protestant poet, wrote such famous and complex war poems as "On Being Asked for a War Poem" (1915), "Easter 1916" (1921), or "An Irish Airman Foresees His Death" (1919). He criticized poets like Owen, Sassoon, and Rosenberg, who "felt bound . . . to plead the suffering of their men. In poems that had for a time considerable fame, written in the first person, they made that suffering their own" (xv). This statement raises troubling aesthetic, ethical, and political questions that still circulate as myths about war writing today.

Why is poetry the privileged genre for representing war? Is all combatant writing necessarily marked by what Yeats calls "suffering," which is now diagnosed as trauma, PTSD, TBI, or "moral injury" and often pathologized as a separate kind of discourse (Scranton)? Can poets or civilians who have not seen combat legitimately write important poetry or prose about war?

Can poems be successfully written from a distance about the experience of suffering civilians in Germany, Iraq, or Afghanistan? A striking, belated response to these questions can be found in W. H. Auden's elegiac meditation on the relationship among literature, language, and politics, written at the end of the Spanish Civil War and on the eve of World War II, "In Memory of W. B. Yeats" (1939).

The revision, reconstruction, and reinvention involved in transforming war experience into literature can also be brought home by reminding students that most canonical World War I memoirs and novels belong to the postwar literary boom of the mid to late 1920s. Much wartime writing can be unvarnished and immediate but, no less important, compared with the more aestheticized perspectives and formal polish of later war writing. The war produced, for example, bestselling soldier memoirs like Donald Hankey's *A Student at Arms* (1917) and Patrick MacGill's *The Great Push* (1916), which give a less literary and more demotic perspective. Rudyard Kipling's wartime short story "Mary Postgate" (1915) is another eminently teachable text, whose misogyny and cheerful callousness shed light into the darker reaches of home front propaganda and jingoism. Rebecca West's marvelous wartime comedy of manners, *The Return of the Soldier* (1918), gives a nuanced sense of the disturbances wrought on both gender and genre by the conflict and is strikingly suspicious of beauty. Other wartime novels, like the American author Margaret Sherwood's *The Worn Doorstep* (1916), provide less canonical representations of nursing and women's war work than Vera Brittain's influential memoirs. Ernst Jünger's much revised combatant memoir *Storm of Steel* (1920) is another remarkable narrative of the conflict, based on the wartime diaries of a highly decorated German soldier who thrived in the bloodshed and hypermasculine solidarity of combat on the Western Front. Here readers can witness Mosse's "myth of war experience" being forged, disturbingly and openly, in the white heat of the narrator's protofascist imagination.

Critics in gender studies, modernist studies, and postcolonial studies have made great strides in revealing the mythologies of gender, class, and race in World War I literature and culture. Students should be encouraged to confront the ways World War I both provided new opportunities for men and women and reinforced traditional, patriarchal gender roles. They can explore the war as a crucible for male heroism, a proving ground for armored masculinity that allowed homosocial solidarity or male intimacy and friendship across class or national identities or provided an opportunity for extreme combat experience that might be translated into literature, stories, or cultural capital. The same texts can show women in wartime acting as matriarchal anchors for a home front, as mothers for future generations of soldiers, loyal wives for absentee husbands, nurses for passively suffering soldiers, suffragists demanding equality, or as empowered wage earners liberated from unpaid domestic labor and temporarily admitted into the industrial war economy. For colonial troops deployed to the various theaters of war, including the trenches of the Western Front, World War I also proved a powerfully contradictory experience. This is evident in both the poignant and fragmentary archive of letters of soldiers in the Indian army recorded by the British officers censoring them (Omissi, *Indian Voices*) and in later historical fiction like Mulk Raj Anand's novel *Across the Black Waters* (1939), which anticipates postcolonial critiques of imperial war.

In striking contrast to Jünger's diaries, Woolf's own diaries make a powerful counterpoint to her shifting novelistic responses to World War I. *Jacob's Room*, for example, is marked by absence and negation as if uneasy about directly representing loss and death, while *Mrs. Dalloway* represents far more directly a postwar London still literally and symbolically haunted by the war. A salutary antidote to the masculine mythology of combat can be found in Brittain's wartime diaries, which Brittain carefully drew on and transformed into her celebrated pacifist memoir *Testament of Youth* (1933). One of the more remarkable examples of the Great War's delayed assimilation is Pat Barker's *Regeneration* (1991), discussed elsewhere in this volume, which draws both on Great War poetry and the military psychiatrist W. H. R. Rivers's wartime case studies.

Reading or rereading Great War literature requires constantly acknowledging and displacing the monumental ways in which texts come to us already imbued with mythic significance. By using digital archives like *The First World War Poetry Digital Archive* to contextualize and show the process of creating World War I texts, readers can also see their publishing history, popular and critical reception, and subsequent institutionalization. Bringing students into contact with archives of the First World War is another powerful strategy for having them think critically about the limitations of canon war literature's availability. The historical distance and continuing timeliness of the war make it an ideal case study for immersing students in questions of canon formation, archival research, and the digital humanities. Amid the digital dazzle and potential sensory overload, however, students may need reminding that the same questions of selection, inclusion, and exclusion also apply to archives. Like World War I writers, they need to be skeptical themselves, in the face of our own technological myths of immediate global access to information or the spectacle of drone warfare waged at a distance.

Here Sassoon's postwar poem "Aftermath" (1919) seems very apropos of the ways that different kinds of traffic can promote amnesia, distraction, or remembrance:

> *Have you forgotten yet?* . . .
> For the world's events have rumbled on since those gagged days,
> Like traffic checked while at the crossing of city-ways:
> And the haunted gap in your mind has filled with thoughts that flow
> Like clouds in the lit heaven of life . . .

Looking back at the German myth of the World War I experience from the end of the twentieth century, Mosse asks similarly haunting questions for our own era of seemingly permanent warfare:

> [D]id the confrontation and transcendence of the war experience and death in war lead to what might be called the domestication of modern war, its acceptance as a natural part of political and social life? Did the Myth of the War Experience entail a process of brutalization and indifference to human life which was to perpetuate itself in still greater mass violence in our own time? (11)

Encouraging students to encounter the clashing national and imperial myths of this global conflict can challenge our conventional modes of reading, teaching, and research in ways that extend far beyond a class on First World War writing.

Part II

Global Narratives

Margaret R. Higonnet

Code Switching and Representations of the Great War

A quintessentially comparative topic, the literature of World War I invites attention to the intermingling of languages that represent the different nationalities, continents, and empires involved in the conflict. The phenomenon of code switching challenges readers by introducing a break or slippage from one language to another.[1] Yet it figures in much of the literature that our students have already read,[2] and it may paradoxically seduce the readers of works such as the Harry Potter series, where the Hogwarts vocabulary helps build a fantasy world of insiders. Code switching is endemic in war literature; as a student in my senior seminar on Great War literature noted, "Wars are the ultimate cultural exchange, not only between enemies but between allies as well," and people "living cheek by jowl in the trenches" borrow each other's vocabulary "seamlessly."[3] Language play figures in particularly interesting ways in colonial texts that "write back" about the imperialist implications of the Great War.[4] Play with creolization can connect linguistic to political borders. In *Borderlands / La Frontera: The New Mestiza* (1987), Gloria Anzaldúa points to the potential for innovation through mixity ("new mestiza"). She invokes a "contact zone" where two or more languages bump up against each other.

Not surprisingly, in fiction about the contact zone that is war, many occasions arise for the overhearing of another language or the interjection of words drawn from a second language (whether spoken by an enemy or an ally) into the narrator's account. Language is an index to identity; it may fit into an us/them mentality (Fussell 78).[5] Monolingualism may foster fear of others and trigger unwarranted reprisals. By contrast, the mastery of a second language and of another culture may suggest one's sophistication and power. While the insertion of words from another language into a narrative may at first seem an impediment to our students as they read, I suggest that linguistic hybridity or code switching plays a rich array of functions in the literature of war.

How do texts facilitate the reader's encounter with a second language? One widely read American war text, Ernest Hemingway's *A Farewell to Arms* (1929), sprinkles in a few Italian words along with technical terminology to establish the military knowledge of the narrator, Frederic Henry, an ambulance driver at the Italian front. With his ambulance, Frederic stops "at the *smistimento* where the wounded and sick were sorted" (33); Hemingway sets up the phrase to help readers grasp the word for *triage center*. Similarly, Frederic sends "a couple of army Zona di guerra postcards, crossing out everything except, I am well." He immediately transposes the simple Italian terms, commenting, "This was a strange and mysterious war zone" (36). In Hemingway, bilingualism serves to mark Frederic's control of his situation among Italians, even when wounded. Like the use of the first person, the device of quasi translation may also encourage the reader to identify with the hero's expertise.

As medical personnel do, soldiers may use a second language to transcend their national identity when they find themselves in a temporary truce. Erich Maria Remarque's hero, Paul Bäumer, trapped in a shell hole with a French soldier whom he has just stabbed, whispers to the dying man in both German and French, "Kamerad, camarade" (156), to soothe him in his final moments. Paul's sympathy for the French soldier, whose family photo he has found in a uniform pocket, finds expression in his paired appeals, which signal the underlying brotherhood of the men at war. The theme of brotherhood is likewise announced in the final chapter of Henri Barbusse's novel *Le feu* (1916; *Under Fire*), when soldiers from opposing sides understand each other without any mediation. The finale describes men buried in mud who are able to communicate across linguistic barriers, in a utopian vision of socialist political unity. First the French ask, "Français?," then, "*Deutsch*?," but hear no answer (352). In this no-man's-land, where the mud has brought an "epic" cessation of war, one of the Germans stumbling past the exhausted French narrator observes cautiously, "*Sie sind tot. Wir bleiben hier*" (354; "They are dead. Let's stay here" [my trans.]). As the German and French soldiers begin to converse, however, they speak in French. After their preliminary inquiry about national identity, the Germans' shift in tongue signals an internationally understood code and a tacit ceasefire. Code switching may then stand as a clue to a potential peaceful resolution of differences.

The strategy of easing the reader into a foreign world and language often draws on recognizable cognates, as well as on explanatory language, to enable a reader's educated guesses. In a class, the puzzle of making those guesses can help students experience the playfulness of language in war's contact zone. In her dramatic suicide narrative "Heroes," Gertrude Stein's friend Ellen La Motte, who nursed in a French hospital in 1915 and 1916 on the Belgian front, follows her patient to "the *Salle* of the *Grands Blessés*, those most seriously wounded" (7). As in Remarque or Hemingway, the reader can readily connect most of the French words to the English that follows. But we may also suspect an ironic pun about the attempted suicide of an AWOL deserter as a "grand blessé." The soldier who seeks a blessed escape in death from the obligation to kill may, as a result, be more heroic than his comrades. We may find dark humor in the term "réformés" for disabled soldiers who have undergone plastic surgery and will be released from service, "mutilated for life" (7).[6] Why, one might ask, did La Motte introduce French phrases that her readers might not understand? Readers may proffer various explanations, beyond effects of authenticity or realism. La Motte's enigmatic voice invites her readers to explore paths such as the defamiliarization of a military medicine that heals a self-inflicted wound so that a man can be "stood up against a wall and shot" for desertion (5).

Film offers an excellent tool for understanding code switching in the classroom, because subtitles can bridge differences among tongues. Alison Smith argues that Jean Renoir's *La grande illusion* (1937) on the one hand infuses language choices with nationalist loyalty (e.g., the English and French singing the "Marseillaise" in defiance of the German soldiers in their audience, during a vaudeville show in their prisoner of war camp).[7] On the other hand, in the language lessons exchanged by the escapee Lieutenant Maréchal and the German farm woman Elsa, Smith suggests that the bilingualism of the farm idyll works "towards the internationalism and pacifism" that Renoir professes (41). While the cosmopolitan aristocrats,

Captains Boëldieu and von Rauffenstein, share knowledge of English (the language of horse racing) as well as French, other scenes highlight difficulties caused by monolingualism. For example, when French prisoners on their way to another prisoner of war camp attempt to inform incoming British prisoners about the concealed escape tunnel they have dug, they are dismissed by an English officer who cannot understand French. By contrast, the wealthy Jewish Lieutenant Rosenthal helps his comrades survive not only through the packages of gourmet food he shares but also through his polyglot background, which has equipped him with a knowledge of Polish, Danish, German, and English in addition to French. Seen from behind the lines in the camps, war appears to be a matter of games and trickery—a situation in which code switching can play a significant role. In this classic prisoner of war plot, multilingualism unleashes "mischief with meaning," as Doris Sommer puts it (xii).

Renoir's ironies about miscommunication and the codes of class resonate in Jean-Jacques Annaud's film *Black and White in Color* (*La victoire en chantant* [1976]),[8] which transposes the problems of communication parodically to Africa. When the French colonists at Fort Coulais[9] discover in January 1915 that war was declared five months earlier, they express their patriotism with a resounding rendition of the "Marseillaise" and plan to attack the neighboring German outpost, using African recruits as their military force; they rename the local creek the Rhine. Rather than an expression of solidarity among allies across linguistic differences or of resistance to their captors, as in Renoir, the song in Annaud connotes the mindless nationalism and braggadocio of petit bourgeois merchants who have themselves no intention of fighting. The colonists' monolingualism in turn permits the bilingual natives to mock them: two corrupt missionaries express their pleasure at a song sung by their porters, but subtitles reveal that the lyrics mock the smell of white men and their feet, in an inversion of white prejudices. The buffoonish colonists exhibit their exploitation of villagers when the missionaries as well as the merchants offer recruits shoes and cooking equipment, along with new, French names. The protagonist, an official geographer and ethnographer, insists that the French must explain in the local language what is happening, but the colonists refuse. Use of the master language permits abuse of the colonized. Annaud bitterly indicts the parody of a "republic" that mobilizes ostensibly consenting recruits, in a process that leads to torture and the corralling of "savages" with ropes around their necks, to replace soldiers killed in the first battles. The war ends a year later with an ironic multinational twist. When British African troops headed by Captain Shashi Kapoor (an Indian) arrive playing bagpipes and announce that they have taken over the German mandate, one of the African soldiers must translate for the monolingual French. When the empire writes back, one of the most telling features of anticolonial narratives is the sophisticated multilingualism of oppressed colonial peoples.

Such writing back can be found as well in "Mutiny" (1919), by Svarnakumari Devi, a political activist, literary editor, and sister of Rabindranath Tagore, who used the mobilization of Indian troops in 1914 both to frame a story of past colonial misunderstandings (a "mutiny") and to interrogate Britain's overdue recognition of the Indians' "self-sacrifice" on behalf of "their mother-land" (389). The Indian narrator exposes the nationalism that colors historical records when a contemptuous Englishwoman labels the great general Kanhoji Angray, who had defeated the British, a "pirate." Her companions boast of British military strength while leaving unacknowledged the national pride of the Indians who "sacrifice our men and money to save the honour of England" (385).[10] The English hostess tells a comic tale within the tale, recounting an armed scuffle between rivals for her Ayah, which "Madam Sahib" had misinterpreted as a sepoy mutiny.[11] Her inability to understand the language of her maid, compounded by the maid's difficulty in understanding the mistress's English, triggered "wild imagination and fears" that could have unleashed military action (388). One road to violence lies in failed communication. In the final lines, after the gentlemen walk onto the verandah talking about the enthusiastic French welcome of Indian troops, the narrator translates the vision of English courage and "honour" (celebrated by the Englishwomen at the outset of her story) into the term "Izzat": the honor of the "mother-land" has been preserved by the bravery of "les Hindous" (389). The Indian woman's linguistic suppleness underscores the sepoys' political claims—claims that readers will realize were not in fact recognized after the war.

Cultural translation and code switching come to the fore likewise in Mulk Raj Anand's rich novel *Across the Black Waters* (1940), which centers on the Lahore division of Indian troops who arrived in Marseilles in September 1914. They experience what readers have described as an encounter with the European "heart of darkness": the horror of modern war.[12] As in Svarnakumari, the French welcome to their war-torn land "an army speaking a hundred different tongues" (5); a quick succession of the men's different prayers underscores the ethnic and linguistic diversity amid unity within their brigades.[13] Before the men enter battle at Festubert, they again prophylactically praise the divine in three different languages, in a "pretence of bravery" to conceal their "private doubts and fears" (218). What Anand calls "pigeon Indian" and the "higgledy-piggledy" intermixture of Indian tongues with European languages have attracted readers' attention as "weird" and "disorienting" (Bluemel, "Casualty" 305).

The linguistic experiment into which soldiers are thrown in wartime marks the role of the young protagonist, Lalu Singh, who has learned English at a mission school. Literate in two languages, he can interpret for his comrades (59). As in Annaud's film, the skilled translators are Anand's sepoys rather than the white officers, most of whom speak an "indifferent" Hindustani (216). Just as the sepoys are mystified by the new world of the French and their "incomprehensible" explanations, the reader may be mystified by Anand's incorporation of Hindi and Punjabi terms, including military ranks and common phrases such as "acha hai" ("how are you?").[14] While this Babel contributes to the construction of a polyglot Indian community with which the reader gradually becomes familiar, Anand's roughly phonetic transcription of what the men hear ("phrunt") also defamiliarizes our own language, to comic effect. In training, the soldiers practice "phormphor" and "stanateased" (82, 133); readers must rehearse the sounds in order to recognize standard military exercises—a good classroom exercise. "Angrezi" and "Francisi" (English and French) reach the "Looa" (Loire). Tellingly, when the men realize that "Jindac" (Jeanne d'Arc [33]) was "a girl Jarnel who drove out Angrezi army!," they consider her a model for rebellion against the British occupation of their country: "And the maid seemed to become a heroine like the Rani of Jhansi" (34). The constant code switching here corresponds to the men's desire to find common ground in France, which they compare with the agricultural world from which they have come. For the idealistic young Lalu, France represents modern technology, clean farmyards, and freedom from distinctions of caste and race. His wise old friend Kirpu, however, reminds Lalu that class (not equality) rules in French railway cars. In a rare direct parody of English officialdom, the boy recounts an English sermon by the Bishop of Chetpur, which he has just heard: "Lord Yessuh Messih, we pray you teach us to hate the enemy and help us to tear out his guts" (254). The transcription of "Jesus Messiah" slides toward "Yes sir, Monsieur," as a cue to authoritarian command structures. When General Roberts, colonel in chief of the Indian corps, declaims at parade what Lalu hears as "meaningless snatches" (192), Anand breaks down military control and questions the meaningfulness of war. Anand's focus on language and difficulties of communication meshes with his judgment of a misconceived British strategy to split up the Indian troops, half under the command of General Allenby and half under General Gough. The men "had come to accept their togetherness as a law of nature" (84) and to expect hearing "calls of battle in their own tongue" (87). Instead they are thrown together with unfamiliar units, compounding the problems of coordination under fire and leading to catastrophic losses.

One aspect of Anand's language that will strike every student is the presence of folk epithets and epigrams and especially of "classical" oaths such as "rape daughter," to which Anand calls our attention (13).[15] These verbal features reflect the oral culture of the sepoys, as well as the universal reliance of soldiers on a vocabulary of curses. The dilemmas of vocabulary and censorship in representing the experience of war have been at the forefront of critical attention since Barbusse's *Le feu*, whose chapter 13 on dirty words ("les gros mots") explains that argot and curse words capture the texture of actual experience: war itself is foul and can be expressed only by appropriate terms, terms that are generally censored as improper. Yet as Matthew Shelton pointed out in a graduate seminar, when a sepoy "affectionately" uses the curse word "rape-daughter" (13), Anand does not use the Hindi word *betichod*, yet he does drop in Kirpu's joking reference to "Lund or Kake Walah" without any further explanation (84).[16] We can ask our classes to consider what political, cultural, or affective reasons might explain the translation of one term but not another.

The struggle to translate across cultural boundaries paradoxically finds expression in texts from the colonies that steer between colonized and colonizers and between oppressive allies and enemies. As we have seen, code switching offers strategies for negotiating the representation of difference—although not understanding may also be the goal the narrator strives to achieve. This linguistic play, I suggest, punctuates war fiction. If an intrusive term becomes a silence or blank for some students, do such moments of rupture offer an analogue to the themes of trauma? Code switching serves metonymically to type characters, to perform mise-en-scène, to define war injuries, and to provide comic relief. It moves easily to the foreground in a course that seeks a global reach. Usually identified with postcolonial literature, code switching is also surprisingly common in World War I literature. It encourages us to ask our students why this hybridity may figure in war (and antiwar) texts, and why the characters within these narratives consider translation to be a tool for shaping what Anand calls "the silence of peace" (250).

Notes

1. Drawing on Susan Gal and Monica Heller, Alison Smith defines code switching linguistically as a phenomenon of "socially meaningful" linguistic variation, often in a "language contact zone" such as a bilingual family (37).

2. A canonical example of resistant bilingualism would be Charlotte Brontë's *Villette* (1853), where the frequent quoting of conversational bits in French evokes the disorientation and alienation of Lucy Snowe.

3. Angelo Manzi, writing about Mary Dexter's *In the Soldier's Service* (1918), noted the seamless use of "Boche," like the casual use of "train sanitaire" or "C'est la guerre."

4. Kristin Bluemel points to the way modernist irony "is put to new, anti-imperialist uses by Anand's adoption of Indian characters" ("Casualty" 308). She argues that our "discomfort" enables "our political education in imperial dissent" (314).

5. In *Monolingualism of the Other*, Derrida interrogates the notion that monolingualism can constitute an identity, calling that notion a "performative contradiction" (3).

6. In an edition such as my *Nurses at the Front*, a glossary of French terms can account for argot, technical references, or military terminology of the period, but La Motte clearly addressed the difficulty directly.

7. Smith cites Noah McLoughlin on the importance of code use to identity and miscommunication (43). See also Heller.

8. The intellectual protagonist's name, Fresnoy, may allude to Renoir's actor Pierre Fresnay. The enemy officers' polite exchanges echo those in Renoir. At the end, clumsy white lookouts in a tree assume the pose of African soldiers in a famous poster.

9. Although Annaud filmed his war story in the Ivory Coast, his fictional setting is modeled on the historical conflict between German Neu-Kamerun and French Equatorial Africa or Cameroun.

10. According to Teresa Hubel, the narrator's reflective silence is itself a kind of code, one that conveys trauma and "unspeakable" rage as well as power (178). The meanings of silence are a productive question for the classroom.

11. Like the Englishwoman's fearful misunderstanding of the local language, in much war fiction we find the menace of overheard foreign words. Thus in Anand, Lalu is "terror-stricken" when he overhears incomprehensible German ("Hokh, ho, hoi!") from a sap attacked by Lieutenant Hobson, who is immediately killed (236, 238).

12. Santanu Das, for example, writes that "hundreds of thousands of non-white men sailed to the heart of whiteness and beyond to witness 'the horror! the horror!' of industrial warfare" ("Sensing" 9).

13. Anand himself wrote that he sought to record "the collective unconscious of our own people, from the inherited oral cultures" (*Sources* 1). Katie Nunnery in her paper for our graduate seminar notes the excitement generated through the colliding celebratory shouts in different languages but also comments on the silent language of mimicry that permits a sepoy whose flute imitates a cobra's movement to communicate with French children.

14. One way to frame the novel is to juxtapose it with letters (and a vocabulary list) from David Omissi's collection *Indian Voices of the Great War*.

15. Anand uses "rape daughter," the literal translation of *betichod*, a slang expletive common by 1800 that can be interjected into conversation as an equivalent of the English *damn* or *motherfucker*.

16. Shelton explains that Kirpu has here not only inserted "lund" ("penis") but also transposed the name Wallon Cappel to "Kake Walla" or "shit" (84), slipping the term under the threshold of our awareness, unless perhaps the reader calls up the use in romance languages of *caca* for excrement. The scatological dimension of soldiers' argot, he suggests, loses its offensiveness when set next to the explicit physical horrors of wartime dismemberment and mutilation. Kristin Bluemel notes that unfamiliar metaphors and curse words "defamiliarize" the war (309).

Pearl James

World War I Regenders America

The United States of America plays a pivotal but minor part in most historical accounts of the First World War: its late entry tipped the military balance in the Allies' favor but limited the role of the United States in the conflict. Either because memories of the American Civil War still lingered or because its leaders were more focused on imperial conquest closer to home, the country avoided war until 1917, when the older European countries had begun to exhaust their resources. These accounts suggest that at the critical moment, the impetuous but untried United States military rode to the rescue, broke the stagnant front, and with plenty of grit and relatively few casualties chased the German army back within their own borders. Fighting quickly turned to occupation, and American soldiers had an easy job, as the popular song went, "winding up the watch on the Rhine" (Thompson and Davis). According to this narrative, the war's negative impacts are measured in terms of the European exhaustion and Russian Revolution, which paved the way for United States economic, military, and cultural ascendency. European disaster provided Americans with a positive masculine rite of passage. In short, American virility and vitality superseded European decadence. Ground lost to a whole generation of European men was gained by their

American peers. The war demolished traditional beliefs, clearing the way for European avant-garde artistic movements and a permissive American youth culture epitomized by sex, jazz, and alcohol. One of the most striking aspects of this stereotypical narrative of American involvement in World War I is the extent to which it is organized around tropes of gender and sexuality. American military intervention in Europe proved the nation's manhood, as it were, and secured the nation's role as a world leader. Another popular song wondered whether young American soldiers could be "[kept] down on the farm" once they had seen the lights—and the ladies—of "Paree" (Donaldson): in that version, war was an adventure that gave men a new level of sophistication and sexual experience.

In both comparative and American literature courses, the governing assumption that the war reinforced hegemonic American masculinity—the narrative I have been describing here—needs to be identified, scrutinized, and complicated. This oversimplified historical narrative creates problems for teaching American literature of World War I and for teaching American modernist writing more generally in relation to its historical moment. The axiom that "World War I was good for American men" makes the American experience out to be unlike that of other nations and their writers. Such a starting point makes it hard to move back and forth between American war writing and, say, the British soldier poets or even Virginia Woolf; it also guides students toward superficial readings of familiar American writers such as Willa Cather, F. Scott Fitzgerald, and Ernest Hemingway. The axiom renders several American war novels and narratives, such as William March's *Company K* (1933), anomalous: while it is impossible to say for certain why March's work has not entered the American literary canon, its biting irony and focus on the suffering of American soldiers puts it out of step with the dominant notion of American war experience. The axiom, in short, makes it hard to connect various strands of American writing to each other, their British counterparts, and to the war. In the course outlined here, I use literary and cinematic texts to pursue a series of questions, many of which hinge on gender: Did the war mean something different for men than it did for women? What did it mean, on balance, to Americans? How did it change gender roles, and how were those changes perceived from different perspectives? How do different writers, and writers of different sexes, register the war's impact? In so doing, I draw on several canonical and recent studies of American modernism that make either gender or war central.[1] Before we can pursue the questions raised above, we have to examine and disabuse ourselves of the familiar narrative: World War I was not good for American men. Why was—perhaps is—the notion that it was good so powerful?

One way of familiarizing students with this dominant narrative is through Charlie Chaplin's 1918 comedy *Shoulder Arms.* In this humorous film, the Tramp joins the American Expeditionary Forces and soon finds himself in the trenches, where he experiences in quick succession lice, rats, homesickness, flooding, bombardment, sniper fire, gas, and trench foot. These miseries leave him unscathed. Before long, he goes behind enemy lines and rescues France (personified by a young peasant woman) from the Hun (personified by a stereotypically degenerate troop of soldiers and a lascivious, authoritarian, and humorously mustachioed leader). He uses radio technology, camouflage, and Yankee pluck to capture the kaiser and save France. This triumphant comedy ends with the Tramp waking up, still in his bunk at a training camp: he looks into the camera and we realize, with him, that it has all been a wonderful dream. This film's gags are organized around stereotypes that 1918 audiences had about the war. (For instance, one German soldier throws a block of Limburger cheese into no-man's-land; having caught its scent, the Tramp rushes to put on his gas mask.) The film thus provides an easy way for students to encounter these aspects of war in their stereotyped form, transformed through exaggeration into satire. Best of all, Chaplin's Tramp provides a wonderfully ambivalent portrayal of American manhood: he wins the war and saves feminized France, but his heroism is bracketed both by Chaplin's performance of awkward—and therefore dubious—masculinity and by the film's dream vision plot device. The widely held myth that the war would turn boys into men, latecomers into victors, tramps into heroes, is introduced as just that: a myth, a dream. I use this film's motifs throughout the course as I try to move my students through and beyond stereotypical thinking about World War I.

First I ask my students to think about the escape the Tramp's dream offers its audience. Where does it invite its viewers to escape to, and by implication what does it allow them to escape from? First we tackle the second question, which guides our reading of F. Scott Fitzgerald's *This Side of Paradise* (1920) and Willa Cather's *One of Ours* (1922). Both texts, I argue, capture in literary terms their era's perceived national crisis of masculinity by problematizing the male coming-of-age narrative (P. James, "History" and *New Death*). Fitzgerald's Amory Blaine cannot find a structure, routine, or marker that secures his manhood. Unlike the Tramp, he has no clear mission to pursue. He has no damsel to rescue, no enemy to vanquish. Instead, he seems adrift in a series of adventures that go nowhere. Though he is not literally a tramp, he has fallen into a lower economic station than his peers and cannot move back up. Fitzgerald's novel, in other words, elaborates the fears that Chaplin's training camp dream allows the Tramp and its viewers to escape. I ask my students to imagine Amory as the target audience for *Shoulder Arms*: the film makes light of all his difficulties and would offer him a comic escape from his uncertain future. Chaplin's performance of awkwardness makes normative masculinity look fluid and easy in comparison. At the same time, the film's visual narrative of the war insists that every man is fit for the draft and that even the clumsiest recruit can become a hero. The familiar, exaggerated eloquence of Chaplin's pantomimes suggest every role, no matter how awkward, even modern masculinity, can be performed successfully. Having made this comparison in class, students can write about how Amory Blaine views the war, how his participation in it changes his masculinity, and how the novel portrays the process of acting like a man. Tropes of theatricality pervade the novel, and students will have new ways of thinking about them. Chaplin's self-reflexive presence on film functions as a cinematic counterpart. If the class includes both British and American war writing, a writing assignment might also ask students to interpret why Amory likes the war poet Rupert Brooke. What sort of model does Brooke provide, and why is that model so appealing? How is Brooke's war poetry like Chaplin's dreamscape? How would the novel change if instead Amory idolized Wilfred Owen? Such assignments can show students that the notion of war experience is constructed through processes of textual imitation, identification, selection, and exclusion. They can catch Amory in the act of constructing a glamorous account of what war did for men and contextualize his fantasy in the novel's larger portrayal of his uncertain masculinity. He, like the Tramp, dreams idealistically about the war and what it will do for him. But as in the film, those dreams prove illusive.

This same point of departure can lead to rich readings of Cather's fiction, particularly her novel *One of Ours*. It portrays a male protagonist, Claude Wheeler, who brings stereotypical American values to the project of growing up: hard work, inspiration, innocence. But he too finds it difficult to achieve a stable masculine identity. For him, adult manhood turns out to be a trap: he finds himself locked into a loveless marriage, more alone than ever. Students can analyze particular problems—sexual, financial, technological, educational, and so on—that the novel's protagonist faces. They can also connect the novel's depiction of masculinity back to Fitzgerald's or to the wider culture of the 1910s and 1920s. For instance, students can work individually to find and present an artifact (such as an advertisement) that their chosen text alludes to, implicitly or explicitly, and then interpret the artifact's appeal and meaning. What does the cultural artifact assume or suggest about masculinity or manhood? Students can also collectively produce an online wiki for the text. In any case, discussing Claude Wheeler's fraught masculinity and his "queer[ness]" (to use the novel's word) in the first half of the novel makes its turn to the war as a heroic adventure more comprehensible and less propagandistic to students (138). Just as Amory reads Rupert Brooke, and just as the Tramp dreams of heroism, so too Claude goes to war in search of an experience that will make his empty life meaningful. His desire for that is strong. Whether and how the war fulfills his desire is an excellent topic for class discussion and can require students to take on the difficult task of separating Claude's free indirect discourse from the narrative as a whole.

Tropes of manhood and masculine sacrifice can also provide a way into talking about the African American experience of World War I.[2] In 1918, W. E. B. Du Bois famously called on his fellow black Americans to "close our ranks" with white citizens and "the Allied nations who are fighting for Democracy" ("Close Ranks"). He acknowledged that he was calling for "no ordinary sacrifice" but that it was necessitated by the fact that blacks had "no ordinary interest" in the American fight against "German militarism" and despotism. When the war ended and black soldiers returned, he connected the manhood proven in France with the ability to fight racism at home. "Tens of thousands of black men were drafted into a great struggle," he writes, and "fought gladly to the last drop of blood" ("Returning Soldiers" 13). These same men must now fight for civil rights. The rhetoric of sacrifice made and yet to be redeemed, of virile masculine power proven in war, dominates his writing about the war, most of which was published in *The Crisis* and is available online.

Similarly, Claude McKay's short story "The Soldier's Return" (1925) draws attention to the odd place black soldiers occupy in the dominant narrative of American masculine achievement. On the one hand, black soldiers rank among "our American boys" who had "smashed the Kaiser and now were returning home in triumph" (191). On the other hand, returning black soldiers are told to take off their uniforms and called "boys"—not men—to their faces (192). White citizens in the story view black manhood, displayed by military uniform, as a sexualized threat to white women.

When the main character is accused of rape and nearly lynched, McKay makes it clear that his captors cannot abide the claim to manhood made by his uniform. The story's biting irony illustrates again the inadequacy of the stereotyped account of American triumph in the war.

What else does *Shoulder Arms* invite its viewers to escape? Certainly, it minimizes the brutality and costs of war. It is useful at this point to teach an example of the combat narrative, the genre that *Shoulder Arms*'s dreamscape slapsticks. I focus specifically on how fighting and being at the front impacts soldiers' masculinity. There are any number of texts that work well here: John Dos Passos's *Three Soldiers* (1921), William March's *Company K*, Thomas Boyd's *Through the Wheat* (1923), or Hervey Allen's nonfiction memoir *Toward the Flame* (1926), to name a few. The World War I combat narrative as a genre follows a predictable pattern that stages and questions the cultural assumptions that warfare provides opportunities for men to perform heroically. The genre typically traces one or more characters through the dehumanizing processes of training, enduring bombardment and other fearful experiences at the front, loss of comrades, debilitating injury, and an anticlimactic and psychologically difficult return home. These narratives both detail the soldier's humiliations and work to imply his toughness as a survivor. They simultaneously reinforce and question elements of the myth of the heroic soldier, and I focus on this contradiction. *Company K* deviates from the genre in ways that make it singularly instructive. For one thing, March's novel (if we can call it that) focuses on an entire company of men rather than a single soldier. As such it emphasizes the variety of war experience and at the same time avoids the bildungsroman development narrative that so often justifies war as a coming-of-age experience. Each episode is named for an individual soldier, and so the table of contents reads like a roll call or, alternatively, like a monument to the dead. While each episode stands on its own, there are a few connections between the stories that make the book more than merely the sum of its parts. From the contraction of sexually transmitted disease, to conflict with French civilians, to souvenir hunting among German corpses, March's small narratives provide fictional examples of the historical experience Jennifer Keene explores in *Doughboys, the Great War, and the Remaking of America*. This is a good point to replace the idealized narrative of American war experience with elements of Keene's and other recent revisionist accounts of American involvement in World War I.

In *Shoulder Arms*, even as the Tramp wakes, he remains in an idealized version of military life. I use the film's vignette to transition to a new unit in the course that focuses on another devastating aspect of American experience during World War I, the flu pandemic that killed more than 500,000 Americans (see Jane E. Fisher's essay in this volume). Katherine Anne Porter's *Pale Horse, Pale Rider* (1939) provides a fascinating opportunity to analyze the portrayal of weakness, disease, and psychological suffering in conjunction with gender norms. I use the book as well to introduce several aspects of total war beyond the crowded conditions of a mass civilian army and the influenza pandemic that resulted from the war. It also portrays the mobilization of the home front and particularly the way media brought European war into American hearts and minds. Porter answers a call H. L. Mencken issued in 1922 when he hoped an American writer would produce a "genuinely typical American story of the war" that does "not deal with the fighting at all, but with the . . . loan drives, the cadging for the Y.M.C.A. and the Red Cross, the looting of enemy nationals, the spy-hunt, all the other patriotic whoop-las of the period." Porter's story evokes precisely this "whoop-la." Seedy war-bonds salesmen bully the story's protagonist, Miranda, who is also targeted by propaganda both at work and as she moves through the streets. Porter portrays how propaganda circulates in Miranda's thoughts and registers the ways that total war has flattened language:

> These vile Huns—glorious Belleau Wood—our key word is Sacrifice—Martyred Belgium—give till it hurts—our noble boys Over There—Big Berthas—the death of civilization—the Boche . . . the war, the war, the WAR to end WAR, war for democracy for humanity—a safe world forever and ever—and to prove our faith in Democracy to each other, and to the world, let everybody get together and buy Liberty Bonds and do without sugar and wool socks—was that it, Miranda asked herself. (175)

If *Shoulder Arms* makes comedy out of Americans' clichéd understanding of war experience, Porter's stream-of-consciousness litany conveys instead the nightmare of a total media war. Each student can be assigned to research and present or write about a different item in Miranda's list and can then collectively describe the wartime media environment. Point them to easily accessible visual material such as propaganda posters, postcards, and photographs from your institution's library, or from the National Archives, the Hoover Institution at Stanford University, the Imperial War Museum, the National World War I Museum, and other online archives. In *Shoulder Arms*, war is a man's affair, and the film's only woman is a French refugee in need of rescue. The reality of total war, as we have already seen, was more complicated and involved women in complex ways, not just as victims but also as agents. Next in my course I move to texts that deal explicitly with American women's war experience abroad. I ask students to consider whether our reading continues to elaborate or to break down apparent differences between male and female experience of the war.

Dorothy Canfield's story "A Little Kansas Leaven" (contained in her short story collection about the war, *Home Fires in France* [1918]) portrays a female character, Ellen Boardman, who goes to France as a volunteer in the war effort. The story celebrates her ethical sensibility and her agency, which it portrays as decidedly feminine traits. While her fellow Kansans (read Americans) "thrust the disagreeable subject [of the war] out of [their] mind[s] with impatience," Ellen acts (141). After the sinking of the *Lusitania*, she takes a series of wholly unconventional steps: she withdraws all her money, takes a leave from her job, heads to France, and soon becomes essential to a voluntary refugee resettlement program in Paris. A version of the stereotypical narrative of American involvement in the war resurfaces here but in feminine form: in this story it is American womanhood that saves the day. In her portrayal of what is needed, Canfield offers a curious blend of modern and traditional femininity. One thing, however, is clear: there is no romance or sexuality in Canfield's portrait. Ellen is "respectable to her last drop of pale blood. And yet *was* it quite respectable to go off offering chocolate and writing-paper to soldiers you'd never seen before?" (162). With this, Canfield both raises and assuages the sexual anxiety provoked by the spectacle of female war workers. Ellen Boardman's "queer," asexual femininity emerges from the social pressure that frames Canfield's self-assigned task of justifying new roles for single women in and around the sphere of war. If the story stakes out new roles for women in modern war, it also limits the terms of their agency. Put simply, Ellen gets to participate in the war and to act like a hero but forfeits sexuality. Canfield's story provides an opportunity to reflect on the stereotype that women cannot understand or experience war and therefore cannot write about it. It is worth telling students that the idealistic elements in *One of Ours* have long been critiqued as a result of Cather's femininity, which supposedly limited her understanding of war. As if to anticipate and counter such criticism of women writers, Canfield portrays the unique power with which Ellen tells her story. This story defends new roles both for women war workers and for women war writers. Thus the story revisits and revises the oversimplified narrative of American experience of World War I. The fact that Canfield's story is out of print and that students will most likely read it online or in a photocopy makes questions of canonization materially palpable.

Mary Borden's *Forbidden Zone* (1929, subtitled *A Nurse's Impression of the First World War*), poses more stylistic and generic challenges than any text discussed so far, but because it follows Canfield and Porter, students have been prepared for it. Its challenges are interpretive opportunities for students who have become more familiar with the wartime tropes of heroic manhood. Borden's text portrays the debilitating effects of injury as a negation of manhood: "Once they were real, splendid, ordinary, normal men. Now they mew like kittens," the narrator reflects (44). She portrays the double effects of modern warfare on male flesh and on the psyches of the women who treat them. Borden refigures the sexual opportunities supposedly enjoyed by soldiers by portraying pain as a "harlot" who "[plies] her trade" in the beds of the hospital wards (45). She uses tropes of gender and sexuality to measure and convey the war's violence to the body and to human relations. Both this and the text's structure can be profitably compared with Hemingway's *In Our Time* (1925). Both texts present their reader with a series of stories with loose, subtle connections and understated meanings. One can ask students to compare the ways in which these two texts use fragmentation and innuendo to imply war's effects. I also use these texts to introduce the term *modernism* and to describe why it has been seen, by many, as the best means of writing about war.[3] I suggest that, according to both Borden and Hemingway, war destroys normality and conventionally realistic narration.

When the Tramp awakens in his tent at the end of *Shoulder Arms*, he has been to war and fought, only to find himself safe at home again. The film's dream implies that men return from war unscathed, almost as if they never left. Once again, the film's conceit works well to introduce yet another important topic of American war literature: soldiers' difficult homecomings. For this I use Hemingway's story about a returned veteran, "Soldier's Home" (1925). Its protagonist, Krebs, has returned from the war "much too late," after "the greeting of heroes [is] over." He seems marked by war in ways that are hard to see or measure. His war experience remains sealed off behind a wall of silence, because "no one want[s] to hear about it" (*In Our Time* 69). War has isolated him from everyone but particularly from the girls he watches and from his mother, who attempts to break through his silence. At this point on the syllabus, literature of World War I can be seen to double back on a longer pattern in American literary history, the tradition that Nina Baym has identified as the "melodrama of beset manhood" (224). In much American literature of World War I, women come to stand for an ignorant home front, for those who did not fight and so are neither willing nor able to understand war and its costs. I ask students to question how the gender opposition between men and women works in Hemingway's story and how that differs from texts we have read so far. In "Soldier's Home," the rift between men and women comes into being through a particular exclusion: the exclusion of war stories. What is "it," we might ask, that "no one want[s] to hear about"? "It" is hinted at in distinct ways but never named directly. Hemingway's language suggests that Krebs is unable to specify his war experience even to himself; Hemingway the author refuses to describe it even to a careful reader. What is missing from this story is the story of the war itself, which is only implied by what it does to Krebs (and men like him): it leaves him silenced, isolated, and unwilling or unable to make commitments that would lead to "consequences" (*In Our Time* 71). Having read more explicit texts such as *The Forbidden Zone* and *Company K*, students have an easier time making inferences about the details Hemingway's text withholds.

Having traced the interior logic of Krebs's male melodrama, we can develop its meaning in the course's larger literary and historical frame. Hemingway's story's gender binary—men fight, women stay home—will have already been contradicted by many readings. The war put enormous pressure on the notion of heroic masculinity and at the same time provided unprecedented opportunities for women in the labor market, in the military sphere, and in civic leadership. As my last several examples have suggested, literature by both canonical and now less familiar authors reflect these and other changes with portrayals of damaged and queer masculinities, with nontraditional femininities, and in the symbolic contests that these new gender roles created. But while Cather, Borden, and Porter all portray the war as a situation in which women take on new roles, they also emphasize its costs for women. These and other literary texts also suggest that, despite the upheaval of the war, traditional hierarchies of value were reasserted in its wake, often with exaggerated emphasis. My essay's title invokes and distorts the common wartime trope of "regen(d)eration" to indicate this complex of both new growth and reiteration. The impossibility of deciding whether the war ultimately changed or reinforced gender norms offers a learning opportunity: students can appreciate literature's unique ability to capture complex social realities. Making arguments without the certainty of a "right" answer forces them to become both better readers and writers.

I conclude this course where most would say American literature of World War I begins, with Hemingway's *A Farewell to Arms* (1929). The readings done before this point estrange the students from this narrative, which now reads very differently than it did in high school (or than it did in one of the various film versions they may have encountered). Frederic Henry's hospital stay and affair with Catherine Barkley will strike students who have read Mary Borden as wishful indeed. I tell students how important Hemingway has been to the understanding of World War I and its literature and invite them to analyze the narrative's meaning and power. I focus on its famous passage railing against the "big words" of propaganda and then on the way it turns away from war and the wounds of men to portray the vulnerability of women. This novel is powerful precisely because it shows the pain of war in such powerful metaphoric ways. What I hope my students can do is untangle the text's metaphoric uses of gender and sexuality in more useful ways than they would have been able to a few months earlier.

Notes

1. Most useful to mention in the context of this essay are Forter; Gilbert and Gubar; Haytock; Limon; Strychacz; Trout; and Vernon.

2. For more on this topic, see Whalan; Schneider; and Chad Williams.

3. Fussell; Winter; Eksteins; Cobley; and Sherry (*Great War*) all figure prominently in this debate.

Richard Smith

The Impact of the First World War on Pan-Africanism: The Transcendence of National and Imperial Boundaries

This essay discusses resources that can be used to study the growth of Pan-African ideas among British West Indian soldiers during and after the First World War. My intention is to encourage learning that recognizes the global nature of the conflict and its consequences. That West Indian ideas of race and identity were increasingly informed by exposure to philosophies beyond the limits of the British Empire is particularly evident in the interaction of West Indians and African Americans. The wartime voices of British West Indians and African Americans are to be found in poems, political pamphlets, newspapers, and periodicals. These materials provide evidence of the desire among black volunteers to have their military service rewarded with social justice and equality, either by a reformed British West Indian colonial administration or by the United States government. The sources can also reveal the transnational and global Pan-African affiliations that transcended the boundaries of nation, state, and empire when local reforms did not materialize. At the same time, it is also important to recognize that many of the texts' bellicose, hypermasculine pronouncements could equally be deployed in support of continued imperial allegiances and privileges for veterans in excess of those for noncombatants who also performed significant roles in the war effort.

The experiences of West Indians in the First World War provide an opportunity to explore the role of the mass media in producing and rehearsing ideas of race and national identity. The conflict itself defined imperial and national character. The experience of both West Indian and African American servicemen, therefore, allows students to consider the impact of key historical moments, events, and processes in identity formation. Diasporic identities are constantly in a state of fluidity and contestation, but war and conflict can intensify these processes.

Historical Background

The early twentieth century was an era of increased geographic mobility for West Indians and African Americans. West Indians traveled to neighboring islands, South and Central America, and to the United States in search of employment, most notably for the United Fruit Company or on the Panama Canal construction (Chomsky). In the United states, southern rural to northern urban migration patterns combined with West Indian migration flows to create what may be regarded as Pan-African communities in the northern cities. At the forefront of these communities was the Harlem neighborhood of New York, which formed the largest concentration of black people beyond Africa (Locke). These demographic developments underline the importance of using comparative approaches when presenting material on West Indian and African American responses to the First World War.

During the war, and in the following two decades, fledgling West Indian nationalist organizations adopted the masculine discourses of military sacrifice and citizenship to support political changes, which ranged from limited constitutional reform to full independence. When the United States entered the war in 1917, African American organizations, such as the National Association for the Advancement of Colored People (NAACP), linked military service with a vocabulary of blood sacrifice to strengthen claims for equal citizenship and civil rights. Expectations of improved social and economic conditions for black people were not met in either the British West Indies or the United States.

Over the course of the 1919 Paris Peace Conference it became apparent that the right to self-determination for small nations, enshrined in Woodrow Wilson's Fourteen Points, did not extend to nonwhite peoples. Thereafter, the cross-fertilization of Pan-African ideas was more evident among both

West Indian and African American movements and activists. West Indians in the United States agitated for global black mobilization alongside African Americans or developed programs for West Indian self-government and confederation away from the watchful eye of the colonial authorities.

West Indian Support for the War

The outbreak of war in August 1914 was met with prowar enthusiasm in the British West Indies. Despite the poor economic and social status experience by the black majority, many retained a faith in the purported British values of justice and a sense of loyalty to the monarch. This enthusiasm was evident not only among volunteers for military service but also in short stories, poems, and letters submitted to the press. Thomas MacDermot, writing as "Tom Redcam," and Henry Shirley Bunbury of Jamaica were at the forefront of this movement (see "A Chant" and "Arouse Jamaica"). William Raglan Phillips's "De War Time Solo" and "Victoria Gran-Pickney" (both 1914) illustrate attempts to encourage support for the war through use of the Jamaican language. Rose de Lisser's "The Appeal" (1915) shows the contribution of women writers to the war effort. A West Indian example of the invasion scare story can be seen in Harry Morgan's "When the Germans Took Jamaica" (1914). Many West Indian veterans were subsequently radicalized by discrimination during enlistment and military service. Nevertheless, ideals of heroic military sacrifice emblematized the development of West Indian national identities.

A key document from the early months of the war is a resolution passed by the Universal Negro Improvement and Conservation Association and African Communities League (UNIA) on 15 September 1914 at the Collegiate Hall, Kingston, Jamaica, which was forwarded to Lewis Harcourt, the British secretary of state for the colonies, the following day. Founded on 1 August 1914 by Marcus Garvey shortly after his return to Jamaica from England, UNIA proposed a number of social and economic measures, including improved education and the promotion of entrepreneurship to instill "the Spirit of Race Pride and Love" among all those of African descent to "help them to a state of good citizenship" (Letter to Booker T. Washington 117). The resolution declared that

> being mindful of the great protecting and civilizing influence of the English nation and people, and their justice to all men, and especially

> to their Negro Subjects scattered all over the world, [we] hereby beg to express our loyalty and devotion to His Majesty the King and Empire. . . . We sincerely pray for the success of British Arms on the battlefields of Europe and Africa, and at Sea, in crushing the "common Foe," the enemy of peace and further civilization. (Letter to Lewis Harcourt)

The resolution demonstrates how at this point Garvey and UNIA were primarily concerned with the betterment of peoples of African origin in the British Empire. The document illustrates how many West Indians held a deep attachment to empire because of its stated values, such as freedom and democracy. British propaganda asserted that a German victory would entail the reintroduction of slavery. UNIA's loyalty also safeguarded the limited rights of black subjects, implying the possibility of military enlistment for that cause. The series Marcus Garvey and Universal Negro Improvement Association Papers, edited by Robert A. Hill, provides the most exhaustive range of documentary material through which to trace the emergence of nationalist and Pan-Africanist politics.

Formation of the British West Indies Regiment

Statements such as the UNIA resolution encouraged West Indians to volunteer in the cause of empire. Many traveled directly to the United Kingdom and attempted to enlist in British army regiments. These volunteers were accepted at the discretion of local recruiting officers on arrival. Others were rejected outright on the grounds that military law regarded black men as aliens and placed limits on the number of them that could be recruited. In October 1915, the British West Indies Regiment (BWIR) was an infantry regiment established to accommodate West Indian volunteers for the duration of the war. The subsequent experiences of West Indian volunteers, including the discriminatory practices they faced, can be found in several accounts, including Glenford Howe's *Race, War and Nationalism* and Richard Smith's *Jamaican Volunteers in the First World War*.

West Indian newspapers from the war period provide useful teaching materials, among them letters and poetry from soldiers. For further discussion, the online *British Newspaper Archive* (www.britishnewspaperarchive.co.uk) gives access to a wide range of national and local newspapers, such as the *Daily Mirror* and *Western Mail*, that provide articles on the contribution of the West Indies to the war effort. The United Kingdom National

Archives has an ongoing program to digitize and make available online battalion war diaries, including those relevant to the British West Indies Regiment. Digitized images and film of the BWIR can also be accessed through the Imperial War Museum collections catalogue. Encouraging students to reflect on their own family histories could also familiarize them with primary source materials. Students of West Indian heritage may have ancestors who served in the British West Indies Regiment. Family history guides, like Guy Grannum's *Tracing Your Caribbean Ancestors*, and digitized military records accessible through the National Archives and its commercial partners, such as *Ancestry.com* and *Findmypast*, will allow students to develop both genealogical interests and case studies of individual West Indian soldiers. These case studies can help students to consider possible motivations for West Indians to volunteer, including the social and economic pressures as well as ideological reasoning.

African American Connections

When the United States entered the war in April 1917, African American organizations also sought to demonstrate masculine self-sacrifice in the pursuit of postwar equality. The NAACP was at the forefront of the campaign to secure black enlistment. *Crisis*, the NAACP's journal, printed many poems and articles encouraging African American military service as an effort to gain political enfranchisement and economic progress. Under the terms of the military service convention between the United States and Great Britain, British subjects resident in the United States could be recruited to the British army. From June 1918, this recruiting effort was extended to British West Indians living in the United States.

In the same month, the *Crisis* published a special issue dedicated to African American troops that was also circulated among West Indian migrants eligible for military service. A poem from the issue by Fenton Johnson exemplifies the crosscurrents in African American and West Indian identity formation evident in literary appeals for black volunteers. Johnson encouraged African Americans to enlist by invoking the Haitian Revolution of 1791 to 1804. The poem can be seen as part of a broader tradition in which the revolution became central to Pan-African identity during the Harlem Renaissance and culminated in the publication twenty years later of C. L. R. James's seminal text *The Black Jacobins* (1938). By this stage James had recognized the pivotal importance of the First World War in the emergence of West Indian nationalist sentiment. Johnson's poem imagines the spirit of Toussaint L'Ouverture, the most renowned leader of Haitian independence, stirring African Americans to enlist in a conflict that would similarly radicalize them:

> Toussaint, old man of the mountains,
> Is tramping through the streets of Port au Prince.
> "Whither do you go, Graybeard?" challenges the sentry.
> Toussaint's voice is soft and low.
> "I go to arouse the sleeping men of Ethiopia,
> "This is the hour that tries the nations and the races." (Johnson 65)

The *Crisis* for the First World War period is available online as part of the Modernist Journals Project (library.brown.edu/cds/mjp).[1]

Poems in *Crisis* show the important influence of Irish republicanism on black political activism at this time, particularly the belief in bloodletting as a purifying precondition for liberty and nationhood. Particularly significant was the conversion of Pádraig Pearse to armed struggle, which he announced with the words, "There are many things more horrible than bloodshed; and slavery is one of them" ("Coming Revolution" 99). At the graveside of the fellow Irish patriot O'Donovan Rossa, Pearse asserted that "Life springs from death, and from the graves of patriotic men and women spring living nations" ("Graveside Oration" [136–37]). Verse written in support of black enlistment took up this theme. Joseph Cotter, Jr., declared:

> They shall go down unto Life's Borderland.
> Walk unafraid within that Living Hell . . .
> All this to them shall be a glorious sign,
> A glimmer of that Resurrection Morn,
> When age-long Faith, crowned with a grace benign,
> Shall rise and from their blows cast down the thorn
> Of Prejudice. E'en though through blood it be,
> There breaks this day their dawn of Liberty.

Demobilization and Postwar Politicization

The aspirations of Africans for self-determination were unanswered by the peace settlements of 1919. Figurative calls for a blood sacrifice in the pursuit of independent African nationhood increasingly appeared on the pages of Pan-African publications. At the forefront of such pronouncements was Garvey, who had reestablished UNIA in the United States. He dedicated

UNIA's Harlem headquarters, Liberty Hall, to the memory of the Dublin Easter Rising, asking "the Negro race to offer up its martyrs upon the altar of liberty even as the Irish have given a long list from Robert Emmett to Roger Casement" ("Liberty Hall").

Pan-African interpretations of military sacrifice became particularly significant following the Italian invasion of Ethiopia in 1935. West Indian veterans of the First World War demanded the right to defend Ethiopia, the primary symbol of African self-determination after Haile Selassie was crowned emperor in 1930 (Weisbord; Yelvington). The Foreign Enlistment Act (1870) and the Ethiopian Order in Council (1934), however, forbade the intervention of British subjects in the conflict. In October 1935, 1,360 members of Kingston UNIA petitioned King George V as "members of the Negro Race, and the descendants of African slaves" anxious to ensure "the preservation of any part of Africa which is free of foreign domination" and to defend "our ancient and beloved Empire" ("Petition to King George").

Another petition collected by St. William Wellington Wellwood Grant, a veteran of the First World War, and L. P. Waison, for the Bustamante Industrial Trades Unions, laid claim to Ethiopia as the "only relic of the great African Empire" ("Petition"). Directly referring to the West Indian contribution between 1914 and 1918, the petition demanded "that in the same way as we helped to safeguard the integrity of other races, we are asking that our race be protected at this crucial moment." Examining documents such as these will enable students to explore how the colonial government apparatus was manipulated to anticolonial ends.

The West Indian War Memory

Media productions and materials produced during the centenary commemorations from 2014 to 2018 provide an opportunity to consider the contemporary inflections of West Indian war memory, particularly in media and literary portrayals. These sources can be found in the Library of Congress, Veterans History Project, and the BBC World War One Web site. There is also an emerging body of dramatic work dealing with the West Indian experience, including *At the Gates of Gaza* (Gilkes).

British memories and commemorations of the First World War still focus around an understanding of the conflict as tragedy, which runs parallel to the national melancholia associated with the loss of empire. These two strands of cultural memory increasingly converge around attempts to remember the First World War as a shared effort involving Britain and her imperial subjects, including volunteers from the West Indies whose descendants may now form part of Britain's multicultural society.

From the perspective of West Indian war memory, the service of volunteers who fought in the name of empire, and who may later have become affiliated with Pan-African and nationalist causes, has now been incorporated into the memory of independent nations (R. Smith, "TV Documentary"). More recently, commemoration of the First World War in Britain has tended to conflate empire and commonwealth, which may result in the expunging of the more painful and difficult histories of the former. A special service was held in Glasgow Cathedral to mark the centenary of the war's opening day and was broadcast live by the BBC. Military representatives from countries who had provided volunteers for the war effort offered speeches and readings, and the service included a contemporary setting of Pericles's funeral oration by Peter Aston, with the words, "So they gave their bodies to the commonwealth, and received praise that will never die" ("World War One"). These aspects of war memory provide fresh ways for students to engage with the long-term impact of the war on West Indian nationalism, Pan-Africanism, and contemporary multicultural societies.

Note

1. Another invaluable collection, which contains numerous interwar African American publications and which details links between African Americans and West Indians, is "Correspondence of the Military Intelligence Division relating to 'Negro Subversion,' 1917–1941."

Stephen Cloutier

For King and/or Country: British Dominions and the Literary Interplay between Imperial and National Identities

Participation in the First World War has become an important factor in helping British colonies fashion their own national identities. The sacrifices made during the war allowed colonies to renegotiate their relationships with Britain. Colonies such as Canada and Australia were able to define nationhoods that were at once independent and yet still firmly part of the existing imperial structure. Both countries celebrated those who fought in that war and used it to impose white, British-centric narratives of their nations, legitimizing their position as senior if independent partners in the British Empire. Ireland, on the other hand, used the war to establish an identity separate from Britain, considering those who fought as little more than traitors. Through this process, nationalist forces in each colony forged what Antonio Gramsci calls "a single cultural 'climate' " (349) that created an official narrative of the war, which the nations disseminated through various cultural channels.

Attempts to push alternative narratives to the social margins merely papered over the cracks in the colonial societies. In Canada, for example, writers consistently challenged the accepted view of the war. In Ireland even a poet as great as W. B. Yeats found himself torn between his political ideals and his personal experience. Any pedagogical approach to the colonial response, then, must take into account not just the wide range of responses between the colonies but also the very different responses in the colonies themselves.

Canada and Newfoundland

In Canada, the historical narrative that has coalesced around the war is that the war established Canada as a mature nation no longer dependent on the mother country. The Canadian victory at Vimy Ridge (1917), a battle that for the first time in history was organized and fought solely by Canadians, has become a particularly potent symbol of Canada's new national identity. In 1967, Greg Clark, who won the Military Cross at Vimy, wrote that "[a]s far as I could see, south, north, along the miles of Ridge, there were Canadians. And I experienced my first full sense of nationhood" (321). Canada was largely a nation of immigrants who looked back to their mother countries for their national identities. The war unified these disparate claims of national identity by forcing soldiers to fight in a Canadian uniform, creating an identification, through shared experience, with a notion of "Canada" that previously did not exist.

The link between the war and Canadian nation building crystallized in the immediate postwar period. G. D. Roberts, one of the preeminent Canadian poets of the period before and after the war, incorporates the sacrifice of the war into his construction of "Canadianness" in his poem celebrating Canada's Diamond Jubilee. In "These Three Score Years" (1927), he writes that "Dying, [the soldiers] live imperishable, and proclaim / Our manhood's stature to the world" (lines 52–53) and ends with "*Canadian* am I in blood and bone!" (66). Thus by the late 1920s, a Canadian national identity had clearly formed, an identity that was definitive enough for Roberts to assert it with some force (as evidenced by the italics).

Linking the notions of Canada strictly with Vimy Ridge may form an important part of Canadian national identity formation in the popular imagination, but the seeds of this shift in identity can be found in the early response to the outbreak of war. The poet William Wilfred Campbell began articulating a conception of a Canadian national identity even before the war; his poems are strewn with images of empire as he urges, "Britons, along the mighty world's highway, / Waken and throng, from mart and field and glen" ("Summons," lines 1–2) and argues that "Our dead, they are ours and the Empire's" ("Our Dead," line 1). Campbell's political positioning is typical of the emerging Canadian identity. The possessive pronoun "ours" clearly identifies the dead as Canadian (Campbell was born in Canada West—now the province of Ontario); yet they also belong to the empire. This then is the new Canadian nationalism, a nationalism based not on complete independence but on a limited autonomy in an imperial structure.

This view of the war, however, privileges an English Canadian formulation of national identity, important in maintaining English Canadian hegemony in conflicts with non-English-speaking Canadians (most notably French Canadians). Other voices responding to the war are pushed to the margins, where they can be easily ignored. While French Canadians did fight in the war, many Francophones saw the war as a European affair that had nothing to do with Canada. When Canadian Prime Minister Robert Borden instituted conscription in 1917, many French Canadians rioted, believing that they should not be forced to fight. As a result, there is little French Canadian literature of the First World War; francophone literature of the period typically escaped into Quebec's past to explore the nationalist ideas sparked by the conscription crisis. French Canadian literature that does deal with the war, such as the novel *Trente Arpents* (1938; *Thirty Acres*), by Ringuet (Philippe Panneton), uses war to illustrate the differences between French and English Canada.

First Nations Canadians similarly get pushed to the margins in an English Canadian formulation of the war, and First Nations writers focused on more urgent sociopolitical matters. Joseph Boyden, in his novel *Three Day Road* (2005), has recently refocused the spotlight on First Nations' participation in the war. The novel recounts the tale of two First Nations' snipers, Xavier Bird and Elijah Weesageechak, in World War I. Boyden shows the destructive power that white Canadian society wreaks on the First Nations, as Elijah is killed in the war and Xavier returns home badly injured and addicted to morphine.

Not all English Canadian writers accepted the established idea of the war; the struggle for the war's legacy is fought out in large part in the literature produced by veterans. *Generals Die in Bed* (1930), by Charles Yale Harrison, stands alongside the brutally frank novels of writers like Remarque and Sassoon; controversially, it includes scenes in which Canadian soldiers loot a French town and kill unarmed prisoners, clearly at odds with the developing positive view of the war. Robert W. Service, who served as stretcher bearer for the Red Cross and is famous for his poems of the Yukon, strips away the sense of patriotism in poems like "The Volunteer" (1916), in which his speaker says, "Them politicians with their greasy ways; / Them empire-grabbers—fight for 'em? No fear!" (lines 5–6). The speaker consciously rejects patriotism as motivation for joining up. Instead he says that when he saw the returning wounded soldiers, he "couldn't look 'em in the face" (35). Personal, not political, reasons push the speaker to enlist. Another veteran, Philip Child, deals directly with identity in his novel *God's Sparrows* (1937); Child's main character, Dan Thatcher, is torn between his American relatives on one side and his British relatives on the other. The political and cultural positions of republicanism and empire that vie for dominance in the Thatcher family become empty and meaningless under the pounding barrage of artillery.

Newfoundland, as an independent country during the war, had a strong sense of its identity separate from the Canadians. The Newfoundland soldier Francis "Mayo" Lind made this distinction clear when, writing to the Newfoundland newspaper *Daily News*, he complained that a Scotland band had played the Canadian song "The Maple Leaf," mistaking the arriving Newfoundland troops for Canadians (3). The war left a different legacy in Newfoundland, one of lost nationhood, as Newfoundland's independence was stripped in the war's aftermath. If the victory at Vimy Ridge symbolizes the war for Canadians, the loss at Beaumont-Hamel (1916) is the touchstone for remembrance in Newfoundland. It is such a devastating event that in Wayne Johnston's novel *The Custodian of Paradise* (2006) one character, never named and rarely seen, feels so ashamed at surviving the war that he breaks off all contact with his family, becoming a representation of the ghostly figures of the past who continually haunt the present. In spite of this loss, or because of it, there is little Newfoundland literature devoted to World War I, especially when compared with that of the rest of Canada. The novel *No Man's Land* (1995), by Kevin Major, picks up this note of sadness. Focusing on the lead-up to and the battle of Beaumont-Hamel, Major relies on the reader's knowledge of the battle's consequences to convey the sense of inevitable tragedy. Mayo Lind, who died in the battle, even makes an appearance to underline the impending disaster. Major's evocation of the Newfoundland identity that the soldiers so deeply held reinforces the futility of their sacrifice in fighting for a nation that would lose that identity.

Australia

With fewer competing voices than in Canada, Australia was able to fashion a coherent, unified national identity that relied on the notion of the

Australian soldier not as the equal of the British soldier but as his superior. This idea coalesced around the image of the "digger." The digger army emerges as a self-reliant force that created a camaraderie unique among the armies that fought in the First World War. An important part of this camaraderie was the fact that the Anzacs were volunteers throughout the war. While other countries initiated conscription at some point in the war, the Anzacs declined to do so, meaning that the digger army was always a volunteer army. The Australian view of its soldiers links the individual with the collective. In this formulation of national identity, the soldiers create unity from their shared individualism, a result of the self-reliance forced on them by the harshness of the trench landscape. Thus the national myth is internalized in the individual soldier and links him to the idea of nation in much the same way that the Canadian Greg Clark can, looking back on Vimy Ridge fifty years later, link his personal experience to a sense of Canada.

As it did in Canada, the outbreak of war sparked a resurgence of imperial feeling. The poem "Irish to English" (1916), by Christopher Brennan, adopts the persona of an Irish rebel who admits that "I am not of your blood; / I never loved your ways" (lines 1–2) and that he is "Irish and rebel both / And both unto the end" (5–6). But he vows to put aside those traditional conflicts: "And here I pledge you troth, / And here I stand your friend" (7–8). The poem takes the British side so ardently that the Germans (never named) become "the scum that blights our land" (9). Similarly, Henry Lawson would invoke images of England to support the war. In "England Yet" (1916), he writes, "We learn our England, and in peace forget, / To learn in storm that she is England yet" (lines 19–20). The Australians, or "Our own" (25), are not fighting for glory; they "reck not of a king's regalia, / Tinsel of crowns, and courts that fume and fret" (25–26). Like Brennan in "Irish to English," Lawson recognizes the conflicting identities, in this case Australian and English; the soldiers "Are fighting for her—fighting for Australia— / And blasphemously hail her 'England Yet!' " (27–28). Stating that it is blasphemy for an Australian to hail England may seem at odds with the pro-English sentiment, but the poem ends by reasserting the loyalty to England: "She's England yet, with little to regret— / Ay, more than ever, she'll be England yet!" (9–30). The notion of England and empire silences other considerations.

The most famous Australian novel of the First World War remains *Her Privates We* (1929; also known as *The Middle Parts of Fortune*), by Frederic Manning, although there is some debate over whether or not

Manning should be considered part of the Australian tradition given that he moved to England at the age of fifteen. However, one can still see the digger mythology at work in his novel as he celebrates the Australian soldiers' grit and self-respect. Another veteran who explores the life of the Australian soldier at the front is Harley Matthews, who was wounded at Gallipoli. His poem "True Patriot" (1938) celebrates common soldiers and links them to the idea of diggers: "Our eyes, all they saw now, / Was earth. Digging, we felt, smelt, tasted it—Earth" (lines 27–29); the term *digger* originally referred to miners. The soldiers in his poem seem to rise out of the Earth: "When we rose to watch, the dead men lay / There in the periscope" (29–30). The verb "rose" is ambiguous in this context. It can suggest "rising" as in waking in the morning, but the reference to the periscope suggests that they are rising from the earth. The poem ends with the collective individualism of the Australian soldier:

> We filed into the trench.
> No destiny
> Ruled us, but our own intelligence.
> Whoever else, whatever it might be,
> It was not himself now that a man doubted. (342–46)

The poem begins with the collective we, which suggests the togetherness of the soldiers. The final line roots the war experience in their separateness. It is their individual experience that allows them to have the shared, collective experience.

The digger ideal, originating as it does from Australian miners and possibly Kauri gum-diggers, carries with it associations of the land and landscape that easily translate to the subterranean world of trench warfare. David Malouf's *Fly Away Peter* (1982) reflects the uniqueness of the Australian experience that stems from the landscape. Ashley Crowther, who has just inherited a farm, observes that it "was a landscape . . . that could accommodate a good deal. . . . It wasn't so clearly defined as England or Germany; new things could enter and find a place there. It might be old, even very old, but it was more open than Europe to what was still to come" (13–14). The Australian landscape opens up the future by creating an egalitarianism that breaks down class barriers. Crowther the landowner builds a friendship with Jim Saddler, the young man he hires to be the warden for his bird sanctuary. Meeting later at the front, the connection between the two remains even though Ashley is an officer, and he is there when Jim dies at the novel's end. As Jim dies, his final thoughts are of the land and the comfort it provides him: "The earth was rich and warm, it smelled of all that was good." The connection with the earth seems to take away the pain of dying, as he reflects that "his back did not ache as he expected" (128). The man who lived on the land returns to the land.

Ireland

If Canada and Australia were able to formulate coherent national identities coming out of the war, the war complicated national identity in Ireland. Ireland had a much longer history of resisting English colonization, and Irish nationalists defined their identity in opposition to British imperialism. If the war caused rioting in French Canada society, in Ireland it led to open rebellion. Irish nationalists had been agitating for independence for years, but, in the years immediately before the war, partial autonomy seemed possible when the British government introduced a Home Rule Bill in 1912. The 1914 Government of Ireland Act, which would have given Ireland home rule, passed the House of Commons, but the outbreak of war postponed the bill before it could reach the House of Lords. This disappointment resulted in a deeply divided reaction to the war. Many Irish men joined the British army, arguing that helping the British would advance the Irish nationalist cause, while many others saw joining up as betraying it. Ultimately, Irish nationalists would attempt an armed revolt during Easter 1916. The Easter Rising was put down and seven of its leaders executed. Partition would ultimately follow the war in 1922, leading to the Irish Civil War (1922–23). Because of these deep divisions in the postpartition period, Irish participation in the war and the literature that emerged from it were often forgotten as Ireland focused on building a new unified state.

That Irish First World War literature is often ignored stems, in large part, from attitudes expressed by W. B. Yeats. Yeats's two famous comments on this topic, often quoted, are "passive suffering is not a theme for poetry" (xxxiv), written when justifying his exclusion of First World War poetry from his edition of the *Oxford Book of Modern Verse* (1936), and the lines from his poem "On Being Asked for a War Poem" (1915): "I think it better in times like these / A poet's mouth be silent" (lines 1–2). Yeats may well have had literary and aesthetic reasons for his hostility to First World War poetry, but there were also clear political reasons. In the battle for "true" Irish identity, Yeats sided with those who opposed fighting for the British rather than those who went to war. Famously, he would celebrate the Easter Rising and its leaders in his poem "Easter 1916" (1916), in which even "[a] drunken, vainglorious lout" who "had done most bitter wrong / To some who are near my heart" (lines 32–34) is raised to the pantheon of heroes.

Even when Yeats was moved by personal circumstances to write a war poem (the death of Robert Gregory, the son of his close friend Lady Augusta Gregory), he removed any notion of British imperialism. In "An Irish Airman Foresees His Death" (1918), Yeats's speaker refuses to identify himself as British in the lines "Those that I fight I do not hate, / Those that I guard I do not love" (lines 3–4). He may fight for the British against the Germans, but he does not see himself as a part of the two countries' national rivalries. Rather he still reflects an Irishness separate from Britain and its empire, stating, "My country is Kiltartan Cross, / My countrymen Kiltartan's poor" (5–6). Kiltartan here acts both in terms of national identity (a barony in County Galway) and personally (being the home of Lady Gregory). This collapsing of the political and the personal is not without tension in the poem. Yeats must resolve why someone who self-identifies as Irish would fight in a war in which he claims to have no political motivations. Ultimately, the airman explains it in personal terms: "A lonely impulse of delight" (11). Even as Yeats celebrates the son of his friend, he is careful to put the airman on the "right" side in the conflict of Irish identity.

The poet Francis Ledwidge, who was killed in the third battle of Ypres, exemplifies the tensions created by the conflicting Irish identities. His poetry is often the sole example of Irish war poetry on a syllabus and therefore bears the weight of critical examination. Ledwidge felt he could best serve Irish nationalism by serving at the front. His poetry would reveal his conflicted attitude toward the war and his love for Ireland. Seamus Heaney memorializes Ledwidge in his poem "In Memoriam Francis Ledwidge" (1979), in which he calls Ledwidge "our dead enigma" (line 41). The poem, imagining Ledwidge in his uniform with his "haunted Catholic face" (26), attempts, if not to reconcile the competing identities in Ledwidge's poetry, at least to examine them.

Ledwidge's early poetry encourages his fellow Irishmen to join up: "It's time to be up and be doing" ("Call to Ireland," line 1). The call is not to empire, but because "We have fought so much for the nation / In the tents we have helped to divide," the poem casts the war as something to unify the country (9–10). Although the poem does not specify who the divided tents represent, its invocation of Irish history rather than British

Empire suggests that the tents refer to Ireland and even the divided nationalist movement. The Easter Rising, which showed so clearly that the war had failed to unite Ireland, deeply upset Ledwidge. His support for the uprising is shown in poems like "Thomas MacDonagh" (1916), which celebrates one of the leaders; yet he maintained that those Irishmen serving in the British army deserved respect. The poem "The Irish in Gallipoli" (1917) affirms the right of Irish soldiers who died to be remembered by their country: "Let Ireland weep but not for sorrow. Weep / That by her sons a land is sanctified / For Christ Arisen" (lines 15–17).

As Ledwidge honors his fellow soldiers in his work, he recognizes that those who served in the war ended up on the wrong side of the debate. In his poem "After Court Martial" (1916), he writes, "And though men called me a vile name, / And all my dream companions gone, / 'Tis I the soldier bears the shame / Not I the King of Babylon" (lines 9–12). While the offense the soldiers bear is ambiguous, the reference to Nebuchadnezzar (the Old Testament king of Babylon who attempts to execute Shadrach, Meshach, and Abednego in the fiery furnace) points to a possible interpretation. Ledwidge was court-martialed himself after he overstayed his leave following the Easter Rising. The Irish soldiers in the English army must have looked to other Irish nationalists as the Babylonian soldiers looked to Nebuchadnezzar in binding and casting the three Jews into the furnace.

What the colonial response to the First World War shows us, then, is the profoundly different ways it helped colonies shape their national identities. The colonies may have come out of the war with a greater sense of themselves, but the war also revealed some colonies' deep divisions. By looking at the war through the colonial lens, students can see the ways in which the war continues to influence nations as they formulate and reformulate their places in the larger world.

Wolfgang Natter

Beyond *All Quiet on the Western Front*: Representations of the First World War in Germany

Embedded reporters at the front; the collection and publication of "authentic" letters and reports from combat troops; book editions about combat exceeding 500,000 copies each; procedures to ensure the availability of "good" reading materials for "our fighting men" and support for the production of inexpensive paperbacks and the consolidation of a mass reading public; declaration of a "state of siege" that authorized ever-widening censorship regulations applied to newspapers and books, which increased from 26 to 954 ordinances over the course of the war; efforts by the military to write its own history during and after the war—to be sure, similar measures have had some currency in conflict zones since 1918, but what I have listed here are initiatives planned and orchestrated during the First World War in Germany. They are instances of the relation between culture and warfare that I find are remarkably illuminated in the study of German texts written about, and institutions deployed during, the First World War.

Several thousand *Kriegsbuecher* ("war books") were written in Germany about the First World War between 1914 and the outbreak of the Second World War, the majority of them during the First World War itself. The scope of wartime activity leading to this book production and reception is remarkably modern, even while the war books partake little if at all of a modernist aesthetic. That juxtaposition—modernist and modern—is a valuable starting point for classroom presentation. It can be undertaken in part through the war books themselves, albeit supplemented by contextual material in order to convey a sense of the centrality of cultural mobilization efforts during the war years and their consequent impacts (Natter).

All Quiet on the Western Front is often the only German book about the war that is taught. Without contextual elaboration, reading that work in isolation can mislead students into thinking that most German citizens were pacifist, antimilitarist, and critical of the country's wartime political leadership. Further, we often assume that the conditions of literary production at the time of the book's publication (1929) were identical or similar to the ones in force during the First World War, when the experiences Remarque narrates occurred. Both assumptions are pointedly not the case, and students interested in German literary responses to the First World War will benefit if they are taught about this more complex state of affairs. In approaching it, teachers may therefore find it helpful to begin their discussions by differentiating and contextualizing German conditions of production and reception during three periods: the war years, those of the Weimar Republic (1918–33), and those following the ascendancy of National Socialism in 1933.

To start with the Weimar years, it is worth noting that, alongside Remarque's book, several hundred other war books were published in Germany between 1928 and 1933, and tellingly there is a four-to-one ratio between books that continued to affirm the war and ones that were critical of it.[1] That is, for every work like Remarque's, four others by the likes of Werner Beumelburg, Hans Carossa, Ernst Jünger, Heinrich Lersch, Boerries von Muenchhausen, Hans Friedrich Blunck, Josef Magnus Wehner, or Hans Grimm appeared. And after 1933, the above-named authors became cultural icons of the new Nazi regime, enthroned in the newly re-formed Academy of Arts in Berlin. The career of Beumelburg is particularly symptomatic of how "properly" written war literature intersects with the cultural politics of National Socialism. He began as a semiofficial military writer and went on to write four best-selling war novels during the Weimar period before becoming corresponding secretary of the Academy of Arts (Brenner). The soldier-writer, in turn, whose moral and aesthetic mission derived from his wartime experiences, became a model for the next generation of aspiring soldiers and authors.

Further, during the war itself, censorship and self-censorship on the part of authors and publishers ensured that anyone who might have been inclined to write with gritty realism about combat in Germany, as Henri Barbusse was in France with his *Le feu* (1916), would not be published and indeed would be subject to further punishment as specified by the state of siege (see Deist; Natter; Nelson). Censorship, however, was but one of very many wartime features of the literary mobilization to produce and support the affirmation of the German war effort. Unparalleled book sales dissolved after August 1914 the significant resistance previously encountered within the ranks of the book trade—in particular toward demands for inexpensive books by proponents of the popular education movement. Publishers embraced the national imperative to provide "our fighting men" with textual evidence of the culture they were fighting to defend and to provide civilians with a taste of "the Spirit of the Trenches" as penned by contemporary soldier-authors (Natter 122–73). The technological capacities for production and distribution of war books published in Germany about the First World War demonstrate a high degree of modernization that is, however, in stark contrast to the overt content of the works themselves.

In order to convey a sense of actual wartime literature published in Germany, one might refer students to a particularly popular series of war books published between 1914 and 1918 by Ullstein, which happened to be the same publisher for *All Quiet on the Western Front.* These forty-five books, glorifying in equal measure the heroes and technologies of the war, while also providing valuable geopolitical instruction, achieved sale levels that fully marked the arrival of the popular best seller in a contemporary sense.[2] Individual volumes in the series addressed new forms of technological warfare—submarines, automobiles, airplanes, zeppelins—as well as global sites of conflict around the world. In formal terms, these works, written by previously well-known authors, including Walter Bloem, and new authors who had become military heroes or diplomats, combined elements of adventure and travel narratives with contents sanctioned by the military and foreign ministry's censorship agencies. In them, both the technological and the spatial pointedly underscore national identity. This wedding of nationalism, war technology, and heroism recurs too frequently in the series for it not to have been by editorial design. The series included works by Karl Doenitz—who in World War II was admiral of the navy and the last chancellor of the Third Reich—and the Red Baron, Manfred von Richthofen. Gunther Plueschow's chronicle of his airplane flights in China was the single largest best seller of the group, at 621,000 copies, while Richthofen's book sold 520,000. Other volumes in the series took place in the Middle East, in Cameroon, Greece, and Siberia, or, in the case of submarines, in the Atlantic or the Mediterranean.

In the pages of *Mit U39 auf Jagd im Mittelmeer* ("U Boat Number 39: Hunting in the Mediterranean"), Captain Walther Forstmann outlines the simultaneous and interconnected struggle for spatial hegemony on two surfaces of the earth, the oceanic and the morphological. In creating an imaginary German imperial space, Forstmann's narrative begins with the German labor and engineering know-how of the "warriors at home" who craft the submarine. He emphasizes the Germanness of this technology and production over and against earlier French advances. Forstmann's plot continues with his submarine's departure amid salutes and music, remembrances of the comrades on both fronts following the successful torpedoing of Allied troop and munitions transport ships, and the returns of the sub to home port to be welcomed by waving flags and cheering countrymen. Although separated from one another by large distances, a unity of purpose links the various sectors of the war effort into a narrative synchronicity.

Paul Hoecker's and Paul Grabein's travelogues open with experiences that simultaneously involve distance and technology. The train—or, in Grabein's case, car—ride across Germany to the front describes a journey consolidating national and collective identity in spatial terms, whose crystallizing moment in the narration is crossing the Rhine River. The border demarcates a definite inside-outside topography, separating friend from enemy. The now collectivized soldiers sing "Die Wacht am Rhein," acknowledging their new consciousness of the boundary's significance, not as a barrier but as a crossing that solidifies their new identity as Germans rather than Prussians, Bavarians, Hessians, and so forth. The pivotal moment of the border crossing is retold in most of the later volumes in the series as well, recalling the "Spirit of 1914" long after its mobilizing power had waned.

Though the prodigious cultural activities undertaken between 1914 and 1918 did not result in the desired aim of military victory, they left traces that decidedly affected the ways in which survivors would belatedly think—and read and write—about the war. The overall effect of the wartime cultural mobilization in which these and a thousand other like-minded works participated was to heavily freight against—recall the four-to-one ratio—reordering the war in a manner that would have supported the Weimar Republic.

Having established the uneven footing of authors critical of the war, one can, however, show students how various authors (including Remarque) later deployed normative signs and codes generated prior to 1919 as key sites for reworking the memory of the war, refunctioning language, and creating public memory usable—or not—in the service of an antichauvinistic, democratic public sphere.

Exemplified here by the varied emplotments of one particularly resonant war memory—the singing of "Deutschland über Alles" at the battle of Langemarck—the codes, slogans, and signs activated in this process of judgment were well known to a contemporary reading audience: *Verdun*, *Kameradschaft* ("comradeship"), *juli-Geist*" ("spirit of July, 1914"), *Etappe* ("support zone"), *Heimat* ("homeland"), and "November 1918." These signs resonate as potential objects of contestation, as a focus of social struggle and contradiction that is at stake in the charged reception of 1920s war literature (Natter 11–34; Mueller; Hueppauf; and Liulevcius).

Is Langemarck, for example, a glorious symbol of the willing self-sacrifice of Germany's academic (and other) volunteers? Or does it connote a tragic tactical blunder, an early manifestation of the military leadership's ineptness that cost the lives of thousands of poorly trained recruits? An army communique published in German newspapers on 11 November 1914 claimed that the preceding day had brought "good progress" for the Imperial Army. The report also provided the material for the subsequent dissemination of the Langemarck myth: "West of Langemarck, young regiments penetrated the first line of enemy positions and took them while singing 'Deutschland ueber alles.' About 2,000 French infantry were taken prisoner and six machine guns were captured."[3]

In this official report, there is no hint that the German offensive against the West was already acknowledged by the high command to have failed, or that the "young regiments" were young not only in age but also in terms of the limited military training they received, or, finally, that the tactical objective was never taken. As such, the report is a witness to and participant in the conscious strategy of deception practiced by the German High Command following the failure of the Marne offensive. This strategy transfigured a tactical (and costly) military failure into an example of sacrifice, nationalism, and heroism, whose symbolic capital increased in proportion to the growing recognition of the absence of tangible military gains.

Four examples from writings penned during the Weimer Republic illustrate how this capital might be invested or, alternatively, declared bankrupt. In *Mein Kampf*, Hitler was careful to mention his participation in the singing of the song during the war in Flanders. Under attack, surrounded by the first casualties and in man-to-man fighting, he hears the song: "From afar, the sounds of a song approached and came closer and closer, catapulting from company to company, and then, just as death reached busily into our ranks, the song reached us as well, and we passed it further along: Deutschland, Deutschland ueber alles, ueber alles in der Welt!" (180–81; my trans.). Hitler's account replicates the message imposed by the official report on the battle for Langemarck—there is no mention of the tactical defeat but instead a celebration of soldierly heroism, death-defying comradeship, and nationalism—and his writing simultaneously envelops Hitler (as a participant) with the symbolic power of the Langemarck legend.

For Ludwig Renn, the author of *Krieg* (1928) and *Nachkrieg* (1930), Langemarck connotes not only a tragic tactical blunder but, worse, a pernicious legend, which his short story "Deutschland, Deutschland ueber Alles!," published in 1929, is meant to demystify. In writing from the perspective of an infantryman, he, like Hitler, emphatically uses the pronoun *we*, but this *we* imparts a different message. For Renn, the song was sung in desperation that November day to alert the German artillery that it was firing on its own troops:

> We were singing for our lives: But we were lying on our stomachs and the grenades penetrated the ground—Fatsch-Bumm. Over and over again when they hit they took our breath away. I roared as loud as I could. But our artillery had heard nothing of it. They fired and fired. The wounded whimpered. Here and there the song bubbled up again, every more despairingly: Deutschland, Deutschland ueber alles. (qtd. in Klaeber 36; my trans.)

In retelling the story, Renn not only offers an alternative perspective on an isolated battlefield event; he simultaneously attacks one of the central elements of a front mythology created during the war, whose continuing power to define memory is displayed by the Hitler text.

A third and similarly critical denouement of the Langemarck myth is a centerpiece of Bruno Vogel's novella *Es Lebe der Krieg!* ("Long Live War!"), published in 1925. The novella's damning critique of the war-affirmative state and social structure of late Wilhelmine Germany, along with its portrayal of battlefield conditions, led to both its author and publisher being put on trial. One of the novella's episodes, "Father and Son," uses an epistolary form to jarringly convey the contradiction between the father's and son's perceptions of the war's reality and meaning. It focuses on the son's retelling of battlefield conditions, culminating in an expressionistic train of language and a no longer innocent presumption uncovered.

Following a relatively quiet period at the front, the son's unit prepares to go into battle, and the son remarks on the dreamlike sense of unreality that accompanies this activity. The inability to comprehend what awaits them escalates into pure shock as the unit's members are decimated by enemy bullets. The letter writer recounts surprise at stumbling into a ditch and noticing a boot above him containing bones and torn up flesh. A memory of a Christian Morgenstern poem ("The Knee") is rekindled before the son realizes that the boot is his own. He relates the effects of battle in one long expressionistic sentence whose combination of exact and visceral depictions would have been censored in Germany between 1914 and 1918:

> Ungraspable violent orgy of sadism: millions of pain-wincing nerves under yawning wounds. . . . [D]estroyed lungs fight for air, brain porridge and skull shards swirl through the dancing mud; out of turning, slit-open corpses surge slimy intestines over the field of honor whose shame is covered by stinking, dense fumes. (18; my trans.)

The "field of honor" is revealed as a place of infamy whose violence is analogous to the violence of misrepresentation with such euphemisms as "field of honor." The jarring contrast to the father's idealistic image of battle, congruent with the information disseminated by the censored press, is further underlined with the question now asked by the letter writer: "Perhaps you presume, dear father, that now the heroic sons sang with defiantly proud lips 'Deutschland, Deutschland ueber Alles!' and then with teary eyes shouted a final 'Long live the Kaiser!' as it so often was reported in the newspapers." Instead, the son reports having heard cries of "Me—dic, Me—dic," and, "Comrade, shoot me dead, please, please shoot me dead," and "help!" (18–19). Such are the facts of battle, the understanding of which prohibits the son from accepting the euphemisms of the father.

Hitler's and not Vogel's or Renn's invocation of the song proved symptomatic of how Germany would remember the war on the cusp of and after 1933—albeit with an added twist. Josef Magnus Wehner, the author of *Seven at Verdun*, set just this accent in a speech he gave in the fall of 1932. These young soldiers' sacrifices, he declared, incarnated the truth that the German nation had not been morally mature enough during the war to realize the hopes of the "time of greatness." The sacrifice of Germany's soldiers, however, who had gone to their deaths at Langemarck singing "Deutschland über Alles," provided the assurance and the basis of a solemn covenant with the war's survivors to finally realize the nation's promise (1–7).

Wehner's refunctioning of Langemarck would be often repeated by others after 1933. National Socialism profited more broadly from an inherited arsenal of slogans, codes, and historical evidence generated between 1914 and 1918, which they used to compare their current "time of greatness" with that of the First World War. Maintaining the earlier heroic tone while recasting the defeat of 1918 as the seed of national rebirth, the *Frontgemeinschaft* ("soldiers' community") of the trenches would be repositioned as the cradle of a new Germany, one leading to the realization of a class-surmounting *Volksgemeinschaft* ("folk community"). All this would necessitate a teleological shift in the direction indicated by Wehner's text—and of the society interpreting it. In practice, the realization of this idealized folk community under the leadership of some part of a generation "reborn" in the trenches would be defined by the exclusion of (and attempt to annihilate) racially, nationally, sexually, politically, religiously, and biologically defined others. The degree to which state-sanctioned representations of the First World War enabled this outcome after 1933 is a final and significant reason not to limit teaching about our topic to a reading of Remarque's important work.

Notes

1. See the entry "Kriegsliteratur" in the 1933 edition of the *Der Grosse Herder* for a contemporaneous assessment.

2. See *Fuenfzig Jahre Ullstein* for sales levels of individual books; see also Richards.

3. On the reportage of the Battle of the Marne generally, see K. Lange.

Nancy Sloan Goldberg

Challenges and Contradictions in Teaching French Great War Literature

Professors, students, and the general public alike are often surprised that there exists a significant corpus of French novels and poetry written during the period of the Great War. Fortunately, recent scholarship and the conservation projects of online sources now make numerous French wartime authors available for literature courses; nevertheless, the interdisciplinary background required to teach these texts, whether in French or in translation, can be daunting. This essay aims to place French war literature in the social and political context of 1914 to 1918, to explicate the French government's interest in fiction produced at the time, and finally to suggest a few writers who are accessible and will help students understand several of the themes that appear in French prose and poetry of the Great War.

Unlike England or Germany, France was partially occupied in 1914 by a long-standing enemy, while much of the intense and brutal fighting took place on its soil. These facts are important for understanding why French citizens supported the war with near unanimity and how the French government's effort to maintain the cooperation of the home front was largely successful. The idea of the nation, the indivisible synthesis of the individual, the community, and the land, whose survival eclipsed that of any individual person, was concretized in the famous political détente, the *union sacrée.*

This cloak of patriotic nationalism that recalled specifically the territorial losses after France's defeat in the Franco-Prussian war of 1870 took precedence over other issues that concerned the population, such as debates over the condition of workers and the aspirations of women for increased rights. The French government took multilateral measures to maintain this tacit agreement, including strict censorship (until October 1919) that filtered what was printed in the media, assuring that what appeared was conventional, conservative, and supported the wider aims of the government. Adversities such as casualties, civilian financial difficulties, labor shortages, food prices, and questions about the propriety of women's volunteer work were enshrined as evidence of the citizen's willingness to sacrifice for the nation.

Writers were specifically enlisted "to encourage a fervent prowar attitude," and they responded to their government's call to inspire the home front (Collins 161). The themes and ideas of prowar writing in France reiterated and expanded the belief that France was engaged in a war defending both secular and spiritual dimensions against an enemy that sought to destroy the double legacies of Latin civilization and of Catholic France. This blending of the past and the present, the spiritual and the material, was a potent means to create and, more important, to sustain support for the war. Throughout Adrien Bertrand's award-winning *L'appel du sol* (1914; *The Call of the Soil*), it is clear that the soldier-author's characters comprehend the meaning of their mission in this melded context:

> "Like you," said Vaissette, "I feel that we are the heirs of civilization. There is a torch that has been handed on across the ages, from the Hellas of Pericles and Plato to the Rome of the Caesars until, thanks to the light of the Gallici Roman period and despite the darkness of the Middle Ages, it reached the palaces of our kings. Thus the light of this torch has never been extinguished but no Germanic tribe has ever borne it, neither the Saxons nor the Franks, nor the Alamans, nor the Goths, nor the Vandals, nor the Cimbri, nor the Teutons. . . . And it is to safeguard this way of living our lives, to preserve our ancient humanistic civilization and the supremacy of the ideals, that we are waging war. Thus, albeit unconsciously, we are obeying the behest of our immemorial destiny."
>
> "We are," said the captain, "fulfilling a sacred task." (116–18)

Like Bertrand, novelists and poets alike applied an explicit set of expressions that indicated their view of current, "real time" events. They often addressed their readers directly, so that words such as *faith*, *homeland*, *sacrifice*, and *honor* combined to become an exhortation, and images of a glorious death in battle grew into object lessons for ordinary citizens called to action under extraordinary circumstances. The novels and poems stress the common characteristics of these citizen-soldiers, with rare mention of social class or education.[1] Whether tradesman or farmer, factory worker or artisan, the poilu was an average man before the war but was now capable of heroism and bravery. Texts such as Henry Malherbe's *La flamme au poing* (1917; *The Flame That Is France*) show that war provided the stimulus that brought out the best in people, attributes stemming from the centuries-long chivalric ancestry and lineage that would otherwise have gone forever undeveloped:

> We believed, we who fought during the first months of the campaign, that we presented the loftiest spectacles of human sacrifice. It was not so. Today is the time when it is beautiful to fight and to dare. After many months of war great souls alone are not weary. Those in whom the fury lasts and who unite the cunning of the present with the audacity of the past are the first among men. The poignant reality that has for so long scorched their eyes does not discourage their glorious ambition. One stands astounded before this abnegation that grows ever keener, before this tenacious heroism that permits no impairment of a conscience chilled by so many visions of ferocity and death. . . . Of a race [descendance] like ours we can hope everything. (92–93)

The ennobling effect of war is not confined to soldiers. In *Mirabelle de Pampelune*, Colette Yver's characters discover that daily life offers few opportunities for heroism and that women and men can show true valor only in response to a threat greater than that to the individual. Writing in 1917, the time of increasing public dissatisfaction at the lack of visible progress in the war, Yver's novel shows the transformation of ordinary women and men into valiant defenders of Catholic France and its Latin heritage: "Today, as yesterday, I find again among the women the same nobility, the same bravery, and the same idea of honor. Among the men unconquerable courage and sacrifice for the glory of the country" (177).

Poets added beauty and love to the list of war's abstract and intangible benefits, no matter how horrific and ghastly the concrete facts. In "Chant de l'honneur," written at the front in 1915, Apollinaire reasserted the obligation of poets to preserve the truth and simplicity of beauty:

> And even Love as we know is cruel
> That's why we must still consider Beauty

The one thing on earth which is never evil
She bears a hundred names in the French language
Grace Virtue Courage Honor and she's always
The same Beauty. (327)

In her poems about the protracted battle of Verdun between February and August 1916, which resulted in over 650,000 casualties, Anna de Noailles underscored the transcendent power of heroic death as a fusion of love, honor, and resurrection:

And yet, right now, I know that nothing equals
The heroic abandon, supreme and without return;
I know that honor is the pinnacle of love,
And that a young death is a triumphant death. (53)

An important element in the justification for war was the concept of collective culpability for the so-called sins of France, a trope that had played a role after the Franco-Prussian War and would resurface later during the Vichy regime. During the First World War, fiction writers echoed the views of journalists who considered the present war to be divine punishment for excesses. These transgressions varied from the materialism and individualism that resulted in smaller families and the decreased length of military service to the demands of workers and women for increased political rights. Such factors contributed to the appearance of a weakened France, thus enticing a predatory Germany to attack. As Henry Bataille wrote in *La divine tragédie*:

It was said to them:
"This is the punishment.
Man forsook his pact with Heaven.
God punishes him for this criminal renunciation,
Having made a covenant with the Spirit who deceives.
The torch of the Faith was in danger.
But France and the Faith will be reborn ever more thriving
From the trial by fire that purifies the earth.
God commands. Humbly we say: So be it!" (127; my trans.)

Novelists as well as poets subscribed to the notion of collective guilt, and their works often featured deeply flawed characters who redeem themselves through wartime acts of patriotic duty and self-sacrifice. Most of the authors of these object lesson novels were established women writers with a substantial female readership. They place their characters in a variety of wartime situations that both test and reconfirm the protagonists' compliance and acquiescence to the primacy of the national family over the individual family. Based on a maternal ideology that originated during the French Revolution, mothers were called on to sustain the life of the Republic by instilling civic values in their children, yet at the same time they were expected to perform Catholic submission and abnegation in delivering those children, as well as their husbands, into the service of France. War in these novels, however tragic, is also a great teacher of civic virtue and Christian values.

In novels such as Geneviève Duhamelet's *Les inépousées* ("The Unmarried Women"), Marie Reynès-Monlaur's trilogy *Pages de deuil et d'héroisme* ("Pages of Mourning and Heroism"), and Camille Mayran's *Histoire de Gotton Connixloo* ("Gotton Connixloo's Story") and *L'oubliée* ("The Forgotten Woman"), irreversible changes brought by war force the female characters to grasp the depth of their personal flaws. The authors trace the women's struggles to atone for these failings through acts of heroism and selfless dedication to their families, their faith, and to the nation. These stories consistently identify motherhood with Catholicism and France, a symbiotic bond that encompasses many different definitions of mothers and children, from war godmothers to the soldiers, especially the wounded. In *Gotton Connixloo*, Gotton, a Belgian, considers her sterility as divine punishment for her adultery and the German invasion the beginning of the last judgment. Without the children she believes will protect her from certain damnation, she offers her life in an attempt to expiate her sin by saving the village from collective execution.

Despite the government's call for writers to aid the war effort, there were French writers, artists, and other creative people who defied official censorship, endured police surveillance and the threat of arrest and imprisonment to galvanize public opinion for peace. Denied access to the mainstream press, French-speaking dissenters expressed their views in alternative and mostly clandestine periodicals published in France and especially in Switzerland. These publications contained articles, letters, and creative works, such as poems and woodcuts that stated in candid terms the political and economic causes of the war and were designed to stimulate resistance to the continuation of hostilities.

Geneva was the center of French opposition to the war, not only because Switzerland's outwardly neutral position afforded more freedom to the dissidents but especially because of the presence of Romain Rolland. In September 1914, the *Journal de Genève* published Rolland's *Au dessus de la mêlée*, the first in a series of open letters from his self-imposed exile in Switzerland, in which he analyzed the nature of war and urged intellectuals to join him in resisting the hostilities. Whether isolated in France or interconnected through Rolland, poets including René Arcos, Marcel Martinet, Henriette Sauret, Charles Vildrac, and Pierre Jean Jouve stressed the union of life and art and the necessity of the individual to reject war. Moreover, their poems demonstrated how the powerful few manipulate language to create a reality that is against the interests of the many. In stark and often harsh terms, they reproached the French people for not seeing through the deception. As Martinet wrote:

> Poor man, farmer, working man,
> With those who made your soul destitute,
> With the rich man, with the master,
> With those who gunned you down during your strikes
> And then cut your wages,
> For those who built surrounding their factories
> Havens and saloons just for you
> And who made your wife and your little ones cry
> Facing the empty food cupboard without bread.
> . . . .
> With the rich, with the master,
> Against the deprived, against the browbeaten,
> Against your brother, against yourself,
> You are going to fight, you are going to fight! (57–58; my trans.)

While Martinet had adopted a clear antiwar position, several important and prize-winning writers who depicted the reality of battle and death remain classified as antiwar writers. Such designation, despite their collective and long-standing reputations, is problematic. These writers, Georges Duhamel (*La vie des martyres* [*The New Book of Martyrs*] and *Civilisation*), Roland Dorgelès (*Les croix de bois* [*Wooden Crosses*]), and most famously Henri Barbusse (1916; *Le feu* [*Under Fire*]), described the starkness of death but also the resolute dedication of the soldiers, their commitment to their brothers-in-arms, and their well-tuned gallows humor. Given that censorship did not end in France until October 1919 and that these works were published and became famous before that time, we are confronted by an obvious paradox that must be addressed.

These texts were and remain celebrated for their realism, for a representation of war that is filled with soldier slang, lice, and the ever-present and often deadly mud. But a truthful portrayal of warfare's horror does not require that the author oppose the conflict. Rather, the obligation of fighting the war is recognized and accepted as a necessary phase to a larger goal. Throughout *Under Fire* especially, Barbusse reiterated "the spirit of war" and the official justification of the war as necessary to defeat German militarism. For Barbusse, this pre-Wilsonian obligation to fight the war to end all wars fused with the socialist ideal to create a more just and socially equitable society. The poilu is neither vengeful nor bloodthirsty but simply an ordinary man who wants to secure the future for his children, if not for himself. The civilians Barbusse portrays are guilty of profiteering, avoiding enlistment, and self-glorification, equating their minor privations to life in the trenches. Journalists who fill the newspapers with hyperbolic tales of glory and sacrifice are despised most of all. Barbusse's praise of the soldiers and criticism of exploitative and insensitive civilians provide important object lessons in late 1915, a time when the French public had realized that the war would certainly continue. The book's long last scene reiterates and revalidates the need to eliminate oppressive systems of government and their institutions that depend on war to exist. In comparing the present conflict with the French Revolution, Barbusse's characters stress its purpose as the way forward to the new day that dawns as the book ends: "If the present war [advances] progress by [only] a single step, its miseries and its massacres will count for little" (319). Fully in keeping with the stated goals of his government, Barbusse's book promotes an honorable purpose to the war, in contradistinction to antiwar activists such as Jouve and Martinet, who insisted that all warfare was against the interests of every soldier.

As instructors and scholars our awareness of canon formation's biases must continue to inform our teaching. Designating all participant narratives as true documents of the war without problematizing any aspect of the book's genesis can frustrate assessing such war texts. Understanding the political context and the author's place in that framework is crucial to any literary work located in a historical event. Barbusse's portrayal passed the censors in 1915 for its validation of the poilu mission to end war, yet this justification was obfuscated and eventually recast as an antiwar message. Such alteration effectively corroborated the later revisionist and negative reappraisal of First World War politics without undermining the causal factor of realism. Thus *Under Fire* became designated as a classic antiwar novel, similar to Remarque's *All Quiet on the Western Front* (1930), a work that refutes unequivocally any justification for the war.

For instructors teaching the literature of the Great War, *Under Fire* remains an important text that exposes the reality of trench warfare, the concerns of soldiers attempting to understand and justify their sacrifice—but also the processes of canon formation. A class discussion centered on all these issues would enrich any course exploring literary responses to war.

Note

1. The exception is the rare mention of French colonial soldiers. Whether from North Africa or Senegal, these soldiers are depicted as innate warriors, fierce, bloodthirsty, and more naturally suited to combat than soldiers from France. While such characterizations of inborn savagery were commonly ascribed to Germans, authors like Barbusse failed to recognize either the contradiction or the racism in their praise of the foreign soldiers: "We watch them and say nothing. These ones you don't shout at. They are imposing and even a little frightening. Despite that, the Africans seem quite merry and in good spirits. Naturally they are going up to the front line. This is their place and the fact that they are coming past indicates that there will very soon be an attack. They are designed for going over the top. . . . People talk about the character of these darkies, how ferocious they are in attack, how they love to put in the bayonet, how they don't like to give quarter" (41–42).

Glenda Abramson

Teaching Representations: The Jewish Experience in Eastern Europe during the First World War

Most of the principles that apply to the teaching of war—universalism versus particularity, partisanship, patriotism, relativist perceptions of war, the question of *jus ad bello* (just war theory)—cannot easily be applied to the teaching of the civilian experience in war in general and to the complex Jewish experience in the First World War in particular. After the Second World War the Geneva Conventions were established partly to protect civilian populations in wartime, but during the Great War the principles behind the conventions had not yet been invoked. The result was that while civilians in eastern Europe were the casualties of general warfare, Jewish civilians in that region were the subjects of targeted attacks.

I am basing this essay on my own discussions of the East European Jewish experience in the First World War with advanced undergraduates, most of whom included at least one Jewish studies course in their curriculum. They have represented many disciplines: languages, history, literature, and Middle Eastern studies. As a literary scholar the purpose of my teaching has been to contextualize literary texts that relate to the history of Jewish communities during the war.

Jewish studies students are more likely to have studied the Second World War and the Holocaust than the First World War. For this seminar they would therefore have to read First World War historiography in order to provide a context for the particular experience of the East European Jewish community. One problem is that while there are numerous books on cultural, historical, political, and economic points of view, there is no single comprehensive outline of the East European Jewish experience in the First World War, despite the large number of personal testimonies. I would therefore prescribe the following: Martin Gilbert's *The First World War: A Complete History*, which places the Jewish experience in the framework of a history of the war; Jonathan Frankel's *The Jews and the European Crisis, 1914–1921*; and *Glorious, Accursed Europe*, by Jehuda Reinharz and Yaakov Shavit, which discusses the Jewish attitude toward, and relationship with, Europe in the early years of the twentieth century.

The Eastern Front, which stretched from the Baltic Sea in the north to the Black Sea in the south, constituted the battle zone between Germany, Austro-Hungary, and Russia. The toll of human life in this region was massive. More than three million men died in the fighting, over nine million were wounded, and in almost every country in the conflict the government fell or changed. Clearly, suffering was widespread throughout all urban and rural communities because of the conditions of industrialized warfare: occupation, mass displacement, bombardments, rampaging armies, lack of supplies, looting, the destruction of civilians' homes and livelihoods. However, the question to be explored with students is why, in this terrible chaos of suffering, the Jews were singled out for specific oppression. The Jews declared, "While everyone suffered, we suffered more" (Rechter).

The Eastern Front was the homeland of about one and a quarter million Jews, and the war brought relentless tragedy to them. They were primarily victims of the postwar ethnonationalist conflicts, when the anti-Semitism of the Polish and Lithuanian nationalists became overt and violent. Recent reports conclude that there were over 150,000 Jewish civilian deaths and over a million Jews were displaced. The Jews were accused of having started the war and then enriching themselves at the expense of their patriotic countrymen. Cossacks orchestrated a reign of terror over the Jewish population with officially sanctioned pogroms. Jews survived in only a few towns, thanks to protection by civilian police. The war and its aftermath almost completely destroyed the Jewish infrastructure in eastern Europe, socially, economically, culturally, and religiously, and eroded the norms of Jewish life. In Russia the Bolshevik Revolution, which White Russians depicted as a Jewish conspiracy, attempted to obliterate the very practice of Judaism.

In spite of the devastation inflicted on their communities throughout the Russian Empire, almost 300,000 Jewish soldiers served in the czar's army. The national loyalty of these soldiers attracted international praise. Rabbis marched with them and delivered patriotic speeches. Nonetheless, Jews were accused of treachery to the empire, of avoiding military service, and of causing Russian defeats. Jews were therefore expelled from towns and villages near the front lines, and some were deported to Germany to be used for forced labor. S. Ansky (1863–1920), the Russian Jewish ethnographer and playwright, accurately predicted that after the war old enemies would live in mutual peace, but "when they remember their neighbour, the Jew, who fought none of them, who killed none of their people, they will nevertheless unanimously agree that the Jew is the one responsible for everybody's misfortune" (115).

Ansky's memoir *The Enemy at His Pleasure*, published in 2002 in English translation, is a fundamental work for students' understanding the situation of the East European Jews during the war. In late 1914, Ansky organized desperately needed relief for Jews who were caught between the warring armies in Galicia, the region of the Austro-Hungarian Empire occupied by Russia. He traveled for four years to towns and shtetls, hearing the stories of troop-led massacre, rape, torture, expulsion, and displacement. Through anecdotes of personal experience, statistics, dialogue, and reporting, his book chronicles in detail the lives and misery of the Jews he encountered. Even after one has read descriptions of the Holocaust, Ansky's accounts have the power to shock.

Until recently the personal has been largely ignored by historians, yet life writing and autobiographical fiction illuminate fragments of history from daily life that we are unable to find elsewhere.[1] Soldiers' tales in personal diaries have been responsible for a renewed interest in the war. Therefore memoirs and diaries should be explored as sources for the eastern European Jewish experience, and the question should be asked whether, taken cumulatively, these sources provide a broad understanding of it. Memoirs such as Ansky's and *The Great Madness*, by the Hebrew writer Avigdor Hameiri, who served in the Austro-Hungarian army in Galicia, help convey to students the intensity of the wartime Jewish experience throughout the Russian and Austro-Hungarian Empires. In addition, students should read some theories of life writing.[2] Unfortunately few Russian, Hebrew, and Yiddish war diaries and memoirs have been translated into English and are therefore unavailable for study. In principle, however—and as such works continue to be translated and digitized—I would recommend the reading of accessible diaries, which are an important source both of information about individuals' war service and for discussions about the value of life writing texts.

Fiction and poetry have been at the center of the courses I taught. Historians may regard these media as controversial choices for teaching war, and therefore one of the main points of discussion with students should be the legitimacy of using belles lettres in an investigation of historical events. The question of whether this medium can legitimately convey historical experience raises the theoretical question of the comparative truth of literature, life writing, and historiography. How can the reader distinguish between historical truth and fiction? If we are left with the "truth" of the fiction, as opposed to the "facts" of the war, do we get a trustworthy picture of the war? Is belief in the truth of fiction at the center of our evaluation of this literature?

I raise these questions to explore with students the matter of literature as an accurate source of historical knowledge. In a discussion about using literary fiction to convey historical experience, a few students told me that they had learned a great deal from seeing the play *War Horse*, which tells the story—through the ingenious use of puppets—of a horse on the Western Front. The play is perhaps overly filled with pathos, being the story of a suffering animal, but it does convey something of the experience of young men in battle conditions. More elevated works of fiction do the same. While memoirs and diaries may be a better source for examining responses to the war, fiction could convey life in battle with even greater vividness, historical accuracy, and minute detail. As the war receded from memory into history, the war fiction assumed growing importance. Because of the need to remember, in the interwar period all war books, even fiction, were primarily considered as documents (see Klein 7). A privileged place was given to belles lettres beside the historiographical narrative.

Bearing all this in mind, and given all the anomalies I have mentioned, I have used fiction and poetry to explore the experience of eastern European Jews during the First World War. While Ansky's memoir personally chronicles his experience and temporally contextualizes the war in eastern Europe, a novel by the Hebrew author Samuel Joseph Agnon, *A Guest for the Night*, provides an equally personal illustration of the war's destruction but in the framework of fiction. Agnon was born in eastern Galicia in 1888, and his novel was published in 1938. He spent twelve years in Germany, four of them during the war, and produced two autobiographical novels dealing with his sojourn in wartime Berlin and Leipzig. *A Guest* provides a picture of Jewish life and its devastation in eastern Europe after World War I. It tells the story of a writer, now living in Palestine, who visits his hometown, a literary version of Agnon's Galician hometown of Buchach. The narrator, clearly a version of Agnon himself, finds that the war and the postwar pogroms have taken friends and families, annihilated towns, and destroyed people's settled way of life. His hometown has changed, its once thriving Jewish population having been decimated. During his stay he attempts a form of redemption by reviving the old house of study (*beit midrash*) and restoring the basis of Jewish life but fails to do so.

Although a work of fiction, embellished with symbolism, it teaches students not only about the aftermath of the war but also about Judaism, Jewish life, loss, and redemption, seen through a largely autobiographical prism. In a kind of proleptic pessimism, many Jewish writers felt that postwar hostility to Jews signaled the end of European Jewish life, and I have questioned students about whether they think the First World War initiated the long and terrible road to the destruction of Europe's Jews.

Perhaps the best known author to read in the context of our topic is Isaac Babel, particularly his *Red Cavalry* (1926). Students should read all the stories but concentrate on one in particular, "The History of My Dovecote." This simple tale of a boy who longs for a dovecote is also a reflection on the Jews in Russia, anti-Semitism, and the pogroms that followed the Great War. The story, said to be based on Babel's diary, offers the immediacy of involvement in the terrible events, from the point of view of a child who is confronted with death and destruction without understanding it. These stories do not directly concern the First World War, but given Babel's service as a journalist with the First Cavalry in the 1920s, they are infused with his consciousness of his own Jewishness and its consequences for him in Russia at that chaotic time. His portrait of the Russian peasants, the Cossacks, and the small East European towns and villages with their variety of Jews, is unequaled.

Agnon and Babel are canonic writers whose works are studied in many languages. Perhaps less accessible for students, but nevertheless of vital importance, is poetry in Hebrew and Yiddish written during and after the war that also explored the experience of pogrom and displacement. Poetry presented individuals' responses to the war and commented on the collective agony. For example, a long poem in Hebrew, "The Melodies of the Time" (1915), by Shaul Tchernichowsky (1875–1943), who served as a military doctor on the Russian front, was created during the persecution of Lithuanian and Galician Jews in 1915. Tchernichowsky expressed the outrage of the Jewish soldier who has shed his blood for his country, which now savagely persecutes his brethren. Joseph Klausner, Tchernichowsky's biographer, describes how the poet and his wife wept helplessly when they heard the news of the expulsions (147). The poem is a furious outburst against the "rulers" who have inflicted yet another catastrophe on the innocent Jews. Tchernichowsky makes it clear that the Jewish soldier was fighting on two fronts: against the enemy and against his own compatriots. The poem unites the disparate elements of First World War poetry in general and Jewish poetry in particular: it extends the elements specific to the battlefield to a meditation on the condition of East European Jewry in the early years of the new century.

Similarly, "The Heap," by the Yiddish poet Peretz Markish (1895–1952), who fought on the Eastern Front, was published in 1921 and dedicated to the victims of the Ukrainian pogroms. The central image of this iconic expressionist work is a heap of corpses of murdered Jews. The poem begins with a dedication: "To you, the victims of the Ukraine / Where the earth is filled with your remains / And to you as well, the slaughtered in 'a heap' / in the town of Horoditchtsh at the Dnieper." Other Yiddish writers, such as Halpern Leivick (1888–1962) and Aaron Leyeles (1889–1966), perfected the so-called pogrom poem in various styles of modernism. Unfortunately these poems are not available in their entirety in translation, and my students had to be satisfied with excerpts that gave a sense of the variety of responses to the terrible events of the wartime and postwar periods.[3] However brief the passages, the students appreciated the unsentimentalized horror of the sight, sound, and smell of mass death. In addition, I have taught a few poems that relate to the topic from Benjamin Harshav's anthology of Yiddish poetry (with translation into English). These can be studied in their entirety (see 9). The work of the Hebrew poet Uri Zvi Greenberg, some of which has been translated into English, is a further autobiographical source. Greenberg served in the Austro-Hungarian trenches and narrowly escaped being killed in one of the postwar pogroms. He is therefore a witness to the worst excesses of the period.

I have cited works I have taught that relate directly to the Jewish experience at the time of the war. Portraits of Jewish life in eastern Europe before and after the war appear in numerous other works, such as those by Isaac Bashevis Singer and Joseph Roth. If all this literature is not historically accurate in locations and dates, it attempts at least to answer the question of what it was like for the Jews as individuals or as a group at a time of turmoil and destruction.

Notes

1. Hermione Lee includes autobiographical fiction in her survey of life writing (see 100).

2. For example, *Life Writing: Essays on Autobiography, Biography and Literature*, edited by Richard Bradford, and Max Saunders, *Self Impression: Life-Writing, Autobiografiction, and the Forms of Modern Literature*. Both define and analyze literary and life writing genres.

3. I gleaned these excerpts from Roskies.

Santanu Das

South Asian Literature of the First World War

If the global turn has been one of the most important developments in First World War studies, how do we communicate it to the students? I was introduced to the literature of the First World War as part of my English degree at Presidency College, Calcutta. Founded in 1817 to disseminate the fruits of Western learning, it regarded itself as Oxford of the East and claimed to have the oldest English department in the world. However, instead of producing Lord Macaulay's dream generation of a class "Indian in blood and colour, but English in tastes, in opinions, in morals and in intellect," the college became the center of the anticolonial nationalist movement, and through the long twentieth century it continued to train generations of distinguished students, from future political leaders, revolutionaries, and writers to academics such as Amartya Sen and Gayatri Spivak. I was a student in the nineties, when the college was already in decline. Every Thursday during our second year, the majestic colonial edifice of the English department, with its sweeping balcony, resounded with the notes of First World War poetry. At Presidency—as across most parts of India—First World War literature meant English literature and in particular English poetry. I diligently thumbed through my father's copy of Jon Silkin's *Penguin Book of First World War Poetry*. "I am the enemy you killed, my friend," I still remember my English professor say, his voice choking with pity. Our teenage hearts bled. Our "postcolonial" identities had not dulled our empathy for these doomed British youths; and the statues of the two English Tommies, who stood on either side of the cenotaph-like Calcutta First World War memorial, blended in my mind with the figures of Wilfred Owen and Siegfried Sassoon, whose poetry I could recite by heart. I did not know that undivided India contributed so heavily to the conflict, that one million Indians actually served on the various battlefronts. And South Asian literature of the First World War: did such a thing exist?

Even today, in classrooms around the world, First World War literature speaks with a British accent. The Victorian cadences and overarticulate intensities of Owen and Sassoon are somewhat broken by the modernist silences of Septimus Smith, and one can even hear poor Rezia in the background. A hundred years after its outbreak, the war has powerfully come home; Pat Barker's *Regeneration* is wholly set in the home front (see Cohen). But the color of memory of the First World War remains largely white in a way that memories of other conflicts are not. One of the most significant legacies of the centennial commemoration will be the burgeoning interest in the experiences and writings of colonial and nonwhite troops, from television and radio programs such as *The World's Wars* to dedicated Web sites and *YouTube* videos. Yet more continues to be researched, written, and taught on the four major English war poets, enshrined by Paul Fussell in his epoch-making *The Great War and Modern Memory* (1975), than on the four million nonwhite men who served from different parts of Asia, Africa, and the Pacific islands (see Das, *Race* and "Experiences"). If Anglocentrism determined the historiography of the war and the school syllabi for decades, it is not the only cause for the continuing marginalization of the conflict's colonial dimensions. Most of the colonial troops who served—the Indian sepoys, the senegalese *tirailleurs*, the North African spahis, the South African laborers—came from semiliterate or nonliterate communities and did not leave behind an abundance of diaries, memoirs, poems, and novels. In the absence of texts, how can we promote and teach the extra-European and colonial literature of the First World War? Such recovery—or indeed, trying to encourage a more global perspective on World War I literature in the classroom—puts pressure on the very scope and definition of the word *literary*. For being nonliterate does not mean being nonliterary, just as *amnesia* does not mean absence.

Colonial memories and literature of the war exist obliquely, stubbornly, serendipitously. Thus, on a shell case recovered from the Western Front one finds a peony rose, a butterfly, and a short poem engraved by a Chinese laborer; in the Esplanade museum in Canada one can see the "war deed" of Mike Mountain Horse, a First Nations Canadian soldier narrating his experiences visually on a cowhide; in a small archive near Calcutta I discovered the broken and bloodstained glasses of Private "Jon" Sen, the only nonwhite member of the Leeds Pals battalion.[1] These objects, almost bequeathed with the pulse of their owners and carers, are immensely moving; the archives of touch and intimacy are mute witnesses to the experiences and sometimes final moments of these people. In a context where the soldiers were largely nonliterate, it is particularly important to go beyond the textual and engage with these other modes of cultural production—the material, the visual, the auditory—through which the literary breathes. An interdisciplinary pedagogical approach becomes not an option but a necessity if we are to understand and communicate to our students the world of the colonial troops. But the main problem is one of access: how do we obtain these trench artifacts, archival photographs, and obscure texts? One of the most valuable legacies of the various centennial commemorative projects has been the creation of a number of important online resources: from photograph banks and short documentaries to podcasts and *YouTube* videos such as "Whose Remembrance?" and "From Bombay to the Western Front: Indians in the First World War" to education packs, dedicated Web sites, and digital sourcebooks.[2] Throughout 2014, the electronic media have been an invaluable rudder behind the globalization of First World War memory.

Of all the colonies in British, French, and German empires, undivided India (which would include today's India, Pakistan, and Bangladesh) along with Nepal and Sri Lanka—that is, today's South Asia—contributed the highest number of men. More than a million men, including 600,000 combatants and 450,000 noncombatants, served in places as diverse as France and Flanders, Mesopotamia, Gallipoli, East Africa, Persia, Egypt, and Palestine. To follow the Indian sepoy (from the Persian *sipahi*, meaning "rifleman") is to follow the global course of the war. He hovers on the fringes of European texts—by writers as diverse as Sassoon, Edmund Blunden, Rudyard Kipling, and Ernst Jünger—but is there an Indian Owen, a Pakistani Graves, or a Bangladeshi Vera Brittain? The question, often asked, is based on a reductive conflation of war literature with a peculiarly English trajectory of trench writing. War writing is often more diffused in the colonial literary sphere. To excavate it requires a new methodology, going beyond familiar genres and modes of analysis.[3] In this brief essay, I investigate some of these issues through the rich and varied corpus of South Asian writing of the First World War—by combatants, noncombatants, and civilians—and address how it does not merely add to what the students know about the war but can also lead them to reconceptualize in the classroom what is meant by "war literature."

Combatant and Noncombatant Literature: Letters, Songs, and Writing

A poignant photograph from the Imperial War Museum shows a nonliterate sepoy dictating a letter to a fellow soldier or scribe: this is how the letters were often written (fig. 1). The letters were then translated by the colonial censors, and copious extracts were prepared from them. The original letters are now lost, but the translated extracts survive. They are housed in the British Library, London, and an excellent selection, *Indian Voices of the Great War: Soldier's Letters, 1914–1918* (Omissi), is available. These letters are our most substantial and tantalizing sources about the Indian war experience. Neither the direct transcript of trench experience nor just scribal embellishment, they are some of the earliest encounters between textual form and South Asian subaltern history: they vary from the sepoy's first impressions of Europe to observations on issues of gender, marriage, and educa-

Figure 1. Photograph of a wounded soldier dictating a letter, Brighton 1915, © IWM.

tion to life in the trenches. There is often thickening of language as emotions such as horror, resignation, or homesickness are not expressed directly but erupt through images, metaphors, and similes:

> Cannons, machine guns, rifles and bombs are going day and night, just like the rains in the month of Sawan. [Havildar Abdul Rahman, France, 20 May 1915]

> There is conflagration all round, and you must imagine it to be a dry forest in a high wind in the hot weather, with the abundance of dry grass and straw. No one can extinguish it but God himself—man can do nothing. [Sowar Sohan Singh, Kitchener Indian Hospital, Brighton, 10 July 1915]

> As tired bullocks and bull buffaloes lie down in the month of Bhadon so lies the weary world. Our hearts are breaking. . . . Germany fights the world with ghastly might, harder to crush than well-soaked grain in the mill. [Santa Singh, hospital in Brighton, 18 August 1915][4]

These letters are in many ways the Indian literature of the trenches. The images of "dry forest," "hot weather," or "tired bullocks" are repositories of feeling: they show how the cognitive and narrative processes of these men, transported thousands of miles, are still shaped by the agrarian culture of their native Punjab. These letters are often treated by scholars as linguistic bubbles on the dark sea of South Asian plebeian history, but they are rooted in the rich literary formation of the Punjab through its various sites of oral circulation: the everyday world of chants, prayers, songs, poems, and stories in village fairs, social festivals, and religious rituals (Mir 91–122). What we have in the letters is the remarkable transition from a vibrant and robust oral culture to a textual culture of letter writing: a whole generation of men who had grown up listening to myths, legends, and *qissas* ("stories") are now forced to write or dictate letters shaped by these oral narrative traditions.

We have insights into some of these rich oral cultures through an extraordinary archive that has recently come to light: a collection of over two thousand sound recordings of prisoners of war conducted by the Royal Prussian Phonographic Commission. Around three hundred of the recordings are of South Asian POWs: the men were made to stand in front of a phonograph and asked to read out a text, narrate a story, or sing a song. This was part of an ethnological study at the time, conducted by a team of thirty German academics comprising linguists, ethnologists, and musicologists (see Ahuja et al.). The sound recordings are now housed in the

Humboldt Sound Archive, and there is currently a project to digitize, transcribe, and translate part of this vast collection.[5] One of the most poignant recordings is by the twenty-two-year-old Jasbahadur Rai, a Gurkha sepoy who adopts a form of Nepalese folk song called *jheyru* in order to tell his life story. Consider the following extract:[6]

> Hai suna suna, sun lāune didī, mon rūnchha durūrū
>
> Listen, oh listen, gold-wearing elder sister, the heart cries, sobbing
>
> Pāniko bulbul, yo manko chulbul, bujhāũchhau katin din
>
> The bubbling of water, the restlessness of this heart, how many days will it take to console yourself?
>
> Hai suna suna, sun lāune kānchhī, bujhāũchhau katin din
>
> Listen, oh listen, gold-wearing little one, how many days will it take to console yourself?
>
> Dui paisa bache tabalmar sigret salkāula mārchisle
>
> If I save two cents, I'll light a Tabalmar cigarette with matches

A desolate male voice rises and falls as Jasbahadur sings this lament, with partly remembered, partly made-up words, stitched together through refrain, alliteration, and onomatopoeia. Blurring the boundaries between song, reportage, lament, *j'accuse*, and compulsive testimony, the lament is also the birth of the lyric subject. The *jheyru* is called on to bear lyric testimony to historical trauma; it also gives a certain material poignancy to Gayatri Spivak's famous rhetorical question: "Can the subaltern speak?"

But what about literature with a capital *L*? Much of the most important literature is in the regional languages and is being slowly unearthed. Though Bengalis were barred from joining the army and served largely as noncombatants, a disproportionately higher number of memoirs come from them because of higher literacy rates in Bengal. These include *Kalyan Pradeep* (1928), a memoir in Bengali by an eighty-year-old woman, Mokkhada Devi, about her London-educated grandson, Kalyan Mukherjee, who served as a doctor in Mesopotamia and died in captivity. The other remarkable Bengali war memoir is *Abhi Le Baghdad* (*On to Baghdad*), by a middle-class Bengali youth, Sisir Sarbadhikari, who volunteered as a stretcher bearer in Mesopotamia, was taken prisoner of war, and made to go on the traumatic five-hundred-mile-long march to Ras-el-Ain.[7] If *Kalyan-Pradeep* weaves in the extraordinary letters of Captain Kalyan Sen—discussing his views on colonialism, nationalism, and warfare—*Abhi Le Baghdad* is the only full-length Indian record we have so far of life in Mesopotamia. However, the only major Indian literary figure who joined the army (the 49th Bengali) and underwent military training (though his battalion was never mobilized) was the Bengali rebel-poet Kazi Nazrul Islam—today regarded as the national poet of Bangladesh. Nazrul was an anticolonial revolutionary poet with socialist sympathies. What is remarkable about his war writings, which include a number of short stories and poems, is the way the First World War gets fused with other events, such as the October Revolution, the Third Anglo-Afghan War, and the Indian nationalist struggle, to form a vision of revolutionary violence, incandescent for him with a terrible beauty. Consider his most famous poem, "Bidrohi" ("The Rebel"):

> I trample on bonds,
> obey no law,
> recognise no rule.
> I sport with loaded boats
> In my revels
> And send them down to the sea's bottom
> Without mercy.
>
> I'm a torpedo
> An explosive mine.
> I am the Spirit of Shiva, the destroyer. (Islam 20)

In India during the war years, stories of the German cruiser ship *Emden* torpedoing boats created widespread panic. The images of boats, torpedo, mine, and "subterranean volcanoes" all come out of the war, but what is extraordinary is the way the accoutrements of an imperial war are pressed by this sepoy turned rebel, with an acknowledged debt to Walt Whitman, into the service of revolutionary nationalism.

The Indian Home Front

As in Europe, war literature in India was produced not only by combatants. When the war was declared, the responses in India were largely enthusiastic: even nationalist leaders, including Mahatma Gandhi, threw themselves into the recruitment effort. Contribution to the war, it was widely believed, would be rewarded with greater political autonomy. The Punjab was the main recruiting area, and Punjabi folk literature was mobilized by the colonial officials and local chieftains for recruitment purposes. Fresh verses and songs were commissioned, and a popular recruiting song, "Rang-Root," gives insight into some of the incentives promised to these naive young men: "Here you get old shoes, there you'll get full boots, get enlisted / Here you get torn rags, there you'll get suits, get enlisted" (Das, *Indian Troops* 22). As the men left home for battle, the womenfolk from villages wove their desperation into heartbreaking songs:

> My husband, and his two brothers
> All have gone to laam. [l'arme]
> Hearing the news of the war
> Leaves of trees got burnt.
>
> Without you I feel lonely here.
> Come and take me away to Basra.
> I will spin the wheel the whole night.
> . . . .
> War destroys towns and ports, it destroys huts
> I shed tears, come and speak to me
> All birds, all smiles have vanished
> And the boats sunk
> Graves devour our flesh and blood. (qtd. in Chandan)[8]

These are subaltern songs of protest: in a context where almost nothing is known about the responses of the women in these far-flung villages, these songs pierce the silence.

The majority of the wartime writing that has survived is elite in nature, however, and was produced by the educated middle classes and the political bourgeoisie. They range from essays, poems, and short stories to anecdotes and vignettes. Some of them were published in the short-lived journal *Indian Ink* (1914–16) and in the compendious war volume *All about the War in India* (c. 1915). Even when they are written in regional languages, there is often an anglicized, bilingual consciousness at work, as in the Bengali recruitment play *Bengali Paltan* or the short story "Mutiny," written by Swarnakumari Devi, the sister of the celebrated Indian poet and Nobel laureate Rabindranath Tagore. There are also poems in English, including "The Gift of India," by the Indian poet, feminist, and political leader Sarojini Naidu. An internationally known figure, she was christened Bharat Kakila or the Nightingale of India by Mahatma Gandhi, and she wrote the poem for the Hyderabad Ladies War Relief Association in December 1915. Consider the following extract:

> Gathered like pearls in their alien graves,
> Silent they sleep by the Persian waves.
> Scattered like shells on Egyptian sands
> They lie with pale brows and brave, broken hands.
> They are strewn like blossoms mown down by chance
> On the blood-brown meadows of Flanders and France.

The most articulate of Indian women-nationalists seem to be ensconced in the English patriotic and pastoral tradition through colonial education. Images such as "pale brows," the euphemistic strewn "blossoms," and the labials and sibilants are strongly redolent of Tennyson and show a shared Georgian heritage with Owen. But this poem by Naidu is also the standard English war lyric turned upside down, as she at once inherits and interrogates the stock images of Victorian verse. "To be Anglicized is *emphatically* not to be English," notes Homi Bhabha (85–92). In the poem, the nation is not Britannia but "Mother India" as she calls on the empire to remember and honor her colonial subjects who lie on the blood-*brown*—not blood-red—battlefields: "Remember thy martyred sons!" While prowar and seemingly derivative, the imperial panegyric is fractured by a nationalist impulse. But the rhetoric of martyrdom is also worlds away from the Punjabi folksongs, pointing to the diversity in responses—emotional, political, literary—in the Indian home front.

India on the International Stage: Rabindranath Tagore and Mulk Raj Anand

The two Indian intellectuals who were most visible on the international stage during and after the war were Rabindranath Tagore and Mulk Raj Anand, respectively. Both had a complex engagement with the war, its aftermath, and its relation to empire and Indian nationalism. The more famous of them was Tagore. He received the Nobel Prize in 1913 and was one of the most feted literary figures at the time, lecturing to packed audiences from Japan to Argentina. Wilfred Owen read his prize-winning poetry collection *Gitanjali* in the trenches. Tagore's poem "The Trumpet," written just before the outbreak of the war, was coopted for imperial propaganda and published in *The Times* in 1915 alongside poems by

Kipling and Laurence Binyon. Tagore's "Crossing," composed on 22 August 1914, adopts the metaphor of a lone boatman crossing the "wild sea at night" amid "stormy winds" and "black fear," particularly resonant in the context of the one million Indians journeying across the *kalapani* ("black waters") to war. Tagore returns to the metaphor a couple of months later in his poem "The Oarsmen," where, with almost messianic zeal, he notes:

> The sin has been yours and ours.
> The heat growing in the heart of God for ages—
> The cowardice of the weak, the arrogance of the strong, the greed of
> prosperity,
> the rancour of the deprived, the pride of race, and the insult to man—
> Has burst God's peace, raging in storm.

The war for Tagore was the symptom of a greater spiritual malaise; the immediate context for the nexus among "arrogance," "greed," "pride of race," and "insult" would have been British colonial rule. In his celebrated lectures—"Nationalism in Japan" and "Nationalism in the West"—delivered in Japan and the United States, respectively, in 1916, he launched on one of the most sustained and searing critiques of war, colonialism, and nationalism, which were for him intimately connected (*Nationalism*). For Tagore, the war was the logical, inexorable climax of Western materialism as well as aggravated nationalism, which he loathed in all its forms, whether in Europe or in India. These essays, in which the argument is conducted through metaphors and allusions, collapse the boundaries between philosophy, politics, and literature and were deeply controversial at the time. As with Virginia Woolf in *Three Guineas*, empire, nation building, and war were for Tagore related in a vicious cycle of violence. Yet, curiously, Tagore never refers to the Indian sepoys fighting and dying at the time.

To understand the emotional world of the sepoys, one must turn to Mulk Raj Anand's *Across the Black Waters*, the only full-length Indian war novel. It was written at the time of the Spanish Civil War and published in 1939. In contrast with Tagore, who was widely viewed as some sort of Eastern sage, Anand had established himself in literary London as a cosmopolitan intellectual and straddled both British and Indian modernism: he worked for some time as the private secretary to T. S. Eliot and hovered on the fringes of the Bloomsbury group. However, he grew up in the Punjab and belonged to the same agricultural-martial community from which the sepoys came. *Across the Black Waters* is dedicated "to the memory of my father Subedar Lal Chand Anand, M.S.M, (late 2/17th Dogra)," who worked in the British

Indian army. The middle novel in the Lalu trilogy, *Across the Black Waters* opens up a whole new world in war fiction, as we see the protagonist, Lalu, and his fellow sepoys from a Punjabi village arriving in Marseilles:

> "Marsels!"
>
> "We have reached Marsels!"
>
> "Hip, hip, hurrah!"
>
> The sepoys were shouting excitedly on deck.
>
> Lalu got up from where he sat watching a game of cards and went to see Marseilles. (7)

For the writer of pidgin English, linguistic and cultural difference is inscribed in the very opening word through the robust (mis)pronunciation. Few novels in English have so inexhaustible or exuberant a fund of swear words: rape-daughter, son of sea-cow, one-eyed son of a gun, cockeyed sons of blind bastards, gum-eyed bastards, hinneying like donkeys. Stubborn to translation, these swearwords become the repositories of a range of feelings, from the evocation of an almost inarticulate intimacy (as in Kirpu's constant address to Lalu as "Beta," meaning "son") to linguistic *jouissance* as defense against everyday violence. Anand is one of the first writers to launch a sustained experimental attack on standard English, a practice more associated with postcolonial novelists.

Following in the footsteps of the soldier-writers such as Owen, Erich Maria Remarque, and Richard Aldington, Anand gives us the trench experience in all its gory detail. But the delicacy of the novel lies in the way he exposes the effects of colonialism—not as event or drama but in the intimate regions of the self:

> Lalu felt guilty at having averted his eyes from them [African troops]. At Marseilles he had seen a few African soldiers talking openly to girls in the cafes and the French sahibs did not mind, though he himself was rather surprised, for the English did not like even the brown-skinned Indians to look at white women. He wondered how the English liked the French being so free and easy. And if the French liked the blacks, why shouldn't he like them? Why had he thought himself superior [to the blacks]? He felt ashamed. (77)

Anand shows the weight of colonial history as internalization of the racist ideology. But the war becomes a site of politicization for Lalu as he begins to question both colonial and racist hierarchies. Anand's novel is not an aria for the death of European bourgeois consciousness but rather a voice for the working-class Indian sepoy, a tradition that has been carried forward in *A God in Every Stone* (2014), a novel by Kamila Shamsie, a British Pakistani writer. Shamsie combines historical thickness with postcolonial and queer insights, as she layers the war experience with the history of the country's nationalist struggle.

Shamsie puts her finger on a debate that has marked South Asian (and, more generally, much of colonial) war commemoration: Should the postcolonies, now nation-states, commemorate the men who took part in an imperial war at the time of the first nationalist struggles? Indeed, to understand and analyze the region's participation in an imperial war alongside the history of its anticolonial movement remains a provocation and a challenge for the current generation of students. For, as we move through the centennial commemoration, a sole focus on the English trench poetry of the war—of the kind we had at Presidency College in the early nineties—would no longer do. Fresh research, digital archives, and online resources have firmly established the full global scale of the war and its literature. The onus is now on the classroom—on both teachers and students—to challenge the color of First World War memory, embed it in a more multiracial and international framework, and carry the debates forward.

Notes

1. The first two artifacts are illustrated in Dendooven and Chilens's *World War I*; for a full report on Jon Sen's glasses, see www.telegraphindia.com/1150307/jsp/frontpage/story_7306.jsp.

2. For a good list of online sources, refer to the fascinating First World War in the Classroom project (ww1intheclassroom.exeter.ac.uk/resources). Also see Imperial War Museum's educational pack: www.iwm.org.uk/learning/resources/how-did-people-share-their-cultures-and-traditions-during-the-first-world-war. Some of the relevant Web sites are *The Great War in Africa* (gweaa.com), *Cultural Encounters in the Time of Global Conflict* (www.cegcproject.eu), *The Guardian's* First World War (www.theguardian.com/world/firstworldwar), and the BBC iWonder *Was the Western Front the Most Multiracial Place in the World?* (www.bbc.co.uk/guides/z2bgr82).

3. For recent historical works, see Buck, *Conceiving*; Das, *1914–1918*. For online resources, see the short documentary *From Bombay to the Western Front: Indian Soldiers of the First World War* (www.youtube.com/watch?v=6stybO5v7SY) and *"In Pictures": Indian Soldiers in the First World War* (www.bbc.co.uk/news/world-asia-india-31937266).

4. Omissi, *Indian Voices* 61, 77, 91. Also see Omissi, "Europe"; Das, "Indian Sepoy Experience."

5. Some of the transcripts of the sound recordings should soon be available on the *Cultural Exchange in the Time of Global Conflict* Web site (www.cegcproject.eu), and the recordings of the Sikh songs should be available on the Web site *Empire, Faith, and War* (www.empirefaithwar.com).

6. Jasbahadur Rai, "Song," Humboldt University Sound Archives, PK03080100. I am very grateful to Anne Stirr for transcribing and translating the song. Also see Britta Lange.

7. Translated extracts from both memoirs are available in Das, "Indians at Home, Mesopotamia and France" (*Race*) and in Amitav Ghosh's excellent post "On to Baghdad" on his Web site (amitavghosh.com/blog/?cat=12).

8. The poem can be found at noglory.org/index.php/multimedia/poetry-and-spoken-word/259-international-wwi-poetry-month-the-gift-of-india-by-sarojini-naidu.

The Great War in the Middle East: Two Perspectives

T. E. Lawrence's Lessons

Stephen E. Tabachnick

Because of the large amount of excellent poetry and prose produced by soldiers on the Western Front, most discussions about World War I in English literature classes inevitably bypass the war in the east, except perhaps for a brief mention of the British defeat by the Turks and Germans at Gallipoli. But this focus on what T. E. Lawrence, two of whose four brothers were killed in France, called "murder war"—static trench warfare, artillery barrages, gas attacks, and the resulting huge casualties—neglects the war of high mobility, surprise tactics, and cultural nuances that took place in Palestine, Arabia, and Syria and that is detailed in Lawrence's great *Seven Pillars of Wisdom* (1926), which has never been out of print since it was published for the general public in 1935. While historical events are an essential element in this book, Lawrence himself wrote that "[i]n these pages the history is not of the Arab movement, but of me in it" (22). This statement is often forgotten by those who claim that he did not offer an objective history of the Arab Revolt, but it reveals that the book belongs in a course on World War I British autobiography, along with the works of Robert Graves, Edmund Blunden, and Lawrence's armored car driver, S. C. Rolls, among many others. (I prefer the term *autobiography* to *memoir* in the course title because in my view only *autobiography* includes the whole spectrum of first-person testimonies, from the most searchingly personal like *Seven Pillars*, Graves's *Good-Bye to All That*, and Blunden's *Undertones of War* to the more objective but still personal work of Rolls and others. And *autobiography* also fits because war is a situation in which many soldiers discover their true selves for the first time, as their works often show.)

Given the length of *Seven Pillars of Wisdom* (seven hundred pages in the Penguin paperback edition) and its depth, I have devoted five hour-and-twenty-five-minute classes to it, and what follows is an enhanced and up-to-date vision (which is, however, based on past experience) of how I would teach Lawrence in the future as part of such a course.

The first class session on Lawrence is the story of his multifaceted life and career, which has been told in over fifty biographies, many works of historical and literary scholarship, doctoral dissertations, and exhibitions such as "Lawrence von Arabien: Genese eines Mythos," which took place at the Landesmuseum Natur und Mensch in Oldenburg, Germany, during 2010 and 2011, and the resulting extraordinary catalog (Fansa and Hoffmann). Perhaps because of the West's continuing and not always pleasant involvement with the Middle East as well as Lawrence's own achievements in multiple fields relating to war and politics, he remains an object of enduring interest to students as well as to the general public.

Lawrence's achievements, in addition to the leadership recorded in *Seven Pillars of Wisdom*, include an often republished Oxford Bachelor of Arts honors thesis that resulted from his solo walk through what are today Lebanon, Jordan, Israel, and Syria to study thirty-six crusader castles; the solution of an important biblical problem when he worked with C. Leonard Woolley in late 1913 to early 1914 on an archaeological survey of the northern Sinai desert (and also covered up a British spying expedition mapping Turkish fortifications while doing so); the failed attempt in 1916, when he was working in Cairo intelligence, to bribe the Turks into letting go fourteen thousand British troops at Kut-el-Amara (now in Iraq) with one and then two million pounds sterling; the mediation at Versailles that led Chaim Weizmann, the head of the Zionist movement, and Emir Feisal, the leader of the Arab nationalist movement, to sign the only peace treaty between the two groups until the Sadat-Begin accord of 1979; the writing of *Seven Pillars of Wisdom* and his memoir of his postwar service years, *The Mint* (completed 1928, published 1955); one of the best prose translations of *The Odyssey* (1931); and work on a prototype of the PT boat of World War II. Despite the contentiousness that has surrounded his career and is evidenced in the many biographies and other works, there can be no argument about the fact that Lawrence was a brilliant polymath whose legacy continues to enhance our understanding in many fields to the present day.

The second class session on Lawrence tells the history of the war in the Palestinian, Arabian, and Syrian theater, focusing, but not exclusively, on his campaign and the political consequences of the war, as told not only in *Seven Pillars* but in excellent multinational scholarly histories of the campaign, including the work of Jeremy Wilson, Maurice Larès, Konrad Morsey, and Suleiman Mousa, among many others. This history includes the Arab Revolt against the Turks by the Sherif of Mecca and General Edmund Allenby's parallel Palestine campaign, which together resulted in the expulsion of the Turks from the Arab lands and Turkey's defeat in the war, depriving the Germans of an important ally. The military high points of Lawrence's untraditional campaign were his development of guerilla warfare's principles, which are still studied at war colleges around the world; his conquest of Akaba after a several-hundred-mile trek by camel through the desert; his many hit-and-run attacks on the Hejaz Railway and the Turkish fortifications along the railway's route; and the Arabs' triumphant entry into Damascus. Allenby's more traditional campaign included two deceptions of the Turks and Germans, the conquest of Beersheba by Australian light horsemen in one of the last great cavalry charges in military history (reenacted by the Australians in Beersheba in 2007), as well as Allenby's conquest of Jerusalem, which Lawrence—whose parents attended an Evangelical church in Oxford and who won a prize for his religious knowledge at the age of sixteen—said was the high point of the war for him. In comparison with the murderous slog of the Western Front, Allenby's and Lawrence's campaigns were exciting and even inspiring, a point that American journalist Lowell Thomas made in his popular multimedia show *With Allenby in Palestine and Lawrence in Arabia* (1919–20) and his biography of Lawrence, *With Lawrence in Arabia* (1924). Students writing about the accounts of Graves, Blunden, and Siegfried Sassoon, among others, inevitably point out the contrast between the Western Front and the eastern campaign as described by Lawrence.

The political consequences of the war also deserve attention, especially the fact that the secret Sykes-Picot Agreement signed by Britain and France in 1916 led the French to evict Feisal from Damascus in 1920, and they, not the Arabs, ruled Syria until 1943. As Lawrence states in *Seven Pillars*, he was aware of this probable outcome during the war although he hoped to avoid it, and he therefore felt guilty even though he had informed Feisal of the agreement's existence early on. In this context, the biblical phrase "Seven Pillars of Wisdom" conjures up a ruined temple lying in the desert rather than a complete structure. However, after his eviction from Syria, Feisal was placed on the throne of Iraq in 1921 by the British, and his brother Abdullah was allowed to continue ruling Transjordan—now Jordan—which his descendants have ruled to this day, a monument, at least in part, to Lawrence's service as a diplomat there after the war.

The third class session on Lawrence is devoted to the literary aspects of *Seven Pillars*, including the influences on the work, its composition, and its style(s). The most important literary influence on Lawrence was his mentor Charles M. Doughty's *Travels in Arabia Deserta* (1888), which Lawrence called the bible of travel books. Doughty's style is a mixture of contemporary English, older English, and Arabic, making it one of the few truly bilingual works in British literature. During the war, Lawrence carried with him the *Oxford Book of English Verse* as well as Malory's *Morte d'Arthur* and Aristophanes. To demonstrate the result of all of these literary influences (and particularly the poems of Ernest Dowson, D.G. and Christina Rossetti, and William Morris, which Lawrence loved), passages from which I read and explicate in class, I quote examples of the spectrum of the eight styles which I have detailed in my *T. E. Lawrence.*

After this introduction to Lawrence's influences and their stylistic effect on *Seven Pillars*, I move to the story of its composition. Lawrence worked on his book from 1919 to 1926. The 1926 text, originally sold to a select group of subscribers in a sumptuous edition, is the final draft found in the Penguin and other editions since 1935, when the book was published for the public at large. Wilson's edition of the longer 1922 draft is now available in major American university libraries, and it can be compared with the 1926/1935 text by students—particularly graduate students—with no need to visit a rare books library.

Students react with great interest to Lawrence's self-characterization and his characterization of other combatants, which we discuss in the fourth class. They are usually surprised to see how introspective and self-critical he is, thinking him only a heroic commander before reading *Seven Pillars.* Here William Howarth's analysis of the different types of autobiography is particularly useful, since Lawrence—unlike Rolls, for instance—writes what Howarth has termed a "poetic" autobiography, in which the autobiographer searches for himself and never quite finds it. In particular, Lawrence's many contradictions come to the fore. Lawrence models his writing at least in part on the *Morte d'Arthur* and the *Odyssey*, since the Arab Revolt for him was an epic adventure pitting a weaker power—the Arabs—against a stronger one, the Turks and Germans. So his Arab characters, outside of a few exceptions, are strongly and colorfully drawn and exhibit energy and will and often—as in the case of Feisal, for instance—complexity. Interestingly, the British, including even Allenby and his intelligence officer Richard Meinertzhagen, while often heroic and brilliant, are less excitingly portrayed than the Arab characters. Students notice this, and the question of whether Lawrence favored the Arab or the British side more makes an excellent paper topic, especially since it also includes the cultural clash with which Lawrence contended. Lawrence saw himself through both Arab and British eyes, the "two veils" as he names them in *Seven Pillars*.

In addition to this conflict within Lawrence, there are the other conflicts from which he suffered during the Revolt. He exposes these conflicts especially in his famous chapter 103, "Myself," in which he tries to understand himself on his thirtieth birthday. Do his military victories justify the loss of his moral integrity, as well as the loss of his personal bodily integrity owing to his rape by the Turks at Deraa? Why was he inevitably disappointed by his victories instead of being overjoyed by them? Can he as a man of thought ever feel comfortable as a man of action? Did he prefer to lead or to follow? Does he desire fame or despise it? In their papers, students can investigate both sides of one (or more) of these contradictions and decide how Lawrence resolved it, if indeed he did, and whether or not some of these conflicts were the result of PTSD. A comparison with Graves's (and others') postwar PTSD is also an excellent topic.

What do interested students who take English courses—including, for instance, not only English majors but also students in history, political science, Middle Eastern studies, psychology, and ROTC—learn about war and politics from Lawrence's book and from his life? Their responses, whether in papers, exam essays, or class discussions, show that they gain great insight into how cultural differences can influence people; how intelligence work and guerrilla warfare are seen from the inside; how politics and war can impact one another, and how the Middle East might be different now if Lawrence's vision of cooperation between Arabs and Jews had been realized; how involvement in war can transform an intellectual—albeit an unusually sensitive, complex, and talented one; and what are the wrenching mental and physical costs of such an involvement. Few other books, including most of the Western Front autobiographies, and few other lives, teach these lessons as powerfully.

The 1962 David Lean film—which students can view at home—provides a valuable comparison with the text and is worth a fifth class session. Because it is dependent on visual action, the film cannot reproduce *Seven Pillars*'s long philosophical meditations—such as Lawrence's painstaking development of his guerrilla strategy—and nowhere does Lawrence state in *Seven Pillars* (or elsewhere) that he deliberately burned his finger with a match or enjoyed killing people, as the film claims. On the other hand, the match burning symbolically represents Lawrence's lingering guilt and the masochism that resulted from his campaign, and it is effective visually and intellectually. (The psychologist John Mack's superb *A Prince of Our Disorder* is extremely useful for class discussions about Lawrence's personality.) A comparison between Lawrence's literary self-portrait and writer Robert Bolt's and Peter O'Toole's representation of him in the film inevitably evokes interesting essay responses. My midterm examination on Lawrence's life and work consists of an identification and short answer section, to test whether the students have listened to the class discussions and read Lawrence's work carefully, as well as an essay section, which examines how well they have thought about the issues that Lawrence's text and the film raise. But even if the film is not used, Lawrence's book, whether on its own or in comparison with other World War I autobiographies, teaches students—and teachers, who have to figure out how to present such a complex text—many lessons that they are unlikely ever to forget.

Note

Quotation of or reference to Lawrence's *Seven Pillars of Wisdom* is made from the Penguin 1983 edition.

Fictional Representations of the War and of Its Consequences

Amaya Martin

The romantic Lawrence of Arabia stereotype of the Arab Revolt against the Ottomans has dominated the English-speaking world's imagination about World War I in Arab lands for decades, especially after the release of the epic 1962 film. This image, however, was created about but not by Arabs and at best is applicable to specific events experienced by relatively few people in a limited geographic area.

The deprivations and battles of World War I affected urban as well as rural Arabs throughout the Middle East. When the Ottoman Empire entered the war on the side of Germany and Austria in 1914, the Arab Middle East became both home front and battlefield. French, British, and colonial troops were deployed to Turkey, Egypt, Iraq, and the Levant (today's Lebanon, Syria, Jordan, Israel, and the Palestinian territories) to fight enemy forces. Arab residents thus perceived the war in terms of both their prewar relations with these foreign powers and the new reality of conquest and occupation. Cairo, for example—a major urban center whose residents had little in common with the Bedouins of the Arabian Peninsula portrayed in *Lawrence of Arabia*—experienced the war mainly through British occupation. The city's residents generally resented and opposed British power. Jerusalemites, however, cheered the British armies as liberators when they entered the city in December 1917, for the locals had suffered almost four years of shortages and hardships under harsh Ottoman military authority.[1]

Authors from the Middle East incorporated their perspectives and experiences of World War I into their literary works. Their local views offer modern Western educators and students valuable insights into the war outside Europe, as these portrayals differ from those of European and American authors. Particularly resonant in the classroom are three novels by Arab writers. The works of two Egyptians, Naguib Mahfouz and Tawfiq al-Hakim, are translated into English and readily available; the third, by the Lebanese author Tawfiq Yusuf Awwad, has not yet been translated, but professors should be alert for its appearance because of the remarkable pedagogical opportunities it offers.

Mahfouz (1911–2006), winner of the Nobel Prize in 1988, defined himself as a child of the revolution, referring to the 1919 revolution against the British occupation of Egypt. Britain had declared Egypt a protectorate at the beginning of World War I, but at the war's end a group of Egyptian politicians led by Saad Zaghlul expressed their right to participate in the Versailles Peace Conference to demand full sovereignty and independence. The British arrested and exiled these Egyptian nationalists, whose constituents revolted in reaction. The first part of Mahfouz's *The Cairo Trilogy*, entitled *The Palace Walk*, is set during the First World War and the 1919 revolution. *The Palace Walk* was published in 1956, four years after the 1952 coup that abolished Egypt's British-backed monarchy. In addition to analyzing the novel's material on the last stages of World War I and the revolution of 1919, students can also use it to study modern Egyptian history. For example, they can evaluate how the fictional portrayal of Saad Zaghlul mirrors the 1952 Free Officers' actions against British occupation.

For Western students, *The Palace Walk* is an accessible literary text in translation. Other World War I Egyptian literary works, such as Mahmud Taymur's *al-Masabih al-Zarqa'* ("The Blue Lights") were never translated into English, but Mahfouz's status as a Nobel Prize winner ensures relatively inexpensive and widely available editions. Mahfouz masterfully intertwines the lives of members of a traditional Egyptian family with the social and political events of their time. In the beginning of the novel the war is merely a backdrop, but by its end the war takes a major role in the plot and completely alters the life of the family. Students reading this novel, including those unfamiliar with the Arab Middle East, will be able to perceive the events of the war at the "street level" while learning about Egyptian society at the time.

Mahfouz's engaging style and vivid characters attract students' interest. The people and events of World War I appear on page after page, while Mahfouz engages readers with dramatic stories. For example, the public protests against the British occupation go hand in hand with the soap-opera-style double life of Ahmad Abdel Gawad, strict and cruel with his wife and children but generous and licentious outside his home. Characters regularly refer to Australian soldiers in the streets of Cairo, raising readers' awareness of the non-English troops in British units. The characters also show their sympathy for the Germans, as they expect that German victory will free them from the British, who are shown slaughtering the Egyptian population. Some of the characters portray their acts of resistance against the British as Islamic "holy war," the now famous jihad concept in the West. Mahfouz's novel can introduce concepts related to postcolonialism, since Egyptian nationalism can be used as a case study. Indeed, the 1956 publication of *The Palace Walk*[2] strengthened the new Egyptian republic of 1952—free of British occupation—by popularizing depictions of resentment against the British presence.

A powerful classroom complement to Mahfouz's *The Palace Walk* is al-Hakim's novel *The Return of the Spirit*,[3] a pillar in the self-construction of modern Egyptian nationalism. Though not as focused on World War I as *The Palace Walk*, *The Return of the Spirit* presents the end of the war and the 1919 revolution in a way that calls for Egyptian national unity against foreign powers, a national unity that brings together Christians and Muslims, rural peasants and city dwellers, rich and poor.

Born in Alexandria, al-Hakim (1898–1987) became one of the most famous Arab writers of his time. Gamal Abdel Nasser, one of the Egyptian army officers who led the 1952 coup and became president of Egypt from 1956 to 1970, reportedly said that *The Return of the Spirit* inspired him. University students today may draw parallels between the 1919 revolution as al-Hakim depicted it and the demonstrations in Cairo's Tahrir Square that overthrew Mubarak in 2011 and Morsi in 2013. Instructors can present media articles from these two events and ask students to compare them with the portrayal of Egyptian unity in the 1933 novel. Instructors can start the discussion by showing or mentioning the 5 July 2013 cover of the Egyptian newspaper *al-Masri al-Yawm*, which shows massive Tahrir Square crowds under the headline "The Return of the Spirit."

Students will need some preparation to fully appreciate al-Hakim's symbolism and allusions. The author links ancient Egyptian folkways and mythology to Egyptians in his own time, and such back-and-forth references may confuse a reader who has no background knowledge. The ideal way of presenting *Palace Walk* and *Return of the Spirit*, then, is by offering Mahfouz's novel first. While gaining familiarity with the events of World War I in Egypt by reading *Palace Walk*, students should consider their relevance, analyze their literary representation, and relate them to the 1919 Egyptian revolution. Al-Hakim's *The Return of the Spirit* is a very suitable follow-up with its emphasis on popular mood rather than events. From analysis and comparison of the two novels, students should gain insights on how identical events were perceived and presented differently.

For students who can read Arabic, the novel that most directly addresses the developments and deprivations of World War I in the Middle East is *The Loaf of Bread* (*al-Raghif*), written by Tawfiq Yusuf Awwad, a Lebanese, and first published in Beirut in 1939. Unfortunately the novel has not yet been released in English translation, but it is such a fundamental work about World War I in the Levant that, without describing it, any program teaching fictional representations of the war and its consequences would be incomplete.

Awwad (1911–88) was born in Mount Lebanon, where he grew up under Ottoman occupation during World War I. Although he was very young at the time, the war greatly influenced his writing, especially his first collection of short stories, *The Lame Boy*, published in 1936, in addition to *The Loaf of Bread*. *The Loaf of Bread* portrays the repressive military government established by Ahmad Djemal Pasha, a senior Ottoman official infamous for personal cruelty. The title alludes to the terrible famine that the residents of Mount Lebanon suffered during those days, a calamity that led to hundreds of thousands of deaths. Sami, the main character, experiences Ottoman repression and joins the rebellion against the Ottomans. Like Awwad himself, Sami is an Arab Maronite Christian.

The Loaf of Bread is valuable to modern students because it depicts the hunger, oppression, and suffering of the Arab population in Lebanon and Syria during the war and the simultaneous emergence of Arab nationalism. It also introduces students to the religious diversity in the Middle East and the ties between European powers and the different religious communities there. Students can approach these ideas by analyzing the main characters' varied identities and finding instances where the novel resists the equivalence between Arabs and Islam and rejects the existence of a single Islamic identity. Like Mahfouz's *The Palace Walk*, *The Loaf of Bread* weaves fictional stories into actual events, political currents, and social causes. Awwad transforms dialogue into political oratory. Note the call for Arab nationalism in Sami's speech and the reasoning against the Ottomans' call for an Islamic holy war:

> No, there is no religious struggle between Arabs and Turks. Most of the Turks are Muslim too. The issue is not Muslims and non-Muslims but rather Arabs fighting Turks to regain their freedom and Turks fighting Arabs to maintain their authority. The real Arab nationalism was born today, and its mother is this revolution in which I, an Arab Christian, walk next to you, Arab Muslims, fighting against a common enemy, the Turk, whether he follows Muhammad, Jesus, or the devil. And its father is the martyrdom of young Arabs and previous heroes. The Turks took them away just because they were Arabs, without asking the Muslim about his Qur'an and the Christian about his Gospels. . . . As for us, in this era, we are ashamed to build our new state on a religious basis. Our Arab nationalism, born today . . . cares about the caliphate only as

> much as Italians care about the papacy. Those who fight today against the Turks fight against the Germans, too, and they are not in dispute with them about the caliphate; and they may fight against the English and French tomorrow if the English and French have the greed to take their countries or to humiliate them. (309; my trans.)

Professors can employ this passage to stimulate student discussion about how World War I magnified ethnic and linguistic Arab identity as anticolonial nationalism. The passage demonstrates that, to an Arab nationalist, religion is not important when fighting a common enemy, and students should analyze the Arab nationalist's perspective on the historical roles and power relations of Arabs and Turks. Assignments in international relations, history, and literature courses could ask students to discuss the implications of Awwad's placing his small, Christian-majority country as part of the greater Arab community rather than focusing on a more local Lebanese nationalism. The passage above is only one of several monologues in the novel that stand on their own, suggesting that instructors can select fragments without assigning the whole novel.

The story "The Winter Rat," from Awwad's first published collection, *The Lame Boy*, may serve as a shorter alternative to *The Loaf of Bread*. As in *The Loaf of Bread*, the wartime famine drives the plot, but the main characters are children. Awwad himself was less than ten years old during the war, and his descriptions of children's feelings and suffering are heartrending. While "The Winter Rat" does not touch on the emergence of nationalism and the great leaders and battles of World War I, it transmits the suffering of the population and the human consequences of the war more poignantly than any other work by Awwad. I taught it in an Arabic short story class to illustrate the consequences of the war in Mount Lebanon and have seen that even students familiar with Middle Eastern history are moved by its all too real and intensely sad descriptions of the slow death of children from hunger.

To best appreciate these works of fiction, students will require some familiarization with the Ottoman Empire and the European presence in Arab lands before the war. Many Arabs perceived the events of the war as a continuation of preexisting rivalries between foreign actors already competing in the Middle East and saw the war as an opportunity to assert their own interests. One novel, for example, portrays the population of Cairo aligned against the British and favoring the Germans; another, the population in Mount Lebanon strongly opposed to the Ottomans and favoring the Allies. Before students read these novels, the instructor might assign selections from Albert Hourani's *Arabic Thought in the Liberal Age, 1789–1939* (1962), a classic work of history. Chapter 2, "The Ottoman Empire," and chapter 3, "First Views of Europe," are especially useful.

Teaching Arab literary works gives voice in the classroom to those who might otherwise not be heard. When European capitals and battlefields become the background to a Middle Eastern foreground, the study of World War I reaches new depth and complexity. In reading works by Arab authors, students will have the opportunity to appreciate the truly global nature of the world war and its legacy.

Notes

1. *Jerusalem in World War I: The Palestine Diary of a European Diplomat*, by Conde de Ballobar, is a valuable resource that describes how locals and visitors of many faiths felt toward the foreign soldiers who occupied the holy city, including Turks, Germans, Englishmen, and Australians. This diary was published in English in 2011 and includes personal accounts by a Spanish consul who was neutral toward the war's events and personalities.

2. There are a number of English translations of Mahfouz's *The Palace Walk*—in Arabic, *Bayn al-Qasrayn* (literally "between the two palaces," the name of a street in Cairo).

3. Al-Hakim's *The Return of the Spirit*—in Arabic '*Awda-t al-Ruh*—was published in English by Three Continents Press in 1990 and by Lynne Rienner Publishers in 2012.

Part III

Cultural Motifs

Wyatt Bonikowski

Shell Shock as a Narrative Paradigm in Great War Psychiatry and Fiction

Teaching shell shock in a course on the literature of the Great War asks us to pay attention to the intersection of the physical and psychological experiences of war. The symptoms of shell shock included both bodily and mental dysfunction: paralysis, tremors, anxiety, loss of speech and memory. From early in the war, psychiatrists noted the similarity of these symptoms to those of hysteria, in which visible functional disturbances signified invisible psychological processes. Symptoms had to be read and interpreted in order to be understood and treated. These acts of reading and interpretation occurred in the real encounters between doctors and soldiers behind the lines and in the fictional representations of conflicts between soldiers and civilians in literature. Reading case histories and literary texts together can show how far-reaching the meaning of shell shock is. We learn about not only the immediate effects of war on the body and mind but also the larger historical context out of which shell shock emerged, including issues of gender and class that informed how it was understood and represented.

Students might come to a lesson on shell shock understanding the term as a synonym for posttraumatic stress disorder (PTSD), which has its own historical specificity. The opportunity arises, then, for a discussion about how far one can assume continuity between terms separated by decades and with different origins. Tracey Loughran provides a useful caution not to ignore the specificity of each term, arguing that "the historical construct of shell shock does not correspond to the historical construct of PTSD" (103). Judith Herman presents the history of trauma as one of "episodic amnesia," a historical repetition compulsion in which questions have been raised, provisionally answered, then forgotten and repressed, only to return and be asked again in a new context (7). The field of trauma theory, as it has developed through the work of Herman, Cathy Caruth, Ruth Leys, and others, suggests that the history of trauma has itself a traumatic structure.

Shell shock was introduced into medical discourse by Charles S. Myers in the 13 February 1915 issue of the British medical journal *The Lancet* ("Contribution"). Only in the Anglo-American context does a term used casually by soldiers become an official medical diagnosis, favored in popular discourse even after it was officially dropped as a diagnostic term in 1917. By the end of the war, the British military was using the general term "nervous" in the acronym "N.Y.D.?N.," or "Not Yet Diagnosed ?Nervous" (*Shell Shock* 97). But in 1922, the War Office Committee created to investigate the lessons of shell shock returned to the term in the title of its report (*Report of the War Office Committee of Enquiry into "Shell Shock"*). Perhaps the informality of *shell shock*, its poetic grouping of sound and meaning so different from standard medical terminology, was what made it stick. Jay Winter argues that the "linguistic compression" of associations in the term enabled it to travel from medical discourse to metaphor, becoming a "representation not solely of damaged soldiers but more generally of central facets of the war itself," such as "its scope, its scale, its repercussions" ("Shell Shock" 7–9).

Case histories of shell shock show students how soldiers struggled to communicate their experiences and how doctors attempted to understand and treat this new disorder. This knowledge can productively inform students' reading of literary works about shell shock, which highlight its social and cultural meanings and show how it becomes a metaphor for the extensive reach of war's effects.

Case Histories

In introducing the study of shell shock to students, it is helpful to inquire into the implications of the term itself. What do these two words mean when put together, and what associations do they raise? *Shell shock* implies a narrative: an event of war followed by a series of effects. In the process of telling different versions of this narrative over the course of the war and beyond, psychiatrists, soldiers, and writers, both combatants and civilians, complicated the seeming simplicity of the narrative at every point. Did the shell blast alone cause shock, or did other events or even predisposition to illness cause it? Could a specific cause even be pinpointed? Was the shock physical, such as concussion, or psychological? How should the symptoms of shock be treated, and was shell shock even possible to cure? The beginning of the narrative might stretch as far back as the soldier's childhood, and the resistance of the symptoms to treatment and cure might make the narrative endless, leaving the soldier stuck in a repetitive middle space of nightmares, trembling, mutism, and amnesia.

While *shell shock* was used only in the Anglo-American context, terms from other national contexts reveal similar questions about cause and treatment. Knowing how French and German doctors, for example, discussed war trauma provides students with both a broader understanding of medical and military discourse in Europe and an opportunity for comparing the meanings and implications of these terms across national contexts. These terms drew on the nineteenth-century history of medical investigation into hysteria and traumatic neurosis. (For a brief overview of this history, see B. Shephard 5–20). German doctors used terms like *Granatkontusion* ("shell concussion") and *Granatexplosionslähmung* ("exploding-shell paralysis") before settling on the more general *Kriegsneurosen* or *Kriegshysterie* ("war neurosis, hysteria," also used in Britain and America; Lerner 61–62). French doctors used *obusite* (from *obus*, meaning "bomb"), *l'hypnose des batailles* ("battle hypnosis"), *syndrome commotionnel* ("commotional syndrome"), and *traumatisme* (G. Thomas 20–21, 56–58).

As the terminology shows, some doctors believed the cause to be physical—Frederick Mott in England and Hermann Oppenheim in Germany, for example—but over the course of the war the debates gradually resolved in favor of a psychological interpretation. Depending on which terms were used, diagnoses had real effects on soldiers' future lives. A term that implied physical or psychological wounding as a direct result of war might lead to a war pension. A term that implied chronic hysterical symptoms often suggested to doctors a constitutional predisposition, which not only negated the possibility of a pension but also branded a soldier with stigmas of cowardice, weakness, and effeminacy. These problems of diagnoses and their effects provide an important lesson for students about the ways in which the ideologies of gender and class inform medical knowledge. Not only were shell-shocked soldiers often viewed as examples of damaged masculinity, they were also split along class lines in terms of their symptoms. The British psychiatrist W. H. R. Rivers, for example, argued that hysterical symptoms were more common in soldiers of the general ranks, while anxiety neuroses were more common in officers, associating the former with the body and the latter with the mind (*Instinct* 207).

Styles of treatment followed from ideas about causation. Doctors who viewed symptoms as hysterical and viewed hysteria as a form of self-suggestion advised disciplinary measures, such as forceful verbal persuasion (Joseph Babinski in France) or the application of electricity to the body (the infamous Kaufmann cure, after Fritz Kaufmann in Germany; G. Thomas 38–41; Lerner 102–113). In these forms of treatment, the doctor acted as the superior military officer who viewed the often lower-ranked soldier as deliberately evading his duty and commanded him to give up his illness. Hypnosis was also widely used, because, like the more direct disciplinary measures, it was considered a rapid method to eliminate symptoms, which suited the military's desire to return soldiers quickly to battle.

Case histories by doctors using disciplinary methods are useful for showing students how some forms of treatment silenced the voice of the soldier. Teachers might ask whose perspective is more prominent in the narrative and whether we learn more about the soldier's experience or the doctor's authority. A particularly stark example is the case presented by Lewis Yealland in *Hysterical Disorders of Warfare* (1918), in which Yealland subjects a mute soldier to electric shocks to the neck and back of the throat for a number of hours (7–15; Leed 174–75). Students are likely to find this case disturbing, but its extreme nature caused it to become an infamous example of disciplinary treatment. Elaine Showalter argues in her writing on the case that shell shock can be interpreted as a form of unconscious protest against the war and rigid definitions of masculinity (170). Unable to protest consciously, the soldier's symptoms spoke for him. Yealland presents his cure of the soldier's mutism triumphantly, but he eliminates the unspoken meaning of the soldier's symptom. The soldier recovers his ability to speak, but, one might say, at the cost of his own voice.

Drawing on both Eric Leed and Showalter, the novelist Pat Barker highlights the narrative implications of such a treatment by staging a fictionalized version in the novel *Regeneration* (1991), which she contrasts with the more humane approach of Rivers. The scene occurs at the end of the novel, after we have witnessed how Rivers treats his patients sympathetically, listening to their dreams and memories and encouraging them to come to terms with their traumatic experiences. We watch through his eyes as Yealland applies electric shocks to the soldier and are horrified along with Rivers at this silencing of the soldier's mute protest. Rivers realizes that he, too, is responsible for silencing a soldier's protest, that of Siegfried Sassoon, who was sent to him for treatment as an alternative to court martial after Sassoon, a decorated officer, had written a scathing protest of the war. The novel ends with Rivers's regretting the fact that, under his treatment, Sassoon has given up his opposition to the war.

Barker's novel brings together two different forms of protest, the public outcry about war's destruction and the silent speech of symptoms, and offers two different approaches to dealing with them: authoritarian silencing and psychoanalytic listening. Ideally, psychoanalysis offers a space in which not only words but also symptoms can communicate a meaning. But while essays by psychoanalysts treating shell-shocked soldiers at times reveal the ways in which symptoms can communicate (see Ferenczi et al.), Freud's own theories present traumatic symptoms as a more intractable problem. Although Freud never treated shell shock himself, his writings on the subject have become influential for understanding not only shell shock but trauma in general (see, for example, Cathy Caruth's *Unclaimed Experience*). His "Introduction to *Psycho-analysis and the War Neuroses*" (1919) represents his first thoughts, and his "Memorandum on the Electrical Treatment of War Neurotics" (1920), included as an appendix to the introduction, expresses his opposition to disciplinary measures. But *Beyond the Pleasure Principle* (1920) is where Freud presents his most far-reaching theory of trauma. He describes trauma as a shattering of the mind's "protective shield" that filters impressions from the outside world (31). Without this shield, the mind is flooded with an anxiety that manifests itself as "repetition compulsion," which "repeatedly bring[s] the patient back into the situation of his accident"—for example, in nightmares or intrusive thoughts (13). Further, the repetition compulsion for Freud was evidence of an underlying "death drive" in the psyche, a primordial impulse toward self-destruction.

Here we have two ways of reading the symptoms of shell shock: as carriers of unconscious meaning and as a resistance to meaning making and communication. In some case histories, we see the latter: soldiers' symptoms resist treatment and cure as well as the doctors' efforts to reconstruct a coherent narrative (see, for example, the second case in Myers, "Contribution"). In Rivers's essay "The Repression of War Experience," we see both. Rivers gradually helps a soldier who had frequent nightmares after witnessing the death of his friend by shell explosion. In order to lessen the terrifying aspect of the memory, Rivers asks him to focus on the fact that his friend was spared pain by the suddenness of his death. Under Rivers's guidance, the soldier's nightmare is altered and a new dream is produced, one in which the soldier speaks with his friend without fear (199). This classic psychoanalytic resolution is based on Rivers's ability to hear what the soldier is trying to say through the symptom and to respond appropriately. But another case shows the limitations of this approach when Rivers is faced with the resistance of symptoms to treatment. The soldier, whose story is fictionalized in Barker's novel, was blown up by a shell and landed headfirst in the rotting corpse of a German soldier. Despite Rivers's efforts to guide him to face the memory, his symptoms of nausea and vomiting continued (Rivers, "Repression" 200). The inconclusive nature of this case leaves the reader of Rivers's narrative with the image of the soldier locked in a repetitive loop, the traumatic memory too present ever to be consigned to the past.

Yealland's and Rivers's case histories are clear in their approaches, which makes them accessible to students and useful to contrast with each other in the classroom. Teachers might find it productive to compare Barker's staging of this contrast with works of the period that also present the ethical failure of doctors to understand shell-shocked soldiers' suffering. In Virginia Woolf's *Mrs. Dalloway* (1925), Sir William Bradshaw treats Septimus Smith's fragmentary speech as a mere "symptom, to be noted on the card" (96). Woolf critiques Bradshaw's rationalist approach to mental illness as an example of the powerful imposing their will on the powerless and connects Bradshaw to the larger forces of patriarchy and imperialism (99–102). Dorothy Sayers's detective novel *Whose Body?* (1923) pits the shell-shocked soldier and detective Lord Peter Wimsey against the nerve specialist and villain Sir Julian Freke. As Ariela Freedman writes, "The shell shock victims in Sayers's novels are heroes or innocents. Doctors, on the other hand, often turn out to be frauds and criminals" (373).

Not all case histories present such a straightforward contrast in approaches, and many provoke questions that undo their neat opposition. Case histories of shell shock can be found in out-of-print volumes, a few of which are available in free online editions. In addition to those already cited, I would recommend books by Millais Culpin, M. D. Eder, G. Elliot Smith and T. H. Pear, and E. E. Southard. The works of cultural historians such as Peter Barham, Jason Crouthamel, Peter Leese, Paul Lerner, and Gregory M. Thomas contain useful information about cases in different national contexts.

Fictional Representations of Shell Shock

Shell shock's representation in fiction is a primary way in which shell shock has become a cultural metaphor whose meanings have traveled far beyond the military-medical context. Teachers can use fictional war narratives to show students how literary devices and formal techniques often reproduce the symptoms of shell shock in order to communicate the disordered experience of war. Jane Robinett describes the narrative discourse of Erich Maria Remarque's *All Quiet on the Western Front* (1928) as "almost entirely lacking in ordinary transitional devices": Remarque "shifts from present to past tense, frequently relying on casual lateral shifts, repositions, and alternate scenes whose rhythms echo the troop movements to and from the front and in and out of battle, with sudden dislocations triggered by hyperarousal, intrusion, and constriction" (305). Ford Madox Ford structures the first novel of his tetralogy *Parade's End* (1924–28) on the symptom of amnesia, not representing the event of war that causes Christopher Tietjens's memory loss but rather unfolding it for the reader after the fact through conversation and fragmentary memory. This technique mimics the belatedness of traumatic experience: the trauma is "missed" at the moment of its occurrence, but its effects repeat long after the event (Caruth 62). Ford himself suffered memory loss after a shell blast and described his subsequent difficulty writing about war as an "invisible barrier in my brain" ("Arms" 37). These novels suggest that in order to render the traumas of war, narrative itself must be shocked, upending cause and effect and leaving gaps in knowledge that might never be filled.

Women who served as nurses and ambulance drivers used similar narrative techniques of fragmentation and disjunction to represent their experiences of war trauma. Both Mary Borden's *Forbidden Zone* (1929), a hybrid text of fiction, memoir, and poetry based on her experiences as a nurse, and Helen Zenna Smith's *Not So Quiet . . .* (1930), a novel fictionalized from the diaries of Winifred Young, who served as an ambulance driver, communicate the intensity of women's experiences during and after bombardment, highlighting through experimental form and graphic and repetitive language both bodily suffering and the perceptual overload of mental trauma. Critics such as Margaret Higonnet, Jane Marcus, and Laurie Kaplan draw attention to the difficulty women writers faced in daring to write in frank terms about their experiences. While the narrative of the soldier feminized by war trauma has become familiar, the narrative of women's war trauma is still marginalized, as Hannah Groch-Begley reminds us in a recent article in *The Atlantic*.

While the narratives above attempt to recreate the symptomology of traumatic war experience, other novels use the shell-shocked soldier as an embodiment of cultural anxieties about the relations between soldiers and civilians, shifting gender roles, and the general instability of postwar society. Rebecca West's *The Return of the Soldier* (1918) places the burden of dealing with the shell-shocked soldier on the women who care for him, reversing the normative scenario in which the soldier, like Odysseus, returns from war to reclaim his rightful place as head of the house. In Woolf's *Mrs. Dalloway*, the relationship between the shell-shocked Septimus Smith and Clarissa Dalloway figures the difficulty of communicating the traumas of war to the home front. Both these novels, written by women and featuring female protagonists, can reveal to students the conflicts of gender and class that the war highlighted. They also exemplify the writers' desire to understand, through a variety of discourses, the meaning of shell shock and to communicate it to the larger public.

Meg Albrinck

Resisting the Call to Serve: Mutiny, Pacifism, and Conscientious Objection in the First World War

Understanding the cultures of resistance that operated during the First World War is no easy task, for the reasons men resisted the call to serve may be more varied than the reasons they enlisted. This presents both a challenge and an opportunity for any teacher hoping to include representations of resistance in discussions of the war. On the one hand, the complexity of the topic may suggest that it is impossible to cover literatures of war and peace in a single term or to address the historical context adequately without sacrificing a literary focus. On the other hand, the variety of materials available ensures that it is possible to incorporate some discussion of resistance in almost any course, whether the focus is national or international, whether the time available is one day or one term.

Indeed, it would be difficult to discuss literature of the First World War without addressing the distinctly antiwar attitude that emerges in much of the canonical literature of the period, particularly works published after 1916. However, it would be inappropriate to suggest that all antiwar texts model resistance for the same reasons or from the same vantage point. While all the texts I reference here exhibit an oppositional perspective, more nuanced understandings of the term *antiwar* may emerge in courses where instructors provide reading lists and assignments that invite students to explore resistance in varied forms, such as mutiny, pacifism, and conscientious objection.

Discussion of resistance in representations of the war can begin with classroom staples such as Erich Maria Remarque's *All Quiet on the Western Front*, Wilfred Owen's "Dulce et Decorum Est," and Henri Barbusse's *Le feu*, all of which include a character or speaker who develops an antiwar attitude as a direct result of his service. Almost any of war's difficulties can produce this attitude—its brutality, the miserable conditions of life at the front, the bureaucratic injustices of the military or service organizations, the disruptions to family life and relationships, the tragedy of life lost, the impact on noncombatants. Popular anthologies (such as those published by Norton, Dover, or Longman) guarantee that teachers have access to many texts that follow a similar trajectory, and increased attention to women's wartime literature has ensured that women's narratives employing this strategy—like Vera Brittain's *Testament of Youth*, Helen Zenna Smith's *Not So Quiet . . .: Stepdaughters of War*, Mary Borden's *The Forbidden Zone*, and Ellen La Motte's *The Backwash of War*—are also available for course adoption. Thus, attention to antiwar attitudes is possible with use of canonical First World War texts, given that many include moments where chivalric notions of glory are rejected through exposure to the brutality and futility of battle.

For those who wish to consider antiwar attitudes globally or visually, I highly recommend Craig Yoe's *The Great Anti-war Cartoons*. Yoe's collection includes images that date from the 1600s through the late twentieth century, with a large number of cartoons from the early twentieth century. The volume is divided into topical chapters focusing on depictions of officers and enlisted men, women and children, and profiteers and peacemongers, and includes the work of famous cartoonists such as Louis Raemaekers (Dutch), Bruce Bairnsfather (British), and Winsor McCay (American). Exploring cartoons allows students the opportunity to absorb a large number of texts and a wide variety of styles with relative ease, thus fueling their ability to identify not only antiwar themes that cross conflicts but also subtle differences in antiwar messaging. Using a collection of visual texts diversifies a course in productive ways, engaging those students who are not as comfortable with literature and stretching the analytical capacities of those who are.

Once students begin to understand that *antiwar* can be applied to numerous experiences and attitudes, they can then distinguish among specific oppositional behaviors or events while also seeing how *mutiny*, *pacifism*, and *conscientious objection* all fit under the umbrella of *antiwar*. For many of the writers named above, this perspective is acquired only after direct experience of battle or service near the front. In fact characters or speakers may not question war in general, or even this war in particular—rather, they may be opposed to their circumstances, or to their commanding officers, or to their jingoistic relatives. Owen, for example, finds value in separating his distaste for the blindness of the home front from his admiration for his comrades. In the case of Remarque, Paul Bäumer's devotion to Kat contrasts sharply to his hatred of the home front warmongers like Himmelstoss. Students thus come to realize that an author may expose the horrific experience of war without questioning its causes or aims.

In some cases, an antiwar attitude emerges from experiential differences between the conditions of war for soldiers and those for officers. Knowing that students readily identify these differences, instructors might include discussions of the mutinies that occurred in France and in Germany as the war dragged on and the conditions for the fighting men became more dire. Few students are aware of the degree to which insurrection and collective indiscipline erupted in the later years of the war, in large part because combatant nations often suppressed information about these uprisings in order to avoid alarming the home front or alerting the enemy to potential weaknesses. However, recent scholarly and popular histories of the war provide helpful discussions of these uprisings, whether among the French at Aisne (April 1917), the British at Étaples (September 1917), or the Germans at Wilhelmshaven (October 1918). Stuart Robson's *The First World War* is a concise historical complement and offers source texts and overviews of the failed Nivelle Offensive and subsequent mutiny of French troops at Aisne.

For instructors who use Brittain's *Testament of Youth* or Siegfried Sassoon's "Base Details," discussion of the Étaples mutiny provides a direct historical context for the literature. In September 1917, approximately one thousand British soldiers passing through this base camp rose up against the military police in opposition to their treatment of enlisted men. By the end of September, Brittain reports, "Étaples was in an uproar" (372). The uprising was contained within a month, but the perception that commanders had less insight and more comfort than those who battled the enemy is captured in Sassoon's poem. Brittain's account of the response to the mutiny emphasizes three dichotomies that may be useful in a broader discussion of war literature: divisions based on gender, on proximity to the front, and on ethnicity or race. First, Brittain records clear distinctions between the experience of men and women during the mutiny, noting that the nurses were "shut up within [their] hospitals" because "the village was no place for females" (372). Second, she notes that few at home knew the truth of the mutiny, saying that no mention of it appeared in the British media until 1930 (426).[1] Finally, she identifies the mutineers' identity as Anzac troops, pointing not only to rank privilege as a factor in the mutiny but also to imperial identity. In the cases above, the primary trigger was experiential—namely, unrealistic expectations and poor living conditions (Gill and Dallas). However, Brittain's insistence that the Étaples rebellion was spurred by "a number of Australians and New Zealanders, always ready for trouble" (372) points to another reason for mutiny or resistance to military service: refusal to serve an imperial power. Thus I find it helpful to orient students to at least two other reasons for resistance that were operating in Europe during the First World War: debates over empire and debates over economic models.

For Britain and France, a strong military force depended on the enlistment of troops from colonial nations. For Britain specifically, the recruitment of colonials for military service came at a particularly troublesome time. In the eastern reaches of the empire, Britain's call for Indians to serve king and country was challenged by the alliance of Turkey's Muslim leader with Germany. In February 1915, Indian Muslims in Singapore mutinied against the British forces there, allying themselves with their religious leader in Turkey rather than with their imperial one in England. Although the Indian soldiers requested assistance from Germans in the area, they were not heeded and the mutiny was quelled. More than two hundred sepoys were court-martialed for their role in the uprising, with forty-seven executed publicly by firing squad (Grant 119).

In Ireland, the circumstances of political resistance differed: although religion was certainly a factor, many opposed Britain's entry into war because it slowed progress on the establishment of Irish home rule. Political, human, and material resources were diverted from the establishment of an Irish free state to the waging of war on the Continent. For Irishmen seeking home rule, service in the British army took the focus away from the quest for self-determination and the capacity to self-govern. Providing a brief overview of the imperial complexity known as "the Irish problem" positions the Easter Rising of 1916 in a broader context. With this wartime frame, students wrestle more productively with W. B. Yeats's poem "An Irish Airman Foresees His Death," in which Yeats foregrounds the ambivalent position of the

Irish airman: "Those that I fight I do not hate / Those that I guard I do not love" (lines 3–4).

In addition to encountering resistance from colonial forces on political grounds, combatant nations encountered resistance from citizens on economic grounds. It was no secret that war brought the opportunity for significant financial gain to financiers and manufacturers alike. Socialists opposed the war because it required working-class soldiers and munitions workers to endanger themselves for the sake of a social system that would never adequately compensate their labor. Emily Orr's poem "A Recruit from the Slums" provides a helpful resource for discussing socioeconomic status in the context of service:

> What has your country done for you,
>   Child of a city slum,
> That you should answer her ringing call
> To man the gap and keep the wall
> And hold the field though a thousand fall
>   And help be slow to come? (lines 1–6)

Will Self's complex novel *Umbrella* (2012) engages the same topic by exploring the war experiences of siblings from a working-class family in London, starkly comparing the experience of the daughter who works in a munitions factory to that of the son who rises to power in government offices that oversee wartime production. Instructors may encourage students to consider this type of resistance as fuel for the rise of Lenin and the Bolsheviks in Russia, with Russia ending its war against Germany once the interests of the czarist state were removed from consideration. Yoe's collection includes a chapter focused on the profiteers of war and can serve as a helpful text for economic discussions.

I have included trench poetry, memoirs, and fiction from the Great War in a variety of college literature classes over the years, and no matter what the level of the course, it is not uncommon for someone to describe canonical texts such as Sassoon's "Glory of Women" or Robert Graves's *Good-bye to All That* as pacifist, an interesting but inaccurate label. While the texts certainly reveal an antiwar attitude, they would not have been considered pacifist by early-twentieth-century audiences, given the word's specific connotations at the time. Those who participated in mutinies or questioned the war's capitalist motives may not have questioned the need to fight. For pacifists and conscientious objectors, however, war of any kind and fighting of any sort was unconscionable. For a pacifist, deeply held religious beliefs or intellectual principles provide the foundation for rejecting military service, regardless of the conflict.

To illuminate these distinctions, it may be useful for students to explore two separate strains of pacifism. For some (like Quakers, Seventh-day Adventists, and Christadelphians), the call to military service challenged religious beliefs about conflict resolution and violent action. The opening chapter of Martin Ceadel's *Pacifism in Britain, 1914–1945* provides an overview of various Christian arguments against war; Ceadel also distinguishes among different sects' approaches to wartime service, indicating that the Christadelphians were less absolutist in their resistance than their Quaker or Seventh-day Adventist compatriots.

For others (like members of the Bloomsbury group), resistance was born out of intellectual arguments exposing the irrationality of war and its expressed end goals. Bertrand Russell's collection *Justice in War-Time* contains several essays that provide accessible examples of intellectual pacifism, including his 1915 essay "War and Non-resistance." In it, Russell proposes that pacifism (or nonresistance) is a practical, logical tool for nations that wish to refuse entry into war. With fortitude and a shared will, he argues, a nation that refuses to retaliate may make the actions of an aggressor nation seem ridiculous. In "Is a Permanent Peace Possible?" he argues that words like *glory* and *patriotism* must be redefined and revaluated in order for peace to develop, an argument that anticipates Woolf's 1938 work *Three Guineas*. Russell notes, "If a better and saner world is to grow out of the horror of futile carnage, men must learn to find their nation's glory in the victory of reason over brute instincts, and to feel the true patriotism which demands that our country should deserve admiration rather than extort fear" (99–100).

Both strains of pacifism contributed to the rise of conscientious objection in Britain following the enactment of conscription in 1916. Students may be surprised to learn that approximately 16,500 British men objected to military service on the grounds of conscience (Ceadel 43). Many applicants were willing to work with the Non-Combatant Corps in lieu of military action, and they were engaged in transportation and construction support (Brock 245). However, approximately 1,300 requested absolute exemption from any kind of service (Ceadel 41).[2] Only members of the religious groups identified above could request exemption for religious reasons, leaving those who opposed the war for other reasons or who were from other religious sects to pursue alternative approaches. Those who refused their assigned service were court-martialed, and more than six thousand were imprisoned (Hochschild 188). Conscientious objectors, also known as "conchies" or "COs," were subjected to significant ridicule and public condemnation. Such accounts are recorded in *We Will Not Cease*, the autobiography of Archibald Baxter, a CO from New Zealand, and *We Will Not Fight,* Will Ellsworth-Jones's history of Bert Brocklesby, a CO whose two brothers fought for England. Almost fifty COs, including Brocklesby, were sent from prisons in England to army camps in France; when they refused to perform the duties assigned, thirty-four of these men received the death sentence, which was commuted to ten years' imprisonment, and fifteen received lesser sentences (Hochschild 202). Literary representations of conscientious objectors appear in May Sinclair's *Tree of Heaven* and Rose Allatini's *Despised and Rejected.*

Sassoon's declaration against the war, originally published in the *Bradford Pioneer* in 1917 and subsequently reprinted in Graves's *Good-bye to All That* (260n), is a readily available example of conscientious objection. Sassoon was due to be court-martialed for the statement, but the intervention of friends allowed him to be treated as mentally ill and moved to a psychiatric hospital. In addition to Sassoon's declaration, Graves includes a clipping about imprisoned COs (259) and a jingoistic piece decrying pacifism from "A Little Mother" (229). When invited to compare Graves's description of Sassoon's treatment to Ellsworth-Jones's description of Brocklesby's, students recognize that more affluent citizens had advantages in navigating the legal and medical systems. For instructors and students who wish to explore the intersection of political resistance and socioeconomic class, Ellsworth-Jones's *We Will Not Fight* provides useful discussions of the treatment of Bloomsbury COs such as Duncan Grant, David Garnett, and Lytton Strachey.

It's clear that there are many texts and contexts to consider when discussing opposition to service. Incorporating an assignment in which individual students or small groups provide brief historical presentations on some of the war's most famous moments of opposition can ensure that students recognize the differences among various forms of resistance. Students could be assigned as focal points the Singapore Mutiny, the Easter Rising, the British culture of conscientious objection, the February Revolution in Russia, the Étaples mutiny, the French mutinies in Aisne, or the Wilhelmhaven mutiny in Germany. Whether the instructor devotes a single class hour to the topic or distributes texts and presentations over several days, this approach offers students a transnational understanding of resistance that also allows for a comparative discussion of reasons for refusing to serve.

Notes

1. Both the suppression of news regarding the incident and the tones of colonial resistance are confirmed by the historians Douglas Gill and Gloden Dallas in their article "Mutiny at Étaples Base in 1917."

2. Documents that outline the Military Service Act, as well as the application for exemption for reasons of conscience, are available for students to review through the UK National Archives Web site.

Bonnie Roos

The Ties That Bind: Modernist Cultures and the Rise of Fascism

> *"The modern temper had been forged; the avant-garde had won.*
> *The 'adversary culture' had become the dominant culture;*
> *irony and anxiety, the mod and the mood."*
>
> —Modris Eksteins

I teach at a regional university that focuses most of its English program on freshman composition, and so it is only once every two years that I have the opportunity to teach an upper-division British modernism course. In this course I spend a week addressing World War I—clearly not enough time to do justice to the subject. I use mainly canonical works, including the World War I poets and Rebecca West's *Return of the Soldier*, in my discussions. But because I use the class's exploration of World War I issues to explain late modernist texts, it is in thinking about how war ends, how it is memorialized, and how it is documented that I find teaching World War I to be a struggle—one that I have worked to strategize for my students in order to explain, in particular, the rise of fascism.

The casual observer often remarks that though Germany and Austria lost the war of attrition, the end of World War I was acknowledged among most participants as a temporary halt in aggression. This point is not strictly true, and indeed such a claim belies the apparent exuberance of the roaring twenties. It does not explain the rise in fascism in Italy, one of the apparent winners, almost immediately at the close of war, even as Vittorio Orlando worked to prevent future wars through peace negotiations at the League of Nations. It also makes it difficult to explain why the most acclaimed novel about World War I, *All Quiet on the Western Front*, was written by a German in 1929: Erich Maria Remarque's *All Quiet* was arguably the first internationally recognized book to break the silence about the reality of war; it was critical of the hypermasculine, militant war rhetoric, becoming a best seller across Europe—particularly in Germany—only shortly before Hitler rose to power. For my students, the end of World War I needs explanation if they are to understand the modernist works and histories that follow.

Sometimes the idea that World War I set the stage for World War II leads my students to assume that we can trace fascism in this first war. But no country was demonstrably fascist during World War I. The hypermasculine, militant patriotism we associate with fascism was not distinguishable between countries that later became fascist and countries that did not. The term *fascist* was not used until 1919, just after World War I ended.[1] Benito Mussolini, with whom we associate fascist Italy, did not rise to power until 1922. Common usage of the term *fascist* refers to centralized, autocratic regimes, usually headed by a dictator, that privilege militaristic nationalism over individuals. In this broader sense, the term might refer to 1930s Nazi Germany or Franco's Spain, explaining some of the affinities shared by the Axis Powers of World War II. As we know, these movements became violently oppressive and anti-Semitic in the 1930s and 1940s. Yet Mussolini's fascist militarism became popular a decade earlier. And so one of the questions I ask my students is, What happened in Italy during World War I that allowed for the subsequent rise in fascism there?

In order to track the change of sentiment, I often set Filippo Marinetti's first futurist manifesto, "Founding and Manifesto of Futurism" (1909), alongside his coauthored "Fascist Manifesto" (1919, with Alceste de Ambris) to demonstrate the way Marinetti's thinking, and by extension Italy's, was transformed by the war. I find the first manifesto to be eminently teachable. For students less familiar with modernist technique or Italian history, I start with the simple question, What is a manifesto? We eventually arrive at some understanding of a manifesto as a document testifying to political or ideological beliefs.[2] Marinetti published his manifesto in the pages of the French newspaper *Le Figaro*—a fitting space for political arguments but a less regular venue for aesthetic ones, at least for students in the United States. I ask what it means for modernists to use art as a venue for their political perspectives or for newspapers to use their pages to host aesthetic discussions. In Marinetti's document, we usually find much of what my students themselves endorse: a love of speed, the latest technology, energy, youth, and danger; an appreciation for late-night study sessions and road trips; a respect for the working classes tempered by criticism of their adherence to tradition. For me, a focus on Marinetti's sense of humor ensures that my students recognize their affinity with these artists, which is crucial for my pedagogy, because if we understand the roots of fascism, with all its ugly hypermasculine, militant prowar rhetoric, as purely evil—and we tend to, given our historical hindsight—we never understand how ordinary people bought into it. This recognition that fascist elements are not so patently obvious reminds us of how vigilant and careful we must be in responding to its beginnings.

I think my students are most surprised to learn that well before the outset of World War I, Marinetti's widely publicized manifesto calls for violent revolution. Marinetti famously proclaims, "We will glorify war—the world's only hygiene—militarism, patriotism, the destructive gesture of freedom-bringers, beautiful ideas worth dying for, and scorn for woman" (140). Already in his words is advocated much of what fascist governments came to represent: violent oppression of undesirable elements and races, duty to country, and dismissal of the feminine. But we might also defend Marinetti's futurist manifestos as demanding an aesthetic revolution, his desire for war naively uninformed by actual war. Still, my students observe that language like Marinetti's sets the stage for the theater of war—and for consciously promoting war as a kind of theater. But certainly Marinetti was not alone. As Modris Eksteins comments in *Rites of Spring*, "The inclination here was to regard the war as a form of art, as superior representation of life. . . . As evocation, as an instrument of change, the war had a positive purpose—that was the judgment of many artists, at least early on" (210).[3] In other words, the notion that the "Futurist Manifesto" is a protofascist document is an oversimplification, for many artists from many countries expressed similar ideas. It is also true, that Marinetti and the futurists were the indirect impetus for many of the artists of which Eksteins speaks.

Because it falls outside traditional literary genres, Marinetti's manifesto is sometimes difficult to treat as an aesthetic object, so I discuss Marinetti as a dramatist, incorporating some of his proclamation's performance art aspects, and I always introduce futurist visual corollaries. He served as the instigator and charismatic voice for his troupe of Italian artists, dominated by male painters, whose representations corresponded with themes espoused in the manifesto. As we see in works like Carlo Carrá's *The Funeral of the Anarchist Galli* (1911), Giacomo Balla's *Dynamism of a Dog on a Leash* (1912), and Umberto Boccioni's *Unique Forms of Continuity in Space* (1913), the futurists aesthetically accentuated speed and diagonal force lines in their move from cubism toward greater abstraction. Together, they advocated Italian renewal and performed an act of implicit cultural imperialism, traveling throughout France, Italy, Germany, and Russia to promulgate their politicized, nationalized, technophilic masculine aesthetic. I often assign my students art projects, asking them to create futurist art objects, writing, or performances and explain how their work draws on futurist principles. They like this assignment and its brash, performative aspects and usually find themselves responding to the sense of play, even satire, often at work in futurism. This assignment reinforces my claim that—in part because it was aesthetic, because there was as yet no World War I to complicate its language, and because of the force of Marinetti's shocking, playful, satirical charisma—futurism was immensely popular. At the same time, and though the futurists never endorsed a political platform, their aesthetic representations heralded ideologies that would become prevalent in upcoming fascist movements—including Marinetti's own.

By 1932, Mussolini's formal "Doctrine of Fascism" looks much more like we might expect fascism to. For example, individual citizens are likened to soldiers in power and obedience to state authority (243). But it was Marinetti's coauthored "Fascist Manifesto" of 1919 that first expressed such views on behalf of the fascist movement. This document is less interesting aesthetically, and it is more serious—perhaps reflecting Marinetti's own wartime experience as a soldier—but it is also more tempered politically than the "Futurist Manifesto." Marinetti calls for an explicit project of Italian cultural imperialism, the institution of a defensive national militia, and the systemization of the railway system (meant to begin to bring Italy's overdue industrialization on a par with the rest of Europe). The "Fascist Manifesto" also calls for—surprising to many of my students—universal suffrage, worker representation in industry, and a high progressive tax on the wealthy. Indeed, the document in many ways advocated socialism, and parts of it might even be endorsed by liberal academics today. Futurist artists did not have the benefit of hindsight about what their political movements would become, though such hindsight does not mean they would have changed their political views. But neither did they suddenly decide to embody Western history's most egregious villains. The danger in tracing a teleology of fascism lies in the facile assumption that its resultant atrocities could never again occur because everyone would see them for what they were.

So how do we teach our students what initially led Italy toward the more frightening aspects of fascism? For a nuanced representation of World War I, I sometimes use the first chapter of Djuna Barnes's *Nightwood*, "Bow Down." We know the difficulty of the book, which is perhaps why it is so rarely taught. But the first chapter offers both a taste of the brilliant complexity of Barnes's writing and a portion small enough to incorporate into a syllabus. Given that "Bow Down" looks back from the brink of a second world war in 1936, when it was published, to the aftermath of a first world war, students can look for evidence of what Barnes might have to say about these events. But because my reading of *Nightwood* is unusual, I outline just a few possible directions that others might take here.

The book's introductory chapter first details Guido and Hedvig Volkbein's relationship. My students know, because I tell them or because it is widely discussed in histories, that the assassination of Austrian Emperor Franz Josef I's nephew and heir, Archduke Franz Ferdinand, ignited the war (though of course the deeper causes are still highly disputed). They also discover in the course of reading this chapter that Barnes's work is temptingly gendered, nationalized, and historically precise. For instance, though his family name, Volkbein, identifies him as Austrian, Guido's Italian name and birth (in 1831), offers a possible parallel to Vittorio Emanuel II, whose name is synonymous with the establishment of the nation of Italy (based on lands taken from the Austro-Hungarian Empire). The history of Vittorio Emanuel II, for those interested in his rise to power, is visible in the portraits Guido purchases to establish his nobility. Through Hedvig, Barnes speaks as well to the patriarchal and capitalist nature of the monarchy, to its women's readiness to be bought and sold in exchange for their access to fortune and to serve as vessels for future kings: like so many queens, Hedvig dies appropriately in childbirth, perhaps taking comfort in her luxurious bedspread with the family's royal crest embroidered in gold. I ask my students what they think, on the basis of this chapter, Barnes believed was the cause of the war. They usually conclude that monarchy, the search for wealth, and patriarchy played some role. It is worth reminding them that Franz Josef had two living daughters (and an ancestral history of female rulers) when his nephew was assassinated, even though he didn't regard them as worthy heirs.

But of course what my students point out, and what critics have observed, is that Barnes makes almost no direct mention of World War I. I ask my students whether such an omission may be part of her point. Why would she begin a book that looks back from 1936 to the first world war without mentioning that it was about to repeat itself? They speculate that trauma may be a reason for silence, and I ask if trauma can be felt by a nation as well an individual and under what circumstances. At least one person will point out that Barnes does mention the war indirectly. In the first chapter, we learn that Felix and Hedvig's son, *Nightwood*'s protagonist Felix Volkbein, possesses a suspect and cyclopean memory of the war—nonexistent because his "blind eye had kept him out of the army" (9). Felix's one eye can be used to explain flawed, romanticized war historiography. His memory of Austria's "military superiority, its great names" (17) in the wake of its recent defeat, for instance, suggests that the Austrians do not wish to remember the war, preferring their more nostalgic, heroic distant past to the ugly reality of the immediate past. Felix's problematic memory explains how, when the story of World War I is told, there is no appropriate mode of writing available to convey his now disenfranchised history. Such willful forgetting and dismissal of truth, along with what my students know about trauma, helps me establish a rationale for the seeming war apathy of United States authors and citizens in the roaring twenties. It also begins to explain why a work like *All Quiet on the Western Front* cannot be written until 1929. Looking back from 1936, Barnes may furthermore suggest that in romanticizing traditions, because no real knowledge of history can be learned, we are destined to repeat history.

The bulk of Barnes's chapter is dedicated to the 1920s in Paris, which is where the peace negotiations that eventually alienated Italy took place. Few of my students know enough League of Nations history to develop this reading without some historical supplements, but it is possible to read Barnes's surrealist circus performers as a satire on the league's proceedings. One simple corollary is based on the fact that, after United States President Woodrow Wilson fought to include the League of Nations in the Treaty of Versailles, he could not convince United States legislators to support it. And so, in Barnes's version, we find a United States "doctor" who is "taking the part of host" (14) because the host could not be present. Despite the rhetoric of peace, this opportunity for league diplomacy was botched, Austria's monarchy dissolved, and the losers made to pay insurmountable reparations—made to bow down, which will eventually mean a return to war. The League of Nations had a particular impact on Italy, which was unable to negotiate for its people a better share of the victory spoils. Italy's people had voted against national participation in the war, but they had been overridden by Vittorio Emanuel II's eventual successor, Vittorio Emanuel III. Though Italy was among those demanding satisfactory compensation for its stunning loss of men and postwar recession, the more powerful England and France laid first claim. In Barnes's take on the event, the German Frau Mann assures a wary Felix that the Italian count attends the party only "to change money—he comes, he goes away, and everything goes on the same, except that people have something to talk about" (14). But Count Onatorio Altamonte interrupts the Paris party by bringing in a girl and demanding that everyone leave. Italy did threaten to withdraw its support for the Paris peace negotiations over its inability to gain the Fiume as part of its victory package, and its failure to do so left its monarchy weakened in the face of an angry populace, improving the position of the outsider Mussolini. In Barnes's version, the doctor doubts Italy will have its way with the other members of the party but politely leaves the proceedings to go to Berlin. There he leaves Frau Mann asleep with the bill, citing popular war slogans as he sneaks out, telling the waiter that "the lady," Germany, "will pay" (28). Asked about a 1936 text that looks back to the 1919 peace processes, my students can trace Barnes's attributions of the failures of peace and the rise of fascism to the common causes of economic inequalities, a literary and journalistic tradition of romanticism, and lack of legislative representation among any number of governmental bodies.

The discussions of Marinetti and Barnes produce a vision of Italy as an emerging nation defined more by its military successes than cultural cohesion. Its leaders maintained an outmoded and autocratic monarchical system instead of creating a modern democracy, and its culturally diverse peoples were working-class and often rural, lacking public education and industrialization. It is no wonder Marinetti espoused the glories of speed and technology and believed that war could change his nation for the better. And when neither the wars of independence against Austria nor the First World War improved Italy's international potential, it turned back to its defining roots, the militarism that had secured and unified it since its inception.

Notes

1. In his 1932 "Doctrine of Fascism," Benito Mussolini claims the Fascist Revolutionary Party was founded in 1915 (235), but I have not found any corroborating evidence for this statement. The earliest *OED* references date the term's association with a political party to 1919.

2. I encourage my more advanced students to turn to some remarkable criticism, including Marjorie Perloff's *The Futurist Moment: Avant-Garde, Avant Guerre, and the Language of Rupture* (1985) and Janet Lyon's *Manifestoes: Provocations of the Modern* (1999) for further research.

3. See, for example, Eksteins on Marcel Proust, Henry James, D. H. Lawrence, Jacques-Émile Blanche (who had promoted the Russian ballet, including Stravinsky's *Rite of Spring*), and many antiwar dadaists, who "despite the purported anguish and rage," Eksteins claims, "seemed to revel in the war" (209–10).

Laura Doan

Inside and Outside Sexual Identity: Queerness, History, and the First World War

In 2006 the University of Newcastle (UK) sponsored an international conference called The First World War and Popular Culture, highlighting the breadth and intellectual promise of an emergent field in First World War studies. As a cultural historian based in an English department, I welcomed this cross-disciplinary event as an opportunity for productive exchange between scholars with mutual interests in the war, especially in relation to gender and sexuality. While disciplinary tensions inevitably surface at such gatherings, I was struck by the differences between the historians, who paid scrupulous attention to publication dates, and the literary specialists, who tended not to notice whether a particular novel appeared in 1918 or 1930. In the realm of sexuality, chronological specificity is crucial, because the modern discourses of sex, taken for granted now in the West, were only just beginning to drift into the collective consciousness during the First World War, becoming more widespread in the interwar era. At the same time, with the gradual emergence of new sexual knowledge, practices organized around categories and identities based on a binary arrangement of normal or abnormal accreted rather than displaced older understandings. This means that reading First World War texts produced in any national context requires awareness of the diverse ways sexuality has been understood and regulated at any given moment.

In my teaching I emphasize this requirement through the three-part structure of my course, entitled The Great War: Culture, History, Theory. Part 1 focuses on close textual readings of materials that appeared between 1914 and 1918, part 2 considers work manufactured in response to renewed interest in the war a decade later, and part 3 looks to cultural representation after the 1960s. My course examines how the war came—and continues—to be represented and imagined in Britain in relation to constructions of gender, embodiment, and sexuality, among other aspects. Rigorous historicization alone, however, does not keep anachronistic readings at bay—students of gender, sexuality, and war also need the powerful analytical tools provided by queer theorists to defamiliarize current ways of knowing the sexual. Organizing class discussion around a queer analysis of lived experience and material culture clarifies both how it was possible or not possible to know and talk about masculinity, femininity, or sex and how ideas about the sexed body, gender and gender variance, sex, and sexuality were continuously in flux.

The First World War, it has been claimed, represented an entirely new experience of war, changing individual lives and entire societies, its impact lingering in Britain well into the twenty-first century. For this reason I have found this terrain an excellent site in which to study gender and sexuality using the tools of queer analysis—not, as commentators often assert, because of the power of queerness to destabilize and loosen social restrictions governing social norms. Rather, the disturbances of war—for civilians and combatants alike—make more visible that the realms of gender and sexuality are fluid, mutable, and unstable, simultaneously coherent and incoherent. This paradox is best discerned through a queer analysis alert to the ways norms intensify and recede, exhibit pliancy and elasticity, rather than dissolve or break. Still, this turn toward queer analysis in the context of the war is by no means straightforward, for at least two reasons. First, the very term *queer* is highly contested and lacks scholarly consensus, its use by queer scholars often making it a difficult theoretical perspective for outsiders to navigate.[1] Second, the handling of *queer* as a tool or method is varied and uneven, with some scholars, for example, treating it as an umbrella term for LGBT communities and politics and others valuing its association with deviance, oppositional stance toward normativity, or disruption of stable sexual identities. Widely misunderstood as roughly equivalent to the modern *homosexual*, no other concept in sexuality studies has so vexed and confused as *queer*, which, whether deployed as a verb, noun, or adjective, revels in open-endedness, its playful resistance to definition rarely deterring ongoing speculation about its capabilities and limitations.

The historian of sexuality Jeffrey Weeks begins his account of the term with a reminder that *queer* originally denoted a figure linked with what was odd, twisted, or bent and would later be appropriated by lesbian and gay activists to describe a militant collective sexual politics ("Que[e]rying" 525). With the advent of queer theory in the early 1990s, the term signaled a privileging of dissidence, subversion, and transgression, and above all a radical critique of sexual identity and an unsettling of the power of the hetero/homo binary. A different starting point for students interested in queering the war would be to interrogate what is at stake in looking for queer beings as opposed to working out the epistemic repercussions of destabilizing the homo and the hetero—and thus the logic of oppositionality itself. This approach takes its cue from the theorist Lee Edelman, who proposes that "queerness can never define an identity; it can only ever disturb one" (17). Thinking about the power of queerness as methodological rather than ontological seems a far cry from current practices, which locate queer in and around same-sex behaviors and desires.

From my examination of materials I have found in the archive as well as published work, I invite students to rethink their assumptions that the poets and writers who produced work during the war and into the interwar period possessed a shared understanding of a "familiar homosexual iconography" or even constructed romantic love between people of the opposite sex as a "heterosexual identity" (Cole, *Modernism* 165, 136). My research suggests that the habit of identifying oneself or someone else as a sexual "something" would not become common among ordinary people until the mid- to late-twentieth century, when sexology became more widely available through sex education and marital advice literature. I remind students that the sexologists and the popularizers of sexological thought did not discover the sexual but constructed a discourse of sexuality. The work of late-nineteenth- and early-twentieth-century sexologists such as Richard von Krafft-Ebing and Havelock Ellis would construct modern sexuality as a hierarchical binary between homosexuality and heterosexuality, but for several decades this way of knowing was accessible only to a small educated elite (see Bland and Doan). This is why it is useful in the classroom to differentiate between queerness as an identity and queerness as an analytical method. Queerness as method is not content with merely extending queer analysis to people's "desires, fantasies, attractions, and gender identifications," as its objectives lie elsewhere (S. Marcus 213). The analytical efficacy of queer methodologies moves beyond the desiring subject toward a new queer critical historiographical purpose divested of an identitarian framework.

In a bold reading of the erotics of male comradeship, the postcolonial critic Santanu Das rightly observes that inasmuch as the war "has become a literary-historical phenomenon, it is perhaps possible to 'queer' it" (*Touch* 117). He argues forcefully for a new category called "*nongenital tactile tenderness* that goes beyond strict gender divisions and sexual binaries" (119). My one reservation with this approach is that it still operates in the epistemological structure of sexology in making sex visible through categorizations of sexual desire. The challenge is to work out the different ways sexuality was configured during the conflict as well as decades later. Let me be clear—I am not saying that this is merely a problem of semantics, as if the job of understanding sexuality were to find better or more historically accurate terms. The task is to discern how words, phrases, or unspoken expressions of sex, love, or intimacy work in the particular logics and circuitries of an epistemological system, often fragmented and patchy. Queering the war demands reading practices that are historically situated and attuned to the ways in which sexual knowledge is produced, thereby clarifying how projects published in the late twentieth century, such as Pat Barker's *Regeneration* trilogy, tell us more about the present than about the past.

I encourage students to develop queer analytical perspectives to heighten their awareness of sexual knowledge as an edifice composed of older residual knowledge regimes but also modern categories and identities built out of a "host of different biological and mental possibilities, and cultural forms—gender identity, bodily differences, reproductive capacities, needs, desires, fantasies, erotic practices, institutions, and values" (Weeks, *Sexuality* 7). Historically minded lesbian, gay, and queer critics have questioned the discursive inadequacies of the infrastructure of sexological knowledge, its modern system of sexual classification, and the vexing problem of identity labels to describe sexual subjects in the past. Yet too often their objectives and interests are already determined by sexology's operational habits of thought in constructing sexuality as categorizable and identifiable. To unravel the literary and cultural meanings and discursive formations of human sexuality—in the early decades and postwar boom of the last century or in the twentieth and early twenty-first centuries—we cannot simply locate lesbian, gay, bisexual, trans, or hetero identities or bodies in the past. What is required is stepping outside the logic of identity and the impulse to identify, while also recognizing that later works invent a past that functions more like the present.

Critically queering Great War literature (as opposed to looking for queer beings) makes it possible to grasp how ideas about sexuality were configured and understood during the conflict and then track change across the decades. Opening the course, for instance, with the most popular wartime novel in Britain, H. G. Wells's *Mr. Britling Sees It Through* (1916), I point out how the narrator's observations of the war's impact on his family and village point less to upended gender norms or new opportunities for sexual promiscuity than to regulatory systems both turned upside down and undisturbed. In this novel Wells captures the contradictory nature of a conflict in which respectable moral restraint jostles alongside old-fashioned values willing to overlook discreetly conducted extramarital affairs. Our critical objective is not to think how illicit desire shapes a sexual identity but to prize apart the conceptual apparatus by which gender and sexuality might be known, thereby discerning the organization of wartime relations between individuals.

In the public sphere, prewar systems of morality continued to govern different-sex relations, though new medicoscientific discourses were filtering into debates on how best to respond to venereal disease. To highlight the differences between the representation of sexual morality in *Mr. Britling* and newer systems arising because of the exigencies of war, I screen a silent film called *Whatsoever a Man Soweth* (1917). Produced by the British War Office to encourage personal responsibility rather than moral goodness, the film sought to educate Canadian troops on how to avoid women willing to make their bodies sexually available to men. In the medicoscientific value system of the film, the regulation of human action and different-sex desire is based on the ethical consequences to the family, nation, and empire. A good text to conclude this section of the course is the pacifist novel entitled *Despised and Rejected* (1918), published by A. T. Fitzroy (the pseudonym of Rose Allatini), which critics often characterize as a depiction of "homosexual" bohemian life. By pairing this novel with the writings of the sex radical Edward Carpenter, such as his *The Intermediate Sex: A study of Some Transitional Types of Men and Women* (1908), I introduce students to expressions of sexual desire that do not evenly map onto the sexological type called the congenital invert. Carpenter's influence on Allatini is unmistakable, virtually verbatim at times, and suggests the importance of stepping outside the structure of sexual identities we know about now.

The second section of the course considers work published in the 1930s, including Siegfried Sassoon's *Memoirs of an Infantry Officer* (1930), Helen Zenna Smith's *Not So Quiet . . . : Stepdaughters of War* (1930), and Radclyffe Hall's *Miss Ogilvy Finds Herself* (written in 1926 and published in 1934). Here I ask students to consider the potential gains in resisting the impulse to classify the narrator as gay or straight, lesbian or transgendered, or to characterize the homosocial communities engendered by war as gay or lesbian. When students assign labels to sexual desires or imagine that minority groups were persecuted for their deviant acts, I urge them to reflect on their own conceptual investments in sexuality as the great classificatory project, sexuality as identifiable and recognizable. Sassoon's reticence about sexual matters might have been a sign of class privilege, but it is misleading to construe his silence as the response of a man closeted or fearful of prosecution under section 11 of the Criminal Law Amendment Act of 1885. This legislation did not outlaw male "homosexuality" but sexual acts between men. Consequently, men of all class backgrounds could pursue pleasure without seeing themselves as possessing an identity (Houlbrook). A product of the elite public school Marlborough College and Cambridge University, Sassoon would have had greater access to new ideas about sexuality than the ordinary reader—the now naturalized habit of sexual identification would have been available to some but not all at the time he published his semifictional account of his war experiences (L. Dowling; Deslandes).

The strangeness of an alien rather than recognizable past is depicted in Hall's story about the bleak postwar existence of the head of a female ambulance unit, Miss Ogilvy. Again I point out how critical readings position the eponymous protagonist as a sexual something—more often than not a lesbian but also the precursor to the stone butch or transsexual (Castle; Franks; Ouditt; Dellamora; Halberstam; and Prosser). My question to students is, What might be gained from resisting the impulse to categorize? Turning to Susan Stryker's powerful theorization of the body as an "interpretive fiction," I encourage seminar participants to take seriously the possibility that Hall's story is not about sexual desire at all (62). Gaining critical purchase on this work as well as Smith's *Not So Quiet* entails keeping all these possibilities in play in order to explore the sexed body, gender variance, gender and sexual inversion, as well as homosexual desire.

Conveying the historicity of sexual knowledge gets more complicated when students encounter Sassoon a second time in the final section of the course, as we discuss Barker's *Regeneration* trilogy. A creature of the

1990s, Barker's Sassoon thinks in terms of sexual preference and acknowledges he has certain tendencies ("My intimate details disqualify me from military service" [*Regeneration* 68]). In effect, Barker's version of Sassoon and his friend the poet Robert Graves closes down all the ambiguity that hovered around sexuality during the war and its early aftermath, fixing the writer as a homosexual. Queering Sassoon as a desiring subject restores the messiness of a cultural moment when sexuality was more often than not conveyed through innuendo, when it was sometimes unspeakable or even unthinkable. Thinking about sex this way also allows students to see it as an "open mesh of possibilities, gaps, overlaps, dissonances and resonances, lapses and excesses of meaning . . . [in which] the constituent elements of anyone's gender, of anyone's sexuality aren't made (or *can't be* made) to signify monolithically" (Sedgwick 8). Similarly, it is important they recognize that characterizing wartime or interwar Britons as homophobic overstates the coherence of deviant sexual beings across public culture. Using words such as *homophobia* or *gay*, which were not common or even invented until the late 1960s, projects our knowledge apparatus onto the past at the expense of understanding how people earlier in the century thought or talked about sex. This is why I am skeptical of claims that the First World War "was the first significant" conflict "following the establishment of the male homosexual as a separate class of being" or that "the homo/hetero schism in male identity and relations had become a phenomenon by the time of the Great War" (Boxwell 2). Whether discussion pivots on the representation of sexuality in the film *Oh! What a Lovely War* (1969) or *Downton Abbey* (2011), materials I often use in the last section of the course, I help students locate archival evidence to support their assertions. Making the past like us, I explain, does not tell us much about life between 1914 and 1918.

Teaching students how to queer representations of war is tricky, since they must learn how to be adept in locating their readings both inside and outside the context of identity. Yet for all its difficult conceptual demands this pedagogical practice is rewarding, because it forces students to confront what they think they know already about the sexual past and present. The realm of the sexual is particularly important, since this modern war—represented in literary and cultural texts across generations and in national contexts—helped shape our view of sexuality as modern, a development best perceived from the analytical framework of queer theory. In my own teaching practices I emphasize the risks in assuming that writers and readers at earlier points in the last century understood sexuality on our terms. My aim is to encourage students to think about configurations of the sexed body, gender, sex, and sexuality in First World War representation by prizing apart the conceptual apparatus by which sexuality is known, thereby discerning how the organization of wartime sexualities and sexual relations changed over time from 1914 to the present.

Note

1. For a good introduction to queer theory and queer studies, see Jagose; see also the edited collection by Hall and Jagose.

Eve Sorum

Thinking about Space: Mapping and Perception in World War I Literature

Within the past decade, critics discussing colonial and postcolonial modernisms, planetarity and globalization in modernism, and the other spaces of modernist experimentation have heralded the spatial turn of literary studies.[1] This critical focus is especially rich and revealing for scholars of World War I literature, whether they focus on anglophone writing or on literature in other languages. Learning to read war spaces and representations of those spaces alongside war literature both enriches our students' experiences of the texts and suggests why writing about war might require new types of languages and literary forms. I have found that showing students maps of the Western Front, whether online images or (even better) the paper copies sold by London's Imperial War Museum, highlights the simultaneous desire for order and the problems with codifying the chaotic and emotionally charged space of war. Maps focusing on battlegrounds in other parts of the world can be found within resources like the National Archive Web site, which has maps of war zones in the Middle East and Africa.[2]

To help students understand why we should look at these maps and images, I bring in the French theorist of space, Henri Lefebvre, and argue that explicating spatial relations helps us read World War I literature because of transformations on three levels: first, in the soldiers' experience of space as a battlefield; second, in their perception of the surrounding land; third, in their literary representations of this space (the imagined space of war).[3] In order to understand modernist narrative and poetic experimentation, we must first understand how World War I literature responded to the subject's disorientation in (war) space, as well as how such disorientation necessitated new modes of representing the trauma done to the idea of a stable, autonomous, perceiving I.

Of the three Lefebvrian categories, changes in the experience of space present themselves most overtly and often horrifically in images of the front lines. Experienced space alters in three fundamental ways during war: in the appearance of the land, in the use of both natural and man-made space, and in the ways in which human beings live in this war space. Placed side by side, as is done in some of the early Michelin guides to the battlefields, before and after pictures of Western Front battlefields do not look like the same landscape.[4] From verdant rolling countryside, the Somme, the Marne, and the northern sector in Belgium (to name a few of the most notorious) became muddy messes of shell craters, mine holes, and trenches. A provocative claim to ponder with a class is Samuel Hynes's statement that "[w]ar turns landscape into anti-landscape" (8). Hynes gestures to the transformed spatial aesthetics and suggests yet another reason why literature must search for new ways to represent the land.

The disbelief and the enormous contrast between what the landscape should and does look like infuses memoirs like Edmund Blunden's *Undertones of War*, which is a text that can introduce students to the war world in more immediately engaging and accessible ways than some other war memoirs. In his first months at the front Blunden was stationed in a quiet sector (though not without its casualties). A rewarding scene to close-read with students is one early on in the memoir as he describes his return to the rest billets:

> History and nature were beginning to harmonize in the quiet of that sector. . . . The empty farmhouses were not yet effigies of agony or mounds of punished, atomized material; they could still shelter, and they did. Acres of self-sown wheat glistened and sighed as we wound our way between, where rough scattered pits recorded a hurried firing line of long ago. Life, life abundant, sang here and smiled. (20–21)[5]

At this point even land that has been the site of war can retain its pastoral character, and the peacetime purpose of the buildings and fields has not yet been emptied of meaning. Not many months later, however, the landscape has been transformed into "a new world," composed of a "succession of sensations": "bullets leaping angrily from old rafters shining in the greenish flarelight . . . bedsteads and broken mattresses hanging over cracked and scarred walls; Germans seen as momentary shadows among wire hedges; . . . a gate, opening into a battlefield" (60). The divisions between inside and outside have dissolved as the houses display their interiors, brutally reminding us that they can no longer be used for shelter. The peaceful fields are now filled with the enemy; the growing wheat—a sign of human partnership with nature—has been replaced by barbed-wire hedges, whose only connection to their natural counterparts is in the ironic name.

Undertones of War shows us that the land changes not only in appearance but also in use. Most profoundly, the natural and the domestic worlds shift in meaning. No longer do houses shelter families or villages act as centers of a community's life; instead, a house may shelter some officers or be the hiding place of a sniper. A village could be a location for rest billets or an eerie skeleton that speaks of unending shell bombardments. All shelters become spots of danger or of possible refuge, depending on their proximity to the front and to which side they belong. This vision of a world turned inside out also emerges powerfully in the first pages of Henri Barbusse's *Le feu* (1916; *Under Fire*), which came out serially during the war and is therefore the earliest literary prose response to the trench experience. Barbusse begins with a chapter titled "The Vision," and the vision in those first lines is of a world perverted by war: "On the fields attacks sweep forward, wave after wave, then come to a standstill; houses are gutted like men and towns like houses; villages appear in crumpled white as though they had fallen to the earth from the sky; frightful loads of dead and wounded men alter the shape of the plains" (4). The normal boundaries between earth and sky, human and inhuman, the dead and the alive are blurred; death transforms the very shape of the landscape.

A few days spent in this hideously reshaped world of the trenches could completely change a soldier's experience of space. The restrictions on the soldiers' line of sight (and the fatal consequences if they forgot those restrictions) produced a world of limited vision. As David Jones writes in his long poem, *In Parenthesis*, the soldiers "were at a loss as to their position and precise direction. . . . They felt only the maze-likeness of all their goings, being aware of nothing much more than the approximate direction of the enemy line" (87). This sense of the enemy position functioned as the primary compass; indeed, everything in the war space gained meaning from its relation to the German lines. Thus T. E. Hulme wrote in a letter home, "[T]he mere fact that in a certain direction there are the German lines, seems to alter the feeling of a landscape. You unconsciously orient things in reference to it. In peacetime, each direction on the road is as it were indifferent, it all goes on ad infinitum. But now you know that certain roads lead as it were, up to an abyss" (164). Not only were the soldiers' lived experiences in war space limited by the confines of their trenches, but they also involved a reorientation around the threat of no-man's-land—what in *Blasting and Bombardiering* Wyndham Lewis remembered as "that arid and blistering vacuum; the lunar landscape" in which the enemy lurked (131).

These changes in experienced space on the Western Front led to transformations in the representations of that space, most obviously in the maps of the area. I usually preface my teaching of books like Erich Maria Remarque's *All Quiet on the Western Front*, Ford Madox Ford's *No More Parades*, and anthologies of World War I poetry by pulling out trench maps and images of maps published in British or German newspapers, asking the students to notice the differences and reflect on how maps are tools for both war and politics.[6] The commanders planned their assaults using the maps of the front line to guide their choice of sites, but the use of maps as strategic tools was flawed. Remarque's protagonist, Paul, notices how this problem pervades even civilian discourse, for his former headmaster tells him that soldiers cannot understand the strategy of the war: " 'The details, yes,' says he, 'but this relates to the whole. And of that you are not able to judge. You see only your little sector and so cannot have any general survey. . . . [T]he enemy line must be broken through in Flanders and then rolled up from the top' " (167).

This one small example shows how the map seen at home becomes more powerful than the reality or, more to the point, how the map becomes the guiding reality. Blunden similarly describes how the "German lines ran out in a small sharp cape here, called The Boar's Head. This was to be 'bitten off,' no doubt to render the maps in the chateau of the mighty more symmetrical" (40). Aesthetic reasons guide the decision for battle—the symmetry of the line—rather than military ones, revealing how much of war may be based on certain abstract and formal choices and ideals.

I find it most important for the students to see how maps, instead of acting as means of orientation, ironically become implicated in the disorientation of the soldiers. As tools for navigating the wilderness of the trenches and no-man's-land, the maps were both just as vital and just as flawed as those used by the generals in the staff rooms. The errors in the maps were due in large part to the rapidly changing terrain—changes that occurred even though the actual movements of the armies were negligible for over three years. As Blunden ruefully remarks, "new roads and railways had changed the map so completely that one was a stranger here" (149).

The disconnect between the war maps and the soldiers' experiences was even more pronounced with maps viewed back in England. Most newspaper maps of the Western Front condensed the actions of war into a symbolic thick line that transected Europe. In his fictionalized account of the war, *The Memoirs of George Sherston*, Siegfried Sassoon muses about one of the armchair generals back in his home in England: "[P]robably he kept a war map with little flags on it; when Mametz Wood was reported as captured he moved a little flag an inch forward after breakfast. For him the Wood was a small green patch on a piece of paper. For the Welsh Division it had been a bloody nightmare" (127). Sassoon's description of the gap between home and the front brings to the fore the division between the war map and the war experience. The map for Sassoon loses its status as an accurate reflection of the terrain of war because it represents neither the physical nor the subjective side of the experience. Newspaper maps did much to perpetuate the sense of a British advantage and a lack of danger. Paul Fussell describes how these mapmakers "became skilled in equivocation," such as by making the Ypres Salient "appear a harmless little protuberance, not at all a vast enclosure of some eighteen square miles in which the British were exposed to shelling from three—and sometimes four—sides" (176).

The actual maps used at the front became spaces on which the soldiers could chart their personal experiences, which most often included violence and injury. I often describe in class one such soldier, a Captain Frisby of the Hampshire Regiment, who kept the map he carried when wounded during the war's first year. In a scrapbook of mementos and reminiscences compiled while convalescing, he included this paper map, marked where he was attacked and wounded, and with a brown stain wrote, "This is my gore!" Despite the seeming flippancy of Frisby's comment, this map reveals how the gore of war adds an affective level to the objective map of war space. Students can see this level also in pictures of the bloodstained map of Belgium carried by Julian Grenfell, a young poet who died in 1915 from a shell splinter entering his head (26). In this instance the stains quite literally transform the mapped image into a bloody testament to one man's death. The map shifts from a representational object to an object of representation—something that has been worked on or changed. As a kind of palimpsest, therefore, war maps must be read for the double text that they inevitably became, whether overtly, as in Grenfell's case, or more silently in the unstained maps.

Another method of addressing the experiential nature of maps is by examining the descriptions and drawings that are included in literary works themselves. The literal bloodied maps of Frisby or Grenfell are profitably paired with the metaphorical map in Ford Madox Ford's *Parade's End*. The shell-shocked main character, Christopher Tietjens, imagines the whole world as "an embossed map in greenish *papier mâché*" (239) that records, with the bloodstain that covers its surface, Tietjens's war trauma and the defacement that must occur to any "objective" chart of war space in order to accurately represent such trauma. With his memory perforated by both personal and battlefield trauma, Tietjens can no longer trust his own orientation as a stable, perceiving subject; the bloodstained map both critiques an objective vision of war and suggests that any attempt to map war must include such defacement of all traditional orienting marks.

While Ford gives us a description of an imagined map, Jones's notes to *In Parenthesis* provide an actual sketch-map that questions the relation between experience and representation. Jones describes how this map was

> made by the author for his own convenience when writing Part 3, as an aid to remembering a typical relationship of trenches and roads. It pretends to no accuracy whatever and was roughly copied from a map of a much later date than the period of the text. The heavy dotted line indicates the imaginary route taken by the troops in Part 3. The numerals along its length refer to page numbers in the text. (vi)[7]

Here he ascribes to the map a different kind of authority and meaning from what we might normally assume. Instead of claiming the map as the ultimate objective power that explains otherwise incomprehensible (and unnavigable) terrain and links it to "real" space, he disconcertingly asserts that the map "pretends to no accuracy whatever" and in fact bears only a subjective relation to the 1916 events that he describes. He reinforces our distrust of the map by pointing out that the journey of the soldiers is "imaginary" and that the numbers on the map (where usually one would find references to latitude and longitude that establish some kind of graticule [Edney 18])[8] actually refer reflexively back to the text. Yet these claims of inaccuracy do not damage the authority of the map within the poem. The text of the poem becomes the map key, and the map gains its meaning in relation to our reading, while functioning as the ordering force behind the poem. As they turn to the map while deciphering the difficult poetry, students will see how a map can create a space that in turn takes on a life of its own and outgrows the constraints of the map.

The maps provide useful methods of ordering and understanding the space of the war but also must always be interrogated and interpreted for the stories that their lines elide and create.[9] Reading the space of war with and in the literature reveals how writers, in their search for aesthetic orders that successfully convey the war experience, expose the porous boundaries among the experienced spaces of the trenches, the perceived spaces of the frontline maps, and the imagined spaces of the literature.

Notes

1. See Brooker and Thacker's *Geographies of Modernism*; Doyle and Winkiel's *Geomodernisms*; Friedman's essay on planetarity; and Hegglund's *World Views: Metageographies of Modernist Fiction*.

2. See www.nationalarchives.gov.uk/pathways/firstworldwar/battles/gallipoli.htm.

3. My translation of Lefebvre's terms follows David Harvey's (218–19) rather than Nicholson-Smith's more literal translation, because Harvey's labels of "experienced," "perceived," and "representational" space are less confusing. Nicholson-Smith calls spatial practices "perceived" space; representations of space are "conceived" space, and representational space is "lived" space (Lefebvre, *Production of Space* 38–39). In the French, Lefebvre provides the labels "perçu—conçu—vécu (spatialement: pratique de l'espace—représentation de l'espace—espaces de representation)" (*La production de l'espace* 50.) That Nicholson-Smith's terms are a direct translation suggests that the confusion exists in Lefebvre's language. Yet Lefebvre's three categories of *perçu*, *conçu*, and *vécu* begin to make more sense if we think of perceived space (in his usage) existing on the level of sensation (the realm in which we live), conceived space on the level of cognition (where human beings order the perceptions that make up their everyday lives), and "acted" or lived space on the level of social behavior. This last term becomes clear when we think of the double meaning of *représentation*: (1) something that symbolizes or stands in for something else; (2) a performance. The space of representation could then refer to the space in which we perform or create roles, both in life and in literature.

4. The Michelin guide to the battlefields of the Somme, published only a few years after the end of the war (and available as a facsimile copy), shows a picture of the town of Ginchy first on 11 July 1916, then ten days later, and finally at an unspecified time when the town is completely destroyed (*Michelin Guides*).

5. Of course, part of Blunden's interest in this contrast results from his reconstituting the landscape through nostalgic reimagination as he writes after the war.

6. Maps were in many ways the instigators of the Great War and were vital in the action that followed. In the decade before the war, Field Marshal Alfred von Schlieffen held "midnight vigils" over maps in his preparation of what became

known as the Schlieffen plan, which Germany hoped to use in its march to Paris (Keegan 33). But the war also inhibited rather than promoted cartographic progress, for it shut down the newly budding International Map of the World project (Brown 305).

7. Disturbingly, the *New York Review of Books* edition that came out in 2003 has left out both the map and this explanatory note. I therefore photocopy the map from the 1937 edition when teaching.

8. Edney usefully explicates in his introduction how the graticule and other elements lend authority to maps.

9. For useful Web sites with representations of World War I maps, see the Imperial War Museum (www.iwm.org.uk/collections/search?query=trench+map&submit=&items_per_page=10), McMaster University (digitalarchive.mcmaster.ca/islandora/object/macrepo%3A49), the map section for *The First World War Poetry Digital Archive* (www.oucs.ox.ac.uk/ww1lit/db/results.php?CISOBOX1=map&CISOFIELD1=objecb&CISOOP1=exact&CISOROOT=%2Fgwa); and map images from *WorldWar1.com.*

Jane Elizabeth Fisher

Teaching the 1918 Influenza Pandemic as Part of a World War I Curriculum

When teaching World War I and its cultural representations, I am always struck by the "unclaimed experience" this era still presents, in Cathy Caruth's resonant phrase. This is especially true of the 1918–19 influenza pandemic, World War I's darker twin, which killed at least eight times more people than the war did, accumulating an estimated eighty million deaths worldwide between 1918 and early 1920.[1] Three to six percent of the world's population died during the pandemic, and an estimated one-third of the world's population was ill with the disease.[2] While scholars may clash over the pandemic's origins, no one disagrees about its path: it followed the war. The first verified cases of influenza occurred in Camp Funston, Kansas, in spring 1918. In the United States, the first wave of the pandemic accompanied the troops to Europe, making some troop ships floating coffins. John Singer Sargent's 1918 watercolor *The Interior of a Hospital Tent*, painted while Sargent was recovering from influenza, represents the first wave of the pandemic, showing one patient recovering and reading, another ill and sleeping, and a third in the background white and still, possibly dead, while a dark storm brews outside the tent.[3] The pandemic's first wave also moved "between countries and continents along the routes of ships and railways" associated with European empires, spreading the influenza from ports throughout Africa (Phillips and Killingray 9). African death rates were higher than European death rates, and Asia, specifically India, had the highest death rates of all during the pandemic (10). A second wave occurred simultaneously with the armistice and the accompanying American and European troop demobilizations; this outbreak dampened victory celebrations. A final third wave occurred in the cruel winter of 1919, killing many already weakened by wartime privations and distracting diplomats during the Versailles Treaty negotiations (J. Barry 381–88). One hundred years after the end of World War I, we are only now beginning to accurately understand the 1918–19 influenza pandemic, as scientists, historians, archivists, and family members assemble their accounts of what precisely occurred during its brief but chaotic fury.

Teaching the pandemic in conjunction with other World War I materials reduces the epic scale of war to a human level and expands the war's temporal range while reemphasizing its international scope. Students should first understand the disease itself, which was unlike the common influenza we are vaccinated against each winter. It often had a sudden onset, and

> [i]n serious cases patients experienced severe headaches, body pains, and fever; their faces turned blue/black, the marks of cyanosis, and they coughed blood and bled from the nose. Death was usually caused as bacteria invaded the lungs, turning . . . [them] into sacks of fluid and thus effectively drowning the patient. (Phillips and Killingray 5)

Death could be rapid, sometimes within a day. Those who survived often suffered from long-lasting cardiac and neurological effects.[4] The 1918–19 influenza was also unusual in the victims it targeted; typically influenza severely afflicts the very young and old, but the 1918 influenza was most often fatal in the young and healthy because it provoked violent overreactions in healthy immune systems. Thus, soldiers, war workers, and pregnant women died at record rates in this pandemic, frustrating doctors who had no methods to treat stricken patients. In October 1918, Herman Biggs, the New York State health commissioner, admitted his proud profession's defeat by the pandemic: "There has never been anything which compares with this in importance . . . in which we were so helpless" (J. Barry 403).

The medical history of the 1918–19 influenza pandemic therefore provides a compelling narrative in itself. After eminent doctors failed to treat the initial pandemic, it was virtually ignored for many decades, only to reemerge in the late 1990s, when researchers at the United States Centers for Disease Control and Prevention sought to sequence its DNA, using a tissue sample dug from the melting permafrost of Alaska. Gina Kolata details the medical history of the 1918–19 influenza pandemic in her book *Flu: The Story of the Great Influenza Pandemic of 1918 and the Search for the Virus That Caused It.* The Centers for Disease Control and Prevention Web site contains a link to the 2005 *Science* article that established the DNA of the pathogen as well as a discussion of the ethics surrounding the reconstruction of history's most deadly virus.[5]

Contemporary historical and sociological research continues to make available more detailed knowledge about how different communities and institutions faced the challenges of such destruction. Recent historical studies by Nancy K. Bristow and by Carol R. Byerly on the pandemic in American society and the American military, respectively, are particularly valuable because they emphasize both the diversity of the influenza's victims and the failures that prominent institutions experienced in addressing it. A special issue of *Public Health Reports* is dedicated to the 1918–19 influenza pandemic in the United States (*Supplement 3*). Given the unplanned extensive mortality caused by the pandemic, doctors, nurses, and other civilian caretakers such as ministers and community leaders played fundamental roles in attending the victims and their families. As Howard Phillips and David Killingray explain:

> The dying and dead placed heavy burdens on families and social institutions. Bodies remained unburied for days; in many towns and cities coffins were in short supply; many victims were buried in mass graves. And throughout the world the brief rage of the flu left in its wake millions of widowed and orphaned, an almost unimaginable burden of personal grief and, of course, poverty. ("1918–1919" 9)

While the war frustrated conventional rituals of mourning by annihilating bodies on the battlefield, leaving no corpses to ship home for burial, the influenza pandemic complicated grieving in the opposite way: through the sheer excess of human remains that must be disposed of and the limited resources available to the survivors. The combination of simultaneous war and pandemic during 1918 to 1919 led to a sort of trauma fatigue, with many trained professionals and family members unable to react to disease and death according to tradition or previous arrangement. The innovative aspects of the 1918–19 influenza pandemic became visible as it forced doctors, nurses, and community leaders to find new ways to treat both the dead and the living. In Willa Cather's *One of Ours* (1922), Claude Wheeler naively perceives the war as generative, breaking open "hard moulds and crusts" (375). The 1918–19 influenza provided the same sort of rough catalyst, mixing society matrons and slum children, soldiers and laboring mothers in the same hospitals. The recently published social histories of the pandemic provide rich materials for students to work with; they might construct patterns of caretaking in one community or compare the approaches of physicians in different cities.[6] A resonant research topic could look at whether quarantines in schools, churches, and public spaces such as libraries and theaters were effective in combatting the influenza.

Studying the literature of the influenza pandemic also introduces one of the major social changes of the World War I era: alterations in gender roles for both men and women. While trench warfare required soldiers to become unexpectedly passive, World War I and its aftermath allowed women unanticipated opportunities for meaningful agency. In both Europe and the United States many women entered nursing during the war, feminizing the profession and providing an essential form of wartime participation for young women. Propaganda posters exhorting women to join the American Red Cross often appealed to their supposed maternal instincts as well as their patriotism, comparing nursing with being "the greatest mother in the world," as in a series of American Red Cross posters. The 1918 influenza literature provides a number of strong female nurse characters, such as Nurse Cornelia Tanner, who saves Miranda's life in Katherine Anne Porter's *Pale Horse, Pale Rider* (1939). Under the strain of the pandemic, however, male soldiers put aside their battle training to become nurses themselves, as the characters of Claude in *One of Ours* and Adam in *Pale Horse, Pale Rider* movingly exemplify. These characters' displays of a masculine ethos of care are particularly notable, since the plots of both narratives foreshadow that they should be patients rather than nurses, indicating the power of the 1918–19 pandemic to challenge gender expectations, revealing possibilities previously unknown to the characters and readers.

Virginia Woolf's imaginative 1923 essay *On Being Ill* provides alternative ways to think about the experience of illness and thus offers a much needed positive framework for teaching literature about the 1918 influenza pandemic. Woolf writes from the patient's perspective, "searching in vain for "[n]ovels . . . devoted to influenza," desiring literary forms flexible enough to contain "[t]hose great wars which the body wages with the mind" (4, 5). She prioritizes the liberating aspects of disability ("Rashness is one of the properties of illness—outlaws that we are"), encouraging her readers to consider disease as an active aspect of human endeavor (22). She especially advocates that patients read poetry and look at familiar objects such as the sky to gain the enhanced sensory experience infirmity can offer (12–16).

Throughout her essay, she balances pain with revelation, acknowledging the former but insisting on the latter's primacy.

The autobiographical American novels *They Came like Swallows* (1937), by William Maxwell, and *Pale Horse, Pale Rider* fulfill Woolf's criteria of "[n]ovels . . . devoted to influenza" by foregrounding both painful and revelatory experiences. Maxwell's elegiac narrative chronicles the death of a pregnant young mother from influenza and its adverse effects on her family. Porter's novel is a modernist, urban narrative set in the final weeks of the war and told from the sardonic viewpoint of Miranda Gay, a young newspaper woman both in love with a soldier and increasingly ill with influenza. Its use of interior monologue, spatialization, and experiments with time allows *Pale Horse, Pale Rider* to include a generous spectrum of period detail and idiom. Through its portrayal of a rally aggressively marketing war bonds as well as its direct allusions to war propaganda, the novel gives readers a sense of inhabiting the final, destabilizing weeks of World War I. Miranda's near death from influenza results in her perceiving the longed-for armistice as painful; she recovers only to discover her soldier-lover Adam already dead. Rejecting her desire for his ghost, she prepares for an unknown future "where there would be time for everything" (208). Both novels convey the abrupt nature of the 1918 influenza pandemic, how—like the war itself, which took unforeseen directions—it unaccountably appeared and transformed countless lives. These two novels movingly portray the human cost of the pandemic, the unexpected suffering it inflicted on an already exhausted population. Porter's work also makes a superb classroom pairing with Woolf's *Mrs. Dalloway*, whose title character is also recovering from a life-altering bout of influenza.

The reanimated voices of the 1918–19 influenza pandemic dominate the American poet Ellen Bryant Voigt's sonnet sequence *Kyrie* (1995), which represents a Tennessee community battered by the pandemic. Both the living and the dead, soldiers and civilians, speak in well-crafted sonnets about this transformative event: "To claim the War alone changed everything / can't be entirely right, too few of us / went over there" (61). Focusing on figures neglected in other World War I literature, Voigt details an entire community during the influenza pandemic, including children, pregnant women, and animals. Particularly strong are the voices of the minister and his congregation, as a community of believers comes to terms with what they view as God's wrath. The sonnet form, which Voigt chose to contain the chaos of the pandemic, makes these poems fine accompaniments to other well-known first-person World War I sonnets. Another sonnet marks the immensity of the pandemic, overwhelming the speaker, urging readers to their own efforts: "I can't remember much—go study the graves" (37). Voigt's poetry can provide the starting point for personal reflective assignments on the pandemic, which students may find had an effect on their families. You can profitably ask students to write about their family or community history involving the pandemic. Alternatively, you can have them go to a large local cemetery and study the grave markers, noting how many deaths occurred in periods corresponding to local outbreaks.

The 1918–19 influenza pandemic also left its traces in the oral traditions and literatures of the Global South, where so many died.[7] Here the colonial dimensions of the pandemic emerge clearly. Two Nigerian novels, Elechi Amadi's *The Great Ponds* (1969) and Buchi Emecheta's *The Slave Girl* (1977), address the pandemic through the matrices of tribal and colonial power structures. In both novels, African communities operate at a dual disadvantage when confronting the pandemic. They struggle to understand the disease that threatens their lives and disrupts their villages. The imperial war that changes their nationality without their consent remains a more abstract, unrecognized threat, however. Both novels offer the double lenses of colonial power and indigenous African culture through which to view the war and the pandemic, contrasting the African communities' internal responses with omniscient narrators' ironic overviews. Amadi's novel emphasizes tribal warfare complicated by tribal belief in native religion, while Emecheta's novel depends on kinship slavery as well as the folk magic *ogbaange*, or spirit child, to stress the social otherness of the main character, Ojebeta.

Amadi's *The Great Ponds* begins with a tribal dispute over the great ponds of the title. Olumba, the chief of Chiolu, has made a bet with the competing tribe of Aliakoro. When his first symptoms appear, his influenza is initially confused with tribal magic from the opposing village. He heroically tries to resist his illness, but a visit to the opposing village reveals they suffer from it as well. A village song illustrates the tribal view of influenza, called *wonjo*: "*Wonjo* the curse of the gods, *Wonjo* will end the world" (209). In the novel's final lines, the omniscient narrator offers a contrasting historic perspective: "But it was only the beginning. *Wonjo*, as the villagers called the Great Influenza of 1918, was to claim a grand total of some twenty million lives all over the world" (217). Amadi effectively offers two conclusions to his novel: a local ending dependent on the tribal interpretation of *wonjo* and the ironic historic conclusion that *wonjo* is also a beginning of an international influenza pandemic. *The Great Ponds* comments primarily on war's futility. Amadi wrote the novel during the Biafran War, and the internal combat between the two villages mimics Nigeria's own civil conflict. The disease's destruction further emphasizes war's absurdity, for the regional war not only fails to resolve the fishing rights dispute with which it began but also causes new devastation. As Chief Eze reminds us, "The war brought *wonjo*" (200), just as World War I brought influenza. In *The Great Ponds*, Amadi carefully details intertribal warfare only to render it meaningless when facing the enormity of global war leading to pandemic disease.

In Emecheta's *The Slave Girl*, the 1918 influenza pandemic acts as a catalyst for the novel's key initial action: Ojebeta's separation from her birth family and entry into slavery when her brother sells Ojebeta to a distant relative. The influenza pandemic is represented in colonial terms as "Felenza . . . a white man's death . . . which is now coming to us" (25). Her character is complicated by her liminal status as an *ogbaange*, which initially brings her special treatment from her parents but later only confirms her subhuman status. She strives to become fully human but finds her efforts frustrated throughout a gendered narrative of "unbecoming," where she is always culturally defined as a spirit child, a slave, and then a wife. Emecheta is particularly critical of European attempts to rationalize colonialism by making claims to abolish slavery and improve medical care in the new colonies. The bitter last paragraph of *The Slave Girl* links British colonialism instead to the continuation of slavery in Africa: "So as Britain was emerging from war once more victorious, and claiming to have stopped the slavery which she had helped to spread in all her black colonies, Ojebeta, now a woman of thirty-five, was changing masters" (179). The narrator's double vision at the novel's conclusion offers a jaundiced colonial view of World War I, reminding us how war can continue after an armistice, destroying without battles. With its critique of Eurocentric war narratives, *The Slave Girl* offers instructive analogies to many World War I coming-of-age novels. I have successfully paired it with Sebastian Barry's *A Long, Long Way* (2005), which also raises postcoloniality but in an explicitly wartime setting.[8]

Given its global reach, the 1918–19 influenza pandemic easily unites literary works from Ireland to Nigeria, America to Europe, because (even more than the war itself) it potentially touched every human being alive between early 1918 and early 1920 (when the pandemic ended).[9] Though it was dubbed the "forgotten" pandemic, repressed because of its awe-inspiring scale and ability to overwhelm our meagre defenses, teaching literary representations of the pandemic can vitally contribute to public memory. Literature provides emotional, aesthetic, and even religious perspectives often absent from starker historical accountings. And comprehending the 1918–19 influenza pandemic contributes to understanding the true magnitude of World War I's destruction, from its gory battles but to an even greater extent from the biological contagion it unwittingly set into motion. As we begin to recognize the authentic dimensions of the 1918–19 influenza pandemic, we can also begin to fully mourn it, almost one century after it began.

Notes

1. For wartime casualty figures, see Hochschild, 347–51. For 1918 to 1919 influenza mortality rates, see Taubenberger and Morens. To define the different waves of the pandemic, consult Taubenberger and Morens; Crosby 203.

2. See Taubenberger and Morens.

3. To access Sargent's watercolor, see the Imperial War Museum London's Web site: www.iwm.org.uk/collections/item/object/23728.

4. For resources documenting the nature of 1918 influenza virus and spread of the disease, see the Centers for Disease Control and Prevention Web site (www.cdc.gov/). The documentaries *The American Experience: Influenza, 1918* and *We Heard the Bells: The Influenza of 1918* (2010) also provide useful interviews and primary materials.

5. See the CDC article "Reconstruction of the 1918 Influenza Virus": www.cdc.gov/flu/about/qa/1918flupandemic.htm.

6. Social histories of the 1918–19 influenza pandemic that detail different communities' responses to the crisis, ranging from treating patients to enforcing surveillance and quarantine policies, include works by Bristow; Ryan Davis; Fanning; Honigsbaum; and Opdycke.

7. See Phillips and Killingray's bibliography, which details the 1918–19 influenza pandemic in the Global South.

8. For an extended discussion of Amadi's and Emecheta's novels, see J. Fisher 177–96 and 187–88, respectively.

9. John Barry discusses Camp Funston as the pandemic's origin (96). For the pandemic's end, see p. 203.

Celia Marshik

The First World War in Consumer Culture

Readers of Great War–era periodicals often stumble across surprising attempts to use the war as a marketing tool for a variety of products. A brand of British toffee called Mackintosh positioned itself "in the thick of the fight" and "always at the front—and right at the front." The company even went so far as to suggest that the candy was "the stuff for Heroes" and offered testimony from "V. C.," who recounted that he "was chewing a piece of Mackintosh's Toffee" during the deed for which he was decorated (Mackintosh's Toffee). Products ranging from candy to clothing to patent medicines were marketed as appropriate for military or civilian use, the suggestion being that the goods that stood the test of the trenches might please those at home. Such advertisements, and the advertising circulars and newspaper "puffs" that reinforced them, indicate that there was no clear line between goods sold to soldiers and ordinary citizens during the Great War; the most extreme cases demonstrate that consumer culture allowed those at home to "put on" the war in their daily acts of eating, dressing, and bodily care.

This essay surveys what students stand to learn about the Great War by studying consumer culture and specifically advertising, the most accessible form of 1914-to-1918 consumer culture. Advertising uniquely complicates the postwar emphasis on a divide between home and front, highlighting the continuity between (for example) London and Ypres. While literature often retrospectively ironizes the Bovril, Burberry, and other familiar brands that combatants used in unfamiliar spaces, what is most striking about period consumer culture is its lack of irony. Moreover, consumer culture provides a venue for examining the national characteristics and values that were mobilized in support of the war, including sangfroid, consistency, and good humor under trying conditions. By studying advertising, students can get a sense of how particular companies employed patriotism to sell products that at the same time sold renewed commitment to the war. Finally, advertising demonstrates the need for members of the Great War military to become smart consumers as a matter of self-protection: the range of products marketed for use at the front demonstrates that companies stepped in to supply items the armed forces did not—gas masks, body armor, and camp buckets, among other things.

The First World War did not initiate the use of soldiers and military campaigns in advertising. As Brent Shannon has demonstrated, in Victorian advertising "the most masculine—and therefore most popular—male figures were athletes and soldiers, and their presence was used to make even ostensibly gender-neutral products masculine and appealing to male buyers" (58–59). Bovril used soldiers in British advertisements at the turn of the twentieth century, depicting the beverage as reviving the wounded in battle during the Boer War (61–62). What one sees in and after 1914 is thus not a new technique but the explosion of similar strategies in Britain, France, Germany, the United States, and elsewhere. In an essay on the United States advertising industry during the war, Daniel Pope observes that "[m]ilitary use was a selling point, for a product worthy of the armed forces surely merited consumer attention" (11). In looking at advertisements that deploy this strategy, students can appreciate the shared experience of life at home and at the front, as military and civilian consumers were encouraged to purchase the same products.

In Britain, for example, readers of the *Telegraph* and other papers might see an ad for Phosferine, a patent medicine for "nerves" and general conditioning, featuring photographs of soldiers on duty and a letter from Private W. G. Amatt of the British Expeditionary Force. Amatt's letter, which is quoted at length, describes his extensive military service, wounding, and subsequent recovery from (shell) "shock" thanks to Phosferine, which he felt had "done me a great amount of good in bucking me up and restoring my nerves." While the ad focuses on the soldier's experience, it concludes with the exhortation to purchase Phosferine "when you need the best tonic medicine" and provides a list of conditions the product treats, which range from "sleeplessness" to "rheumatism." The promotion thus claims that a product that could treat shell shock would help with the more mundane cares of civilian life.

Such strategies were common in France and the United States as well. Lithinés du Dr. Gustin, a French medicinal water additive, opened one advertisement with the observation that "Le soldat n'a pas toujours le choix de l'eau qu'il doit consommer" ("A soldier cannot always choose the water he drinks").[1] By diluting a package of Dr. Gustin's Lithium in a liter of water, the ad continued, a man at the front could instantaneously prepare a safe drink (Lithinés [July]). Other advertisements for Lithinés du Dr. Gustin reinforced this message by depicting soldiers in a range of uniforms raising a glass, and collectively such images suggest that the product was most necessary and useful to those in military service (fig. 1). But like the Phosferine ad, the promotional text for Lithinés du Dr. Gustin moves from soldierly to civilian uses: "This delicious water—either pure or mixed with any drink—is recommended to dissolve uric acid and to heal derived afflictions such as: arthritis, rheumatism, sciatica, gout, gravel (kidney stones), diabetes as well as all diseases of essential organs: kidneys, bladder, liver, stomach" (Lithinés [Aug.]). Merchandise pitched in terms of providing water safety and quality at the front quickly evolves into yet another medicinal product targeted for civilian ailments. While the French company, unlike its British counterpart, did not cite soldier testimony in promotional materials, it invoked martial utility—evidenced in the images that surround the text—as proof of the product's safety and effectiveness.

In general, products aligned (however loosely) with maintaining or restoring health were marketed using similar strategies. In the United States, brands like Colgate depicted their products at the front to sell toothpaste at home. *The Youth's Companion* of 10 October 1918 represents two young soldiers brushing their teeth with Colgate at an army training camp (formations march in the background), and the text exhorts young readers:

> You have surely noticed how strong and well the men in the Army and Navy look. That is because a few simple rules of exercise, sleep, cleanliness, and health are insisted on. One rule is regular care of the teeth. You cannot do a better thing for your own health than to clean your teeth twice a day with the safe, sane, delicious dentifrice—COLGATE'S Ribbon Dental Cream.

Figure 1. Soldiers in a variety of uniforms raise a glass to Lithinés du Dr. Gustin.

Such promotions located a decidedly prosaic consumer product in a military context, aligning, in this case, toothpaste with a militarist precision in the matter of appearance. These examples demonstrate the perceived merits of a consumable's use at the front: if a patent medicine, tonic, or toiletry could assist soldiers in their dangerous duties, such ads suggest, they might do equal good for those at home.

While most endorsements used martial utility to sway noncombatant consumers, the process occasionally worked in reverse. *L'écho de Paris* of 14 April 1915 contained a notice about La Ration du Soldat, milk packaged for use at the front. The advertisement assured *L'écho* readers that Henri Nestlé's products were "bien connu des mamans" ("well known by mothers") and that the firm had now developed special merchandise for soldiers (Nestlé). While the advertisement focuses on the product's packaging—three hermetically sealed little iron containers enclosed in a special cardboard box—it invokes France's mothers as guarantors of Nestlé quality and thus indicates that idealized civilian identities could help render items appealing to soldiers. Nestlé's milk was guaranteed in terms of its purity, preservability, and ease of use, but its alignment with French *mamans* was its affective selling point, a means of communicating the watchful care with which the milk was prepared and packaged.

At times, one firm offered products for a range of locales and roles, complicating the separation of home and front. In Germany, for example, the Franz Sauer company promoted its Regenmäntel ("raincoats") as ideal for "Herren, Damen und Kinder" ("gentlemen, ladies, and children") but also marketed its Militär-Mäntel ("military coats") and Offizier-Mäntel ("officer coats") in the same advertisement. The firm's vaunted "Grosse Auswahl" ("wide choice or variety") suggested that wartime consumers of all stripes might find under one roof garments suitable for their needs (Franz Sauer). Such firms and products assert a national unity in part constructed through experiences of advertising and consumption: if readers wear Sauer's coats under vastly different circumstances, they will be united by (and, in a coat, under) the Franz Sauer label.

The desire to align oneself with the war—to wear the war—even if one is not involved in active service is also evident in period advertising. Promotions effecting this alignment can seem shocking to contemporary students, but they demonstrate that consumer culture allowed civilians, whether they volunteered their service for the war or not, to demonstrate their commitment to country through garments and accessories. These products and campaigns were particularly, albeit not uniquely, targeted at female consumers. The London department store Harrods, for example, promoted three "Ladies' Weathercoats in Trench Twill Cut on Service Lines," vaunting the fabric as particularly "durable." The model names should surprise students: the styles have been dubbed Somme, Meuse, and Perrone (*Harrods Weekly Price List* 32; fig. 2). If one reminds a class that the 1916 Somme Offensive (and the battles that raged around Péronne) resulted in over 1.5 million casualties and that the Meuse was the French department in which the 1916 Battle of Verdun (or Meuse Mill) took more than 250,000 lives, students will be forced to consider why a company would name coats after some of the bloodiest battles of the war. The strategy will make sense, however, if students consider the emotional appeal of wearing attire similar ("cut on service lines") to clothing adopted by soldiers, particularly for women who were involved in war work and needed practical garb. As Camila Loew has observed in an analysis of war posters, World War I was the first conflict in which women "had a right

Figure 2. Wearing the war: trench coats named after battles.

to . . . claim their experience as a part of war" (124). Harrods trench coats let women visually claim their experience. Since Harrods repeatedly promoted the Somme and Meuse models in advertising circulars, most of the British public must have found the coats' names natural or at least unobjectionable.

In France, too, companies advertised products that linked women to country and conflict through clothing or accessories. Titre Goldfilled, for example, advertised "Notre Bague Tricolore!" ("Our Tricolor Ring!") as a beautiful and patriotic "Souvenir de la Grande Guerre 1914–1915." While most of the ad focused on the ring's fabrication—the setting included a sapphire, zirconium, and ruby—this "charmante bague" was, the company asserted, a perfect way to "commémorer l'épisode le plus glorieux de notre Histoire" ("commemorate the most glorious episode in our history"). Unlike the Harrods coats, the Titre Goldfilled ring was not represented as on par with anything worn by the men at the front; as a souvenir, it suggested that the war would soon be over, would soon become a historical event to be commemorated. Of course, this confident supposition was incorrect, and students can see reflected in such advertisements an early faith in the conflict's short duration.

The Titre Goldfilled and Harrods advertisements suggest that women were more likely than noncombatant men to purchase garments and accessories that linked them to the war and to their nations. The scenario in which women become bad (because inauthentic) consumers is challenged by other products and companies. Frenchmen might purchase, instead of a tricolor ring, a pocket watch that serves as a "jolie souvenir de la guerre" ("Comme"; "pretty souvenir of the war"), similarly signaling their association with the conflict if only through the act of consumption. Examining related products and advertisements helps illuminate how consumer culture rendered the emotional attachment to country and history concrete and visible.

Such promotional materials also make plain the wartime values and characteristics that cohered (however unevenly) in each nation at war. In 1917, The United States Cream of Wheat company depicted Uncle Sam (hat off and accompanied by an eagle) lifting a spoonful of the cereal above the simple word "Preparedness." This unadorned message aligned the country, as well as the breakfast food, with a readiness for the challenges of war. As David Clampin has written, "simple sales messages [were] devised, which keyed into the popular narrative and reinforced pervasive propaganda messages. Patriotism was a recurring motif in commercial advertising." Cream of Wheat's use of Uncle Sam provides a vivid illustration of this motif.

National ambitions and values were also advanced by wartime advertisers. German advertisements for the Mercedes and Benz corporations, for example, routinely represented each company's motor car near airplanes and placed both types of vehicle in exotic locales. While the images aligned automobiles with modern modes of transport and warfare—the enthusiasm over flight might be transferred to the new German cars, company executives must have hoped—the settings also subtly underline the country's territorial ambitions. Benz and Germany have their rightful place in the land

Figure 3. Advertising colonial ambitions as well as automobiles.

of palm trees and mosques, such advertisements suggest (fig. 3). During the war, the cars would help the country acquire valuable overseas colonies; afterward, these motorcars could serve as yet another "jolie souvenir" of the conflict.

Advertisements also targeted soldier and officers as companies raced to offer products developed for use in conflict. The front cover of the 4 April 1916 edition of *Daily Mail* has a full-page ad for Gamages, listing all the service products it sells. Uniforms, hurricane lanterns, service mess baskets, splinterproof cigarette cases, camp chairs and buckets, as well as other items sprawl across the page, offering a mere taste of all the goods Gamages offered in its "new and enlarged military catalogue." The extensive list of products offered those in the service—as well as those hoping to cater to service members' comforts—equipment most readers now assume were provided by the armed forces. During World War I, however, such advertisements remind students of the bare-bones provisions that most countries offered those at the front.

They also remind students of the desperate hope that soldiers, officers, and their loved ones had that men might return safely from combat. The Gamages spread included the Dayfield Body Shield, a product that was also advertised separately in the *Daily Mail.* Whitfield Manufacturing touted its shield, formed of metal plates that covered the chest and back, as "proof against bayonet, sword, and lance; and also against spent bullets, shrapnel, shell splinters and grenades." Testimonials from Sir Hiram Maxim and "a lady" assert the protective powers of the garment, and readers with loved ones at the front may have hoped that by purchasing the Dayfield shield they could increase the odds that a husband, father, brother, or friend would survive unscathed. At 21shillings and 6 pence (for the single shield) or 53 shillings and 6 pence (for the double), acquiring the product may have felt less like consumption than insurance. Items in the same class were marketed in other countries, including La Sauvegarde, a mask said to protect its wearers against "les Gax Asphyxiants et les Liquides Corrosifs" ("asphyxiating gas and corrosive liquids"). Such advertisements provide students with poignant reminders of the hopes that animated a portion of wartime consumer culture: love, anxiety, and the desperate desire to protect a loved one must have sold countless camp beds, personal protection devices, and other items around the globe.

For many years, limited student access to such advertisements presented a high barrier to classroom use. Some libraries have excellent microfilm and microform resources, but these older technologies are often resisted by students, who find them clunky to use. While there are virtues in sending students on treasure hunts through such media, the increasing number of reputable Internet resources renders student access much simpler. The Newberry and British Libraries, for example, offer curated sites with a limited number of advertisements for students to examine; the Library of Congress offers a deeper archive through its digitization of *The Stars and Stripes*, a newspaper printed by the United States Army for its forces in France.[2] Incorporating consumer culture into the classroom gives students the opportunity to engage in archives large and small and to recover wartime culture, which is often quite different from the culture that looked back on the war in some of the best-known works about the conflict.

Notes

1. Thanks to Nathalie Noel-Marshik and Evelyn Hutter for translation assistance.

2. See dcc.newberry.org/collections/world-war-i-in-us-popular-culture, www.bl.uk/world-war-one/articles/commercial-advertising-as-propaganda, and memory.loc.gov/ammem/sgphtml/sashtml/sashome.html.

Part IV

Genres

Marguerite Helmers

Mud, Machines, and Madness: Teaching the Art of the First World War

In 1918, the British artist Paul Nash completed an oil painting of the sun rising over Inverness Copse, Ypres, Belgium. The rays of the sun illuminate gray-brown mud, water-filled craters, and blackened stumps of trees. He titled the painting *We Are Making a New World.*[1] In the same year, George Matthews Harding, an American, sketched an American tank descending on a nest of German machine gunners. In this charcoal-and-crayon drawing, now titled *Cleaning out Boche Machine Gun Nest*, the tank appears like a great ship obliterating the sky. Below it, two German machine gunners in camouflage helmets leap back in fear. Also in 1918, in Leipzig, Max Beckmann was working on his giant oil *Die Nacht* ("The Night"), a painting of terror and violation: three men have invaded a cottage, raped the women, and murdered the men. The chaos and disorder of the cramped room suggest the chaos and disorder of the postwar society, a place of suffering and disillusionment. These three paintings represent prevalent themes in the art and literature of the First World War: the reduction of the landscape to a mudscape, the reverence for and fear of the machine, and the lasting physical and psychological damage caused by warfare.

Examining the way that war art incorporated physical objects, Fabio Gygi notes that "[t]he experience of materiality—of the 'body' and the structure rather than the idea of things—became of paramount importance, because the things could save one's life after all" (78). Thus objects such as tanks or guns that could tear the landscape and human flesh were also the first line of defense against the onslaught. Objects were potential relics but could also fulfill the sacred duty of protection. This dual relation toward the thing gave rise to thoughtful works of art that interrogated the horror of the front lines. Using the framing device of the soldiers' journeys, art may trace a soldier's tale from recruitment through homecoming, from recruiting posters through trench landscapes, encounters with machines, and scenes of the wounded and dead. While this approach is ahistorical and transnational, it offers a broad way of examining representation, persuasion, and affect. Not only may the students examine works of art from the period but at various points they may also experiment with their own designs and constructions.

For example, before looking at art or reading literature in the classroom, students may try mapmaking. Ask the students to use a pen or pencil and a pocket-sized notebook to map a journey taken on foot. Many diaries taken to the front lines fitted in a top pocket, and thus a three-by-five-inch blank notecard or a sheet of letter-sized paper folded into fourths could approximate the 9.5 centimeter by 15 centimeter standard diary. On this first journey by foot, ask the students to concentrate on the route and the physicality of the experience—the sights, sounds, smells, and feelings. Threats to the personnel on the front lines came from below; soldiers were "eye-deep in hell," mired amid mud, lice, rats, gas, water, rocks, rubble, ordnance, disease, and decay. They walked miles over uneven terrain to towns with unfamiliar names and often had no maps to indicate their direction or location. "Heavy is the tread of the living," wrote Edward Thomas in his poem "Roads." Nash's painting *The Menin Road* depicts the chaos of the bombed sector near Ypres. *Republican Automatons* (1920) and *Street Scene* (1925), by George Grosz, are set in urban Berlin; both feature veterans, scarred and crippled by the war.

The Soldier's Tale

Recruiting posters illustrate the degree to which young men were persuaded to serve king, kaiser, and country.[2] The posters are often used in the literature classroom to illustrate the effects of propaganda on civilians and to demonstrate the disjuncture between the promises of the military and the reality of the military life. They depend on a visual language of a hale and hearty recruit. Frank Brangwyn's posters epitomize the type—a muscular, square-jawed, uniformed man of action (*Fall In*, *Help Your Country Stop This*). In Germany, too, the posters reflected a strong masculine type, notable for a determined gaze outward toward the viewer—see, for example, *Sturmbataillon Schmidt* ("[Join] Schmidt's Battalion") and *Auch du sollst beitreten zur Reichswehr* ("You Too Should Join the Reichswar!"). One of the most recognized French posters from the war, *On les aura!* ("We'll Get Them!"), depicts a youthful and exuberant young man with gun in hand, gesturing toward the front lines.

So much of the war machinery was new—shells, searchlights, zeppelins, tanks, airplanes—that it became the subject of artworks by painters who were also searching for new modes of expression. As Gygi writes, "Every speck of space was taken up by the industrially-produced equipment, tons of barbed wire, endless heaps of metal obstacles and, of course, mountains of artillery shell cases" (79). These material objects worked their way into the paintings. For example, the British artist C. R. W. Nevinson was initially fascinated by the potential for fusing man and machine and celebrated the power in *La mitrailleuse* (1915; "The Machine Gun") and *Marching Men* (1916). By 1917, however, Nevinson was so disillusioned by battle that, in defiance of the British War Office, he painted two soldiers dead in the mud, barbed wire in an impenetrable line in front of them, rifles by their sides (*Paths*).

Despite the initial fascination with war machines, after the protracted entrenchments and the devastating battles of 1915 and 1916 artists began to explore the consequences of the machines on the human body and mind. Red Cross posters attest to the end of the soldier's journey; however, the soldiers who are represented usually have their physical prowess undiminished. For instance, the wounded soldier in the Italian poster *Per la Patria i miei occhi! Per la Pace il vostro denaro* ("For the Country, My Eyes, for Peace, Your Money") is depicted from a low angle that emphasizes his heroic stature. He stands defiantly, hands clenched into fists, and, despite bloodied bandages around his head, stares into the sky. The bandaged head became shorthand for the seriously wounded; it appears in *Mitbürger! Sammelt leere Mineralwasserflaschen* ("Fellow Citizens! Collect Empty Bottles of Mineral Water [for the Red Cross]") and *In the Name of Mercy, Give!*

Wilfred Owen's poem "Disabled" opens with the lines "He sat in a wheeled chair, waiting for dark, / And shivered in his ghastly suit of grey, / Legless, sewn short at elbow." Not only did soldiers lose limbs but also their faces were horribly disfigured by rifles, shell fire, and burns. With facial wounds testing the limits of surgery, artists served in the medical profession to either enable diagnoses or to help with facial reconstruction. The Slade Professor of Fine Art Henry Tonks, before the war a fairly conservative portrait painter, was attached to St. Mary's Hospital in Sidcup, England. Here he assisted Dr. Harold Gillies by completing medical illustrations of facial wounds. Tonks's delicate color pastel drawings showed the damage, disease, and repair needed for plastic surgery better than black-and-white photography. Because surgery could not repair the massive damage caused by the guns, the British sculptors Francis Derwent Wood and Kathleen Scott, together with the American Anna Coleman Ladd, created "tin masks," facial prosthetics designed to cover the horrible wounds. Such art created in the service of the war offers a visual complement to Owen's poem.

But Tonks's images provide a means beyond the verbal or the demonstrative to examine subjectivity. The fine line and color of his medical illustrations reveal the inner anguish of the men, speaking of pain and sadness through colors of green, gray, and vivid crimson. There are many idealized illustrations of wounded soldiers in war bond propaganda and even legless soldiers in wheelchairs appear in hospital photographs, but the wounded soldiers of Tonks's medical drawings were not posed for a society painter, nor were they imaginative recreations of psychological anguish. They operate as documentary images and are all the more persuasive in that they exist as fact. As Elizabeth Kahn notes, World War I portraiture revealed "those aspects of human presence that the war set out to destroy":

> Far more constricted in terms of creative space for resolving the contradiction between modernization and the old, time-honored humanist approach to artistic representation, the frontline soldier, no matter his aesthetic choice, saw in the portrait an icon of resistance to the vast "machine of slaughter" and a means of transcending a self-image as a meaningless cog in the military bureaucracy.

An art historian, Kahn draws attention to the lineage of the portrait, harking back to Théodore Géricault and Eugène Delacroix. Her contention that "this one face should be seen as unique among others at a particular moment in time and for all time" (196) introduces a way of interpreting the portraiture of the war. Students may research, collect, and juxtapose faces of war by drawing from official photographs, illustrations on recruiting posters, medical illustrations and photography, and portraiture. Paired with research and writing that gives voice to soldiers' individual experiences, art transcends casualty lists, which emphasize the losses of nations.

The devastating effects of machine warfare on the human body and mind became the subject of many introspective and disturbing paintings from the Weimar Republic. While portraiture remains a consistent genre, the artists of the Weimar sought out the limits of experience and the troubled legacy of the war years. Movements such as expressionism, dadaism, new objectivity, and verism significantly altered the landscape of twentieth-century art, not least because the artists shocked the viewers with new techniques, such as fragmentation, collage, and the use of found objects. Their art drew attention to the mechanization of war, the dehumanization of the soldier, and the inability of surgery to mask the wounds and scars. No consideration of war art can be complete without an extended examination of the suffering and twisted faces that emerge from the illustrations in Otto Dix's *Der Kreig* (1924; *The Art of War*), perhaps the single most devastating criticism of war in the twentieth century. The fifty-one etchings and aquatints in the series were modeled on the work of the early-nineteenth-century Spanish artist Francisco Goya, who completed *Los desastres de la guerra* ("The Disasters of War") in protest of the Napoleonic campaigns. Illustrating a profusion of bones, fragmented and dissected bodies, bombed houses, craters, trenches, and mud, Dix's work is at once hallucinatory and unflinchingly realistic. His horrific painting *Die Skatspieler* (1920; *Skat Players*) merges men with machines. Ernst Ludwig Kirchner's *Self-Portrait as a Soldier* (1915) juxtaposes two self-images, one blasé, publicly clothed in a uniform, the other naked, exposed and vulnerable. Grosz and Marcel Janco used the mask as a way of exploring that which was unnatural or *unheimlich* in human experience, that which was subsumed to the will of the army or masked by artistry and artifice.

Through the work of the Weimar artists, students can consider much larger questions about art and war: What can art represent and what is it unable to express? What experiences does art represent that writing cannot reach? The American writer Tim O'Brien asked a related question in *The Things They Carried*, his 1990 novel about the Vietnam War. O'Brien posed a problem for readers: How do you tell a true war story? Listening closely to that question, we can hear two important words: *tell* and *true*. These words are complementary but not equivalent, for to tell a story involves giving voice to experience, expressing the details of one's involvement in war, a process of selecting and presenting information. The truth is another matter entirely, as scholars who study life writing recognize, for the emotional truth of a matter may not reside in factually accurate details or indeed be represented at all. As O'Brien notes, there are times when "story-truth is sometimes truer than happening-truth" (171). These ideas encourage students to examine the relations between fine art and writing by asking questions about representation, communication, and persuasion.

There is perhaps another, more troubling question related to the pity of war that we should introduce to students. While the prevalent mode of representing the First World War in the classroom has emphasized the horror of the Western Front, there were in fact many types of direct witnessing. For example, direct witnesses painted factories, shipyards, and munitions works. Many of the women painters of the time, such as Mabel May, Anna Airy, and Norah Neilson Gray, were witness to the large social and industrial changes on the home front. Yet the mud, blood, and gore of no-man's-land and the iconic status of the trench have come to eclipse these other experiences. As the historian Margaret Higonnet has pointed out, "authentic speech, it has often been repeated, could only come from the trenches in the disabused words of a man who had 'seen' combat" ("Women" 205). Thus we can ask students what value the art offers the study of war. In the twenty-first century, does our fascination with what Mark Selzer has called a "wound culture" influence our desire to single out paintings of trauma as the most authentic representations of war? Do modern viewers find in the images a certain truth that is ratified by literature?

The hazard, then, is limiting the myriad experiences of the conflict to the single emotion of horror. The prolonged boredom and inaction for combatants are represented in witness art from behind the lines; the hospitality huts, brothels, and billets offered comforting, salacious, and enticing entertainments to officers and soldiers. Even so, ethnicity and religion played a role in who had access to these entertainments—the Chinese, indigenous Australians, Maori, African American, and Muslim workers and combatants cannot be said to have the same experience as a painter such as Paul Nash or Fernand Léger.

Paul Fussell famously claimed that the First World War was "a literary war," but it was also a visual war. The British Expeditionary Force included a regiment called the Artists Rifles, and issues of the influential art magazine *The Studio* published the names of artists who had enlisted. War is a traditional subject for art, and the combatant nations of the First World War quickly grasped the opportunity to merge art and propaganda. The Allied nations created offices for war art that produced illustrated recruiting posters, many of which remain distinctive examples of twentieth-century typography, lithography, and graphic design. In addition, through an early effort of what we now know as embedding reporters, artists joined troops in the front lines. Official war artists hired by the governments of England, Canada, Australia, New Zealand, and America were given the freedom to represent landscapes and people in their own stylistic idiom.

George Orwell claimed that "[a]ll art is propaganda" and that "every writer, especially every novelist, *has* 'a message'" (47). The language of poetry, for example, presented a message by examining and representing frontline experience in the Great War; the canonical British war poets expressed a message that was profoundly antiwar. And while the poetry is not propaganda in the sense of a skillful manipulation of a reader's sympathies, it is nonetheless rhetorical. The war poets hoped for social action—changed attitudes, changed actions. War art is also rhetorical. Art of the First World War engages students with the questions of audience, style, and message. Just like poetry or famous novels such as *All Quiet on the Western Front*, the fine arts of painting and drawing represented time and place, encoded personal reactions to conflict, and sought to persuade viewers of the less than heroic consequences of war.

David Roberts observes that the English war poets Siegfried Sassoon, Wilfred Owen, and others, "whether civilian or military personnel, were almost all writing from a personal motive to express and describe their experiences and feelings in response to the war." The official war artists, on the other hand, "were limited in their powers to interpret the war by the subject matter they were required to record" (15). It is telling that Roberts uses the terms *interpret*, *subject matter*, and *record*, for those suggest that the art of the war was predominantly illustrative and representational. However, as the war progressed, the art becomes darker and psychologically richer as those affected by the prolonged engagements pursued their haunted inward visions. Thus the classroom exploration of war's visual culture suggests self-reflective questions: What do we expect to see when we look at war art? Do viewers seek a representation of scenes or an emotional truth of combat experience? Whose experiences do we seek or to which country do we default when we examine the art? Whose experiences count as authentic? Finally, are we seeking paintings to ratify literature, particularly the emphasis on "the pity of war" represented by the English war poets?

Beyond the initial mapping exercise, the curricular activities suggested by this essay depend in large part on using a computer or library to locate images by internationally recognized artists. However, students also may find original artwork close to home, in the diaries and sketchbooks housed in local archives. The private diaries and sketchbooks of combatants often contain maps, scenes of camp life, sketches of planes and tanks, and caricatures or portraits of comrades. After the war, some of the creators donated their diaries to the regiments; some gave them to local historical societies; others put them away in trunks, where they have only recently been rediscovered. Their sketches attest to the need to witness trying times and extraordinary events.

Notes

1. Collections of paintings and etchings in digital collections include the Anne S. K. Brown Military Collection, at the Brown University Library; Archives of American Art, Smithsonian Institution; the *Art of the First World War* Web site, published by the Caen-Normandie Memorial; Australian War Memorial; Canadian War Museum; National World War I Museum at Liberty Memorial, Kansas City; UK Ministry of Defence Art Collection; and Archives New Zealand.

2. Posters may be viewed online at the *Library of Congress* and *Eurpeana* Web sites.

Elizabeth A. Galway

A "School of Arms": Teaching Children's Book Culture of the First World War

Through school plays and textbooks, games and toys, and works of fiction and nonfiction, young readers could not escape the pervasive influence of the First World War. The conflict affected every aspect of the child's life at home, at school, in play, and in the work children performed as part of their support for the war effort. The vast array of anglophone literature that was published in Britain, Europe, America, and Canada from 1914 to 1919 encompassed a variety of representations of the war that contributed to a generation's understanding of this military conflict.

Though a great deal of material for young readers was published during the war years, it has largely been omitted from the teaching of World War I literature. This omission results in part from the fact that many have dismissed children's literature as unworthy of serious academic study. But for those seeking to be comprehensive in their approach to teaching World War I literature, the inclusion of literature for young readers is essential. This significant body of work can be helpful for us in understanding the complex attitudes toward war, nationhood, empire, gender, religion, citizenship, and childhood that existed throughout the war years.

One assumption that is shattered when students begin to study children's literature is that war, violence, and death are considered unsuitable topics for children. Even the most cursory glance at literature from the period reveals that World War I was a key topic for children's authors, and it can demonstrate for students the ways in which definitions of children, childhood, and children's literature have changed over the years. It also shows some of the ways in which children's literature served as propaganda, with authors seeking to instill a particular set of values and attitudes in young readers. My first experience teaching World War I children's literature was in a course on Canadian fiction. The inclusion of noncanonical children's texts enabled students to question some of the dominant narratives of the war that have been presented over the last century and to see that literature from the war, and the attitudes reflected in it, were more varied and complex than they may have originally thought.

Genres and Forms

The wide range of material for children that was published during the First World War included everything from ABC books for very young readers to pamphlets and textbooks aimed at high school students. Book culture included fiction and nonfiction, poetry and songs, novels and short stories, periodicals and magazines, games and crafts, advertisements and textbooks.

Works for early readers, such as *The Child's ABC of the War*, show how the war could serve an educational purpose, as well as the ways in which books could be used to cultivate support for the war and the nation. For example, the letter *L* stands for "the Life we are ready to give / That what we love more may continue to live" (Whitworth, n. pag.): in addition to teaching the alphabet and vocabulary, this book provides a didactic lesson about the importance of making sacrifices for one's nation. ABC books can be used in the classroom to reveal the extent to which the war quickly crept into all aspects of children's lives. In *A to Z in the Puff-Puff*, for example, in which some letters stand for familiar objects, such as "B for Bridge," other letters, such as *M*, which stands for "Military Train," show that elements of warfare quickly became normalized as part of the child's world (R. Williams). Such examples can generate discussion on how a normative childhood is defined and how this definition, and understandings of a child's relation to warfare, may shift over time.

Children of various ages had access to anthologies, some of which were sold to raise funds for the war effort. *Princess Mary's Gift Book*, for instance, contains poems and stories for young readers, some of which were originally published before 1914 but which took on new meaning in the context of war. One example is Rudyard Kipling's poem "Big Steamers." First published in 1911 in *A School History of England* as a celebration of "imperial economic integration" (MacKenzie 112), in the context of the wartime anthology it celebrates the strength of Britain's navy and the loyalty of its empire.

Other anthologies were designed for use in schools and contained a mix of prose, verse, and nonfiction, including excerpts from longer works, such as wartime speeches and historical accounts of events. These anthologies and textbooks are a good source of primary materials and can also foster discussion about how the conflict impacted curriculum and about the role that schools played from 1914 to 1919 in encouraging particular attitudes toward the war.

Periodicals and annuals, which tend to contain a variety of material—advertisements, nonfiction, songs, poetry, serialized novels, and short stories—are among the best resources for those looking to teach a sampling of World War I children's literature. Because they rely on a large number of authors for their material, they provide a broader range of perspectives on the war than a single novel or monograph can.

For American readers, one popular periodical was *St. Nicholas.* Material pertaining to the war could be found throughout this publication, but beginning in September 1915 it included a special section titled "The Watch Tower," which was intended to help readers "learn month by month much about the great things that are happening in all parts of the globe" (Forman 963). From 1915 to 1919 the war was the primary topic of this section. Instructors may find this section particularly useful for comparing how the war was presented to American children before the nation's entry in 1917 with how it was portrayed after.

Chums, *The Boy's Own Paper*, and *The Girl's Own Paper* circulated throughout the British Empire and were read by children in places like Canada and Australia. Instructors can use these resources to consider how British publications may have impacted attitudes toward the war, the empire, and national identity throughout British Empire.

Periodicals are a good source of nonfiction, containing articles on topics such as military heroes and battles and on popular pastimes such as stamp collecting and the making of model ships, planes, and other military objects. Nonfiction accounts of the war, like Stephen Paget's *Essays for Boys and Girls* and Herbert Strang's *Great Britain and the War*, appeared in the form of histories.

Some reading material crosses into the realm of toys and crafts and can be useful for instructors wishing to include discussion of children's material culture. The painting book *Defenders of the Empire*, for example, allows readers to color a series of postcards featuring militaristic images that can then be mailed to friends. This focus on children's play and its connection to the war is apparent in works like the anthology *French Toys* (published in Paris for anglophone readers), which encourages young Americans to help the people of France and Belgium by boycotting the German toy industry.

Children also read and participated in dramatic works, performing in school plays that focused on the war. For example, in an effort to cultivate support for the war in Canada, plays like E. L. Groves's *The Making of Canada's Flag* were performed by schoolchildren, while works like H. J. Bulkeley's *Four War Plays for School Children* were published in Britain.

Novels and series books, of course, adapted to the war. In some cases writers of children's novel series published before 1914 simply altered their tales and characters to reflect the new wartime realities. For example, the illustrated Peek-a-Boos series for young readers, centered on humorous, childlike creatures that were doll-like in appearance, began before 1914 but later included titles such as *The Peek-a-Boos in War Time*, by May Byron. Much fiction was heavily influenced by existing genres such as the spy story and the adventure story, and the war became another backdrop against which to set such tales of adventure. Clair Hayes's *The Boy Allies with Haig in Flanders; or, The Fighting Canadians of Vimy Ridge* (part of his The Boy Allies with the Army Series) is one example that instructors can use to discuss representations of Canadian and American identity, masculinity, and violence in boys' fiction. For an example of how some authors satirized the popular spy story, instructors might use "How We Caught the Spy," by Edward Shirley.

Themes and Topics

Because it is important to situate World War I children's literature in its original historical context, as well as to consider it in relation to changing perspectives on the war over the course of the past century, students should be taught some of the historical facts about the war's origins, its major developments, and its final outcomes and lingering repercussions. Children's literature can be understood as part of the propaganda effort, and there are relatively few pacifist children's publications from the period. Authors attempted to bolster support for the war through cultivating particular attitudes in young readers. At first glance children's literature might appear uniform and purely propagandist, but the variety of themes and topics pervading this material can teach students that the genre was in fact one of great complexity.

The role of religion in the conflict is one theme that instructors can address in relation to prowar sentiment. For example, authors like Robert Harvie used religious doctrine and imagery to argue for the just nature of the Allied cause, claiming that "the cause of Britain to-day is the cause of Christ" (7). Instructors can consider how Christianity impacted (and was in turn impacted by) portrayals of the enemy, notions of military sacrifice, and the desire for peace.

Wartime children's writing also gives voice to changing notions of gender and some of the anxieties these produced. World War I brought about major social changes as women were increasingly required to work outside the traditional domestic sphere, and it played a key role in the eventual success of the women's suffrage movement. Some works, like the article "Women and Patriotism," reinforce traditional notions of femininity and gender roles for young readers. Others, such as Margaret Vandercook's novel *The Red Cross Girls in Belgium*, present female characters as capable and responsible citizens who can serve their nation outside the domestic sphere. Tales of girl munition workers, nurses, Red Cross workers, and ambulance drivers both challenged and sustained traditional notions of femininity. At the same time, masculinity was the focus of much writing, often defined in terms of physical strength, military skill, bravery, and sacrifice. Yet the millions of young men slaughtered, maimed, or injured in the war, which children were made aware of through literature and through their own life experiences, problematized this notion of masculinity, making representations of boyhood and manhood key topics for discussion.

The world's first global conflict cannot be understood without paying attention to questions of nationalism and imperialism. Studying children's works comparatively can reveal the surprisingly nuanced contemporary attitudes toward the war found in a body of literature that was, on the whole, prowar and patriotic. For example, a comparison between American children's literature and that from Britain and Canada illuminates a range of views on the role of the United States during the war. Likewise, comparing American literature published before American entry into the war with that published after reveals some very different attitudes and allows for a consideration of American prowar and antiwar sentiment.

Similarly, much British wartime children's literature celebrates the loyalty of Britain's colonies, but works published in places like Canada provide useful material for comparative analysis. Canadian literature highlights conflicting attitude toward empire: some works champion it, as in Ralph Connor's poem "Canada's Word," and others see it as a hindrance to Canadian national progress. These competing attitudes are sometimes evident in a single work, such as Edith Lelean Groves's play *The Wooing of Miss Canada*.

Discussions of nationhood should also include consideration of race, class, and ethnicity, and there are a range of portrayals of the German enemy. George Orton's 1916 novel *Bob Hunt in Canada*, for example, displays a degree of ambivalence toward Germany that can foster classroom discussion of American neutrality, while Arthur Pier's 1918 novel *The Son Decides: The Story of a Young German-American* outlines concerns about the allegiance of so-called hyphenated Americans. Meanwhile, Charlotte Schaller's book *At War!* and E. V. Lucas's *Swollen-Headed William*, provide examples of humor in promoting anti-German sentiment.

Many wartime children's authors focused intently on cultivating good citizenship in young readers, and teachers might focus on the wartime role of children: Were they seen as victims, or were they seen as productive citizens? Both images are prominent in the literature. Even while some authors highlighted the child's lack of agency during the war and suggested that children needed protection, as seen in Annie Franchot's novel *War Babies*, much literature teaches children that young people played a crucial role in the war—Carroll Smythe's anthology *Mother Goose's Garden*, for example, outlines their responsibilities as citizens. Children were asked to make sacrifices and to serve in numerous ways such as practicing thrift, growing food, contributing money, sewing, and preparing themselves for future service as nurses and soldiers through organizations like the Junior Red Cross and the Boy Scouts. Works such as Ascott Hope's *The School of Arms* even suggest that children could make contributions on the battlefield. Published in New York around 1915, this is a collection of stories about boy soldiers from different historical periods, including World War I, and it suggests that there is a long tradition of young boys fighting in service of their nations.

Resources for Teachers

One of the biggest challenges of teaching children's literature of the First World War is the fact that so much of it is out of print and not readily available. While poetry by the likes of Wilfred Owen and John McCrae has been preserved and canonized, becoming a standard part of the curriculum for courses on twentieth-century literature, much of the children's literature produced between 1914 and 1919 has been forgotten. Children's literature is susceptible to changing market demands and shifting definitions of childhood (and, consequently, changing ideas about what constitutes appropriate literature for children), so many works do not remain in print. The bulk of this material remains housed in historical children's literature collections in Canada, Britain, and the United States, but in recent years there has been an increase in the children's literature available online, making the teaching of this work somewhat easier.

It is not possible here to provide a full bibliography of World War I children's literature, but Michael Paris's *Over the Top* and Susan Fisher's *Boys and Girls in No Man's Land* may provide a starting point for children's titles to teach, as might my own article on boy soldiers. For more about pacifist children's literature, instructors should see Kimberley Reynolds's discussion of antiwar sentiment.

Andrew Maunder

Staging the First World War

> Put your hands up—above your head. They've answered. They're safe! Thank God! Now, you damned spy, your game is up. (*She staggers a little.*) They'll be—all right—they've got my—signal—My God!—it's getting dark again.
>
> —Leslie Styles, *The Day* (1914)

Leslie Styles's *The Day* is just one of over one thousand war plays, pageants, and revues submitted to the theatrical censor in Britain in the years 1914 to 1918. These texts remain a neglected source for understanding how the conflict and its challenges were represented at the time. Yet in the war years these works filled the cultural space inhabited by the many people who flocked to the theaters. When Mary Frobisher, the heavily pregnant heroine of Styles's play, denounces her neighbor William Brown—now revealed as Karl Kruger, a German spy—and foils his wireless invasion signal to a waiting U-boat, it is not too far a stretch to picture hundreds of audience members applauding and cheering enthusiastically. When she slaps him across the face, as she does later, they would have cheered even harder.

These days, few people have heard of Styles or his play. First World War drama has come instead to be represented by R. C. Sheriff's *Journey's End* (1928) and Joan Littlewood and Charles Chilton's *Oh What a Lovely War* (1963). These works are indisputably powerful pieces, but there is something a bit odd about the way they've come to stand in for wartime drama as a whole. They're both postwar pieces written with the benefit of hindsight.

Since 2011, the World War I Theatre Project at the University of Hertfordshire has been attempting to reintroduce the experience of British wartime plays to modern audiences. It has also used these plays as teaching texts in the classroom. There are obstacles to this, of course. Despite the value of such work in a survey course of World War I literature or culture, even if that course has a British focus, it is difficult to justify the inclusion of nakedly jingoistic hacks like Styles or equally unknown playwrights like John Brandon, Berte Thomas, or Gladys Ungar when much of Wilfred Owen, Siegfried Sassoon, and Isaac Rosenberg may have had to be jettisoned because of time constraints.

One of the challenges of teaching wartime theater is that of legacy. Many of the writers we study and whose work has come to dictate our sense of what the war was like were less than complimentary about theater's role. Thus we see Sassoon attacking theater and its "prancing ranks / Of harlots" in his 1917 poem "Blighters" (Walter 181). In "Concert," Richard Aldington records feeling unstirred by the "naked" chorus girls prancing on the stage; "instead of women's living bodies / I see dead men . . . / With sullen dark red gashes / Luminous in a foul trench" (Taylor 197). The trench poets' unappreciation of theater's wartime activity is theater's seeming failure to tell it like it is—its unreality; another is theater's seeming callousness. Given the store we set by these poets' opinions, their words have discouraged us from taking this theatrical world and its wartime activity seriously.

An initial step toward getting students to take such theater seriously is to let them see its presence on the wartime cultural landscape. Wartime diaries and letters can build a picture of theater's role in the lives of individuals. Owen's correspondence with his mother is scattered with his attendance at all kinds of theatrical events, including those that Owen acted in himself. Students could be asked to read or research what he watched. Alternatively, even the most cursory glance at classified advertisements from national or local newspapers of 1914 to 1918—many now available online—confirms the extraordinary liveliness of theatrical activity and the different kinds of entertainments on offer. Sourcing them can be a useful, research-driven way for students to picture the cultural scene and reappraise their sense of life on the home front. "London theatres and halls are full to overflowing," reported the *Bystander* in October 1914, "and never were there such crowds in the streets and cafes" ("War Comments"). Rather than heartless, such activity was conveniently cast as a patriotic determination to carry on as normal and not be bullied by the Germans. Theatrical entertainment was also sold as escapist and therapeutic, and this argument was often used to explain the popularity of musicals and revues: "positively pouring on," as the *Bystander* reported in March 1915, "and without even a particle of a pretence of seriousness of purpose about them" ("In England"). Revues were collections of topical or comic sketches performed by an ensemble cast, interspersed with music. *The Bing Boys Are Here* (1916), *Zig Zag* (1917), and *Hullo America!* (1918) were three of the most popular. It is also still possible for students to hear on the Web songs from Walter Ellis's *A Little Bit of Fluff* (1915; 1,239 performances) or Oscar Asche and Frederick Morton's *Chu Chin Chow* (1916; 2,238 performances) and for them to think about the kinds of representations being offered, particularly as those representations relate to wartime debates about gender. It was this kind of "childish" work against which Sassoon and later George Bernard Shaw reacted so strongly and that helped fix wartime theater in people's minds in the years that followed. Students might be asked to consider whether these songs are childish or whether other adjectives better describe them. John Mullen's recent work on popular song also asks us to consider singing style and the kinds of emotional cues offered in these recordings. What kind of song is it? Is it sung as an anthem? A lament? Does the fact that "Keep the Home Fires Burning," one of the war's most famous songs, was often performed with a hymn-like quality say anything to students about the values being propagated?

An effect of all these seemingly frivolous shows was to make the business of writing a war play, that is to say a play that dealt directly and seriously with warfare, a challenging task. Would commercial managements even take on such a play? In the spring of 1915, Derek Ross lamented how "we are still without a war play of any merit" and how the plays of daring deeds given this label fell short: "We cannot take *The Flag Lieutenant* seriously—West-End drawing-room stuff dished up with a naval sauce and some fuzzy wuzzy shooting. . . . *The Man who Stayed at Home* is the ordinary stage detective story cast in a war setting to fit the moment." In this latter play, a "silly-ass" Bertie Wooster–type hero investigates espionage at a coastal boardinghouse. As Ross saw it, only Thomas Hardy's Napoleonic epic *The Dynasts*, revived in 1914, came near what was needed. Others suggested that the British were "afraid of khaki on the stage—properly handled" and that this fear, linked with the censoring of wounded or dying soldiers on stage—or indeed any kind of soldier, unless he was a stiff-lipped officer or cheerful cockney "Tommy"—was casting a long shadow ("Dramatic Gossip").

In the years from 1914 to 1918 the phrase *war play* meant different things to different people: it suggested something topical that advocated resistance to the enemy; in other contexts, the term indicated a play about war, but this could include a revival of an older production, including Shakespeare; it could be a production that flagged up a particular historical legacy; it could be a play that concerned the impact of the conflict on the individual, even if this was not the main driver of the plot. The plays that the World War I Theatre Project has introduced to students tend to be texts of this last type: thirty-minute plays produced for home front audiences, the short running time a reminder that many were initially staged in variety theaters and music halls. A century later, it has the advantage of making them fit into a seminar. Students can read them out loud and have time to discuss them. In their original theatrical spaces, of course, the plays would form part of a larger program, squeezed in between comedians, acrobats, and dancing dogs.

Edmund Goulding's *God Save the King: A Play of the Moment* is allegedly the first play written in direct response to the outbreak of war. When it premiered on 14 August 1914 at the London Palladium, it was part of a program that included the comedian Little Tich (Harry Relph [1867–1928]) and *Up the River*, billed as a musical aquatic comedy revue most notable for the scanty costumes worn by its chorus. The production of *God Save the King* starred Goulding himself as the young working-class hero—also christened Edmund. The hero is unprepossessing, a man with a "weak heart" (11) on the verge of betraying his country for money, who is roused to action when reminded of the sacrifices made by gallant Englishmen before him—Laurence Oates on Captain Scott's ill-fated polar expedition, and John Phillips, the Marconi Operator of the Titanic, images of whom are projected on the stage's backdrop like specters. Instead of becoming a traitor, Edmund dies a hero. He kills with his bare hands Heinrich Schultz, the family's lodger who reveals himself as a German spy. Edmund then dies of a heart attack brought on by his exertions.[1]

God Save the King is a reminder of the importance of melodrama during the war, in particular the ways in which its traditional emphasis on the struggle between good and evil was reconvened. Students can be asked to think about the role wartime drama played in creating a set of images that could be used in promoting the cause and about the relation between an early play like *God Save the King* and the ideals of courage, sacrifice, and patriotism being popularized at the same time by Rupert Brooke and others. Discussions can also be had about the extent to which *God Save the King* subverts dominant cultural perceptions of World War I, particularly the idea of the conflict as communal. Goulding's play is not as simplistic as might first appear and dispels the idea that the plays of 1914 to 1918 were pure propaganda pieces created to produce docile or compliant minds. Theatergoers were expected to think. The kinds of plays that generate most discussion in the classroom seem to be ones like Gwen John's *Luck of War* (1917), about a returning soldier who discovers that his wife has remarried. The soldier is a brute; the new husband is a decent man. Whom should the wife choose? The play poses a moral dilemma. What would I do in X's situation? Other striking examples are John Brandon's *The Pacifist* (1918) and Berte Thomas's *For My Country* (1917). Both plays show how melodrama maintained its grip on wartime playwrights, but they also pose topical and still relevant questions about the claims of personal relationships versus those of the state. In *The Pacifist*, a doctor poisons her fiancé when she discovers he has been signaling to German ships ("England must come first, always always" [28]). *For My Country* asks whether you, as a mother, would turn over a German spy to the authorities, knowing that if you did so, your son (held hostage by the Germans) would be killed. If you did nothing, your son would be returned to you safely. The play, a two-hander, seems intended to remind audiences that national warfare affects more than just those serving in the army or navy. It is an instance, too, of the ways in which theaters were socially aware spaces. As Susan Grayzel has noted, there was widespread "British confusion about women's . . . contributions to the war" (91). *For My Country* encourages the audience to work through this confusion. In order to compare messages across genres, the play might also be usefully read by students alongside other texts dealing with this issue: Katherine Tynan's poem "The Mother" or Rudyard Kipling's "Mary Postgate" (1915).[2] Another play worth noting here is Maude Deuchar's *The Handmaidens of Death* (1919). As well as considering the strains of munitions work, Deuchar articulates a feeling, voiced by other thinkers of the time, of "incongruity that the mothers and nurturers of the race should also be the primary arms producers" (Ouditt 77). The irony, of course, is that the women in this play are surplus to requirements. Once the war ends, no one will need them, neither men—of which there aren't any—nor other women. Deuchar's pessimistic play captures this dilemma, which is a far cry from the romanticized image of women seen on wartime recruitment posters.

There were plays that questioned the war. These tend to fit more neatly with the narrative of trench poets, and antiwar sentiment was later picked up in the play and film versions of *Oh What a Lovely War!* Miles Malleson's *Black 'Ell* (1916) was initially banned in Britain. It is about a shell-shocked, decorated Englishman, Harold Gould, who is haunted by his killing of a German soldier and who questions the idea of self-defense, on which the war was supposedly launched. Harold's well-meaning parents and fiancée don't understand his anguish, and the play stresses the distance between those who have served and those who haven't. Elsewhere the character of John Woodhouse in Ernest Temple Thurston's three-act play *The Cost*, first performed in London's West End in October 1914, is an early attempt to show shell shock onstage—perhaps the first piece of creative writing to admit its existence. While the play, written when it was widely believed that the conflict would be over in a few months, appears to endorse the war ("War is strife, and strife is the striving of men's souls, and without that striving we should all wither into nothingness" [Maunder 105]), the ruination of the hero's mind and body encourage a resistant reading. His disablement invites criticism of how the war is being run and its long-term effects long before Ivor Gurney's "Strange Hells" or Wilfred Owen's "Mental Cases," texts with which it can usefully be compared in the classroom.

J. M. Barrie's *A Well-Remembered Voice* (1918), about the ghost of a soldier who appears before his father after a séance, is an example of a text that students can research from various perspectives. Students can be asked about the mixed messages coming from the play. Is it propaganda? Biographically the play seems to have been inspired by the death, in Flanders in 1915, of George Llewelyn Davies, one of the original models for Peter Pan and the lost boys of Neverland; students might debate how the play could be seen as Barrie's writing out his own grief. The same play could also prompt them to consider other products of the war—spiritualism and mourning, for example. When it appeared, people were beginning to think about how the generation of dead should be remembered and the necessary process of grieving. The World War I Theater Project's recent production decided to move away from the play's realist aesthetic, to make cuts and have actors step out of character to comment on the action, and the question arises of how these wartime works might be staged now. Do we need to try and recreate what the initial audience would have seen? Or do these plays lend themselves to other kinds of treatments? How could technology help?[3]

Given that in Britain, one result of the recent centenary commemorations of the war has been an interest in the stories that haven't—or have rarely—been told, it seems a fitting time to rediscover some of these theatrical voices. They allow students to explore more of the relations between the home front environment in which our ancestors lived and the cultural signposts they used to find their way through the war's events. For those students more willing to speak in someone else's character and idiolect, there's a potential freshness to such works, whether British or American.[4] We can think not only about their social and cultural significance but also about the methods used by these forgotten playwrights. The naïveté of their voices sometimes stands out to students, but students should be invited to consider the reasons for this naïveté.

Notes

1. A film of the 2011 version is available on the Web at heritagehub.herts.ac.uk/projects/staging-world-war-1.htm.

2. A film can be seen at www.herts.ac.uk/heritage-hub/heritage-and-history-projects/world-war-i-theatre.

3. A clip is on view at researchprofiles.herts.ac.uk/portal/en/activities/a-well remembered-voice-by-jm-barrie-1918(007eec68-91dc-4602-94c6-68d277c300a0).html

4. This essay focuses on Britain, but audiences in New York, for example, saw similar kinds of entertainment. Spy plays such as Berte Thomas's *Out of Hell* (1917), F. Tennyson Jesse and H. M. Harwood's *Billeted* (1917), and Walter Howard's *Seven Days Leave* (1917) were hits in both countries, although, as was often the case with British plays, the New York versions were tweaked to appeal to American sensibilities. More obviously political American plays were Marion Craig Wentworth's *War Brides* (1914), Beulah Dix's *Moloch* (1916), and Alice Dunbar-Nelson's *Mine Eyes Have Seen* (1918), the last a rare onstage discussion of the conscription of black Americans for the war. America's stance during the war is also presented (unsympathetically) in Sewell Collins's one-act play *The Quitter*, produced in London in 1917. The works by Wentworth and Dunbar-Nelson are available in Claire Tylee's anthology *War Plays by Women*.

Carol Acton

Life and Death at the Front: Life Writing, Literature, and the Language of War

In 1915 a young British officer, Roland Leighton, finding the decayed bodies of German soldiers in a trench, writes a letter home angrily denouncing the abstract rhetoric of "Honour" or "Love of Country" that sent these men to their deaths, declaring that only those who "have known and seen" can reveal the horror obscured by the abstraction (qtd. in Brittain, *Chronicle* 198). This rejection of war propaganda emphasizes the power of language to conceal or reveal. An English literature course necessarily lends itself to examining the way language constructs war and, more specifically, how life writing allows us to enter, as far as possible, the subjective experience of knowing and seeing war.

My own course uses life writing along with more conventional literary texts to show students the power of language to articulate war and consider where language breaks down in conveying the experience to those outside it. In addition to canonical war writing, such as the poetry of Wilfred Owen and Edmund Blunden's memoir *Undertones of War*, the course analyzes the often less publicly acknowledged experience voiced in letters, diaries, and memoirs to explore how language constructs war and the wartime self. While the primary texts are British (the course fulfills a British literature requirement), I manage this limitation by asking students to consider a much broader range of writings from different theaters of war, backgrounds, sex, and age range, including translated texts, in their research assignments. Students then present their research to the class in formal presentations and more informally in small discussion groups so that life writing from other nationalities and locations, such as North America, Russia, Italy, Germany, Switzerland, and Turkey, allow us to explore a world war experience at the local and personal level. Three collections of extracts from memoirs, letters, and diaries have been especially useful for this purpose: *Lines of Fire: Women Writers of World War I*, edited by Margaret Higonnet; *Intimate Voices from the First World War*, edited by Svletana Palmer and Sarah Wallis; and Zlata Filipović and Melanie Challenger's collection *Stolen Voices: Young People's War Diaries from World War I to Iraq*. From raw diary entries to literary memoirs, these writings offer an entry into war as a lived experience in the front lines, at casualty clearing stations, in hospitals behind the front lines, and on the home front. Focusing on the private subjective experience allows students to consider war in terms of Margaret Higonnet and Patrice Higonnet's call for understandings of war to move past "a specifically militarized front or . . . institutionally defined arena, to include the private domain and the landscape of the mind" (46).

The range of writings we examine allows us to consider common themes across different classes and nations, for example the role of witnessing injury and death in questioning the war. Thus the German nurse Käthe Russner asks if "our charges yearn for just one thing, peace. . . . Why, then, the sacrifice of all these lives?" (qtd. in Higonnet, *Lines* 226). The Canadian nurse Clare Gass describes the wounds and the mental exhaustion of her recently arrived "convoy of patients":

> Some terrible cases, oh so much better dead (one young lad with eyes & nose all gone—one blur of mangled flesh—& body whole and sound.) heads shattered to pieces or limbs hanging by a thread of tendons. Oh why must such things be [sic] All are so brave, & yet those who are not badly wounded are so tired of the war . . . tired in such a hopeless way. (Mann 32)

Eric Appleby, a British artillery officer, writes to his Irish fiancée, "It's nearly nineteen long months since I came out here. I seem to have lived this kind of life all my days, and everything that came before seems like a dream. When will the nightmare end?" (qtd. in Kelly 270). The Turkish officer Mehmed Fasih at Gallipoli mourns his dead sergeant: "Oh my Lord!

How many more tragedies will you make me witness? Nuri has injuries to his chest, head, one arm and both legs. His head and chest are ripped wide open. . . . He seems to be cursing those who destroyed him. I can't stand it anymore" (qtd. in Palmer and Wallis 137–38).

As these extracts show common (as well as differing) responses across different allegiances, so the writings transcend the gendered boundaries that often define war. Nurses may not be combatants, but they bear witness to the horror of massive injury and death; women at home may be removed from the physical actuality of war, but they participate emotionally, through anxiety, fear, loss, and grief. They also come to know war in the letters from husbands, sons, and lovers at the front. Combatants such as Appleby often confide their emotional pain to women at home, as well as describe death and injury in graphic terms.

Such exchanges challenge the gulf between home and front that many canonical memoirs emphasize and break down binaries that separate ally and enemy. Medical personnel writings especially allow us to see a story that is even more rarely told: that of the soldier once he becomes sick or wounded and is no longer a combatant. The title of the volunteer nurse Mary Borden's *The Forbidden Zone*, for example, claims a legitimacy of her witness to war in a space forbidden to women because war is defined as an exclusively male endeavor.

Bringing this range of writings to the classroom works best in my experience when the class is small (approximately fifteen) and can be conducted as a seminar. This format allows for assignments that rely on strong working relations between students that continue outside the classroom. While students do write conventional essays, the emphasis is equally on presentations, group work, and creating a classroom environment that facilitates discussion in a way that is not possible in a much larger class. The model for the group work end product came out of an original World War I nurse's album, owned by a student's family and brought to class by the student at the beginning of the term as an artifact that represented a very specific human experience. Each student contributed a section, either digital or hardcopy, of an album that reflected on their group discussion and group research. In these discussions students brought research conducted outside class back to a weekly in-class meeting of twenty to thirty minutes so they could exchange ideas in their groups. This collaboration allowed them to share research and thus increased their exposure to more primary and secondary texts than they would have had time to research on their own. While the group work focused on oral discussion, students submitted individual reflective journals to me over the term. The journals allowed me to see how they were responding to the readings and to the group discussion as well as allowed them to choose topics outside the formal structure of the essay. Responses ranged from the personal—for example, examining a family connection with the war (I encourage this examination as a further means of engagement with the material)[1]—to thinking about the politics of war and commemoration and the relation between that politics and firsthand experiences of those who participated in the war.

We begin the course with *The Forbidden Zone*, a modernist rendering, in what Borden calls "fragments," of her work as a volunteer nurse on the Western Front. In pointing to the problems of war writing, which paradoxically communicates and fails to communicate an extreme and often traumatic experience, her preface frames our thinking about the course material. The preface draws students into this paradox through her articulation of the connections among the writer as witness, the representation of the experience and the limitations of language, and the position of the reader.

Borden opens by claiming her legitimacy as witness to war: "I have not invented anything in this book. The sketches and poems were written between 1914 and 1918. The five stories I have written recently from memory; they recount true episodes that I cannot forget." She then points to the limitations of expression, which, she implies, are both psychological and linguistic:

> To those who find these impressions confused, I would say that they are fragments of a great confusion. Any attempt to reduce them to order would require artifice on my part and would falsify them. To those on the other hand who find them unbearably plain, I would say that I have blurred the bare horror of facts and softened the reality in spite of myself, not because I wished to do so, but because I was incapable of a nearer approach to the truth.

She closes by emphasizing the relation of the uninitiated reader to the text:

> I have dared to dedicate these pages to the Poilus who passed through our hands during the war, because I believe they would recognise the dimmed reality reflected in these pictures. But the book is not meant for them. They know, not only everything that is contained in it, but all the rest that can never be written. (6)

Through discussion of this preface I introduce students to ongoing questions that must be asked of war writing: Who is authorized to speak? To what extent do writers use a perceived breakdown in communication to sustain their legitimacy as carriers of ineffable knowledge? These concerns about the limitations of language allow the class to grapple with the idea that war writing is often as much about what cannot be (or is not) communicated as what can. During the most recent iteration of the course, this problem made its way into discussion of the relation between the combatant and the civilian in Phil Klay's *New York Times* article "After War, a Failure of the Imagination" (8 Feb. 2014). Klay argues that the imagination is the point where war veteran as writer and civilian as reader can meet to try and overcome the supposed incommunicability of the war experience. His discussion brought to the class a timely reminder of the connection that is often ignored in our culture between politics and the role of literature and the imagination.

The relation between politics and the imaginative recreation of war in poetry was a concern in many works we now consider canonical, such as Blunden's memoir and poetry by the best known of the war poets, including Owen, Siegfried Sassoon, and Isaac Rosenberg. We look at poets' letters and diaries, where available, alongside the poetry to examine how certain incidents translate from the immediate capturing in a letter or diary into the poetic. Sassoon, for example, often includes early drafts of poems in his diary. To begin our reading of war poetry and to discuss the translation of extreme experience and bearing witness to horrific events into an aesthetic form, I use Seamus Heaney's discussion of the relation among poetry, aesthetics, and traumatic experience, what Heaney calls "song and suffering," in his essay "The Interesting Case of Nero, Checkhov's Cognac and a Knocker." Reading life writing and poetry (as a representative of the aesthetic) in the same course, where the focus on both is language, allows for comparison of very different forms: for example, by juxtaposing the representation of death by gas in Owen's "Dulce et Decorum Est" to Vera Brittain's experience of nursing gassed men in *Testament of Youth*.

To create the theoretical framework in which to read this varied material without employing a hierarchy of literary aesthetic, and through which students can engage with this immediate and disturbingly graphic writing, I make use of secondary readings: Elaine Scarry's *The Body in Pain*, Kali Tal's *Worlds of Hurt*, Judith Butler's *Frames of War*, and Sidonie Smith and Julia Watson's *Reading Autobiography*. Scarry asserts that the "[t]he main purpose and outcome of war is injuring" but that public representation of war "disowns" injury, asserting that "the perpetuation of war would be impossible without th[is] disowning of injury" (63–64). We examine how these writers own injury and death and the emotions that attend witnessing. In reading Tal, we consider how language attempts to overcome such disowning and articulates trauma, as well as how gaps and silences can reveal what cannot be adequately expressed. Tal also points to the problem of communicating trauma because of the "transformation of meaning" between signifier and signified, such that the reader or listener cannot hear the meaning carried in the words of the survivor. She writes that "[t]raumatic experience catalyzes a transformation of meaning in the signs individuals use to represent their experiences. Words such as *blood, terror, agony* and *madness* gain new meaning, within the context of the trauma, and survivors emerge from the traumatic environment with a new set of definitions" (16). Language also informs Butler's question, "When is life grievable?," where Butler confronts the othering that makes war possible. Arguing that societies accept war because it is framed through language that allows us to ignore the common precariousness and grievability of all lives, valuing only that of our own side, she asks, "[W]hat would it take not only to apprehend the precarious character of lives lost in war, but to have that apprehension coincide with an ethical and political opposition to the losses war entails?" (13).

In applying life writing theory, we explore how language and narrative create a relation between writing and the ordering and controlling of a physically and emotionally demanding experience, especially how the self in extremis is constructed. In the case of medical personnel, such a reading is complicated by the fact that these men and women often foreground the suffering that surrounds them, representing their own experience only obliquely. In this context, life writing theory as outlined in Smith and Watson's *Reading Autobiography*, together with recent work on the psychology of war experience and the construction of memory (see, e.g., Hunt), can offer ways to think about how language articulates or fails to articulate the subjective experience. Importantly, these theoretical approaches work across genres and translated texts and also make connections between the more literary critical analysis and a broader cultural studies approach that can include historical, sociological, and psychological perspectives.

I encourage students to consider subjectivity as a crucial position from which to understand the war as a lived experience in a particular cultural context and as a way of engaging with it at our own historical moment.

One student's journal response captures such a connection and affirms the success of this approach:

> I seriously doubt the significance of Remembrance Day. It fails to help me remember. You know what does: learning about war two days out of every week.
>
> There is no grandiose celebration in class. Students do not bow their heads every day before the lesson begins and raise a collective patriotic voice of thanks to the invisible soldiers of WWI. We get our noses right down in the books. None of the students stay in absolute silence. We talk about what we have learned from what we read the day before. I have found that I remember the soldiers of WWI, but in a way that actually matters to me.
>
> When I am in class, talking and listening about the conditions of the trenches, the letters writers sent to their loved ones, and the recorded memories of a fallen friend, that is when I sense that the concepts of duty, respect, and gratitude become more tangible. This happens because I come to love these men through their words.[2]

Notes

1. After posing some probing questions to her family, one student uncovered a background worthy of fiction: a missing soldier returned to find his wife remarried with two children.

2. I would like to thank Amber O'Brien for permission to reproduce these comments.

David Williams

Representations of Time: Film and Great War Writing

To students who can't wait to text or tweet before they're out the classroom door, the Battle of the Somme can seem as remote as the Battle of Waterloo once did to British and dominion troops who fought and died at Beaumont-Hamel on the First of July 1916. More remote, perhaps, since the boys of 1916 had at least encountered Napoleon and Wellington in the fixities of print. But in the relentless now of electronic information networks, history is that nebulous time before there were status updates on *Facebook*.

Yet tell your class that 19,240 British soldiers were killed on the first day of a five-month battle, with twice that many wounded, and there's a flicker of interest. Show a clip of "A Sunken Road in No Man's Land," from Charles Urban's *The Battle of the Somme* (D. Williams, "Film" 170), and the past comes back to life in three slow shots of seated boys staring out of frame, rifles bristling with bayonets, most of them about to die within minutes. You remind the class that, while we are looking at ghosts, they are present to us in ways that no soldier at Waterloo ever was. Remember, you say, though you see them, they can't see you.

Cut to "The Attack" (likely faked), where, safely back of the line, you watch men who have "Leaped over the Trench Parapets" now clamber over barbed wire and "Advanc[e] towards the German Trenches under Heavy Fire." And then you read "British Tommies Helping a Comrade," followed by the sight of men coming up a trench, one hatless soldier in khaki carrying a dying comrade on his back, his eyes staring soulfully up into the lens, imploring help from above. By this time, every eye is transfixed, and no one is surprised to learn that this film is still the greatest box office success in British history, drawing half of Britain's forty-three million people to see it within six weeks of its release. Why the public hysteria, given the glacial pace of its editing? Maybe, a student timidly offers, it allowed audiences to see what they had only read about in newspapers. Doesn't the face of that man carrying his buddy cry out for help? A more advanced student invokes a rudimentary theory of interpellation. Then a young woman asks, Were viewers maybe hoping to catch a glimpse of a loved one? And the point is made. Film is a window into time; we are looking at time in these scenes.

So why did soldiers mock the film? The poet Wilfred Owen wrote to his mother, "Those 'Somme Pictures' are the laughing stock of the army" (Letter to Susan Owen 429). A young woman in a freshman class called Literature and New Media wonders aloud if it was because soldiers felt as if they were reduced to factory workers. And someone else recalls the scene of men unloading trucks and stacking shells like cordwood. Aren't those "Canadian 60 Pounders" just more machines waiting to be fed, their casings removed, as artillerymen rush to and fro, blasting explosives toward the horizon? Another voice cracks with sudden excitement: So Owen must have felt like they were cogs in a wheel, even interchangeable parts! This is a good place to show a four-minute clip called "Taylorism on ABC World Report."

If it's an upper-year course on media and literature of the Great War, you might show Elizabeth Cornell's video *The Ford Motor Co. and Taylorism* and repeat Henry Ford's line about cars rolling off the assembly line "like the successive negatives on a motion picture film" (qtd. in Grierson 27). Isn't film assembled out of a myriad of parts like cars on the assembly line? And you can finally introduce Michael Hammond's idea that the "Somme picture" belongs to the genre of "industrial process films," which follow "an object through the series of tasks necessary to its creation" (111). Still, you need to ask why this "industrial process" ends in a long shot of German prisoners marching to boxcars for transport to England. What did the British War Office want us to see as the finished product? Prisoners of war, the class agrees, the product of an efficient British war machine. And what did soldiers think was the finished product? A lot of rubble, one boy says to hoots of laughter. Answers vary from the literal to the poetic: a muddy wasteland, the Four Horsemen of the Apocalypse.

But on occasion an attentive viewer will recall an eight-second shot of a burial detail laying out dead bodies. The camera angle of that image of bodies laid side by side evokes an earlier image of artillery shells laid out in rows. Corpses were the finished product, a voice drips with irony. No wonder the film was a joke! No wonder soldiers grimaced at what the film let slip. To them, corpses were the sole product of the war machine, both German and British corpses.

To sum up what audiences saw in this film, they were hoping back home for a glimpse of Tommy before he died, to see his ghost. There he is, waving at us as they march by on that dusty road; now he's kneeling to wash at the edge of that stream! But frontliners steadfastly refused to see this ghostly time on screen, only the finished product. Not the one envisioned by the War Office, either, of that finished product of assembled prisoners. To the men in the trenches, film was no ghostly presence of another time but the deadly mechanization of time, a mere illusion of movement produced by mechanical means.

So why, you ask at the start of another class on *All Quiet on the Western Front*, does Remarque show those coffins stacked up beside "a shelled school-house," then have his narrator add, "The coffins are really for us. The organization surpasses itself in that kind of thing" (100)? While German troops were unlikely to view the British film, the incident reveals a recurring animus against industrialism and its mechanization of time in canonical Great War novels. Could that explain the present tense of Remarque's narrator, who dies a page before the novel's end, since his camera eye continues to run? From the first page, this relentless present tense of verbal cinema lends sharp immediacy to everything and everyone. And time is further flattened in flashbacks by Remarque's cinematic straight cuts that continue the present tense of the verb; differing times are conflated as they are in motion pictures. Given a total suppression of the future tense, the primacy of present over past in this novel supports its valorization of images over language, aiding and abetting the relentless attack on authority that turns on an older generation's falsifying of language. "We had suddenly learned to see," Paul Baümer says in what is a true leitmotif in the novel (13).

American and Canadian teachers might add or substitute *Generals Die in Bed* (1930), a vivid novel by the New York writer Charles Yale Harrison, who served with the 14th Montreal Battalion until he was wounded in August 1918. One advantage of *Generals* is the likelihood that the narrator has seen, and is actually responding to, Urban's film. Like Remarque's novel, *Generals* is narrated in the present tense, jumping in chapter 1 from an embarkation parade in Montreal to the trenches in chapter 2. Do these titles remind you of anything: "In the Trenches," "Out on Rest," "Back to the Round," "Bombardment," "Béthune," "London"? By now a chorus exclaims, the intertitles in Urban's film! And from this point on, there's a broad menu of scenes that parody the British propaganda film. In one scene, for example, five men fight over scant rations before a sniper shoots one of them, leaving extra rations to be divided up—a particularly bitter comment on Urban's cheery scene titled "The Royal Warwickshires Having a Meal." In another, the men ride to and fro all night in the back of a lorry, still unfed and forced to defecate over the side of a bouncing vehicle. Urban's scene of men in "Seeking Further Laurels," grinning and waving helmets as they march past, turns into a sick joke.

And how might this scene from the novel be a comment on the film? "The lorry rumbles and bounces on. We are tossed about like quarters of beef on the way to market" (123). The class shouts: The assembly line! The slaughterhouse! The meatpacking plant! But is it markedly different from this episode in the novel? Outside a French bordello, there waits "a long line of avid men who stare hungrily at the brightly lit door of the house as it opens every now and then and emits a khaki-clad figure which hurries off into the dark. The line moves up one pace" (81). Most agree that the sexual act is here reduced to automation, or, as one student puts it, to conveyer-belt sex. So you return to the idea of the mechanization of time, and the germ of an idea begins to grow: Great War writing is often about the cultural disturbance of industrial production as much as it is about the war.

If it's an upper-year class, you ask, Could film be complicit in this mechanization of time? And you show a clip from Lewis Milestone's film adaptation of *All Quiet on the Western Front* (1930), with its panning shot of Allied troops advancing on a German machine-gun emplacement. From the view of the attackers the gun appears in a static shot as a machine spitting death; from the outlook of defenders, it sweeps across the line of vision as if the camera itself were cutting the swath of death (Eberwein 70). Neither Arthur Edeson's cinematography nor Lewis Milestone's editing draws back from implicating the camera in the industrial production of corpses; to their credit, they identify their own medium with the cultural disturbance of the war.

The narrator of *Generals* similarly identifies the war with cinema in his dugout, where candlelight, wavering from artillery blasts, turns into "a steady rapid flicker. We look like men seen in an ancient, unsteady motion picture" (53). Perhaps it's more than the threat of immediate death that makes him say, "We do not know what day it is" (14), thereby emptying *now* of its significance. Is his cinematically styled narration just a symptom, or is it also a cause of his inability to imagine past or future? "I try to imagine what Montreal looks like. The images are murky. All that is unreality. The trench, Cleary, Fry, the moon overhead—this is real" (10). What are we to think of his refusal to see any time but *now*? Does he think of time as an automated process? Is it really more to him now than passing frames of film drained of meaning?

And does this mean that viewers have no choice? Must we conflate his loss of the past as past—distinct in time and place—with both the medium and its antiwar message? Here is a good place to read the passage where Harrison's narrator rages against a crowd of civilians laughing at a London stage show about his war. "They should be made to remember," he snorts at the suggestion that they want only to forget the war (89). By his choice of means to make them see what he has seen, has he not turned his past into the universal present? Could this be an attempt to prevent "viewers" from exposing one final lie—not the "old Lie" of Wilfred Owen's anti-Horatian ode—in the novel's climactic event?

In a Canadian context, this ultimate lie is doubly complicated because of the myth of the Canadian peacemaker who has worn the blue beret of UN peacekeepers in every conflict from Suez in 1956 to Cyprus to Bosnia to East Timor. Students, in fact, are often surprised by Harrison's account of Canadians as fierce fighters. Some will protest, "But we're peace*keepers*, not peace*makers*, like they are down south," although Canada's role in Afghanistan has begun to soften such attitudes in the last decade.

So what is the big lie in *Generals* and how is it related to the book's cinematic style? At the end, the narrator is haunted by a war crime playing endlessly in the cinema of his mind: "I remember the funny jerky steps of the prisoners as they came running towards us with their hands held high above their heads—I see the clasped hands lifted over the lip of the shell hole as we fired into it—clasped hands silently asking for pity" (152). The scene is shocking, because it implicates Canadians in the sort of war crime we have witnessed from Auschwitz to Cambodia to Rwanda. And seeing is believing, at least until you check the facts (Cook 426; Nicholson 398) and notice the flattening effects of *General*'s presentism, with its motivated refusal to set the scene in a longer time sequence.

But is film to blame for the oversimplifications of Harrison's prose cinema? Has its mode of production or its mechanism of presentation rendered it unable to represent any time but the present? Or do prose cineastes like Harrison and Remarque also betray an ideological bias in modeling their narratives on film? Here, "The Return of the Dead," a fourteen-minute sequence from Abel Gance's Great War film *J'accuse* (1919) offers a different vision of time on film and of the time of war. And it helps explain the conflicting responses of soldiers and home audiences to Urban's film.

Gance's sequence begins with the protagonist, Jean Diaz, returning from the front to his lover, Edith Laurin, who struggles to understand his fevered musings: "The nightmare . . . the dreams . . . life . . . the war . . . the dead . . . and the living . . . I no longer know! I accuse!" But as she begins to see what Jean sees, we also watch the dead rising from the cemetery where he stands sentry—see them in their thousands forming up on parade. Later, Gance cut into this scene postwar footage of the Victory Parade of 1919 through La Place d'Étoile, splitting the screen horizontally into a bottom half of the French army filing through L'Arc de Triomphe, and the army of Jean's dead marching in the upper half of the frame above the victorious French army, until the marchers converge in single plane of tree-lined roads in the Midi.

A *PowerPoint* image of Édouard Detaille's *Le rêve* is useful at this point to recall the dream of defeated French soldiers in 1870 sleeping in a field as bannered columns above them parade across the heavens to the stars (en.wikipedia.org/wiki/%C3%89douard_Detaille#/media/File:Detaille_Le_R%C3%AAve.jpg). What, you ask the class, is the greatest difference between this painting of Napoleon's ghostly troops and Gance's use of it? Someone invariably notices how painted soldiers don't move; just the ones on film do. The truism points to something essential about each medium: the past is always inert on canvas, but it lives again on film. Gance's dead may return to be seen by their loved ones, but they also come to learn if their deaths "have been to any purpose."

So you ask: Does it matter that Gance's dead were real French soldiers, two thousand of them loaned out on their precious week of leave to shoot these scenes? Many of them went back to die at Verdun in the last month of the war, turning the film into a literal haunting. But hasn't the medium always enabled the filmmaker to raise ghosts at will, to close that gap you see in Detaille's painting between sky and earth? While the villagers can't cross the barrier of death, don't they stare for a moment into eternity? And don't we see what they see: the face of time in this fourth dimension of film? Isn't this what home front audiences glimpsed in *The Battle of the Somme*, even when the War Office tried to show them German prisoners, while British Tommies saw only corpses at the end of the assembly line? Each of these outlooks, it appears, is determined by ideological differences more than by properties inherent to the medium.

In another long-lost classic of the Great War, the plot of Will R. Bird's memoir *And We Go On* (1930) parallels Gance's "The Return of the Dead," not as celluloid fantasy but as perceptible reality, verifiable by the senses of sight and touch. The ghost of Will's brother Steve, who was blown to bits in 1915 by a trench mine in Flanders, appears to save Will's life a dozen times between his entry into theater at the end of 1916 and the Armistice in 1918. Still more remarkable is Will's sense of the war taking shape under the hand of "some master director" (149) as he witnesses a cavalry charge in the breakthrough at the Battle of Amiens. Four decades later, he explicitly likens the cavalry pursuit to "a grand movie scene" (*Ghosts* 147). Even more telling, in the revised text of 1968, entitled *Ghosts Have Warm Hands*, the voice of this apparition now speaks aloud (169), as he never did in the silent film era, where he simply "faded" or disappeared into thin air (*And We* 48). The point is not just that Bird was now acclimated to the talkies or using differing resources available to silent cinema and sound-era film. Rather it is the sense that in either era there is always "a ghost in the machine" (D. Williams, "Spectres" 120).

So what do Bird's revisions finally say about memory? And how do differing media affect our recollection of events? Do differing media environments alter our sense of time? Is the past over and done with? Or could it still exist in a hidden dimension of space, like film's fourth dimension of time? In what ways does the written word also change in response to new media like film or that smartphone you have in your hand? Post your answers, please, once you are completely clear of the classroom door.

Deborah D. Buffton

Memorials as Text: Debating the War's Meaning through Monuments

War memorials fill our world to a much larger degree than peace memorials. The former are so common that they can become almost invisible to us. And yet war memorials provide a wealth of information about how a major cataclysm such as World War I has been remembered. Teachers in political science, history, women's studies, art, and sociology can use memorials to illustrate or explore a variety of questions or topics relevant both to their disciplines and to understanding World War I itself.

War memorials are physical reminders, portraying a particular idea or narrative about the war to people who may never have experienced it. While students may know about the surface aspects of war—battle strategies, generals, lives of individual soldiers—they rarely learn about war's deeper cultural and social meanings and effects. Studying memorials helps them understand why we, as individuals and as a society, see wars in particular ways ("the Good War," "the Lost Cause," a fight for democracy, etc.). Further, looking at the memorials, along with the process of their creation, can help students see postwar values, ideals, and tensions in the time and place in which the memorials appear.

Following World War I, local and national politicians, families of soldiers, artists, veterans, and the general public understood the power of memory and the need to preserve the war's lessons for future generations. There was obviously more than one lesson to be learned, and often the lesson one group wanted to remember was at odds with the lesson of another. Establishing memorials became an important part of determining which lessons were passed along and which were not. In some cases, the memorials were constructed (i.e., monuments or statues). In other cases, certain places, such as battlefields (Verdun, France, for example), were declared to be themselves monuments (Prost, "Verdun" and "Monuments"). Many of these monuments and places became sites of pilgrimage and tourism for veterans, their loved ones, and ultimately the general public (Lloyd 1–2). These structures and sites taught the visitors about the meaning of the war, about the virtues of a good citizen, and also, sometimes unintentionally, about the political and social concerns at the time the memorials were established. It is important to remind students that memorials, whether constructed or designated, were created after the event they commemorated—in some cases decades later. Thus they reflect not simply feelings at the time of the event but also the issues that were important to communities and nations later on.

The process by which these memorials were created was anything but straightforward. Often initiated in a top-down manner, the projects nonetheless had to take into account local concerns. Monuments and statues came about through the work of local committees, through artistic competitions, and through government initiatives. In many countries, as in France, building monuments was an industry; there were catalogs from which towns could select mass-produced, interchangeable pedestals and statuary (Sherman 145–46). So the process was a complicated one, in which artists, national and local politicians, businesses, community leaders, veterans, and the families and friends of those being honored all tried to have a voice. The creation both opened up and closed down dialogue about the war. Monument building opened up spaces in which to grieve, to honor the dead, to celebrate national values, and in some cases to eschew war. But the process could also close off the individual experiences as well as the opportunity to question the war's causes, consequences, and necessity. Monuments often provided a single narrative that allowed the state to justify itself and its reliance on war. The creation of war memorials, then, offers important questions for educators to raise with students. Whose voices were heard in the creation, and whose got lost? Is there a way to recapture the voices that were muted in the process of remembering the past? Whose past was remembered, and whose was not? Who made the decision? Beyond portraying the war experience, what else was reflected in these monuments, either intentionally or not? And why is it significant that we remember the war in this particular way?

To get at these larger questions, teachers might ask students to explore some more specific ones. Who paid for the memorial? Who designed it? What can we say about the design? Does it reflect a particular artistic style? It is striking or conventional? Who built it? Where was it located? Who determined the location? What sorts of ceremonies accompanied its dedication, and what sorts took place in later years? Was it a scene of any acts of political (or other) defiance? Does the memorial continue to resonate, or has it come to be irrelevant to the life of the community? What symbolic messages did the monument send, and were these intentional or unintentional? Did the messages change over time—that is, did later generations understand the original message from the memorial or a different one? What questions does the memorial raise about the political process? What message do World War I monuments offer us today about commemoration, politics, the social fabric, World War I, and war in general? Students today have grown up in a world in which war has been a constant reality. The questions they raise about World War I, and the answers they find, can help them understand the ways war and memory work in their war-torn world today.

World War I monuments serve a variety of purposes. Some memorials teach particular civic virtues (e.g., the Monument aux Fusillés). Other memorials make statements about gender roles and expectations (e.g., the Monument à Louise de Bettignies). Still others, through the process by which they were created, reveal values and conflicts in a particular society at different times (e.g., the Monument Foch). The following sections offer examples of the kind of close reading of monuments that teachers might engage in with students. This general approach can be taken with any monument, including, perhaps especially, local monuments.

Monument aux Fusillés

In the northern French town of Lille, there is a popular monument called the Monument aux Fusillés ("monument to those who were shot"), created in 1929 by Félix-Alexandre Desruelles (1865–1943). It commemorates five local men who were shot by the Germans in 1915 for espionage. The monument shows the men at the moment of execution. Four of them stand facing the firing squad, while the fifth, an eighteen-year-old named

Léon Trulin, lies dead next to them. This is a dramatic scene but, interestingly, historically inaccurate. The four men who are still standing were actually shot six weeks before Trulin. Moreover, they never worked with him. Trulin worked separately, was arrested separately, charged separately, and executed separately. This is the first clue that the purpose of this monument was to portray not historical truth but something else. So we need to raise some questions: Why did the sculptor choose to show all five men together and to show Trulin being killed first, when he was actually killed last? Why does the sculptor portray these five and none of the other civilians shot by the Germans during the war for various crimes of resistance? What did the five represent that the sculptor wished to remember or have others remember about the war?

In fact, the portrayal of the five men was a source of a great discussion that included the families of the men; the Lille Municipal Council, which gave permission for the monument to be built; the editors of the local newspaper; prominent citizens; and the sculptor himself. The questions to discuss in class become, Whose voice got heard? Who was silenced, and why? Who was permitted to write this chapter in the history of World War I in Lille?

By examining minutes of municipal council meetings, sculptor's sketches, and local newspaper accounts, we can begin to approach these questions. Trulin was the youngest of the five. His family initially complained that he was shown blindfolded, which they believed made him look cowardly. It was also inaccurate, as eyewitnesses confirmed that he'd rejected the blindfold at his execution. He was also portrayed in short pants, which they believed made him look like a little girl. Ultimately, the artist removed the blindfold in the interests of historical accuracy but refused to change the pants, which he claimed were not short pants at all but a soldier's leggings (Archives Municipales de Lille [AML], box no. 3 M 27).

We can make more sense of this disagreement when we discover that the press clearly wanted to emphasize Trulin's youth as a way to heighten the perceived cruelty of the execution. Trulin was regularly identified as being fifteen rather than eighteen, for example. While his age would have been easy enough to confirm, portraying him as a young boy served a purpose. It is one thing to execute men in their forties and fifties, who know what they are getting into with resistance work; it is quite another to execute a child. So the family's desire that Trulin be remembered as a brave young adult conflicted with the desire of the sculptor and the municipal council to comment on German cruelty.

The portrayal of Eugene Jacquet, the leader of a resistance network, also created debates. The monument committee explicitly directed the artist to portray him "with his hands in his pockets in an attitude of fierce disdain, showing this to all by bravely exposing his chest to enemy fire" (AML, 3 M 27). The family complained that this posture was completely uncharacteristic of Jacquet; however, the municipal council sought to show a national hero, not necessarily to immortalize a local man as he was in life. The artist explained the "proper" interpretation of each man's demeanor in a statement published in the local paper. In the monument, each man represents one of the following values: defiance of the enemy, Christian faith and humility, military bravery, youthful innocence, and humanity. This monument, then, was created less to help people remember five brave men from World War I than to provide a sort of textbook showing the virtues that future generations should practice. Ironically, the process of teaching that lesson erased the actual identity of the men, and they became symbols instead of real people. Teachers might introduce local monuments and ask students what messages they find and what those messages reflect about the values of the larger society.

In an interesting coda to this story, the Germans destroyed the monument in 1940 when they invaded the region in World War II. It was recreated in 1960 by Germaine Oury-Desrouelles but was defaced in 1970 by opponents of the Vietnam War, who saw the monument as promoting militarism, not civic virtue in defiance of militarism (AML, 3 M 28). Exploring this monument and its life cycle offers an opportunity for teachers to address the ways monuments insert political messages into civic life and illustrate the political ideals of a society. In addition, this is a fine way to examine the role of dissent. Teachers can use the example to get students to think about the ways the original meanings of certain things (statues, rituals, etc.) get lost as societies change over time.

Monument à Louise de Bettignies

A second monument in Lille can teach students about gender roles and expectations in war. The Monument à Louise de Bettignies was erected in 1927 by Maxime Réal del Sarte to celebrate a local woman who ran a British-led espionage network in northeastern France. Bettignies crossed enemy lines dozens of times before being captured by the Germans in 1915. She was held in Siegburg Prison in Germany, where she led hunger strikes to protest conditions. She died in September 1918 in a German hospital, probably from tuberculosis. The British posthumously named her an Officer of the British Empire, claiming that her work for them had been "invaluable," and the French government awarded her the Croix de Guerre and named her a Chevalier de la Legion d'Honneur. However, the monument that was erected to remember this intrepid spy captures none of the remarkable nature of her life.

The Monument à Louise de Bettignies shows a traditionally feminine woman standing with her eyes cast heavenward while an old soldier kneels at her feet and kisses her hand. It could be a courting scene. It is significant that the monument is nearly identical to another monument the same artist created earlier to celebrate Joan of Arc (Darrow 281–84; AML: 3 M 53). And that is part of the key to understanding its message. In press accounts of Bettignies, she was repeatedly compared with Joan of Arc, both explicitly and implicitly (AML: 3 M 53). The comparisons frequently stressed the women's obedience to directives that came from God. But the truer connection is that both women defied gender expectations of their times to venture into "men's work" (espionage or combat). But such gender bending could not be celebrated in postwar French society because of anxiety about changing gender roles and the emergence of the "new woman," who rejected traditional expectations and thus threatened the core of French civilization (M. Roberts). The creators of the monument faced a problem: How could they recognize Bettignies's obvious contribution to the French war effort without encouraging dangerously unconventional behavior among other women? The answer was to portray a pious, loyal, and traditionally feminine figure receiving the courtly gratitude of a soldier. As with the Monument aux Fusillés, this monument erased the true identity of its subject in order to teach a lesson more in keeping with the needs of the state and society. It also glossed over a part of the history of World War I—the active participation of thousands of women in espionage (Proctor). Teachers might use this or similar monuments to get students to question gender expectations as well as the often complicated roles women play in war. They might engage students in debates about what roles women currently do or should play and how our society views women's participation.

Monument Marechal Foch

At first glance, the Monument Foch, created in 1936 by Edgar Boutry (1857–1938), seems uncontroversial. It is a typical nineteenth-century-style equestrian statue of Marshall Ferdinand Foch (1851–1929) set high atop a pedestal. But debate surrounded its creation and location, revealing the strong feelings of both pro- and antimilitary factions in Lille. The city's first two attempts to create this monument (1929 and 1933) both failed to raise the necessary funds because of disagreements over the appropriateness of the location and of honoring someone from outside the region. Finally, a third, more modest proposal in 1935 succeeded. But the debate continued.

The proposed location, a small rectangular park known as Jussieu Square, already had a twelve-foot sculpture dedicated in 1902 to a nineteenth-century local poet, Alexandre Desrouseaux. It shows a seated woman cradling a child, while a bust of the poet looks down benignly on the tender, maternal scene. Next to it looms the sixty-foot monument to Foch. According to the local communist paper *L'enchainé*, the Foch monument represented a militarism that threatened the comfort and protection of hearth and home; the paper referred to the monument as a "menace" and to those who were building it as "vandals" ("Vandales"). Not so, said the more conservative *Réveil du nord* ("Monument au Foch"). Instead, "the conqueror of Yser [i.e., Foch] offers his protection in his great shadow to the mother and child." *L'œuvre* in Paris, however, sided with *L'enchainé*, sarcastically suggesting that perhaps a new monument should be erected in the Jussieu Square to replace the monument to the poet. In this one, the mother would "heroically" offer up her son to Foch "as the Italian mothers offered their sons to Mussolini" ("Monument du marechal Foch").

Part of the controversy relates to the style of the monument. In 1935, when the Foch statue was completed, some perceived its style to be anachronistic at best—a throwback to an earlier century when the military, and warfare in general, was seen as glorious and honorable. At worst, after the bloodbath of World War I, such a portrayal was offensive. Although the dedication ceremonies in 1936 included both military and civilians in an attempt to recreate the *union sacrée* of the war ("Homage"), this artificial appeal to an earlier, more united time did not work. Violent confrontations broke out between veterans' groups and antimilitary protesters. Significantly, at least one confrontation occurred at the Monument aux Mort—the monument to honor all the dead of the region, civilian and military, rather than simply one high-level military officer.

Thus this fairly unremarkable monument to a familiar World War I commander revealed strong divisions in Lille over the role of the military in society and the changing views of warfare that World War I had produced. Teachers might use this conflict to explore the process by which public spaces are filled, how dissent can simmer just below the surface of society and suddenly erupt, and how governments use public monuments to make political statements. Art history teachers can look at the various design styles of memorials and the degree to which they reflect contemporary styles or earlier ones. If an earlier style is used, why is that? Students might consider how the styles of monuments change and what the artist's message might be in returning to a design associated with the past. Teachers might then ask students to consider whether there are contemporary disagreements over other monuments to war and what those disagreements tell us about divisions in contemporary society.

Far from simply adorning public spaces, World War I (and other) monuments provide a wealth of opportunities to get students to think deeply not only about the meaning of World War I but of war in general and, certainly, in our own time.

Note

Images of all of the monuments discussed in this article are available at the following URLs: Monument des Fusillés: www.cheminsdememoire.gouv.fr/fr/monument-des-fusilles-lille; Monument à Louise de Bettignies: http://statues-monuments-npdc.pagesperso-orange.fr/louise-de-Bettignies; Monument Foch: http://statues-monuments-npdc.pagesperso-orange.fr/foch; *Sculpture to Alexandre Desrouseaux*: http://statues-monuments-npdc.pagesperso-orange.fr/le-p'tit-quinquin-lille.

Scott D. Emmert and Steven Trout

In Their Time: Teaching First World War Short Stories and the Case of Richard Harding Davis's "The Man Who Had Everything"

As Anne Marie Einhaus explains in *The Short Story and the First World War* (2013), an illuminating study of the relation between canon formation and collective memory, the phrase "First World War literature" has become, especially for American and British readers, all but synonymous with poetry and, to a lesser extent, book-length works of fiction or autobiography. Short stories, she notes, only rarely figure in First World War scholarship, and those that do typically represent authors better known for their novels. Consequently scholars have fallen into the habit of ignoring a rich lode of cultural evidence. Indeed, in Great Britain hundreds if not thousands of short stories addressed the war while it was under way or grappled with its memory during the decades that followed. Since most of these stories appeared in long-forgotten magazines or now-obscure collections, Einhaus persuasively argues that mining these neglected artifacts—no matter how fleeting their topicality or dubious their artistic merits—yields a fuller picture of a society struggling to draw coherent meaning from a war unprecedented in its scale and carnage.

Although Einhaus focuses on short fiction published in Great Britain, her conclusions also apply to the vast trove of First World War short stories published in the United States. Like their counterparts in Great Britain,

American writers mobilized the short story genre, then at the peak of its popularity, in the service of conflicting ideologies and competing constructions of the past. For example, while many American stories published after November 1918 registered disgust with modern industrialized warfare and protested its lingering effects, others celebrated military service as an expression of manhood—precisely the kinds of stories that members of the American Legion, the largest and most powerful veterans' organization in American history, read throughout the 1920s and 1930s. Among the dizzying array of stories published between 1917 and 1941—many by long-forgotten writers—one finds works by members of the Anglo male elite as well as by African American soldiers and by women of all races who either assumed new wartime roles or remained bound throughout the conflict by cultural tradition.[1]

When incorporated into a First World War literature course composed of upper-division English majors (or even graduate students), such stories could serve as useful prompts for original research on material culture. Imagine an assignment in which each student examines a story's original appearance, together with any subsequent reprintings. Such an assignment might pose the following questions: Where did the story first appear? Was it illustrated? If so, what do the illustrations tell us about its then contemporary interpretation? What sort of textual materials surrounded it? What do these materials, which might include advertisements or opinion pieces, have to say about the war? If published in a book, did editorial apparatus seek to shape the story's reception? Did the story inspire any sequels, parodies, or counter-narratives? And so on.

Students could, of course, complete some of this detective work online. However, in most instances the assignment would require time in a research library, perhaps a dreaded prospect but one that students might find absorbing for its sheer novelty. Having students share their results in class, through discussion or presentations, would add another layer of intellectual complexity to the project. Two key questions might be raised at this point: Did different genres of stories have different publication histories? And, what ideological factors apparently determined a work's eligibility for reprinting or canonization?[2]

To illustrate this assignment, we offer the following analysis of Richard Harding Davis's story "The Man Who Had Everything" as a case study in how a work's passage through material culture intersects with issues of ideology. Davis's potentially subversive narrative quickly became mediated by other texts, which attached themselves to his original work like editorial suckerfish. At stake was nothing less than a construction of wartime manliness identified with a major American role model.

Most students have probably never heard of Davis (1864–1916). They may, however, find his image familiar. A friend of Theodore Roosevelt and archetype for the clean-shaven look that became popular among World War I–era American males, Davis was an international celebrity whose public image as a dashing man of adventure—as a kind of journalistic Indiana Jones—both derived from and transcended his work as a war correspondent and author of popular magazine fiction. During a career spent largely on the edge of various battlefields, he helped create the myth of the Rough Riders' charge up San Juan Hill, covered the Anglo-Boer War in South Africa, and, of course, threw himself into the war to end all wars, which he observed for two years before dying of a heart attack in 1916.

Ironically, Davis did much of his First World War reporting on the Macedonian front, which from a journalistic perspective was a bit of a dud. Stalemate and anticlimax defined the military situation there. The Allied campaign in the region where Greece, Serbia, and Bulgaria met began in the fall of 1915 with the landing of British and French troops, sent to aid the Serbs. These forces arrived too late to save the Serbian Army from disaster at the hands of the Bulgarians. Thus, instead of advancing into Serbia as planned, the Allied troops dug in amid the mountains north of the Greek port of Salonika, where—much to the chagrin of many members of the ostensibly neutral Greek government—they would remain for most of the next three years.

Davis reached this obscure corner of the war in November 1915 and secured lodging in a large room in the Olympos Palace Hotel, where he joined fellow American journalists John McCutcheon, Jimmy Hare, William G. Shepherd, and John Bass (Lubow 320–21; Richard Davis, *With the French* 145). On trips to the front, the great reporter found few truly engaging stories. One day, however, back in the Olympos, a story found him, a story so good that Davis immediately claimed it as his exclusively. Precisely what happened will never be known, but the bare essentials of the episode seem to have occurred as follows: apparently nearing a breakdown after months at the front line, an American volunteer in the British Army walked into the journalists' hotel room and pleaded with his fellow countrymen to help him secure safe passage to Athens. Though sympathetic, the reporters ultimately talked this would-be deserter out of his scheme. Angry and bitter, the volunteer then grudgingly rejoined his British unit and disappeared back into the war, leaving Davis and his companions to ponder the man's fate—and the ethics of their actions.

Davis quickly transformed this memorable incident into a compelling and uncharacteristically ambiguous short story that would prove to be his last and most celebrated work of fiction. He completed the narrative in March 1916, just two weeks before his death. Although he gave the story the working title "The Deserter," it was published in *Metropolitan* magazine in September 1916 as "The Man Who Had Everything" and instantly hailed by the press as the greatest American short story of the war.

To understand the intriguing twists and turns in the story's subsequent history, one must first recognize the narrative's potentially subversive features. As he translated his original encounter with the volunteer into fiction, Davis emphasized three themes. First, he turned the would-be deserter, named Hamlin in the short story, into an image of himself. Once a reporter for the *Kansas City Star*, Hamlin, we are told, joined the British army in order to acquire war stories for future publication. He is, in other words, an author and adventure seeker, not unlike his creator. Thus the story implicitly questions the costs versus the benefits of a strenuous life spent observing violence and death—precisely the kind of life that Davis had theatrically staged for his admirers.

Second, Davis used Hamlin's claims on his fellow countrymen to explore the ambiguities of American neutrality in the midst of the Great War, a pressing topic for readers in 1916. Indeed, the suspense in the story derives from the ethical conundrum presented by Hamlin's situation. Should the journalists help him desert or not? What exactly are their obligations, as representatives of a supposedly neutral power, to this fellow American and to the British Army? Davis provides no clear-cut answers to these questions.

The story's third theme represented its most provocative departure from standard wartime fiction—and from Davis's neomasculine writings and persona. When the first-person narrator (one of the American reporters) first meets Hamlin, he notes that the latter looks "like a young business man from our Middle West" (315). Further evidence of the volunteer's credentials as a respectable, middle-class American male—of the clean-cut Davis variety—comes with the disclosure that Hamlin was once a fraternity brother to one of the other journalists. Soon, however, this all-American image begins to crumble. Hamlin reveals that the horror and discomfort of trench warfare have become more than he can bear. He describes a gruesome scar across his torso that also symbolizes his psychic and emotional wounding. The war has, in effect, unmanned him. As he describes the misery of the Macedonian campaign, for example, he lapses into a state of hysteria: "'The cold gets into your blood, gets into your brains. It won't let you think; or else you think crazy things. It makes you afraid.' He shook himself like a man coming out of a bad dream" (325).

In response to this neurasthenic spectacle, the journalists do more than simply work to convince their fellow countryman of his self-interest as a would-be author; their language bristles with claims that desertion will place Hamlin in a no-man's-land of gendered abnormality. For instance, one of the reporters remarks, "When you reach home, if you can't tell why you left the army, the folks will darned soon guess. And that will *queer* everything you've done. When you come to sell your stuff [i.e., war stories], it will *queer* you with the editors, *queer* you with the publishers" (327; emphasis ours).

Of course, claiming in 1916 that the stresses of industrialized warfare could potentially "queer" an American male—that, in effect, emasculating shell shock spared no one—was one thing; allowing that message to stand after April 1917, when the United States launched its crusade to make the world safe for democracy, was quite another. Suddenly Davis's acclaimed study of the moral haze presented by neutrality became a threat not only to his larger-than-life image as a reporter and adventurer but also to the public ideologies that promoted service in the Great War. As a result, William Gunn Shepherd and John T. McCutcheon, two of his companions in the Olympos Palace Hotel and witnesses to the original events that Davis fictionalized, quickly stepped in to tell their version of the rest of the story—namely, the tale of how the supposedly real-life Hamlin became a decorated war hero.

Shepherd was the first to reclaim the Hamlin story, with a piece titled "The Scar That Tripled." Published in the July 1917 issue of *Metropolitan*, the article begins, "He is over at the front in France now, if he is still alive, with three scars across his stomach instead of the one Richard Harding Davis knew" (7). Shepherd supports this claim with an account of meeting Hamlin in London, where he learns that the now gung-ho volunteer has received medals for valor, in addition to two more scars on his midriff. In Shepherd's story, Hamlin, a proud "youth," accosts the journalist on the street and warmly clasps his hand in "a college-boy clinch" (60). Hamlin then enthusiastically fills Shepherd in: "I'm still in the British army, and I'm a sergeant once more, and I've got the D.C.M. And next week my regiment goes to France and I'm going with them. My girl wants me to come home, but I'm going to see it through. I don't want to quit in the fifth inning" (60). Shepherd's sequel to "The Man Who Had Everything" conveniently ignores the trauma and despair depicted in Davis's narrative. Magically cured of his crippling neurasthenia—apparently through sheer force of will—Hamlin now comes across as a character straight out of a boy's novel, a high-spirited youth as eager to perform his war duties as he would be to finish a baseball game.

Tellingly, Shepherd calls the Davis story about Hamlin "The Deserter," even though the *Metropolitan*, the very magazine for which Shepherd wrote, published it less than a year earlier as "The Man Who Had Everything." Shepherd thereby closes off part of the story's subversive irony. One can read Davis's original title at least two different ways. "The Man Who Had Everything" may refer to Hamlin, who will lose his chance at journalistic greatness should he desert, or to the narrator, who, unlike his shell-shocked fellow American, has not made the mistake of surrendering his freedom in order to join a pointless war. Shepherd calls the story "The Deserter" to emphasize the path that Hamlin did *not* take—and the greater glory that he achieved as a result.

"The Man Who Had Everything" was published under that title twice, first as a magazine story and then in Davis's collection *Lost Road* (1916). In 1917, the story appeared again, this time as a separate book titled *The Deserter* and featuring a lengthy introduction by McCutcheon. Like Shepherd, McCutcheon tries to rewrite the original story by adding information to it, and he enjoys a distinct advantage in this regard. Since his piece introduces Davis's, it cunningly sets the terms by which the reader will interpret an otherwise troubling and ambiguous narrative. For McCutcheon, Davis's story is a "literary monument" that "presents a wholesome lesson to young soldiers who have taken an oath to do faithful service to a nation" (v). Indeed, he even goes so far as to claim that *The Deserter* "belongs in patriotic literature by the side of Edward Everett Hale's 'The Man without a Country!' " (vi).

McCutcheon also never refers to the story as "The Man Who Had Everything," and he summarizes Shepherd's preposterous tale about Hamlin's having been decorated and gone willingly to the Western Front. Going a step further, he diagnoses Hamlin's neurasthenia in a way that erases any negative implications for young American men on their way to the battle: "In view of what we now know of Hamlin's physical condition at the time his mind was obsessed with the idea of deserting, both Mr. Shepherd and

I are glad to believe that his decision to desert was the consequence of physical rather than mental or moral weakness, for his stamina was at its lowest ebb because of a weakened body" (xvi).

Arthur Lubow notes astutely that Shepherd and McCutcheon sought to give "The Man Who Had Everything" a happy ending not only because of the narrative's incongruity with prowar propaganda but also because "[t]hey saw it as a Richard Harding Davis story" (326). Enamored of the Davis myth (as was the rest of America), they could not allow this literary monument to their friend and journalistic idol to memorialize anything less than high ideals and indestructible masculinity. Through their rewriting of the tale, however, they concealed an arguably true act of heroism—namely, Davis's artistic confession that his widely imitated model of strenuous masculinity might not survive the horrors of a world war.

Needless to say, not every American short story of the First World War has a back story as juicy as the one offered above, but the history of "The Man Who Had Everything" reveals issues for which students should be on the lookout. As Peter Widdowson reminds us, works of literature never reach their readers as pure, unmediated "primary material" (43). There is no such thing. Texts are packaged from the outset; printed and laid out in a certain way; illustrated (or not); framed by prefaces, forewords, or afterwords that attempt to head off certain interpretations while encouraging others (as in McCutcheon's anything but innocent introduction); and, in the case of short stories published in magazines, situated among discourses ranging from advertising to explicit political commentary.

As we have tried to demonstrate through this discussion of "The Man Who Had Everything," the story of a literary work's interface with material culture can sometimes be as revealing as the work itself. Research in this area need not, of course, be limited to American short stories. Consider for example Richard Aldington's well-known story "At All Costs," which appeared as both a freestanding, signed, limited edition in 1930 and as part of Ernest Hemingway's 1943 anthology *Men at War*. What was it about this story that set it apart from Aldington's other antiheroic depictions of British soldiers on the Western Front? Why did it enjoy multiple reprintings? And what were the implied criteria for inclusion in Hemingway's collection, which appeared at the height of the Second World War?

Advanced students of First World War literature and cultural history need to do more than simply read the versions of works packaged in twenty-first-century anthologies. To gain a fuller understanding of the complexity of literary history and canon formation, as well as the ideologies of war and remembrance, students could be directed to century-old books and magazines. By poring over such texts, teachers and students can come closest to seeing First World War short stories *in their time*.

Notes

1. Our collection *World War I in American Fiction: An Anthology of Short Stories* places twenty-six of these thematically varied stories side by side.

2. For examples of this type of analysis, students may be directed to David M. Earle's *All Man! Hemingway, 1950s Men's Magazines, and the Masculine Persona* (2009); Robert Scholes and Clifford Wulfman's *Modernism in the Magazines: An Introduction* (2010); and *American Periodicals: A Journal of History and Criticism*.

Marlene A. Briggs

The New Great War Novels: Revisiting the War's Myths through Contemporary Fictions

Despite increasing temporal distance from the conflict, contemporary novelists continue to investigate the sociopolitical relevance of the period between 1914 and 1918. In particular, I teach *Another World* (1998), by Pat Barker, and *A Long Long Way* (2005), by Sebastian Barry, in a senior undergraduate English course on twentieth-century British and Irish studies.[1] Multidisciplinary scholarship on memory inspires my approach. Each of these two novels engages critically with a national myth, a simplified story that plays a dominant role in the collective reception of the past.[2] Ross J. Wilson deduces that such myths "provide society with a frame through which to construct and align present concerns with the events of the Great War" (129). He classifies myths as modes of "intangible" cultural heritage subject to ongoing negotiation and renegotiation (131). As Laurajane Smith summarizes, "Heritage is about negotiation—about using the past, and collective or individual memories, to negotiate new ways of being and expressing identity." By invoking material and immaterial forms of heritage, writers may reinforce as well as resist "received values and identities" (4). More broadly, the study of historical consciousness, which fosters an awareness of changing perspectives on the past associated with archives, commemorations, myths, symbols, and other mediations, underwrites my pedagogy, implicating literature in shifting frameworks of interpretation. Accordingly I encourage students to become self-conscious about their own assumptions and expectations through encounters with historical documents, sound recordings, war memorials, and portrait photographs. These examples of aural and visual culture serve as intriguing points of departure for class discussions. Next, close readings of specific passages apprise students of the volatile interactions among history, literature, and mythology. Lastly, a spectrum of critical opinion facilitates open-ended explorations of each book's conclusion. Even as Barker and Barry address pivotal events, memorial sites, and popular songs, they emphasize repressed and unresolved issues. As these contemporary writers mobilize intangible and tangible modes of heritage, they configure-reconfigure the legacies of the Great War, enlisting the reader in ethical inquiries about the present.

Nearly one hundred years after the Easter Rising in Ireland (24–29 Apr. 1916) and the Battle of the Somme in France (1 July–19 Nov. 1916), Barker and Barry challenge abstract conceptions of collective violence. In *Another World*, a novel set in the 1990s, Barker confounds received narratives of the Somme, a notorious site of mass carnage that encapsulates the futility of the Great War in British popular culture.[3] On the first day of the battle, widely known as the worst "tragedy" in "national military history," nearly sixty thousand men became casualties, as the historian John Keegan indicates (295). Barker, however, disrupts synoptic accounts of passive soldiers consigned to slaughter in a micronarrative that juxtaposes the plights of two brothers on the eve of the action (22 June 1916). By entangling international hostilities on the Western Front with the interpersonal strife of the brothers' Victorian family, she embeds the aggressions of the war in the institutions of the peace. In turn, *A Long Long Way* revisits the revolutionary period in Irish history through the experiences of a Great War volunteer, contesting unitary versions of the Easter Rising in the process. This armed insurrection against the British colonial administration was largely confined to Dublin and resulted in three thousand civilian and military casualties (Jeffery 51).[4] The execution of fifteen leaders within weeks of the revolt (3–12 May 1916) confirmed their status as Irish martyrs, consolidating popular opposition to British rule. Subsequently, sectarian memorial cultures elevated the sacrifices of the rebels above the services of the soldiers from the south. In different ways, Barker and Barry complicate dominant myths of events through marginal figures who defy social typologies.

Geordie Lucas, an elderly working-class veteran from Northumberland, survives the Somme after killing his injured brother in *Another World*. And Willie Dunne, a naive young private in the Royal Dublin Fusiliers, the Catholic son of a policeman, unwittingly participates in the suppression of revolt during Easter week in *A Long Long Way*. Barker and Barry concentrate on issues of class and creed, respectively, provoking timely-untimely debates on the transgenerational dynamics of violence and the exclusionary ideologies of sectarian histories. These contemporary fictions illuminate the contingencies that shaped diverse historical experiences in 1916, a decisive year that had fateful consequences in both Britain and Ireland.

Another World

Why is the Somme such a charged site of memory in Britain? In class, we examine the military history and the cultural reception of this major offensive. More specifically, I draw on historical accounts of zero hour (7:30 am) on 1 July 1916.[5] I talk about my trips to the region, and I show photographs of the Thiepval Memorial to the Missing of the Somme (1932), designed by the British architect Edwin Lutyens. Its complex geometry and architectural mass arise from its intersecting classical forms.[6] Panels mounted on sixteen piers exhibit over seventy-two thousand names of missing soldiers who fought and died in the area: "Here are recorded the names of officers and men who fell in the battlefields of the Somme between July 1915 and March 1918 but to whom the fortune of war denied the known and honoured burial given to their comrades in death." As Jay Winter affirms, "It is unmistakably the names which matter. People come to read the names, and to touch them" ("Pilgrimage" 191; see Laqueur). In order to enhance public awareness of these communal and personal losses, Ken Linge and Pam Linge of Northumberland created a biographical and photographic database at the Thiepval Visitor Centre that features the men whose names appear on the memorial. I share a poster with the class, *Thiepval: The Panel of the Missing*, an assemblage of over six hundred portraits compiled from the database that enables viewers to match names with faces.[7] This painstaking project of digital reclamation contravenes the indiscriminate violence of technological destruction. Students concur that hundreds of these faces, differentiated by caps, moustaches, spectacles, and other marks of individuality, convey the cumulative devastation of the battle. I also provide a series of short commentaries on the Somme by a range of contemporary British writers (c. 1965–2005). This striking compilation catalogs the familial, regional, national, and international legacies of the Somme: Ted Hughes evokes the somatic basis of traumatic memory (70–71); John Harris concedes the inadequacy of speech after mass death (145); Alan Sillitoe condemns the class warfare enacted in the trenches (106); Lyn Macdonald articulates the collective dynamics of mourning (158); Geoff Dyer dwells on the dire precedent of attrition warfare in the twentieth century (128); Barker asserts the limits of working through the calamitous past (qtd. in Thursfield); Christopher Moore acknowledges the haunting afterlife of cultural memory (90); and Nigel Jones relates the gripping experience of walking the battlefields (xx). In short, historical accounts, photographic images, and poignant commentaries bring this battle to life in the classroom.

A multifaceted curriculum on the Somme promotes greater understanding of the variables that constitute and reconstitute the heritage of war. As I guide the students through a close reading of Geordie's visit to Thiepval with his grandson Nick in *Another World* (72–75), I pose several questions pertinent to studies of public memory. How might tensions between official narratives and individual motivations impact veterans who return to the battlefields? Why might members of different generations adopt divergent outlooks on commemorative sites? Will the descendants of combatants preserve or transform memorial observances on the Somme (see Gough 217)? In the novel, Geordie and Nick approach the Memorial to the Missing in distinct ways. The veteran walks "in a straight line" toward it, while Nick, who avoided traveling to the battlefields for many years, "[retreats] to a curved stone bench" (72, 73). Geordie searches for the proper name of his brother. He "stood for a full ten minutes looking up at Harry's name, and his lips moved, causing Nick to wonder what could be left to say after so many years" (74). This compulsion to speak to Harry mystifies Nick. In Geordie's extended family, charged silences shroud the battle: "Why? How? What happened? Nick would ask, but there were no answers" (58). Despite the stock of cultural images that may render 1916 a familiar script for subsequent generations in Britain, the "annihilating abstractions" of the memorial overwhelm Nick (72). He surveys Thiepval from a distance, comparing its empty arches with "Golgotha, the place of a skull," an allusion to the crucifixion of Christ (73). Yet Lutyens's design contradicts a progressive idea of history, prompting Nick to reject a didactic view of its moral significance (73). Grandson and grandfather eventually converge on the steps of the altar. As Geordie lays a wreath, Nick admits its blood-red poppy as a valid symbol of collective remembrance (74). Their journey to the Western Front possibly precipitates the transmission of trauma across the generations: "Something important happened to Nick at Thiepval and he'd never come to terms with it" (74). The legacies of the Somme exceed the conscious direction of survivors and descendants. In this manner, the narrative comprehends the interrelated issues of national heritage, historical consciousness, and traumatic memory.

Another World also dramatizes the complexities of oral histories. Simulated transcripts of Geordie's testimony form an integral part of the novel. In particular, the class focuses on the unexpurgated recording that Helen, an oral historian, plays to Nick after his grandfather's death (257–66). I orient the students to the difficulties involved in historical interviews through a few fundamental questions. How might personal inhibitions and public prohibitions regulate the testimonies of Somme survivors? On the other hand, how might popular representations mediate recollections of battle? Why might a veteran seek to "compose" the past in an effort to achieve psychic equilibrium or social approval (Thomson 11)?[8] In his testimony, Geordie deplores the locally based battalions of "Pals" that permitted brothers to sign up together, a recruitment policy that decimated communities in the north of England (260; see Gilbert, *Battle* 2–5). In the weeks leading up to zero hour, he endures the deafening preliminary bombardments, and he details the preparations of the raiding parties anxious to check the barbed wire before the assault (261). When Harry does not return from the raid because of an agonizing abdominal wound, Geordie risks his life to venture into no-man's-land, where he ends his brother's suffering: "I ram the knife in and the screaming stops" (264). Yet Geordie pauses to gloss his own testimony, divulging the unreliability of his memory:

> GEORDIE: [. . .] It's . . . I know that what I remember seeing is false. It can't have been like that, and so the one thing I need to remember clearly, I can't. Nothing vague about it, you understand. It's as clear as this hand . . . only it's wrong. So how do I *know* I couldn't have got him back?
> HELEN: How do you know it wasn't murder?
> GEORDIE: Yes, that's it. Exactly that. (265)

Ellipses and italics betray Geordie's empirical and ethical uncertainty about his actions. Only the memory of Harry's injuries can justify his (mercy) killing of his brother. Yet Geordie alleges that a fallacious image impedes his recollection of the incident.[9] He dies at the age of 101 without resolving his anguished memories. The novel thus involves the reader in the fraught interpretation of oral testimony without historical or psychic closure.

Barker suggests that "the way you heal the past is through the grandchildren" ("Going" 243). Conversely, the transgenerational dynamics of unconscious transmission may perpetuate the legacies of violence. How, then, do Geordie's anguished memories affect his extended family in *Another World*? To answer this, I ask the students to contemplate the final paragraph, which relays Nick's ruminations in the wake of his grandfather's funeral:

> He remembers the trip to France with Geordie, the rows upon rows upon rows of white headstones, ageless graves for those who were never permitted to grow old. . . . But now, looking round this churchyard, at the gently decaying stones that line the path, he sees that there's wisdom too in this: to let the innocent and the guilty, the murderers and the victims, lie together beneath their half-erased names, side by side, under the obliterating grass. (278)

Is this conclusion upbeat or ominous? Does Geordie's death relegate his psychic conflicts to the past? Or will the interpersonal feuds that plagued the veteran continue to trouble Nick's blended family? This critical exercise generates questions about Nick's actions throughout the novel. For example, why did Nick withhold information about the Fanshawe murder (1904) from his wife and children (115, 277–78)? I supplement this conversation by presenting a range of scholarly perspectives on the ending. David Waterman deems it "optimistic," in part because it blurs distinctions between perpetrators and victims, endorsing a vision of ethical indeterminacy (110). Alternately, John Brannigan detects a "dual function" in the conclusion because of unresolved tensions between human agents and unconscious forces (137). Finally, Anne Whitehead provides a pessimistic judgment on the last scene, contending that its "tentative promise" of "comfort" remains "deceptive" (16). *Another World* rewards sustained scrutiny in a group setting: by delineating the domestic dynamics of sibling rivalry in the catastrophic context of industrial warfare, the novel unsettles standard narratives of national military tragedy. Notwithstanding the death of the last British Great War veteran, Henry John "Harry" Patch (1898–2009), Barker's fiction stimulates reflection on the possibilities and limits of working through the past in ways that are germane to future commemorations on the Somme.[10]

A Long Long Way

Barry derives his title, *A Long Long Way*, from the music hall ballad by Jack Judge and Harry Williams, "It's a Long Way to Tipperary" (1912).[11] This three-verse song, often chanted by soldiers during the Great War, includes a chorus that concerns Paddy's return to Molly in Tipperary, Ireland:

> It's a long way to Tipperary,
> It's a long way to go;
> It's a long way to Tipperary,
> To the sweetest girl I know!
> Goodbye Piccadilly,
> Farewell Leicester Square,
> It's a long long way to Tipperary
> But my heart's right there! (27; lines 5–12)

I distribute the lyrics for the purposes of analysis: Molly, a shrewd young woman set on marriage, and Paddy, a cheerful but dim-witted Irishman, exchange letters. She convinces him to forsake his urban adventure in London, and the chorus heralds his journey home. I play a version of the song by John McCormack, who won the Tenor Solo Medal (1903) at Feis Ceoil, an Irish festival of music dating from the Gaelic revival (M. Dowling 215). His accomplished rendition of "It's a Long Way to Tipperary" (1914), the first recording of the piece, features an orchestra and a male chorus; its lighthearted mood defies grim associations with the trenches (Worth and Cartwright 37). I invite the students to describe what they hear. Typically, they point out the flat tonality of the monophonic record (76 rpm) that precedes stereophonic sound. Paradoxically, electronic files conserve the acoustics of antique technologies, signaling the problems and prospects of the digital classroom. Students note the driving beat of the snare drum as well as the brass instruments that resonate with other military music from the era. Most important, we attend to McCormack's robust performance: even as his lilting voice swells in volume, he maintains remarkable control in his elocution and phrasing. His unaffected verses culminate in the rousing chorus that made this musical composition famous.

Why, I inquire, does Barry refer to this song in his title? To what extent do Willie and Gretta Lawlor, his girlfriend, resemble Paddy and Molly? More pointedly, I propose that the students contrast the content and performance of the song with the plot and style of the novel. Why does Barry undermine the romantic lyrics? How does he frame-reframe the traditional picture of Ireland? Does he cite this piece of cultural ephemera in order to induce nostalgia for the past? Or does he heighten historical irony through his recourse to the song? The lyrics promise a reunion of lovers following a brief correspondence; in the novel, however, letters often instigate misunderstanding and separation. The looming marriage in the original song clashes with the historical trauma of the Great War in Barry's fiction. As the students infer, the novel dismantles the stable image of Ireland: experiential, geographical, and ideological distances ultimately sunder Willie from home. In addition to his physical and psychological ordeals on the Western Front, political developments after the Easter Rising, including the rise of Sinn Féin (1918) and the Anglo-Irish War (21 Jan. 1919–11 July 1921), alter the country beyond recognition. Yet, in the aftermath of a deadly gas attack at Ypres (1915), Willie shouts, "It's a Long Way to Tipperary," along with his fellow soldiers: "Probably every man in the army knew it, whether he was from Aberdeen or Lahore" (57). Despite cultural differences, the song highlights the universal desire for return. Through its popular association with the Great War period, this ballad functions as an ambivalent site of memory in twenty-first-century Ireland. Barry thus enjoins the reader to ponder shifting perspectives on the past, a hallmark of his critical approach to Irish heritage.

After we consider the song, we turn to Barry's depiction of the Easter Rising, a contentious event central to the subsequent formation of the Irish state (85–97). This part of the novel may be placed in dialogue with the "Proclamation of the Provisional Government of the Irish Republic," which Barry's characters struggle to decipher in the midst of the action.[12] Its ennobling rhetoric characterizes the insurrection as a "supreme hour" for the Irish nation in quest of an "august destiny" (Clarke et al. 161). In Barry's retelling, however, the uprising engenders accidents, errors, and miscommunications. Jesse Kirwan, who volunteered for the Great War under John Redmond, the leader of the Irish Parliamentary Party (1900–18), acts as a political counterpart for Willie, who signed up following the massive appeal for manpower by British Field Marshal Horatio Herbert Kitchener (1914).[13] The Irish soldiers watch in disbelief as gunfire brings down dragoon regiments in front of the General Post Office, the building where Padraig Pearse, one of the most famous signatories of the "Proclamation," read this declaration at the beginning of the revolt (87). Initially, Jesse and Willie suspect that Germans occupy the city (88). But the dichotomy of friend and enemy dissolves as German adversaries in the trenches assume the guise of "gallant allies" in the "Proclamation" (Clarke et al. 160; Barry,

Long 90, 95–96). The leaflet circulated by the provisional government to "the people" clarifies the reality of civil war for Jesse, if not for Willie, as exemplified by a shocking assault on a hapless groom and his horses in the Battle of Mount Street Bridge (91).[14] A scene of tragicomic misrecognition follows when a young rebel mistakes Willie for a British "Tommy":

> "You're my prisoner," said a trembling voice.
> "I'm not," said Willie Dunne.
> "I need you for a prisoner, Tommy," said the youngster.
> "No," said Willie.
> The wounded captain behind Willie sort of reached in over Willie's shoulder and fired his pistol. The bullet tore into the young man's neck, and he fell to the marble floor. (92)

As the insurgent dies, his blood sprays Willie's uniform, implicating Willie in the violence despite his disorientation (93). Barry supplants a well-rehearsed tale of emancipation with a scene of chaos: "No one seemed to have the story straight at all" (94). The narrative thus wrests pluralities from polarities. In contrast to the "exaltation" of Ireland through the armed conflict legitimated by the "Proclamation," Barry exposes carnage and confusion, countering the dominant myth of 1916 (Clarke et al. 160).

Buried in the disputed territories of the Western Front before the partisan campaigns of the Anglo-Irish War, Willie disappears beneath the "heaving swell of history" along with over thirty thousand other Irish soldiers (290). As Barry cautions, "there are ambiguities and contradictions in the very idea of war literature for an Irish person. Whose war, whose tradition, whose literature?" ("Reading Guide"). The final page of the novel includes the terse words on Willie's makeshift grave (292):

> William (Willie) Dunne, Private,
> Royal Dublin Fusiliers.
> Killed near St-Court,
> 3 October 1918.
> Aged 21.
> RIP

I ask my students to analyze this inscription, including name, rank, regiment, place, date, and age. Why does the book conclude in this manner? What relation does the standard epitaph bear to the particular story that Barry imparts? Techniques such as foreshadowing, personification, and simile often elicit powerful feelings of identification with Willie; the pathos of the novel complements its ironic slant on Irish heritage (see Fengler 214–15).

Does Barry effectively reclaim the forgotten Irish soldiers of the Great War? Scholars disagree on this question. Roy Foster ascribes a "dark" vision to the author, in which history corresponds to a "juggernaut," an inexorable force that renders his characters "impotent" (195). In another vein, Eugene McNulty honors the "cultural archaeology" that enables Barry to rehabilitate the dispossessed (80). Finally, Liam Harte qualifies his appreciation for the book, arguing that it merely "refutes one partial version of history with an equally partisan rebuttal" (212). Excerpts from these critics generate thoughtful responses to *A Long Long Way*, a narrative that reverberates with recent sociopolitical developments. During the one-hundredth anniversary of the Battle of the Somme (2016), Michael D. Higgins, the president of Ireland, accentuated "the possibility of plural interpretations of the past" in both northern and southern parts of the island (11).[15] Such negotiations and renegotiations of heritage attest to the fluctuating discourses of history, memory, and myth that will undoubtedly influence future commemorations of 1916 in Dublin and elsewhere (see McCarthy).

Contemporary fictions by Barker and Barry arguably contribute to cultures of social repair after historical trauma, mobilizing tangible and intangible heritage to destabilize received narratives of 1916. Students may discover the composite as well as the long-term repercussions of global conflict by grappling with these Great War novels. *Another World* troubles popular perceptions of combat trauma on the Somme, while *A Long Long Way* recasts civil divisions during the Easter Rising. Barker upholds the idiosyncratic resilience of the veteran, although she probes the unconscious processes of repetition fundamental to trauma. In a strategic effort to upset the ideological orthodoxies that sustain sectarian histories, Barry dignifies the afflictions of a humble soldier. The working-class centenarian Geordie Lucas and the Catholic youth Willie Dunne thus disclose the cascading effects of conflict. Critical approaches to the heritage of the Great War reveal its convoluted and protracted legacies of violence, encompassing combatants and civilians, men and women, and ancestors and descendants. Contemporary fictions negotiate and renegotiate the myths of 1916, sensitizing students to their own historically belated positions. Barker and Barry highlight the sociopolitical relevance of the Great War in Britain and Ireland, respectively, even as they anticipate the dynamic contexts of its reception for subsequent generations.

Notes

1. Other acclaimed contemporary novels from Australia, Canada, France, Germany, Russia, and the United States that address the First World War and its contested legacies are, respectively, Keneally, *The Daughters of Mars* (2012); Boyden, *Three Day Road* (2005); Japrisot, *A Very Long Engagement* (1993, translated by Linda Coverdale); Sebald, *The Emigrants* (1996, translated by Michael Hulse); Solzhenitsyn, *August 1914: The Red Wheel, Knot I* (1989, translated by H. T. Willetts); and Vonnegut, *Bluebeard* (1987).

2. In his influential study of English culture, Hynes defines "the Myth of the War" as an "imaginative version" of the conflict that emerged as a standardized set of narratives in the 1920s and persisted into the 1990s (ix, xi). Staples of this myth include disillusionment with ideals, alienation from civilians, and sympathy with the enemy (439). The year 1916 emerges as a "turning point" in his inquiry (97–167). With regard to the Irish context, Longley summarizes the bipartite myths of 1916 for Ulster Protestants and Irish Catholics: "[T]he Somme, 1 July 1916, complicated the politics produced by the Rising on 24 April: two sacrificial shrines—the people crucified, a chosen people massacred—demanded their incompatible due" (78). For a succinct critical overview of key terms in memory studies, including myth, see Beiner.

3. In a contrasting viewpoint, Löschnigg claims that Barker "perpetuates a cluster of myths about the war" in *The Regeneration Trilogy*, the series that precedes *Another World* (227).

4. Over half of those who died in the Easter Rising were civilians. For statistics and records, consult the *1916 Necrology*, an electronic document available from the Glasnevin Trust. Centenary commemorations of the uprising (3 Apr. 2016) included the unveiling of a controversial memorial wall listing the names of all the dead in Glasnevin Cemetery, Dublin.

5. Historical accounts by Gilbert (*Battle*); Keegan; and Middlebrook inform my lecture on the Somme. In this connection, instructors may also wish to devote class time to Sacco's illustrated panorama of 1 July 1916, which features twenty-four meticulously drawn plates.

6. On the design of the Memorial to the Missing of the Somme, see Stamp 129–52.

7. In addition, a catalog from the exhibition *Missing of the Somme*, curated by Linge and Linge at the Historial de la Grande Guerre (19 Apr.–25 Nov. 2012), based on their ongoing research into over ten thousand names listed on the Thiepval Memorial to the Missing of the Somme, includes diligently reconstructed narratives accompanied by photographs ("Missing but Not Forgotten"). Both the poster and the catalog may be purchased from the online shop of the Thiepval Visitor Centre.

8. On the complex interaction of public languages and subjective identities in oral histories, see Thomson 10–17.

9. Nick and Helen develop contrasting theories of memory in *Another World*. However, neither Helen's theory of cultural memory premised on shifting social

norms nor Nick's model of involuntary recall based on a neuropsychological conception of trauma explains Geordie's torment (241). See Rawlinson for commentary on this controversy (106–13).

10. On the interrelated processes of acting out and working through, see LaCapra 65–66.

11. Barry extols song and dance in *A Long Long Way*. In a rich segment, for example, Joe Kielty performs a dance on a table top, showcasing Irish expressive arts (201). As Barry states, "If singing shows the soul of a person, dancing shows the elemental core, the celebratory fierceness, Blake's tiger leaping" ("Really" 47).

12. In this context, de Paor's analysis of the "Proclamation of the Provisional Government of the Irish Republic" may be a helpful resource. See also Gibney 83–87.

13. On Redmond's policies in Ireland during the Great War, consult Finnan 78–116.

14. *A Terrible Beauty*, Farrell's docudrama on the Easter Rising, may enrich class discussions of *A Long Long Way*: both the film and the novel aim to disrupt partisan perspectives on the Battle of Mount Street Bridge.

15. Notably, Ahern, minister for foreign affairs in Ireland (2004–08), mentions Barry in his essay advocating an ethos of historical inclusion in commemorations of 1916 (16).

Jan Baetens and Hugo Frey

Graphic Novels and the First World War

Generally speaking, when one thinks of the representation of war in graphic narratives (comics and, more recently, graphic novels), the first images that come to mind are the mid-twentieth-century war comics featuring American GIs and British commandos fighting stereotypically evil Nazis or ugly Japanese bullies. In brief, examples of depictions of the First World War are rare. This may be because comics, published in serialized form, were intricately linked to the news media and were commonly drawn to use as backdrop news reportage rather than history. Nonetheless, in the past thirty years the rise of graphic novels has altered the context of war comics and specifically opened up new and challenging representations of the period between 1914 and 1918. As comics were increasingly deemed not for just for kids (circa 1986 in the United States, the late 1970s in francophone contexts), graphic novelists have expanded the range of historical subjects discussed through text-image formats. Moreover, the graphic novel has become something of a privileged medium for visual story telling that prefers ambiguous, difficult, or troubling history over images of exciting war actions and stereotypical heroism and villainy.

This essay provides educators and students with a general orientation on the growing field of First World War graphic novels. Of course, it is suitable to use the graphic novel in the way some instructors introduce cinema into their history classes—that is, as a happy break from analysis of written texts. Alternatively, for cultural historians with preferences for unusual or original sources, graphic novels provide a fascinating entrée into other important but underdiscussed visual realms of war: the postcards of battle scenes or destroyed cities that were so popular after the war, sketches from soldiers' autograph books, popular songs, propaganda poster art, book cover design, and now the many museum Web sites that make connective use of word and image. Our students can also study First World War graphic novels as central texts in and of themselves.

The graphic novelist Joe Sacco's *The Great War: July 1, 1916: the First Day of the Battle of the Somme: An Illustrated Panorama* is an experimental addition to the several cultural representations of the First World War being promoted during the hundredth anniversary commemoration period. Sacco's work is a graphic depiction of the battle, folded into a series of conjoined papers that make up a long panorama in which Sacco narrates the experience of the British on the Somme. Included in the book are eight plates depicting trench warfare. Like the Bayeux Tapestry, which Sacco describes as one influence, there are also extended sections of prebattle visualizations.

Perhaps more important than the images themselves, the material presentation of the volume makes for a distinctive object that encourages readers to reflect on the horror of historical violence. Thus Sacco's book is set inside a thick cardboard sleeve. This package is closer to a box or even an arcane military rations canteen than to a normal book cover. The container also includes a separate if slimmer pamphlet of Sacco's essays and an adapted text extracted from Adam Hochschild's history *To End All Wars* (2012). From our experience it is the difficult materiality of the product (the box, the separation of word from image) that encourages a slow and considered student reader response: the awkwardness, deliberate, necessitates reflection. Such a representation also problematizes the positive panorama commemorations of warfare that were common on the eve of the First World War itself. Deliberately or otherwise, Sacco appropriates the style and idea of the 1912 *Panorama of the Battle of Waterloo* (by Louis Dumoulin) that commemorated the hundredth anniversary of that battlefield just outside Brussels, Belgium. Dumoulin produced a vision of grandeur that was housed on the battlefield itself—his panels were "110 metres round and 12 metres high" (*Panorama*). Today, Sacco reduces his landscape battle scenes to a more accessible A4 size. His unique format thereby constantly encourages students to reflect on the nature of format (that is, the very processes of commemoration) as much as on historical content. In a seminar classroom, one can use the materiality of his works to introduce a comparative discussion of other commemorative devices or visual displays—bringing new attention to the idea of war in the panoramas. Literally unpacking Sacco's book across a table with a small group will encourage students to think about the war as a physical, spatial-geographical experience, as distinct from a purely literary or military-historical episode.

Because graphic novels are more commonly narrative than material, student groups are encouraged to discuss what kind of story worlds are featured in this form of representation. In fact, graphic novels often prioritize subjects that are less conventional than those in Sacco's work. For example, the artist Charlie Adlard has worked with Rob Morrison on *White Death* (2002), which focuses new attention on the Alpine war fought between Austro-Hungarian and Italian forces. In the book, Adlard and Morrison introduce the terrifying world of mountain warfare, militarily provoked avalanches, and the freezing conditions of combat that characterized that theater of combat. More recently, Caanan White and Max Brooks's *The Harlem Hellfighters* (2014) provides a representation of a too often neglected subject in traditional British and North American histories of the war: the African American contribution to the United States Army.

The search for original themes is not limited to communities or specific cultural traditions recalling their group's historical experience. One of the most interesting examples is David Vandermeulen's *Fritz Haber* (four volumes to date, 2005–14). This very detailed, long-running biography brings to new light the political and scientific history of the German scientist whose research underpinned the use of poison gas in combat. No conventional French-language biography of Haber existed before the graphic novel, hence the work was utterly original and groundbreaking. Moreover, alongside the graphic novels, Vandermeulen has created an extensive Web site filled with complementary historical information. This tool allows the classroom to compare facts with his creative reinterpretations in *Fritz Haber*, which emphasizes the mythic aspects of the doctor's story. Vandermeulen appropriates images from photojournalism and the codes of silent cinema to contextualize and authenticate his visual storytelling. The title therefore works as a powerful educational gateway to other visual materials that may profitably be taught in higher education.[1]

A corollary to telling forgotten histories or adopting points of view different from conventional military history writing is that the graphic novels about the First World War also offer a generally leftist political interpretation. As such they represent a popular adjunct to the other cultural forms that used the war to either critique military conflict or, as with Marxist-Leninist texts, associate it with bourgeois imperialism. Students will easily be able to place these works in this school of historical interpretation. You can easily demonstrate that the graphic novels sit squarely in the post-1960s neopacifist tradition that uses the conflict as the perfect example of the horrors of militarism. The works from Sacco or Morrison and Adlard should, and could, be compared in the classroom with films like *Oh What a Lovely War* and *Paths of Glory*.[2]

The definitive example of a politically motivated and even, dare one say, propagandistic antiwar graphic novelist is Jacques Tardi. Through numerous fictional and semifactual titles, Tardi's oeuvre disseminates relatively classic leftist binaries about the war: the bloodthirsty generals and industrialists versus naive ordinary folk, pointless military regulations trumping good sense. In his major work—*It Was the War of the Trenches* (1993)—it is the horror of combat conditions on the Western Front that are repeatedly emphasized. Page after page charts the violence and its consequences for the men of both sides. In *It Was the War of the Trenches*, the style is decidedly modernist, despite the self-evident political slant. No consistent narrative carries the reader through the work. Rather, Tardi provides snapshots of different stories and episodes. The work is only really held together as a single graphic novel by its repeated and regular page design—tiers of three landscapes descending down the page and therefore allowing for repeated wide-angle views of trenches. The trenches themselves also repeat over the ninety pages, adequately illustrating the endless monotony of it all. Tardi is quite open about his politics in the introduction to the English edition: "People ask me, 'More soldier tales, Tardi? When are you coming out of your trench?' . . . but I'm afraid we are all of us still down here, down in the trenches . . . East, West. . . . In fact in all of that, it's not so much a matter of the 1914–1918 War as of WAR. . . . From trench mortars to neutron bombs. . . . It's the upcoming one that worries me" (22). While elsewhere Tardi has underlined his personal fascination with the period, he is also willing to use the historical context to speak to the divisions and dangers of later eras. The point of studying him is therefore twofold: he is a major international intellectual voice speaking on the continued meaning of the war, and, even if one does not fully agree with his interpretation, his perspective is a vital point for debate (in the classroom in essay analysis or beyond the classroom in informal student conversations).

A number of artists and writers have used the First World War as an extended backdrop to plot development rather than for their main subject. These titles tend to gravitate toward the genres of horror and science fiction. Here again Tardi is the important forerunner who has developed the field in interesting ways. For several years before the completion of *It Was the War of the Trenches*, he used the eve of the war to recount a series of fantastical stories in the *Adèle Blanc-Sec* adventure series. First published in French in the 1970s by the magazine *A suivre*, the Blanc-Sec graphic novels use the horror genre to make metaphorical criticism of the European governments that plunged the ordinary people into violence in 1914.

To summarize the series's treatment of the war: Tardi implies that nothing he or any other fantasy-horror novelist could imagine would ever be as terrifying as the banal reality of history itself. Thus the keynote is a thought-provoking irony. As readers we can enjoy the thrills and scares of the mysteries he recounts in fin de siècle Paris, but we are also regularly reminded that all his characters will be soon plunged into a very real man-made military disaster—the First World War. Here, students are recommended to revisit comparable titles, such as Mike Mignola, Christopher Golden, and Ben Stenbeck's *Baltimore: The Plague Ships*, and there is also Alan Moore and Kevin O'Neil's series *The League of Extraordinary Gentlemen*. All these works in part satirize the patriotic popular literature of the eve of the war (everything from H. G. Wells to H. Rider Haggard), while, as in Tardi's Blanc-Sec stories, also suggesting that the imagination cannot compete with real history. It is in this synthesis of historical narration and horror genres that Adlard returns to the war as a theme for the first time since *White Death*. Working with the French writer Mathieu Missoffe, he produced *Curse of the Wendigo* (2011), which draws attention to the Native American presence among the United States troops on the Western Front, while blurring this historical restitution argument with straightforward horror and fantasy fiction tropes.

In turning from narrative content to form, it is important to recognize that graphic novels are particularly good at dealing with issues of time and history. As exemplified in Art Spiegelman's world-famous *Maus* (1987), the gridlike organization of a comic strip page facilitates a permanent split screen effect where past and present can be treated together on a single page. Classically, in *Maus* this effect allowed Spiegelman's readers not only to experience a Holocaust memoir but also to encounter the modern-day context for its telling. Even some of the simplest examples of First World War graphic novels are open to this same strategy of handling time on the page. Pat Mills and Joe Colquhoun's long-running *Charley's War* exemplifies the many possibilities for representing the past. A twelve-panel grid is used on most pages to create several important effects: the juxtaposition of time (present-day reflection is offered in the words alongside the historical images of past battles); mixed interpretative modes (images of letters home are drawn alongside the events they describe); and the re-representation of other visual forms inside the strip (official photographs and newspaper cartoons are redrawn on the same page). Of course, other media can achieve similar effects (e.g., multiscreen Web sites; split screen film; flashback and flash-forward sequences in literature), but they are not able to achieve those effects with the same level of communicative efficiency. In that sense the graphic novel is following and contributing to the more general updating of First World War museology that has occurred in the past twenty years, wherein traditional and static exhibition of usually military artifacts has been upgraded to offer multiple perspectives of biography, gender, social, and cultural history.

The changing format of panel organization in a graphic novel further facilitates original and powerful effects. Throughout much of the narration in the account of African American war experience in *The Harlem Hellfighters*, the page is organized in the classic comic-like grid of six to nine panels. Yet consistently when violence or traumatic action is depicted, this organization is replaced. Now a series of single page-size images interrupt the grid to show the most dramatic or important scenes. This is in fact a common convention of comics—the so-called splash page, which magnifies picture size when a superhero is fighting a particularly vicious enemy and the artist needs more space than the constraint of six or nine panels. However, the same device functions perfectly well for the historical graphic novels and indeed does grab the reader's attention when images of violence or tragedy are blown up and no longer held inside grids or panels.

Similarly, it is also common for artists to use sequences of pages that are primarily filled with images and have little or no text—neither direct speech from protagonists nor authorial interventions. This technique of silence in a graphic novel is a further effective rhetorical mode to gain the reader's attention. It is especially effective in the depiction of warfare, as it metaphorically captures the silence of anxiety and anticipation before conflict, and it is again helpful after depictions of violence to suggest emotional impact.

The medium-specific features of graphic novels (page design, text and image relations, silence) are themes for classes to work on. It is by understanding the modes of graphic novels that one can best recognize how they specifically represent the First World War. Writing on literature and culture more generally, the novelist and critic Michael Chabon argues that some of the most intriguing and important contemporary developments are occurring today on the borderlines between forms, in the intermediary spaces that are accessed by adept creators who are equally comfortable with more than one genre or even medium. For Chabon, original creation is found where existing paradigms are remixed, where the old boundaries between high and low culture are placed in flux. Graphic novels such as those described above are especially good at this remixing of paradigms. For this reason, so many of their titles offer new ideas or original representations of the First World War. Publishing houses have therefore given space for several graphic novelists to write new titles that coincide with the war's hundredth anniversary. Over the past ten years, the fields of literature and graphic novels have engaged in numerous interchanges and exchanges that have raised the profile of graphic novels (see Baetens and Frey). This context has no doubt encouraged publishers to believe that First World War graphic novels will be read as much as any new novel, maybe even more so.

Notes

1. At the time of writing, this work has not been translated into English, and so it may be of more value for teachers and students of French studies or comparative literature than to anglophone history or literature teaching groups.

2. For an excellent, more general discussion of postwar images and micropolitical uses of them in Britain, see R. Wilson 57–100.

Peter Grant

From Brel to Black Metal: The First World War in Popular Music and Music Videos

During the First World War, thousands of war-related popular songs were written. In the United States, although the country joined the conflict only in 1917, 36,500 were registered for copyright. Since the late 1950s, though the numbers have been far fewer, there have still been around 1,500 newly composed songs featuring the war in one form or another. They emanate largely from the main belligerent nations, with the majority coming from the winners—70% are French, British, or American—but there are also examples from as far afield as Latvia, Greece, Brazil, Colombia, and Malaysia. They cover virtually every popular music genre, so that one can find a song to match nearly every student's musical taste. Easy access to live performances or official videos online make the task far simpler.[1]

In the classroom, modern popular songs can be used as a teaching aid or an arresting way of introducing a topic. One can turn to the video of Paul McCartney's "Pipes of Peace" (1983) as an introduction to the 1914 Christmas Truce, to June Tabor's haunting "Aqaba" (1989) before discussing the role of T. E. Lawrence, or to one of System of a Down's angry songs—"P.L.U.C.K." (1998) or "Holy Mountains" (2005)—in relation to the Armenian massacres. There are a host of French songs about Verdun, which range in genre from Azziard's death metal concept album *1916*

(2009) through the darkwave band Collection d'Arnell-Andrea's "Villers aux Vents (Fevrier 1916)" (2003) to the more traditional approach of Bernard Joyet, entitled simply "Verdun" (2002). There are as many British songs about the Somme, including Saxon's "Broken Heroes" (1985), Motörhead's "1916" (1991), and the more recent "High Wood Suite," by progressive rock singer Fish (2013). There's even a song about the Schliffen Plan, God Dethroned's "Under the Sign of the Iron Cross" (2010).

But there are more sophisticated ways in which these songs can be deployed, especially when considering the popular memory or cultural representations of the war. One question to ask is whether a song is mirroring or questioning any dominant national myth of the war. In most English-speaking countries the war is strongly identified with futility, military incompetence, and lost innocence. Particularly notable in this genre are the Scottish Australian folk singer Eric Bogle's two songs "And the Band Played Waltzing Matilda" and "No Man's Land" (also known as "The Green Fields of France" or "Willie McBride"), both first recorded by him in 1980, and they appear in numerous cover versions. The former, about a disabled Gallipoli veteran, is best known through the outstanding version by the Pogues (1985). The latter has been covered by artists of all political shades from the Fureys (1981) and the Angelic Upstarts (1986) to Skrewdriver (1988) and Prussian Blue (2005), and it can serve as an effective point of departure for a discussion of the political nature of popular song. Mike Harding's "Accrington Pals" (2005), another song about the Somme, is notable for its detailed description of the protagonists' progress from volunteers to victims, and its use of many well-known images (birdsong, walking toward the guns, mud) raises questions about how these myths relate to the events they depict.

However, the futility myth is not all-pervasive in the Anglo-Saxon world. In Canada, views of the war are often more positive: one can contrast Matthew de Zoete's "Remembrance Day" (2008), referencing "the holy ground of Vimy [Ridge]," or Bryan Adams's anthemic song of the same title (1987), in which most of the soldiers return victorious from the conflict, with more pessimistic approaches. One reason that the myth of futility persisted was its usefulness in the 1960s as a metaphor for contemporary events, most notably the threat of nuclear war and opposition to the war in Vietnam. Bogle has said that when he wrote "And the Band Played Waltzing Matilda" in 1971, he had Vietnam as much as Gallipoli in mind, and Bob Dylan's "With God on Our Side" (1964) and Don McLean's "The Grave" (1971) are other examples of this influence (see

Casimir). In France the war in Algeria played a similar role, and Georges Brassens's satirical "La guerre de 14–18" (1961) references that conflict. When Michael Flanders translated the song three years later, he replaced Algeria with perhaps the first reference to Vietnam in song. The French chanson has a long tradition of political and historical commentary, and the first modern popular songs about the First World War came from that genre in the late 1950s and early 1960s. Of the performers from that era, including Barbara, Leo Ferré, and Jaques Brel, Brel is the best known in the English-speaking world, and his "La colombe" (1959; "The Dove") was covered in an anti-Vietnam context by both Judy Collins (1964) and Joan Baez (1967).

In many countries, more recent conflicts have greater prominence and the First World War is simply a part of history. Most German and Polish examples that reference the war are in the relatively recent genre of martial industrial music, which often uses historical recordings of speeches or battle effects set against a somber musical background of electronic sounds and marching tunes. The genre has been controversial for its adoption of neo-Fascist imagery. Debate can include music's ideological implications.

Popular songs frequently explicitly reference war remembrance and memory. The writer can approach the theme from the point of view of participants looking back (veterans or widows), as in "And the Band Played Waltzing Matilda," Richard Thompson's "The Woods of Darney" (1996), or "Dancing at Witsun," which has been covered by English folksingers from Shirley Collins (1969) to Maddy Prior and Tim Hart (1971).[2] It can be a modern retrospective, as in "The Green Fields of France," PJ Harvey's "On Battleship Hill" (2011), or Radiohead's "Harry Patch (in Memory of)" (2009), or it can incorporate the iconography of the armistice on 11 November. Examples of this iconography range from the death metal pioneers Bolt Thrower's "Cenotaph" (1990) and "Remembrance" (1994) through many songs called "Remembrance Day," from bands including the punk groups Disorder (1993) and Guv'Nor (2009), as well as Leon Rosselson's humorous antiestablishment approach (2004). Gary Miller's 2010 album *Reflections on War* comprises a suite of six songs looking back at the war, which stem from his involvement in a community arts project in York, England. When working with the participants, Miller wrote a set of songs based on their ideas and memories. An alternative approach to memory is taken in Barclay James Harvest's "The Ballad of Denshaw Mill" (1993), which invokes Christmas as a universal image of hope by using the nativity and civilians' thoughts for loved ones at the front. It adapts complex mythical imagery that explores the thoughts of the troops, their loved ones at home, and the way in which memory works.

Song lyrics are not poetry; they are designed to perform different functions, and this holds true even for songs whose words can stand by themselves, for once music is added, new meanings are produced (Frith 182). Nevertheless there are many links between the approach of the war poets and those of popular musicians, and for those who are not easily engaged by poetry, songs can be a way into the poems. "The war poets, Wilfred Owen and Sassoon, they have inspired me," confirms Bolt Thrower's singer and lyricist Karl Willetts, "even if it's not the words it's the rhyming structure, it helps me formulate a plan and a pattern." War poems have also been set to music. Simple musical settings of war poetry include Country Joe McDonald's album of Robert Service poems, *War, War, War* (1971, rereleased in a live version in 2012), and French American Sergerémy Sacré's *War Poems—Siegfried Sassoon* (2011). The famous "In Flanders Fields," composed by Lieutenant Colonel John McCrae, a Canadian medical officer, with its twin themes of remembrance of the dead and defiant belligerence, has been set to music many times. There are choral versions by Alexander Tilley and Barry Taylor (2001), Matthew Ackroyd and Dennis Khvatov (2003), and John Jacobson and Roger Emerson (1994) as well as a bagpipe and choral version by the Bonfire Ensemble (2006) and a pop version by Anthony Hutchcroft (2006), which is available on the Internet together with an associated ballet. With the exception of Jacobson and Emerson, who are American, all are Canadians. There is a rock version by the Russian band Romislokus and written by the Canadian radio DJ Stan Hilborn (2004), incorporating a modern response to McCrae's original poem, and another from the French doom metal band Mourning Dawn (2009).

The poetry of Wilfred Owen has been an influential source for both popular and classical musicians. Some songs take the form of direct translations, such as "Anthem for Doomed Youth," by 10,000 Maniacs (1990), and "Futility," by Virginia Astley in her guise as the Ravishing Beauties (1983). Others take Owen as an inspiration for new interpretations. There are distinct similarities between Bogle's "And the Band Played Waltzing Matilda" and Owen's "Disabled," which is about a legless young veteran, and between "It Was a Navy Boy" and the Decemberists' "The Soldiering Life" (2003). "The Soldiering Life" is a self-declared homoerotic song that suggests that the war was not all mud and blood. Its protagonist finds love and companionship in the trenches, and Colin Meloy's words are both subtle and subversive.

Halfway between poetry and political tract lies Diamanda Galás's "Orders from the Dead," an eleven-minute sound poem of war, murder, and anger about the Armenian genocide. Galás declaims rather than sings the words, and she has recorded both a solo version and one with the Greek extreme metal band Rotting Christ (2010), which is the slightly more accessible version both musically and on CD or the Internet.

The above example indicates that extreme metal not only is a genre well suited to comment on war but also often intelligently reworks material from other cultural sources. In the genre of extreme metal, Bolt Thrower's many songs about the First World War use a considered, objective approach, often taking the soldier's perspective. The lyricist Karl Willetts has reflected, "For me 1914–18 was a time of massive change. A real clash between old and new, both ideology and technology. There was the massive waste of life and massive disaster politically. But it was a fascinating time when things were changing and the world moved to modernity." Their songs reflect this ambiguity: "[W]e don't say war is a good thing, we don't say war is a bad thing, we don't glorify it, we just say it as it is" (Willetts). Bolt Thrower establish their ideas through simple, noneuphemistic language, almost the modern equivalent of trench poetry, notably in the albums *For Victory* (1994) and *Those Once Loyal* (2005). Another song by an extreme metal band, "Poets of the Trenches" (2002), from Denmark's Iniquity, is in two parts. The first is a straightforward reflection on those who fell, on both sides, in the Battle of the Somme, sung in the usual harsh growled death metal style. The second takes the form of a diary entry or letter written after the battle, and it is spoken in clear English. Its powerful language recalls some of the classic wartime novels, such as Henri Barbusse's *Le feu* (*Under Fire*), Ernst Jünger's *Storm of Steel*, or Frederic Manning's *Her Privates We*.

Going one stage further in its radical reinterpretation of popular myth is PJ Harvey's influential and acclaimed album *Let England Shake* (2011). The songs deal with war, both directly and indirectly, through its impact and memory. Throughout the album Harvey interweaves the theme of war as she considers what England means for her, noting how the country's present is inextricably bound to its past. Accompanying the songs is a remarkable DVD containing films by the Irish photojournalist Seamus Murphy. Harvey gave Murphy total freedom; her only instruction was to "just avoid the bleeding obvious," and very few changes were made after she had seen the first cut (PU). They are far from conventional pop videos, instead presenting a vision of present-day England through the lens of the past. Taking *Let England Shake* as a starting point for teaching the First World War will certainly open up a vast range of possible directions for debate.

Notes

1. I host a Web site (blogs.city.ac.uk/sa505pg1955/) that lists over nine hundred songs produced since 1960. Organized alphabetically by artist, the list includes the artist's country of origin, the name of the album in which the song was released, date of release, and the song's genre. The Web site list will be periodically updated.

2. The original lyrics of "Waltzing Matilda" were written by Andrew Barton "Banjo" Paterson in 1895. Paterson served in the First World War first as an ambulance driver and later as a veterinarian. Austin John Marshall, Collins's husband at the time, wrote "Dancing at Whitsun" in 1968, setting new lyrics recalling the lost generation of 1914 to 1918 to the traditional tune of "The Week before Easter" or "The False Bride."

Part V

Places and Pedagogies

Jeffrey Drouin

From the Global Archive: Teaching World War I with Digital Tools

As the centenary of World War I sparks an outgrowth of new online resources, many national archives, museums, and private collections around the world are releasing a wealth of digitized war records, posters, periodicals, photographs, movies, music, matériel, letters, diaries, and other manuscripts. These freely accessible digital artifacts offer unprecedented opportunities for teaching the war and its cultural context through active learning and research. When digital media are used effectively, students may synthesize experiences of World War I with its cultural mediation, while cultivating skills in information literacy and thinking creatively with technology. More important, in breaking down the walls of the classroom, students make real contributions to public and academic discourse about the war, which results in a sense of ownership and pride in their work. This essay covers a variety of practices for teaching World War I through digital research. The following case studies, potential lesson plans, and other projects draw on my experiences and may be adapted by instructors at any level.

Digital technologies can help students contextualize the war along geographic and thematic lines, such as the European and colonial causes beginning in the nineteenth century, the nature of the conflict on all continents, gender and women's issues, economics and labor, political movements, battle history, home front print culture, avant-garde aesthetics from the 1910s through the 1930s, and of course much more. The print media at various international locations allow students to follow political and aesthetic contours, like changes in sensibility and philosophical outlook, from the prewar years through the war's aftermath.

When undertaking digital projects in a course, the technology should integrate seamlessly with the learning goals, readings, and other course activities and not sit on the fringes as an isolated add-on. Using the simplest application possible best ensures that learning the technology does not distract from learning the content and gives each activity a practical outcome. In fact, learning the technology should enhance the learning of content. Students are more apt to become excited about their projects if the technology is a means to achieving an intellectual goal. The following segments suggest ways in which to integrate technology organically with the objectives of a course.

Blog

Teaching World War I with a blog is a great way for students to begin engaging with difficult readings, to process historical or philosophical questions, and to incorporate media for multimodal composition. A blog can be effective as a course site, complete with a schedule page, supplementary downloads, student project pages, and up-to-the-minute discursive writing about course material, and it serves as an excellent building block for interactive activities. Most blogging platforms are flexible enough to allow a variety of writing assignments, from time-stamped journal entries to static documentary pages, and can use syndicated and embedded media content from other sites. It is easy to create a free, customized blog at Wordpress.com. If your institution prefers to keep the site in-house, then a Web administrator can set up software if it is not already available.[1] *Drupal* is another content management system (CMS) that functions very well as a blog and also presents more sophisticated possibilities for instructors who are technically inclined.[2]

A blog's carefully delineated framework allows for open-ended responses to reading-response assignments. Allowing students the freedom to discover their own observations strikes a productive balance between active investigation and synthesizing the unknown with the known—two key ingredients in knowledge production. The list below presents selected blog prompts from a fifteen-week undergraduate English course on World War I. In the full list, the first three prompts are reflective, designed to make students aware of their intellectual motivations and how they can apply those motivations to the war, with the ancillary effect of fostering a community of writers. The rest are designed to process specific readings and make connections among them. In each of the cases below, the required length is one to two paragraphs, enough to begin engaging with the material but not so much that it becomes an onerous task. The goal is to produce process-oriented writing that contributes to in-class discussion and can build cumulatively to a paper or other project.

What aspect of Vera Brittain's experience in *Testament of Youth* is the most significant to you and why? What does it say about the war's effects?

Pick one poster from the special collections exhibit at *Flickr* and embed the image in your post. How do you read the poster in the light of Pearl James's introduction to *Picture This*? Can you tie it to Brittain's *Testament of Youth*?

Browse or search for content related to World War I in *The Crisis* at the *Modernist Journals Project* (MJP), using the Advanced Search tool.[3] Pick one item such as an essay, a poem, a story, an advertisement, a photograph—anything is fair game. Post a link to the item and analyze its stance toward the war vis-à-vis race, taking cues as necessary from Jennifer D. Keene's "Images of Racial Pride: African American Propaganda Posters in the First World War." Be sure to quote from the item to back up your point. If it is a visual piece, then be sure to embed it in your post so your reader may see it.

How does T. S. Eliot use the technique of quotation in *The Waste Land* to critique the Western tradition? How does that in turn form a critique of World War I?

Based on the first two sections of Virginia Woolf's *To the Lighthouse*, how would you characterize its response to the war vis-à-vis narrative technique? In other words, what is Woolf doing with the narrative, and how does it speak to the war and its aftermath?

There are many pedagogical benefits in requiring blog posts before class meetings. That students are prompted to keep up with assignments and have a directed engagement with readings leads to better preparation and livelier in-class discussion. The instructor may identify problem areas to be addressed in class or insightful comments to be woven into the conversation. A sense of community and shared endeavor emerges when students write for one another and respond through the comment features. Students can tag their posts with semantic headings (e.g., "Virginia Woolf," "Chemical Warfare," "War Poetry," "Surrealism"), allowing them to make their writing discoverable through bibliographic and descriptive metadata, which enhances information literacy. The added fact that the blog is open to the wider world inspires them to take ownership of their work. Most important, they realize that learning not only happens between the walls at school but also has a real impact in the world—an especially valuable lesson during the war's centenary, as we collectively remember what the war meant and assess its impact on our own condition.

Time Line

A student-curated, interactive time line is an excellent project for teaching the war's cultural and historical developments. Such time lines are usually media-rich resources offering viewers the ability to scroll forward and backward in time to see chronological relations among significant events. They often provide search and filter functions that use metadata to organize information, and such information may then be used in subsequent projects. The expanded creativity of a time line provides multiple ways for students to find, synthesize, and interpret information relating to a thematic arc of the course and to gain experience presenting it in different formats.

There are many free time-line tools available. Some blog platforms and content management systems now come with time-line plugins that might be used for a project on the war, though there are plenty of options for stand-alone pieces. One of the easiest to use is *Timeline JS*, by Northwestern University's Knight Lab (timeline.knightlab.com/). The setup instructions provide a template for creating a *Google Drive* spreadsheet, where students enter the time-line data without having to know any special coding skills. The instructor may embed code by copy-pasting into a page on the course site (including a blog, wiki, HTML site, or other content management system). A more flexible yet complex tool is the *SIMILE Timeline* widget, which was originally developed at MIT and is now maintained by an open source software community (www.simile-widgets.org/timeline/). The *SIMILE Timeline* is fully customizable, offering color-coded entries, a search field, and filter widgets based on data categories, all of which are supported by Brian Croxall's excellent tutorials (briancroxall.net/TimelineTutorial/TimelineTutorial.html).

A time line is a useful part of the research process when students are investigating questions or topics related to a field of interest. On the most basic level, students might fill in historical events from the war, perhaps enhanced with images or video they found at an online scholarly resource, as a way of presenting a particular angle on the culture (e.g., nursing, women's labor on the home front, the development of poetic expression in camp magazines, the introduction of new military technologies).[4] In my courses, the social value of the time line has been in its exposure of students' findings to one another. A lab setting, where students enter data together in real time, provides an excellent opportunity to discuss the material as well as reflect on the ways in which bibliographic data entry constitutes an interpretive act.

In my courses on periodical studies and digital humanities, students have curated time-line content from the *Modernist Journals Project* (MJP) during research projects. For instance, in an undergraduate course during 2009, students worked in small groups to investigate depictions of World War I in a selection of relevant magazines—*BLAST*, *The New Age*, *The Owl*, *Poetry*, *Scribner's*, and *Wheels*:[5]

> For this assignment, you will work in groups of two or three to study a topic impacted by the Great War in one of the magazines below. Your work will be presented as a minimum seven-paragraph blog post, three time-line entries per person, and an in-class presentation on your findings. Some suggested topics are nationality, imperialism, gender, race, advertising, commerce, art, and literature, though you may cover a subject that falls outside these in consultation with the instructor. Each group will decide on one theme to cover between the years 1914 and 1919.

Wiki

Wikis are the natural choice for collaborative documentation projects. The wiki teaches students to collaborate toward a scholarly goal, increase their information literacy through familiarity with a commonly used platform, and negotiate the balance between respectfully editing previous content and adding one's own contribution. *MediaWiki*, the free software platform on which *Wikipedia* runs, provides several functionalities that make it pedagogically useful.[6] In addition to the flexible document page, which can display images and multimedia, the software's revision history shows which users made which contributions, allowing for comparison among drafts and the ability to roll back to a previous version. It also contains a talk page where students may discuss their writing and decision-making process. These features are useful to them as they reflect on the material and on the ways the technology facilitates critical thinking and useful to the instructor for assessing their contributions and for identifying problems. *MediaWiki*'s flexibility can also be a drawback in that its tagging language, wikitext, presents a learning curve for inexperienced instructors and students. However, tutorials are widely available on the Web, and, once the basics are learned, the platform is very effective.[7]

Wikis are best suited to asynchronous group projects, as well as to those that accrue across multiple iterations of a course. For instance, in a project on *The Waste Land* for a digital humanities course, students used a wiki to compile information and write multimodal essays about the poem's allusions and quotations, its representation of electric media such as the gramophone, and its original instantiation in *The Dial* and *The Criterion*. Students also embedded derivative multimedia works from around the Web that were inspired by it.[8] In a subsequent iteration of the course, students expanded on existing content and added more of their own, including a new section on *Waste Land*–inspired video games. Another group reorganized and extended the magazines topic, adding interactive maps of place-names in the poem and related pieces, as well as authors' origins, in order to establish meaningful geographic patterns that enhance our reading of the poem (modernist-magazines.org/modmag/waste-land-wiki/index.php/Archival_Evidence#Internationality). The maps were made in *Google Maps* and embedded into *MediaWiki*, in yet another example of the platform's flexibility in mixing together various tools from the Web. A similar set of projects could easily revolve around World War I and *The Waste Land*, such as reading the poem's linguistic and allusive jumble along the lines of post–World War I internationalism evident in the *The Dial* and *The Criterion*.[9]

Exhibit

Exhibit projects are great for exposing World War I materials that might be at your campus or, with permission, curating already digitized artifacts from scholarly resources on the Web. An exhibit can be done in many ways—on a static blog or wiki page, for instance—but is best executed in a purpose-built CMS like *Omeka*.[10] One reason to use *Omeka* is that its information architecture is built on the Dublin Core metadata standards used by libraries and museums, rendering it interoperable with other archives and vastly expanding the possibilities for representing World War I. In creating exhibits, students gain information literacy by learning metadata description and its effect on interpreting the material. *Omeka* works well with various media (text, image, audio, video) as well as with matériel and artifacts (gas masks, weapons, uniforms, medals). If compiling exhibits based on digital objects from the Web, such as on an archive's digital repository, students should first seek permission to use any images. In cases where such permission is difficult to receive, a wiki project or other activity that uses linking or embedding might be more appropriate.

I have used exhibit projects in my World War I courses to reinforce the materialist nature of historical analysis and for students to gain practice in writing on the same topic in different formats. The course blog is a *Drupal* implementation with a separate *Omeka* instance as a dedicated exhibit space.[11] The University of Tulsa happens to own a large collection of World War I propaganda posters, equipment, textual artifacts, and media of all kinds. One unit in the course involves the reading of race, gender, and visual or textual rhetoric in recruitment posters. Undergraduates curated a poster from our special collections department as part of an interpretive paper based on course readings. Each student picked a poster on which to build an exhibit and write a corresponding three-page paper, which was supported by a lab in which I taught the students how to use *Omeka*.

A second exhibit project, which was done at both the undergraduate and graduate levels, required students to identify and digitize an object in special collections, create an exhibit about it, and subject it to critical analysis both in the exhibit and in a longer paper. The project garnered a wide variety of material that included six Victrola records brought back from Europe by an Oklahoma veteran, along with his diary describing the songs and why he would listen to them; a historically enhanced reading of encrypted Austro-Hungarian diplomatic communiqués; aerial reconnaissance photos and the trench maps that were made from them, combined with the narrative provided by the pilot's log; a camp magazine produced by nurses; and many other worthy items. The combination of bibliographic description, historical contextualization, and close reading resulted in a collection of insightful exhibits that are now freely viewable on the Web.

With the centenary of World War I under way, digitally enhanced projects allow students to become part of the conversation by engaging actively with war artifacts and presenting them in various online formats. As we digitize the cultural artifacts of our past, it is critical that students' toolsets include practices beyond writing that will be fundamental to their role as citizens. If diplomats and military leaders at the time of the Great War were criticized for not understanding the technology at their disposal, then the onus is on us to make sure that our future leaders understand ours.

Notes

1. See wordpress.org for information about the software and a download link. The site also features numerous themes and plugins for additional features. There are plenty of other free and commercial blogging platforms, such as *Movable Type* (movabletype.org). However, I recommend *WordPress* for its ease of use and its prominence in the world of open source software, which has led to the development of many plugins that are helpful for teaching.

2. My own World War I course blog and project site uses *Drupal* and can be found at courses.utulsa.edu/wwi.

3. The *Modernist Journals Project* is an archive of digitized modern magazines, located at modjourn.org.

4. A list of online World War I resources appears in the back of this volume.

5. The *Modernist Journals Project* now features many more magazines covering the war years, including *The Crisis*, *The Egoist*, and *The Little Review*.

6. The software can be downloaded at mediawiki.org.

7. Wikitext tutorials may be found at en.wikipedia.org/wiki/Wikipedia:Tutorial/Formatting, en.wikipedia.org/wiki/Help:Cheatsheet, and en.wikipedia.org/wiki/Help:Wiki_markup/. Many more tutorials and goal-specific instructions can be found by searching the Web.

8. The *Waste Land Wiki* is located at courses.utulsa.edu/modmag/waste-land-wiki/index.php/Main_Page.

9. Other CMSs like *WordPress* and *Drupal* offer wiki-like functionalities for static pages but without some of the benefits of *MediaWiki*, while *MediaWiki* lacks the blog functionalities that would otherwise make it suitable as a main course site. *MediaWiki* can present exhibits, of course, but does not use the Dublin Core metadata that make it interoperable with other library and archival sites. In other words, each of the CMSs described here may be used for multiple purposes by mimicking the features of other purpose-built systems but may lack certain features that leverage their full advantage.

10. See omeka.org to download a package for installation on a Web server and omeka.net to set up a free exhibit site (similar to the service provided at wordpress .com).

11. The blog is located at courses.utulsa.edu/wwi and the exhibit at courses .utulsa.edu/wwi-exhibit/.

Elizabeth Outka

Teaching the First World War through Community-Based Learning

Community-based learning (CBL) courses have soared in popularity on college and university campuses, and they can be an especially effective way to teach the First World War. The components of CBL courses vary, encompassing everything from semester-long projects to targeted volunteer work to scientific research in a local area, but they generally seek to engage students by connecting classroom work with the history, culture, and environment of the local community. While literature and humanities classes can often be tricky places to implement CBL components,[1] classes that focus on wars or other conflicts lend themselves to community engagement, as few communities, unfortunately, remain untouched by war. In the United States, where World War I is often given scant attention in high school curriculums, CBL approaches are often particularly helpful. They can engage students with a war most undergraduates have not yet deeply considered and give them a multidisciplinary understanding of this particular conflict and its devastating effects.

At the University of Richmond, a colleague and I developed a successful CBL approach for a literature course involving World War I, the elements of which might be adapted to different disciplines and different conflicts (indeed, in this team-taught course, my colleague's section focused on the

Civil War).[2] In addition to a careful examination of the literature produced in both wars, our approach involved three components: first, we invited members of the local community to campus, asking a series of speakers to talk about the conditions and consequences of war for those in Richmond; second, we took the classes out into the community on targeted trips to local war memorials; third, we developed a concluding project that brought the students together with veterans at a local veterans' hospital. By the end of the semester, students who had started the class knowing little about World War I (and who were often initially uninterested in learning more) became deeply engaged in the literature and far more aware of how the war affected—and continues to affect—the local community. Students told us that the class was one of the most interesting and meaningful they had ever taken. Many of the components, though, required trial and error for us to get them right, and some were tricky to implement. In this essay, I describe our strategies in detail and note how different elements might be adapted for various approaches to World War I.

Our first CBL component involved bringing in speakers in our community who worked with or as soldiers. We invited three types of professionals: doctors who treated the physical injuries suffered by soldiers in war, psychiatrists or psychologists who worked with soldiers suffering from posttraumatic stress disorder or other psychological issues related to combat and its aftermath, and individuals who served or had served in various capacities in the armed forces. One semester, for example, we invited a neuropsychologist from the local veterans' hospital to talk about his work with soldiers suffering from traumatic brain injuries and about the consequences, both physical and mental, of being in a war zone. In different semesters, we invited a psychiatrist who spoke about her work training Iraqi citizens to respond to and treat posttraumatic stress disorder and a therapist trained to help military families adjust to deployments and to the many issues they face when soldiers return. While we thought these speakers would fit well with our course, we were stunned at how relevant their talks were to understanding the literature we read. To take just one example, when the psychiatrist spoke of the often paradoxical effects of trauma on memory—the way a soldier might remember constantly and yet still push away the memory of a terrible experience—students discovered in class the next day how a war poet might convey this effect through enjambment. In Ivor Gurney's "To His Love," for instance, the poem's line breaks suggest both how the soldier-poet tried to keep an image at bay and how that image relentlessly rose again in the next line. The literature suddenly became current, and the way that the literature might shape the experience and that the history might shape the literature became much more vibrant for our students.

At the suggestion of several of our ROTC students, we invited soldiers or former soldiers to speak about their experiences. One soldier, who had been stationed in both Iraq and Afghanistan, detailed the challenges soldiers faced in modern warfare and the way they approached some of the cultural differences they encountered. Another year, we invited a soldier who spoke of his work recovering missing bodies as well as of his experience on military bereavement teams. His talk let us consider differences in how the military dealt with bodies and notifying next of kin in World War I and in the United States today and how those differences might grant new insights into our readings. The staccato death notifications of Virginia Woolf's brackets in *To the Lighthouse*, for example, took on new meaning in the light of our discussions of death notices, and students could start to see how military policy and experiences wove their way into literary form—and how literary form could, in turn, show the limitations and costs of such policies. The talks from soldiers also allowed students to see war from yet another perspective, to focus on the motivations of both soldiers and armies as well as on traumatic experiences. Here again, students found immediate connections between the talks and our literature, seeing how the literature spoke both to the importance of a particular cause and to the trauma of what that cause might nevertheless produce. After each speaker, students wrote short response essays that explored a particular connection between the literature and the talk.

The second component of our CBL approach—field trips to various war memorials—might also be adapted to most communities. Since our class focused on investigating how writers remember and memorialize war in literary form, a parallel investigation of how war is remembered and represented through material monuments deepened student understanding of both forms. In the United States, one challenge of this field trip is the relative lack of memorials to World War I; classes taught in many European countries will not face this issue. We discovered, however, that memorials were hidden in plain sight in Richmond (a city primarily dominated by memorials to the Civil War). Our research revealed that a well-known local bell tower, the Carillon, had been built as the city's memorial to World War I, and further research uncovered the motives and history behind its construction. For example, newspaper accounts detailed how, after the completion of the tower, the city held a parade that marched from the Virginia State Capitol to the Carillon, accompanied by planes dropping red poppy flowers in their wake. Women had formed patrol groups to guard Richmond's bridges from German attack, and groups on both sides of the suffragette question had joined together to support various war efforts in Richmond. We brought students to the Carillon site and told some of the history surrounding its construction as they toured. We then gave them time to look closely at the details of the monument and its surroundings. After the class returned to campus, they posted detailed response essays about how the monument's various elements represented and remembered the war—and what elements it might have left out. They also paired the monument with an example pulled from our reading. Many World War I poems address monuments, from Sassoon's searing "On Passing the New Menin Gate" or "Memorial Tablet" to Charlotte Mew's "The Cenotaph." Students could select one of these poems to compare or select an example that related more generally to memory or to grief and loss. Comparing an actual monument in their community to the readings allowed them to understand World War I not simply as a conflict fought long ago in a different place but also as one that continued to impact the local area. The class analyzed how the structure of the memorial and the surrounding landscaping spoke to the same issues found in the poems, including the attempt to balance somber reflection and loss with recognition of heroic effort.

This CBL component could be used with some modifications for communities without World War I memorials. Even in our class, I brought in photographs of different memorials in France and elsewhere, and students analyzed them before the field trip. Comparing monuments such as Menin Gate and the London Cenotaph with each other and to our readings generated conversations about how location, size, materials, and representation might offer different types of consolation and also moments of problematic erasure (which Sassoon so memorably rages against in his work). Other memorials might also be considered from countries on both sides of the conflict and from various ethnic, racial, or religious groups. For those communities without a World War I memorial, photographs of memorials from other places could be compared with local memorials of another conflict, which students could visit and pair with course readings. Even the lack of memorials might become a source of conversation, suggesting that the fears in the World War I literature—that this conflict might be forgotten—were far from baseless.

The third CBL component involved a set of final projects that might likewise be adapted to different communities. Students were given a choice of two projects. Working in small groups, they could select a particular

World War I memorial, ideally in Richmond or in the surrounding area, and do more extensive research into the origins, characteristics, and controversies surrounding it. The groups then had to consider how some aspect of their memorial connected to several of our readings. As their final exam, groups presented their topic to the class, and individual students then turned in a longer essay that considered an issue raised by the research into both the literature and the memorial. The second option asked students to develop and organize a literary reading at a local veterans' hospital. Working in small groups, they considered what themes might speak most directly to veterans (such as the strong bonds formed among soldiers or the pleasures and difficulties of returning home after a war). They prepared a presentation that put the works in context and then selected a mini anthology of our readings that reflected the particular issues they were exploring. For their individual final paper, they wrote on one of their selected themes.

For the veteran reading, we took several critical steps to ensure that the presentations would work smoothly and be appropriate for the given audience—no veteran or soldier needs to be told what war is like by a group of college students who have never seen armed conflict. First, early in the semester, we made contact with the veterans' hospitals and arranged convenient times and meeting places. Because a visit was often challenging to arrange, students could choose this project only if they could be available for the time specified. On the advice of one of our speakers who worked with veterans at the local VA hospital, we visited primarily with older veterans, who might be more ready and willing to process such a reading, rather than recently returned soldiers. In their presentation, students had an introduction explaining the class itself and the particular themes they would explore in the readings to follow. Then each poem or passage was preceded by a mini introduction. Students prepared handouts with all the readings numbered, so the audience could follow along. Finally, we asked all the groups to present for the two of us before going to the hospital. We wanted to ensure the presentation was of high quality and that the students did not seem to be preaching or telling soldiers what the soldiers had gone through. Rather, we wanted students to share passages that might (or might not) speak to a particular veteran's experiences. We accompanied students to the hospitals, and in every case these readings were highlights of the semester, with extremely enthusiastic responses from the veterans in the audience. The class had time both before and after the readings to talk with the veterans, and these talks, along with the readings themselves, made the visits both significant and memorable.

Through the community-based learning elements of the course, our students gained awareness that Richmond and its residents remain marked by World War I and other conflicts. They came to see a condition like shell shock not as a malady lost to history but—now relabeled PTSD—as something ongoing, affecting soldiers today. Whether they read a poem by Wilfred Owen or a novel by Virginia Woolf, they saw how the conditions of war and its aftermath affected the literature's structure, and they realized that the literature in turn shaped the way we now represent the war. They thought deeply about how individuals and communities remember traumatic events, considering what is remembered but also how we remember and why. It was our hope that, by interacting with Richmond doctors, current soldiers, veterans, and material memorials, students would come to see this conflict and its repercussions as a still present force in both their community and their nation.

Notes

1. Susan Danielson and Ann Marie Fallon have edited an insightful collection on general issues and the practical applications of CBL components in literature courses; see *Community-Based Learning and the Work of Literature*.

2. I am deeply indebted to my colleague Kevin Pelletier, who developed the Literature of War course and its CBL components with me and who brought his encyclopedic expertise on the Civil War to bear on his section of the course. We are both grateful to Terry Dolson at Richmond's Bonner Center for Civic Engagement, who deftly guided us through the challenges of creating an effective CBL course.

Laura McLary

Bild und Text im Ersten Weltkrieg: A Genre-Based Approach to the First World War for Intermediate-Advanced Students of German

A few years ago, I began to plan an upper-division German language and culture course focusing on literature and fine arts in anticipation of the commemoration of the First World War's beginning. I originally intended to build upon an existing course centered on depictions of youth between 1909 and 1945. I already had a good body of materials to draw from, and I was prepared to create my usual course around literary analysis in German, providing students with opportunities to practice the metagenres that our German program had defined as essential skills: summarizing, describing, narrating, and comparing. But between my first idea about this class and my first day standing before a group of students, I attended a workshop at Georgetown University that led me to a broader conception of the course that included a variety of texts and images, not just literature and fine arts. Heidi Byrnes and Marianna Ryshina-Pankova in the German Department at Georgetown led the workshop, which was based on their ongoing curricular revisions, intended to overcome the bifurcation between language acquisition and content courses endemic to many foreign language programs in the United States.[1] In particular, their program focuses on developing literacy (in German) and uses a genre-based approach to support students as they work toward achieving advancedness in the language.[2] This approach was developed by teachers and researchers in Australia for the teaching of English as a second language; it applies systemic functional linguistics (SFL) as means of understanding the social functions and stages of genre and uses the texts as models for student writing. Literary scholars are used to thinking about genres in terms of literary genres, but an SFL approach engages with a wider range of text types and defines genre "as a goal-oriented social process" (Martin 10).

From the perspective of second-language teaching and learning, I find this approach at once pleasantly restricting and exhilaratingly liberating. Students can work with text in a clearly defined structure, focusing on development of vocabulary specific to each genre and its topic and thus becoming aware of how word choice affects a text's tone and function, while also tuning into the social interaction between writer and participants. When it comes to text production, students can use our readings (as appropriate) as mentor texts. Once we have identified the stages, the participants, and salient grammatical and rhetorical features of the genre under study, students have a framework for their own writing. In the past, I typically sent students off to write literary analysis papers, expecting that they had experienced this kind of writing in an English literature class. Using a genre-based approach to reading and writing, I construct with them useful templates and linguistic elements through example, and they are then free to develop, for example, a personally interesting semantic field that can be used for a particular genre. The assessment of genre-based writing assignments is logically based on the extent to which the student fulfilled the requirements of the genre, and we can thus avoid the general terms I once attached to writing assessment—for example, organization and content. The rich array of genres from the World War I era provides an excellent opportunity to explore the social function of texts in the context of their time and presents students with literacy-based writing tasks that require them to combine their developing content knowledge with awareness of genre construction.[3]

Course Content

During the summer of 2014, I had the opportunity to visit exhibits on World War I in Vienna and Salzburg.[4] The Georgetown workshop attuned me to the way the texts and images in the exhibits could be potential materials for learning not only about depictions of the era but also about how language was used for specific social purposes. I focus here on text choices for the course on World War I and highlight in the next section how we engaged in particular with one text, a public appeal. In a second language classroom, it is necessary to balance the course content goals with students' language proficiency needs. Using a literacy and genre-based approach to language learning allows these two needs to flow seamlessly into each other, but planning such a course requires careful selection of texts. I chose texts that represented a range of genres.[5] Among the texts we read were Kaiser Franz Josef's declaration of war against Serbia; public appeals; letters between the front and home; propaganda posters and postcards; memoirs from men and women, including childhood memories of the war; literary narrative; poetry; and newspapers. Through close reading of these texts, using semantic field, participants, and tone to guide our reading, I helped students understand how the demands of a genre convey a particular social discourse. A wide range of genres also provided students with maximum exposure to semantic fields and registers, supporting their growth as readers and writers of German striving to achieve advanced ability.

My second reason for choosing a wide range of genres evolved out of my decision to emphasize gender roles during the war years. While it would have been possible to structure the course around a longer reading such as Erich Maria Remarque's *Im Westen nichts Neues*, we read this novel only in excerpts so that we could look at numerous voices.[6] As the historian Christa Hämmerle has documented, there are many memoirs written by women about their war experiences at the home front and as nurses or in combat roles at the front, but many of these documents are not published.[7] Focusing on gender roles during the war allowed my students to organize their readings, class discussions, presentations, and writing assignments in relation to a particular form of identity construction, one of the thematic motifs on which the German program at the University of Portland is structured. It is also a useful means of comparing texts and images, often revealing the many underlying contradictions in the gender expectations of the era. The range of genres allowed us to consider how gender roles shift depending on the intended function of the text. Hämmerle references a rich body of research on the First World War, revealing that the division between the so-called feminine home front and the masculine front was in fact quite porous.

In addition to comparing genres from a variety of authors to understand how the genres function, students require a basic historical fluency in order to place the texts and images in context. I therefore provided, early in the semester, brief lectures in German summarizing the major events and issues for each year of the war. In a follow-up activity focused on new vocabulary terms and on significant content, I assigned pairs of students to research terms and concepts to present in our next class meeting—for example, *Mittelmächte* and *Alliierten*, *Kriegseuphorie*, *Liebesgaben*, *Isonzoschlachten*, *Ersatzstoffe*, and *Hungerkrawallen*.[8] A few students were familiar with some of these terms and concepts in English, and this activity allowed them to tap into their preexisting historical literacy while expanding their semantic field for talking and writing about World War I in German. The terminology provided a basis for future work in the class, as we encountered these concepts in other texts and images.

Comparing a Declaration and a Public Appeal

At the beginning of the semester, we compared two public documents that appeared within one day of each other: a public appeal by Marianne Hainisch (chairwoman of the League of Austrian Women's Clubs) to the women of Austria, asking them to support their sons, fathers, and husbands and their country in the event of war (27 July 1914) and the full text of Franz Josef's declaration of war on Serbia (28 July 1914).[9] We read the two texts together because they demonstrate contrasts in language usage specific to male and female gender expectations early in the war. Though the official languages of the two documents share some similarities, we turned up many differences as we began to analyze the texts. One key difference between the two documents rests on the fact that the kaiser's is a declaration (*Erklärung*): that is, he is telling his audience what he has decided and is not asking for their opinion or their help. Hainisch's document is an appeal (*Aufruf*): that is, her goal is to persuade the women of Austria to join her in supporting the war effort.

We focused first on semantic field and significant structures to understand what kinds of vocabulary appear with regularity in the two texts. We discovered a heavy reliance on nouns and genitive constructions, particularly in the declaration of war, conveying abstract concepts (honor, peace). In the appeal, we discovered also a tendency toward nominalization; but about a third of the way into the document, the emphasis shifts to verbs of action—for example, *to help*, *to support*, *to care for*, *to organize*—as the author makes her actual appeal. We noticed a distinctive use of pronouns in each document, consistent with their social function. The declaration of war relies solely on the first-person singular pronoun and possessive adjective, and these are always capitalized: *Ich*, *Mein*. The appeal reaches out to a collective community in solidarity and therefore makes repeated use of the first-person plural pronoun and possessive adjective: *wir*, *unser*. An analysis of the pronouns gave us a clear sense of the participants in the social exchange created by both documents. One of our final steps was to break down the appeal into stages: the *Anrede* (address: "Frauen Österreichs!"), the description of the situation, a rhetorical question and its rebuttal ("Sollen wir passiv dulden und leiden? Das geziemt der Gattin und Mutter, der Staatsbürgerin nicht, sondern"), a solution ("pflegen," "helfen," "organisieren"), a specific request for action ("bitte ich im Namen des Bundes österreichischer Frauenvereine"), a concrete means of taking action (in this case, a place to volunteer), a final appeal ("Frauen Österreichs sammelt euch"), and finally place, date, and signature.

For our next class meeting, I asked students to think about a cause (on campus, in their community) they felt strongly about so that we could begin to write our own appeals, using the structure provided by "Frauen Österreichs!" In class, I provided them with the bare structure we had created from our mentor document, and using my own cause (a neighborhood clean air group), we constructed an appeal together. Then students worked singly and in pairs to begin building up a semantic field for their appeals. The results showed a high degree of semantic development and a greater level of accuracy than was typically the case for student analysis essays I had assigned in the past. For example, the *zu* + *Infinitiv* construction is often difficult for students to use spontaneously, but when we found repeated examples in our mentor text, students could see where and how it is most effectively employed and were able to use it with a high degree of accuracy in their own public appeals. Our work with the public appeal "Frauen Österreichs!" allowed us to gain insights into expectations for and actions of women during World War I and provided students with linguistic tools for increasing their advancedness in German.

Resources

In commemoration of the beginning of the First World War, many first-rate German-language Web sites documenting the war experience have appeared. For example, the *Süddeutsche Zeitung* is publishing a series of articles related to events from 1914 to 1918, including extensive photo documentation.

The Wienbibliothek im Rathaus and the Wiener Stadt- und Landesarchiv have curated a rich collection of text and images documenting the war. Many of the documents are available as high-quality downloads. Particularly interesting for my course is the extensive collection of posters, public appeals, and public announcements. The posters represent a robust commentary on gender roles and social expectations in wartime. Public appeals and public announcements provide an opportunity for analyzing how these documents use a relevant field of vocabulary, a clear audience address, specific rhetorical devices, and a genre-specific structure to persuade fellow citizens (usually) to contribute to the war effort. Linked to this Web site is a collection of protocols from 1914 to 1918, in which the Viennese police department documented public responses to the war in so-called public mood reports ("Stimmungsberichte der Polizeidirektion Wien"). These very dense and interesting documents provide insights into daily life during the war years. Topics covered include public sentiment about everything from war refugees to prices of food to sectors of unemployment. From a second-language standpoint, these documents are linguistically accessible for students at the intermediate level of German language proficiency and represent good examples of mentor texts from which students can practice the conventions of reporting.

The *AEIOU Österreich-Lexikon* of the *Austria-Forum* provides a comprehensive historical overview of the First World War in German that is accessible to intermediate undergraduate students with some support and scaffolding. A much longer and more detailed historical overview is also available here as a link to the *AustriaWiki.*[10] Much of this material is too detailed and advanced for most students at this level, but it provides an excellent resource for teachers. The article is extensively hyperlinked and contains useful visual materials, such as historical photos, maps, and visual propaganda. The topic page on the First World War of the *Österreich-Lexikon* also contains an extensive list of essays, some video documentation, and a link to photographs, including a dense collection of propaganda and war-related picture postcards.

Finally, the Deutsche Historische Museum and the Haus der Geschichte maintain the Web site *Das lebendige Museum Online* ("Living Museum Online"), covering German history from the nineteenth century to the present, an excellent resource that has been available for nearly fifteen years. Like the *Österreich Lexikon*, it is a dense source of photographs and other images; historical documents in a variety of genres, including eyewitness accounts, such as letters and memoirs; and official documents, such as public appeals and proclamations. Some of the historical, informational text, which is extensively hyperlinked, is accessible for undergraduates. The wide variety of text genres readily available for professors of German makes teaching about World War I from a German-speaking perspective an excellent opportunity to support students' development of advanced writing and speaking skills. Students leave the class with a richer and more nuanced understanding of how text and images shaped the discourse around World War I in the German-speaking world.

Notes

1. The workshop, an AATG faculty seminar, Meeting Tomorrow's Needs in College German Programs, took place 11–13 October 2013 on the Georgetown campus and was attended by representatives from thirteen college and university German programs across the country. In preparation for the workshop, we read an excellent article by Hiram Maxim et al. on the curricular reforms in the German program at Emory University: "Overcoming Curricular Bifurcation: A Departmental Approach to Curriculum Reform." See also the special issue of *The Modern Language Journal*, *Realizing Advanced Foreign Language Writing Development in Collegiate Education: Curricular Design, Pedagogy, Assessment*, edited by Heidi Byrnes, Maxim, and John Norris.

2. Applied linguistics uses the term *advancedness* to refer to the sequenced, supported development of writing skills by second language learners that employs conventions beyond those more typical of spoken language.

3. This particular course employed and practiced the text-based approach used at Georgetown. In our German program at University of Portland, we are revising our curriculum, based on our existing structure, to include a more specifically literacy-based approach in all our German courses.

4. The Salzburg Museum's exhibit focused on the experience of war in Land Salzburg. The Leopold Museum in Vienna considered the role of the artist during World War I. The catalog for the exhibit provides many reproductions of work by Austrian artists of the World War I era, including Egon Schiele and Albin Egger-Lienz. The Nationalbibliothek in Vienna also produced an exhibit entitled *An Meine Völker* with an accompanying catalog.

5. Concurrent with our genre-based reading of texts from the First World War, our class considered the role of images to depict the war experience, also from a gendered perspective. Images from posters, postcards, and newspapers represented the most frequent kinds of materials we investigated, but we also considered the representation of the war experience in fine arts, through works by Egon Schiele, Albin Egger-Lienz, Otto Dix, and Käthe Kollwitz.

6. For the same reason, we read only excerpts of Fritz Weber's *Alpenkrieg* and Ernst Jünger's *In Stahlgewittern*.

7. In her book, she quotes from many such sources, and I brought excerpts for my class to read.

8. "Central Powers," "Allied Powers," "war euphoria," literally "love tokens" or alms for soldiers, "Battles of the Isonzo," "substitutes," and "hunger riots."

9. Franz Josef's declaration of war is widely available in a variety of sources, but we used the typescript reproduced in the catalog of the exhibit in the Leopold Museum in Vienna (Leopold et. al 1, 3, 5, 7). The appeal "Frauen Österreichs!" is reproduced in Hämmerle (84).

10. *AustriaWiki* contains articles that have been taken over from the German-language *Wikipedia* and frozen, meaning that the site does not accept comments or revisions and that the contributions are read and revised by experts in the field ("AustriaWiki: Beiträge mit Österreichbezug").

Mark D. Larabee

World War I Landscapes at the United States Naval Academy

While students today may not arrive at college already well versed in Great War literature or history, the landscapes of that war—dominated in the popular imagination by the trenches and no-man's-land of the Western Front—may offer one familiar locus. Courses addressing these Great War landscapes can follow a variety of pedagogically inviting avenues: interart comparison, for example; aesthetics and epistemology; or comparisons among national literatures, artistic traditions, and identities. Such interests have informed several courses on World War I literature and art that I taught at the United States Naval Academy. On one hand, a military academy offers a uniquely conducive setting for courses on military themes in literature; on the other hand, our students must surely resemble young adults at any other college in terms of learning about literature, history, and themselves. In this essay, I describe those particular courses and my students' unique personal commitment to learning about the landscapes of war, while also indicating potential connections to teaching in other college settings.

The Naval Academy is a four-year coeducational undergraduate college that offers a bachelor of science degree with a choice of twenty-four majors among disciplines in engineering, sciences, mathematics, humanities, and social sciences. Students (called midshipmen) who major in English follow a curriculum that will be familiar to readers: survey courses and Shakespeare, electives in literary periods and genres, and literary theory. The senior year culminates in research-intensive capstone seminars on special topics that vary each semester, and the menu of these capstone courses has a number of times included two of my courses, Literary Landscapes of World War I and The First World War in British Art and Literature.

Our graduates receive bachelor of science degrees but also commissions as officers in the Navy or Marine Corps. Therefore, alongside their regular academics, they study military leadership, ethics, law, and weapons systems. After graduation, they go on to advanced technical training in a particular warfare specialty (such as aviation, surface ships, submarines, or one of many Marine Corps occupations) before ultimately serving overseas. Before coming to my courses, students have all studied and practiced navigation, both at sea and on land. Those who become officers in the navy (whether in aircraft, ships, or submarines) must be able to correlate what they read on maps and charts with what they see in the world around them, even in the age of GPS. For Marine Corps officers, skill in land navigation is essential to success on the battlefield. Thus, for virtually all our future officers, interpreting landscapes is a crucial skill, and studying landscape representations in literature and art offers useful ways to combine their academic and military preparation while demonstrating the immediate relevance of otherwise potentially remote historical periods and literary topics.

Literary Landscapes of World War I centers on ways that the war challenged the representative capacities of maps, language, and visual art. This course explores responses to those challenges, such as how modernist topographies of war in texts by Ford Madox Ford, Edmund Blunden, Rebecca West, and others shaped the meaning of the Great War and offered reconstructions of self and culture. These explorations can expand beyond British literature, however. Novels and poems by such authors as Henri Barbusse, Georg Trakl, Eugenio Montale, Giuseppe Ungaretti, Emilio Lussu, and Ernst Jünger, for example, deepen students' cross-cultural understanding of landscape representation in Great War literature. We use Paul Fussell's *The Great War and Modern Memory* as the organizing text, reading each of his chapters as an introduction to issues in the primary readings and to significant historical themes. The course has four main units on landscapes: maps, verbal descriptions, visual art, and the globalizing imagination.

In the unit on maps, students first read Fussell's chapter entitled "The Troglodyte World," which primes them for a detailed examination of life in the trenches and how the landscapes of the war powerfully shaped soldiers' quotidian experiences. After students receive an introduction to techniques of military mapping in the early twentieth century, they read Blunden's *Undertones of War* (1928) and Ford's *No Enemy* (1929). We focus on the mapping and map-reading skills practiced by Blunden and Ford as British army officers and how topographical representation shapes the themes of those autobiographically inspired texts. Many of our students spent a lot of their childhood in the outdoors, and they in particular find Blunden's sensitive portrayal of natural landscapes under the pressure of mechanized war both understandable and unsettling—such as his aesthetically appealing description of a battle area he was sent to examine (88). A parallel instance appears in Jünger's autobiographical *Storm of Steel* (1920), in the description of what can be seen from the heights "dubbed 'Bellevue' " (38). Meanwhile in the contrastingly mountainous terrain of the Italian front, the battlefield becomes similarly aestheticized in such poems as Ungaretti's "Vanity" (1917) and "Once upon a Time" (1916) and Montale's "Valmorbia" (undated).

All the midshipmen are especially attentive to the divisions of mind that Ford portrays in *No Enemy*. Our students, as people in their teens or early twenties at a coeducational college that combines military training with the liberal arts tradition, frequently grapple with a problem that comes up in many forms here: how to hold together often competing fragments or versions of themselves. For this reason, Ford's account of the narrator's military observation of the countryside from a hill in Flanders—struggling to coordinate visions of landscape inflected by the narrator's divided mind (infantry officer, intelligence officer, and poet all at once)—strikes a resonant chord (38–45). A contrasting narrative about the divided mind of the military observer appears in Lussu's *Sardinian Brigade* (1938). Throughout this novel, the mountains surrounding the front lines complicate soldiers' attention to seeing and not being seen. Furthermore, a notion of the "co-ordination of intellects" in Lussu's novel echoes Ford's description of a tripartite mind but in a comic episode instead (142–44). Reading these accounts gratifyingly leads to conversations about the often unexpectedly competing demands placed on our graduates as leaders and followers, and as warriors and family members, in military organizations that prize both individual initiative and self-sacrificing teamwork. Discussing what Ford's narrator, especially, sees in the landscape through the multiple lenses of his competing identities thus insightfully prepares midshipmen for such challenges.

The second unit focuses on the words that describe landscape, first by comparing the treatment of physical place in Baedeker guidebooks with Blunden's ironic reuse of deictic conventions in his poems "The Prophet" and "Trench Nomenclature" (both 1928). We turn from the nicknames that British troops gave to places (e.g., "Jacob's Ladder," "Picturedome," and "Krab Krawl" [Blunden 221]) to their renaming of foreign place-names ("Ocean Villas" for Auchonvillers) to the naming of places in Iraq and Afghanistan in recent American campaigns (even, for instance, "No Name Canal")—a second naming that can supplement or supersede official nomenclature on maps. Comparisons with naming in nonanglophone poetry are available through readings of Montale's "Valmorbia" and "Distant, I Was with You When Your Father" (probably 1939), both of which, in the words of Jonathan Galassi, "make talismanic use of place-names" (458). Similar effects animate Trakl's "Grodek" (1914) and Ungaretti's "San Martino del Carso" (1916). Monte S. Michele in Ungaretti's "I Am a Presence" (1916) and Bosco Cappuccio in his "Once upon a Time" (1916) exert talismanic effects as well.

A third unit, on representations of landscape in visual art, grounds a reading of Rebecca West's *The Return of the Soldier* (1918) first in the context of Fussell's chapter "Arcadian Resources" and Samuel Hynes's chapter "The Death of Landscape" in *A War Imagined*. We consider how the legacy of the landscape tradition in visual art is called into question by the frontline experience. Students then read Longinus, Burke, and Kant to discern how West portrays the beautiful, picturesque, and sublime in the war-inflected landscapes of home in her country house setting. We also examine references to landscape painting in C. E. Montague's memoir *Disenchantment* (1922) to understand his critical characterization of the war's cultural stakes and outcomes. From a French perspective, Henri Barbusse likewise meditates on ideals and doubts alongside painterly descriptions of the battlefield landscape near the end of *Under Fire* (1916; 306, 314). Especially given the unanticipated outcomes of American military engagements in the Middle East, such uses of art and verbal descriptions provide my students with some terms (e.g., *faith* and *illusion*, *chivalry*, *defense of culture*) with which to express their thoughts about military service.

The last unit, on Joseph Conrad's *The Shadow-Line* (1917) and Virginia Woolf's *Jacob's Room* (1922), explores the globalization of war landscapes through the fictional landscapes of novels ostensibly set outside the front lines. Conrad's method, for instance, of implicitly superimposing the topography of the Western Front over his fictive Gulf of Siam gives us ways to discuss how United States military camps in Iraq and Afghanistan become projected patches of American landscape in the Middle East and how posttraumatic stress disorder can bring the IED-riddled roads and chaotic urban environments of foreign campaigns home in the imaginations of veterans.

The course The First World War in British Art and Literature includes one unit on landscapes. This course incorporates war poems, and it juxtaposes visual art and literature in direct pairings and other combinations. First I orient students to methods of art interpretation, comparative analysis, and interdisciplinary theory. Students read selections from Mary Acton's *Learning to Look at Paintings*, prepare handouts on reading a painting, and then deliver an oral presentation in which they use her formal categories (composition, space, form, tone, color) to analyze a set of assigned artworks that demonstrate a variety of formal approaches. Such works include C. R. W. Nevinson's futurist-influenced *Flooded Trench on the Yser* (1915), for example, among more traditionally composed scenes by other artists. Then students read and discuss the critical considerations of verbal versus visual art contained in Gotthold Lessing's *Laocoön*, Joseph Frank's "Spatial Form in Modern Literature," and W. J. T. Mitchell's "Image versus Text" and "Space and Time: G. E. Lessing" (chapters in *Iconology*), as well as selections from Wendy Steiner's *The Colors of Rhetoric* and a passage from Ulrich Weisstein's "Literature and the Visual Arts."

In the landscape unit in this course, students examine the psychological divisions of landscape observation in Ford's *No Enemy* while also studying Muirhead Bone's *The Battle of the Somme* (1916) and *Road Liable to be Shelled* (1917). We discuss, first, the reliance of Bone on conventions of landscape portrayal as he presents the front lines in ways familiar to civilian audiences. Then we consider Wilfred Owen's condemnation of the drawings as "the laughing stock of the army" because of their artificiality (Letter to Susan Owen 429). Montague's captions and introductions to drawings published in Bone's *The Western Front* (1917), on the other hand, argued for their perceptive uncanniness. We attempt to account for these differences of opinion, considering the effects of varying degrees of battlefield experience between this artist and his critics. Midshipmen are forcefully reminded of the many-sided nature of truths in war; the difficulties, ambiguities, and compromises inherent in any attempt at portraying those truths; and the availability of different artistic techniques for those portrayals. We then embark on a lively discussion of these differences in experience and interpretation, moving outward to consider variations in how the wars in Iraq and Afghanistan are portrayed in popular media, recent literature, and by Naval Academy graduates who have returned to the faculty after serving there. Thus prepared, the class continues to read *No Enemy* while moving from Bone's traditionalist drawings to a variety of more formally experimental landscape works by Paul Nash (e.g., *We are Making a New World* [1917–18], *Sunrise: Inverness Copse* [1918], *The Menin Road* [1918–19], *Landscape—Year of Our Lord, 1917* [1918], and *Ruin: Sunset* [1917–18]), Nevinson (*The Roads of France* [1917–18] and *After a Push* [1917]), D. Y. Cameron (*The Battlefield of Ypres* [1919]), and John Nash (*Oppy Wood* [1918–19]).

Both courses culminate in a topic of acute personal interest to midshipmen: myth and memory, with emphasis on cemeteries and war memorials as landscape features. Cemeteries, memorials, and what they signify are ever present to midshipmen, all of whom are required to live on campus and spend almost all their time within its gates. The Naval Academy's compact grounds (just 338 acres) include a cemetery and columbarium that are home to 4,600 burials, and over sixty monuments and memorials to naval leaders are scattered among the academic buildings and sports fields (Arbuthnot xiv). The remains of John Paul Jones rest beneath the Naval Academy Chapel in a sarcophagus and crypt reminiscent of Napoleon's tomb at Les Invalides. At the ceremonial heart of Bancroft Hall (the nearly two-thousand-room single dormitory that houses all midshipmen), Memorial Hall contains numerous busts, plaques, and paintings dedicated to alumni killed in service and walls engraved with names of the fallen. Many student rooms have citations, mounted just outside the door, detailing the exploits of Medal of Honor recipients (frequently posthumous).

Because these landscape and architectural features make war a visibly present part of midshipman life, we deepen students' understanding of memorial landscape as a cultural signifier by studying such works as Stanley Spencer's *Unveiling Cookham War Memorial* (1922), his paintings for Sandham Memorial Chapel, Burghclere (Malvern 167–73), and Fred Varley's *For What?* (c. 1918), alongside Rudyard Kipling's "The Gardener" (1925). Doing so allows us to consider how personally significant abstractions in war (heroism, sacrifice, loved ones' memories) are both mythologized and brought into concrete existence through statuary, memorial architecture, and the landscape design of cemeteries, both then and now. The conversation thereby takes a turn into how midshipmen are integrated into an ongoing story of heroism defined and asserted through landscape, as they witness their own change from college students into officers with sobering obligations of self-sacrifice.

Yet for all the evident applicability of World War I landscapes to the education of our midshipmen, Annapolis is still a rather unlikely place to study those landscapes. Naval Academy curriculum, history, and lore revolve around ships and the sea, not trenches and no-man's-land, and the city just outside the academy gates prizes its water access to Chesapeake Bay and bills itself as America's sailing capital. Nevertheless, when our midshipmen make the leap from sea to land as discussed above, they follow academic inquiries recognizably applicable at other colleges. Philosophical approaches to landscape emphasizing epistemological limits or the relations between words and images; art history approaches focusing on traditional and experimental styles; or thematic approaches addressing violence, trauma, grief, family, memory, comradeship, and so on can be appealingly taught at a wide variety of institutions. Most important, our students are like others their age in coming to terms with the cultural and historical forces shaping them and in their growing awareness of how they are simultaneously constructed by and constructing their worlds. Representations of those worlds—in Great War landscapes as recorded and created through art and literature—can thus provide endlessly fascinating topics for students, both military and civilian.

Part VI

Web Resources

Douglas Higbee

First World War–Related Web Sites: A Bibliography

Depending on the day, a *Google* search for "First World War" can produce anywhere from 400 million to over a billion results (more than that produced with a search for "Second World War"). This huge number reflects the general public's intense, ongoing interest in the war, the enormous amount of scholarship and research performed by both professional and amateur historians, and the growing amount of material posted online from various archives and universities. This interest, which will surely continue in decades to come, is currently augmented by the centenary.

With this vast Web presence, teachers have the opportunity to bring into the classroom materials that previously were housed in faraway archives or bound in expensive books. Given the globalization of our understanding of the war, this opportunity is both more necessary and, now, more possible. Of course, more doesn't necessarily mean better, and it can certainly mean overwhelming.

What follows is an annotated list of Web sites chosen for their degree of helpfulness to university-level teachers. Sites with substantial primary sources and pedagogical materials were preferred, as well as those that are well organized and easily searchable. Most of the sites listed below are scholarly or archival, but a few have been created by nonprofessionals. Not only do scholarly and archival sites offer many primary sources of various genres suitable for classroom use but also we can expect such sites to be around for quite some time.

I've largely excluded sites with a broad, national focus ("Australia and the Great War," etc.), because an adequately fair representation of them would extend this bibliography beyond anyone's patience and because they are relatively easy to find. The same principle of selection applies to sites dedicated to individuals.

Armenian Genocide

www.armenian-genocide.org/

Sponsored by the Armenian National Institute, a Washington DC–based organization, with content overseen by a board of prominent academics, this site offers primary sources such as photographs, contemporary accounts, and government documents related to the Armenian genocide. It also includes an educational resources section.

Art of the First World War

www.memorial-caen.fr/10EVENT/EXPO1418/gb/visite.html

Sponsored by UNESCO and hosted by the Memorial Centre for History and Peace in Normandy, this site features over one hundred paintings by key European and American artists of the war, searchable by name and topic, and includes a helpful introductory essay.

British Broadcasting Company

www.bbc.co.uk/ww1

This extensive site emphasizes the global nature of the war in offering a number of recordings and transcripts from broadcasts on a range of topics. Instructors might also find useful this site's interactive guides on battlefield communication, medicine, and trench life as well as links to several online courses on various First World War topics offered by prestigious universities.

British Cartoon Archive

www.cartoons.ac.uk/search-catalogue

Hosted by the University of Kent at Canterbury, this site contains over one thousand First World War–related cartoons from British newspapers, categorized by publication, artist, and topic.

British Library: World War One

www.bl.uk/world-war-one

This site features a searchable-by-theme archive of hundreds of primary sources related to many combatant nations (not just Great Britain), including photographs, postcards, drawings, booklets, and books, as well as a number of introductory essays by historians on key topics associated with the war. The site also provides a series of lesson plans for teachers.

Canadian Letters and Images Project

www.canadianletters.ca/collections.php?warid=3

Directed by Stephen Davies, a professor of history at Vancouver Island University, this fascinating and easily searchable site offers hundreds of transcribed letters and diaries, many donated by private families, sent by Canadian soldiers during the war. It also includes capsule biographies and digitized enlistment papers of the soldiers and offers a series of detailed lesson plans for teachers.

European Film Gateway

www.europeanfilmgateway.eu/content/efg1914-project

This site offers thousands of First World War–era films contributed by twenty-one European national archives, including newsreels, documentaries, feature films, and propaganda films, with detailed descriptions of each item and the ability to search by topic, title, and year.

Firstworldwar.com

www.firstworldwar.com/today/index.htm

This site offers a comprehensive overview of the history of the First World War and contains a large number of primary documents. Perhaps most valuable is the site's sizable archive of photographs, maps, posters, diaries, and music from the war—though they are presented without much context or background.

The First World War in Popular Music

blogs.city.ac.uk/sa505pg1955/

This list of over nine hundred war songs (and growing), produced since 1960, was compiled by Peter Grant, a contributor to this volume. Organized alphabetically by artist, the list also gives the artist's country of origin, the name of the album in which the song was released, the date of release, and the song's genre.

First World War Poetry Digital Archive

www.oucs.ox.ac.uk/ww1lit/

Hosted by the University of Oxford, this invaluable resource for the British war experience features profiles of the major war poets (including full texts of their poems and manuscripts), as well as oral interviews, photographs, films, trench newspapers, and propaganda. Each genre is searchable by topic. The site also has an education section with a number of instructional materials for teachers of various levels and *Second Life*, a three-dimensional, interactive portal to the trench experience.

German History in Documents and Images

germanhistorydocs.ghi-dc.org/section.cfm?section_id=11

This site features two sections pertinent to studying the First World War: "Wilhemine Germany and the First World War, 1890–1918," edited by the noted scholar Roger Chickering, and "Weimar Germany, 1918–19–33," edited by Eric Weitz. Both sections discuss key issues of the historical periods in question and offer numerous primary documents (in German and English), including letters from soldiers, newspapers, government documents, maps, photographs, posters, and cartoons. Such materials are helpful in understanding the German experience of the war and its complex aftermath.

The Great War and the Shaping of the Twentieth Century

www.pbs.org/greatwar/

Based on the 1996 PBS television series, this site offers a global historical perspective on the conflict, with an emphasis on the war's complicated legacy. Numerous short essays on various topics by leading historians are supplemented by in-depth lesson plans for teachers.

The Great War in Africa Association

gweaa.com/

This site, coordinated by the independent historian Anne Samson, provides an overview of the war in Africa (in its various sectors) and provides a number of primary sources, including photos, government documents, and newspaper accounts, as well as links to other sites with information and sources about the African theater.

The Heritage of the Great War

www.greatwar.nl/

Edited by the journalist Rob Ruggenberg, this eclectic site is noteworthy for its collection of photographs, some of them in color and many of them quite graphic.

International Society for First World War Studies

www.firstworldwarstudies.org/bibliography.php

Hosted by the key organization for First World War scholars, this site offers an extensive, collaborative bibliography of primary and secondary sources organized by topic, nation, and genre. It is directed by Franziska Heimburger from the École des Hautes Études en Sciences Sociales.

Library of Congress—A Guide to World War I Materials

www.loc.gov/rr/program/bib/wwi/wwi.html#American

This site offers a variety of photographs, documents, newspapers and advertisements, films, sheet music, and sound recordings related to United States involvement in the First World War, as well as links to World War I resources throughout the Library of Congress Web site. In addition, it provides a series of lesson plans for teachers.

Modernist Journals Project

www.modjourn.org/

A joint project of Brown University and the University of Tulsa, this well-organized site features full-text versions of major modernist journals, such as *The Egoist*, *Blast*, and *The Little Review*, and a growing list of full-text books and essays by modernists. The site also features introductory biographies of hundreds of modernists and, most helpfully, an extensive teaching resource section that includes sample syllabi and assignments provided by experts in the field.

National World War I Museum and Memorial

theworldwar.org/explore/online-collections-database

The growing online component of the United States World War I museum features an extensive archive of photographs (with detailed captions), cartoons, posters, and scans of other war-related primary documents and artifacts.

Popular Songs of World War I

cylinders.library.ucsb.edu/wwi.php

Hosted by the library at the University of California, Santa Barbara, this site offers over one hundred World War One–era cylinder recordings of American popular songs about the war, as well as an essay that contextualizes and categorizes the various songs.

Propaganda Postcards

www.ww1-propaganda-cards.com/index.html

Hosted by two amateur historians, this site offers 1,400 World War One–era postcards, searchable by topic, theme, and artist, from numerous countries.

Royal College of Nursing

rcnarchive.rcn.org.uk/

This easily searchable archive includes over one hundred volumes of *The British Journal of Nursing* stretching from the late nineteenth to the mid-twentieth century, including the two world wars.

Russia's Great War and Revolution

russiasgreatwar.org/index.php

Overseen by leading scholars in the field, this site's "Media Content" section includes brief articles (with some primary sources, both written and visual) on key aspects of the Russian war experience (military affairs, revolution, home front, culture, etc.).

Spartacus Educational

spartacus-educational.com/FWW.htm

This encyclopedic site emphasizes the British experience of the war and gas chapters on history, politics, literature, journalism, women, and the home front, each with a number of primary source documents and biographies of major figures.

Wikipedia

en.wikipedia.org/wiki/List_of_World_War_I_films

This extensive (and still growing) list of over one hundred films from the war era to the present is organized by genre, year of release, and country of origin. Each listing is hyperlinked to a fuller Web page devoted to the individual film.

World War I Document Archive

wwi.lib.byu.edu/

Hosted by the Brigham Young University Library and maintained by academics, this site offers a vast archive of primary sources—political discourse on the war, memoirs and diaries, an image archive, and, perhaps most interesting, a large group of documents on the medical history of the war, including psychiatric and venereal treatments.

Web Sites Cited in This Volume

Web sites cited by contributors are listed below, unless already noted above.

1914–1918 Online: International Encyclopedia of the First World War

www.1914-1918-online.net/ (Natter)

AEIOU Österreich-Lexikon

austria-forum.org/af/AEIOU (McLary)

Archives of American Art. *Smithsonian Institution*

www.aaa.si.edu/ (Helmers)

Art of the First World War. *Memorial Centre for History and Peace*

www.memorial-caen.fr/10EVENT/EXPO1418/gb/visite.html (Helmers)

Australian War Memorial

www.awm.gov.au/ (Helmers)

AustriaWiki: Beiträge mit Österreichbezug

austria-forum.org/af/AustriaWiki (McLary)

Canadian War Museum

www.warmuseum.ca/home/ (Helmers)

Commercial Advertising as Propaganda in World War One. *British Library*

www.bl.uk/world-war-one/articles/commercial-advertising-as-propaganda (Marshik)

Cultural Exchange in a Time of Global Conflict: Colonials, Neutrals, and Belligerents during the First World War

www.cegcproject.eu (Buck, Das)

Experiencing War: World War I: The Great War. *Library of Congress*

www.loc.gov/vets/stories/ex-war-wwi.html (Smith)

First World War. The Guardian

www.theguardian.com/world/firstworldwar (Das)

First World War: A Global View, Egypt. *The National Archive*

www.nationalarchives.gov.uk/first-world-war/a-global-view/#Egypt (Buck)

First World War in the Classroom: Teaching and the Construction of Memory. *University of Exeter*

ww1intheclassroom.exeter.ac.uk/resources (Das)

From Bombay to the Western Front: Indian Soldiers of the First World War

www.youtube.com/watch?v=6stybO5v7SY (Das)

Gallipoli Campaign. The First World War, *The National Archives*

www.nationalarchives.gov.uk/pathways/firstworldwar/battles/gallipoli.htm (Sorum)

Imperial War Museum

www.iwm.org.uk/ (Das)

In Pictures: Indian Soldiers in the First World War. *BBC*

www.bbc.co.uk/news/world-asia-india-31937266 (Das)

Lebendige Museum Online

www.dhm.de/lemo/bestand (McLary)

Ministry of Defence Art Collection

www.gov.uk/ministry-of-defence-art-collection (Helmers)

Monument à Louise de Bettignies

statues-monuments-npdc.pagespersoorange.fr/louise-de-Bettignies (Buffton)

Monument des fusillés

www.cheminsdememoire.gouv.fr/fr/monument-des-fusilles-lille (Buffton)

Monument Foch

statues-monuments-npdc.pagesperso-orange.fr/foch (Buffton)

The Newberry Library

dcc.newberry.org/collections/world-war-i-in-us-popular-culture (Marshik)

New Zealand War Art. *Archives New Zealand*

archives.govt.nz/ (Helmers)

On to Baghdad. Amitav Ghosh

amitavghosh.com/blog/?cat=12 (Das)

Prints, Drawings, and Watercolors. *Anne S. K. Brown Military Collection, Brown University*

library.brown.edu/cds/askb/ (Helmers)

Sculpture to Alexandre Desrouseaux

statues-monuments-npdc.pagesperso-orange.fr/le-p'tit-quinquin-lille (Buffton)

The Stars and Stripes. *Library of Congress*

memory.loc.gov/ammem/sgphtml/sashtml/sashome.html (Marshik)

Süddeutsche Zeitung

www.sueddeutsche.de/thema/Erster_Weltkrieg (McLary)

The Trenches at Messines, 1916–17. Map Room

www.worldwar1.com/maptr01.htm (Sorum)

Trench Maps: Western Front. *McMaster University*

digitalarchive.mcmaster.ca/islandora/object/macrepo%3A49 (Sorum)

Was the Western Front the Most Multiracial Place in the World? *BBC*

www.bbc.co.uk/guides/z2bgr82 (Das)

Wienbibliothek im Rathaus

www.wienbibliothek.at/ (McLary)

World War I in U.S. Popular Culture. *The Newberry Library*

dcc.newberry.org/collections/world-war-i-in-us-popular-culture (Marshik)

Notes on Contributors

Glenda Abramson, emeritus professor of Hebrew and Jewish studies at the University of Oxford, is editor in chief of *The Journal of Modern Jewish Studies* and the author of *Hebrew Writing of the First World War* (2008), *Soldiers' Tales: Jewish Soldiers in the Ottoman Army in the First World War* (2013), and numerous articles on modern Hebrew literature and Hebrew literature and the First World War.

Carol Acton, associate professor of English at St. Jerome's University, teaches early-twentieth-century literature, gender and war, and life writing. Among her books are *Working in a World of Hurt: Trauma and Resilience in the Narratives of Medical Personnel in Warzones* (with Jane Potter, 2015), *A Very Private Diary: A Nurse in Wartime by Mary Morris* (editor, 2014), and *Grief in Wartime: Private Pain, Public Discourse* (2007).

Meg Albrinck is professor of literature and writing and provost and vice president for academic affairs at Lakeland University. Her teaching interests include gender studies, cultural studies, twentieth-century literature, and visual culture. She has published articles and reviews on Virginia Woolf, Gertrude Stein, First World War narratives, and popular film and television.

Jan Baetens is professor of cultural studies at the University of Leuven. His scholarly interests include the graphic novel, poetry, and the relation between photography and literature. He is the author of *The Graphic Novel: An Introduction* (with Hugo Frey, 2015) and *Pour en finir avec la poésie dite minimaliste* (2014).

Wyatt Bonikowski, associate professor of English at Suffolk University, teaches twentieth-century British literature and literary theory. He is the author of *Shell Shock and the Modernist Imagination: The Death Drive in Post–World War I British Fiction* (2013) and articles on Rebecca West and Shirley Jackson. He is working on twentieth-century British and American women writers who draw on gothic and folkloric traditions.

Marlene A. Briggs, assistant professor of English at the University of British Columbia, teaches modern and contemporary writing on the First World War. She has contributed essays to *Conflicted Pasts and National Identities: Narratives of War and Conflict* (2014), *The Great War in Post-memory Literature and Film* (2014) and *History and Memory: Studies in Representation of the Past* (2016). Her current research examines the intergenerational legacies of the First World War in British literature.

Claire Buck, professor of English at Wheaton College, teaches First World War writing, women's poetry, modernism, and colonialism and postcolonialism.

Her most recent book is *Conceiving Strangeness in British First World War Writing* (2015). Among her articles is "Counter-Discursive Poetry of War," in *The Cambridge Companion to Twentieth-Century British and Irish Women's Poetry* (edited by Jane Dowson, 2011).

Deborah D. Buffton, professor of history at the University of Wisconsin, La Crosse, teaches world and First World War history. Her research centers on war and memory, and she is the author of "Memorialization and the Selling of War" in *Peace Review: A Journal of Social Justice* (2005), among other essays.

Stephen Cloutier, instructor at St. Mary's University, Canada, teaches twentieth-century British and Canadian literatures. He has written essays on Wilfred Owen and George Eliot and is working on Dan Billany's fiction and Siegfried Sassoon's poetry of the 1930s.

Debra Rae Cohen, associate professor of English at the University of South Carolina, is the author of *Remapping the Home Front: Locating Citizenship in British Women's Great War Fiction* (2002) and the coeditor of *Broadcasting Modernism* (2009). She coedits the journal *Modernism/modernity.*

Santanu Das, reader in English literature at King's College London, teaches First World War literature and the modernist short story. Among his books are *Indian Troops in Europe, 1914–1918* (2015), *Cambridge Companion to the Poetry of the First World War* (editor, 2013), *Race, Empire and First World War Writing* (editor, 2011), and *Touch and Intimacy in First World War Literature* (2006).

Patrick Deer is associate professor of English at New York University, where he teaches war culture and war literature, modernism, and contemporary British, American, and anglophone literature and culture. He is the author of *Culture in Camouflage: War, Empire and Modern British Literature* (2009) and "Mapping Contemporary American War Culture" (2016) and the editor of *The Ends of War*, a special issue of *Social Text* (2007).

Laura Doan is professor of cultural history and sexuality studies at the University of Manchester, England. Her research interests include the history and historiography of sex and sexuality, gender studies, and queer theory; First World War studies; and memory studies. She is the author of *Disturbing Practices: History, Sexuality and Women's Experience of Modern War* (2013) and *Fashioning Sapphism: The Origins of a Modern English Lesbian Culture* (2001).

Jeffrey Drouin, assistant professor of English at the University of Tulsa, teaches modernism, World War I, periodical studies, and digital humanities. He is the author of *James Joyce, Science, and Modernist Print Culture: "The Einstein of English Fiction"* (2014) and is working on the *Ecclesiastical*

Proust Archive, a multimedia database of the church motif in *À la recherche du temps perdu* (proustarchive.org).

Scott D. Emmert, professor of English at the University of Wisconsin, Fox Valley, teaches the American short story, sports literature, and Midwestern literature. He recently coedited (with Steven Trout) *World War I in American Fiction: An Anthology of Short Stories* (2014) and is completing an essay on sports writing for *American Literature in Transition, 1910–1920* (edited by Mark Van Wienen).

Anne E. Fernald, professor of English and women's studies at Fordham University, teaches modernism, women and war, feminist theory, and the essay. She is the editor of Woolf's *Mrs. Dalloway* (2014), the coeditor of *The Norton Reader* (2011), and the author of *Virginia Woolf, Feminism and the Reader* (2006) and essays on modernism and women.

Jane Elizabeth Fisher, associate professor at Canisius College, teaches transatlantic modernism, medical humanities, and gender studies. She is the author of *Envisioning Disease, Gender and War: Women's Narratives of the 1918 Influenza Pandemic* (2012) and articles on Virginia Woolf and women's literature.

Hugo Frey is professor of cultural and visual history and head of the Department of History and Politics at University of Chichester. Among his scholarly interests are the history and politics of visual culture in France—including cinema, comic strips, illustration, art, and design—and North American comics and graphic novels. He is the coauthor, with Jan Baetens, of *The Graphic Novel: An Introduction* (2015) and the author of *Nationalism and the Cinema in France* (2014) and *Louis Malle* (2004).

Elizabeth A. Galway, associate professor and chair of the Department of English at the University of Lethbridge, teaches children's literature, nineteenth-century literature, and Canadian literature. She is the author of *From Nursery Rhymes to Nationhood: Children's Literature and the Construction of Canadian Identity* (2008) and is working on a study of American, British, and Canadian children's literature from the First World War.

Nancy Sloan Goldberg is professor of French at Middle Tennessee State University. Her scholarly interests include French literature of the First World War and the Third Republic. She is the author of *Woman, Your Hour Is Sounding: Continuity and Change in French Women's Novels of the Great War* (1999) and *En l'honneur de la juste parole: La poésie française contre la Grande Guerre* (1993). She is completing a study of Romain Rolland's *Au-dessus de la mêlée.*

Peter Grant, senior fellow in grantmaking, philanthropy, and social investment at the Sir John Cass Business School, City University, is the author of

Philanthropy and Voluntary Action in the First World War: Mobilizing Charity (2014), *The Business of Giving: The Theory and Practice of Philanthropy, Grantmaking and Social Investment* (2012), and *National Myth and the First World War in Modern Popular Music* (2017).

Marguerite Helmers, professor of English at the University of Wisconsin, Oshkosh, teaches Irish and British literatures and cultures, visual culture, and First World War studies. She is the author of *The Elements of Visual Analysis* (2006), *Harry Clarke's War: Ireland's Memorial Records, 1914–1918* (2015), and several essays on the visual culture of the First World War.

Douglas Higbee, associate professor of English at the University of South Carolina, Aiken, is the editor of *Military Culture and Education* (2010), the coeditor of *Hunting from the Ivory Tower: Essays by Academics Who Hunt* (forthcoming), the author of articles on twentieth-century soldier poetry and the British veterans' movement, and the coauthor of *In Their Own Words: Augusta and Aiken Veterans Remember World War II* (forthcoming).

Margaret R. Higonnet, professor emerita of English and comparative literature at the University of Connecticut, specializes in feminist theory and women's literature of the First World War. She is the editor of *Margaret Hall's Letters and Photographs from the Battle Country, 1918–1919* (2014), *Nurses at the Front: Writing the Wounds of the Great War* (2001), and *Lines of Fire: Women Writers on World War I* (1999) and the coeditor of *Behind the Lines: Gender and the Two World Wars* (1987).

Pearl James, associate professor of English at the University of Kentucky, teaches war literature and film, American literature, gender and masculinity studies, and visual culture. She is the author of *The New Death: American Modernism and World War I* (2013) and the editor of *Picture This: World War I Posters and Visual Culture* (2009). She is working on monographs on American First World War film and First World War nurses.

Mark D. Larabee, associate professor of English at the United States Naval Academy, teaches modern British and world literature. He is the author of *Front Lines of Modernism: Remapping the Great War in British Fiction* (2011) and articles on Joseph Conrad, Ford Madox Ford, Yasunari Kawabata, and travel writing. He is also the executive editor of *Joseph Conrad Today.*

Celia Marshik, professor and chair of the English Department at Stony Brook University, teaches British modernism, literature and law, and the literature and culture of the First World War. She is the editor of *The Cambridge Companion to Modernist Culture* (2015) and the author of *British Modernism and Censorship* (2006) and *"At the Mercy of Their Clothes": Modernism, the Middlebrow, and British Garment Culture* (2016).

Amaya Martin is assistant teaching professor of Arabic at Georgetown University. She has published articles on Arabic cultural and literary texts and modern Arabic language and media in *Islam and Christian-Muslim Relations*, *Journal of Jewish Identities*, and *The Levantine Review*. She is working on the influence of the 1952 Egyptian revolution on cinematic adaptations of literary works.

Andrew Maunder, lecturer in the School of Humanities at the University of Hertfordshire, teaches nineteenth- and early-twentieth-century literature and the short story. He is the editor of *British Theatre and the Great War, 1914–1919: New Perspectives* (2015), the coeditor of *British Literature of World War I: An Anthology* (2011), and the author of *Bram Stoker* (2006).

Laura McLary, professor of German and academic associate dean of the College of Arts and Sciences at the University of Portland, teaches second language acquisition and late-nineteenth- and early-twentieth-century German and Austrian literatures and cultures. She coedited *Winning Back Lost Territory: The Writing of Lilian Faschinger* (2014) and is working on a book about Georg Trakl entitled "Objects and Absences: Georg Trakl as Corpus."

Wolfgang Natter serves as the administrative fellow at Wesleyan University's Center for Pedagogical Innovation. He is the author of *Literature at War: Representing the Time of Greatness in Germany, 1914–1940*, "Imagining Mitteleuropa: Conceptions of 'Its' Space in and outside German Geography" (with Hans-Dietrich Schultz), and "Geopolitics in Germany, 1919–1945: Karl Haushofer and the *Zeitschrift für Geopolitik*."

Elizabeth Outka, associate professor of English at the University of Richmond, teaches modernism, the First World War, and the twentieth-century novel. She is the author of *Consuming Traditions: Modernity, Modernism, and the Commodified Authentic* (2009). Her current book project, "Raising the Dead: War, Plague, Magic, Modernism," explores how the First World War and the 1918 influenza pandemic radically shifted perceptions of the corpse.

Bonnie Roos, professor of English at West Texas A&M University, teaches modernism, postcolonialism, and world epic. She is the author of *Djuna Barnes's* Nightwood*: The World and the Politics of Peace* (2014) and the coeditor of *Postcolonial Green: Environmental Politics and World Narratives* (2010) and *Behind the Masks of Modernism: Global and Transnational Perspectives* (2016).

Vincent Sherry, Howard Nemerov Professor in the Humanities and professor of English at Washington University in St. Louis, teaches modernism and First World War literature. He is the author of *The Great War and the Language of Modernism* (2003) and *Modernism and the Reinvention of Decadence* (2015) and the editor of *The Cambridge Companion to the Literature of the First World War* (2005) and *The Cambridge History of Modernism* (forthcoming).

Richard Smith, senior lecturer in the Department of Media and Communications, Goldsmiths, University of London, teaches cultural studies and theories of media and memory, particularly relating to race and empire. He is the author of *Jamaican Volunteers in the First World War: Race, Masculinity and the Development of National Consciousness* (2004) and has published widely about the impact of the First World War on West Indian nationalism and Pan-Africanism.

Eve Sorum is associate professor of English at the University of Massachusetts, Boston, where she teaches modernism, modern poetry, and the literature of World War I. She is the author of essays on World War I poetry and prose, T. S. Eliot, Thomas Hardy, W. H. Auden, Virginia Woolf, and Ford Madox Ford. She recently finished a monograph titled "Modernist Empathy."

Stephen E. Tabachnick, professor of English literature at the University of Memphis, is the author of *The Quest for Jewish Belief and Identity in the Graphic Novel* (2014), *Images of Lawrence* (1988), *T .E. Lawrence* (1997), and *Lawrence of Arabia: An Encyclopedia* (2004) and the editor of *Teaching the Graphic Novel* (2009), *The T. E. Lawrence Puzzle* (2011), and *The Cambridge Companion to the Graphic Novel* (forthcoming), among other books.

Steven Trout, professor and chair of the Department of English at the University of South Alabama, teaches twentieth-century British and American literatures, modernism, and the First World War. He is the coeditor, with Scott D. Emmert, of *World War I in American Fiction: An Anthology of Short Stories* (2014), and the author of *On the Battlefield of Memory: The First World War and American Remembrance, 1919–1941* (2010) and *Memorial Fictions: Willa Cather and the First World War* (2002).

David Williams, retired professor of English at the University of Manitoba, is the author of *Media, Memory, and the First World War* (2009), *Imagined Nations: Reflections on Media in Canadian Fiction* (2003), and *Milton's Leveller God* (2017); monographs on William Faulkner and on the artist novel in Canada; and three novels.

Works Cited

Acton, Mary. *Learning to Look at Paintings.* 2nd ed., Routledge, 2009.

Agnon, Samuel Joseph. *A Guest for the Night.* U of Wisconsin P, 2004.

Ahern, Dermot. "Shared History Can Help Build a Shared Future." *The Irish Times,* 11 Nov. 2005, www.irishtimes.com/opinion/shared-history-can-help-build-a-shared-future-1.517144.

Ahuja, Ravi, et al., editors. *"When the War Began, We Heard of Several Kings": South Asian Prisoners in World War I Germany.* Social Science Press, 2011.

Al-Hakim, Tawfiq. *The Return of the Spirit.* 1933. Lynne Rienner Publishers, 2012.

Allatini, Rose (A.T. Fitzroy). *Despised and Rejected.* 1918. Gay Men's Press, 1988.

Allen, Hervey. *Toward the Flame.* Doubleday, Page and Company, 1926.

All Quiet on the Western Front. 1930. Directed by Lewis Milestone, Universal Classic Cinema, 2007.

Amadi, Elechi. *The Great Ponds.* Heinemann, 1969.

The American Experience: Influenza, 1918. Directed by Robert Kenner, WGBH, Boston, 1998.

Anand, Mulk Raj. *Across the Black Waters.* 1940. Orient Paperbacks, 2008.

———. "The Sources of Protest in My Novels." *Literary Criterion,* vol. 18, no. 4, 1983, pp. 1–12.

Angell, Norman. *The Great Illusion.* 1909. Putnam's, 1910.

Annaud, Jean-Jacques, director. *Black and White in Color (La Victoire en chantant).* 1976. Home Vision Entertainment, 2003.

Ansky, S. *The Enemy at His Pleasure: A Journey through the Jewish Pale of Settlement during World War I.* Henry Holt, 2002.

Anzaldúa, Gloria. *Borderlands / La Frontera: The New Mestiza.* Spinsters/ Aunt Lute, 1987.

Apollinaire, Guillaume. *Calligrammes: Poems of Peace and War.* Translated by Anne Hyde Greet, U of California P, 1980.

Arbuthnot, Nancy Prothro. *Guiding Lights: United States Naval Academy Monuments and Memorials.* Naval Institute Press, 2009.

Arcos, René. *Le sang des autres.* Kundig, 1919.

Arendt, Hannah. "Reflections on Violence." *The New York Review of Books,* 27 Feb. 1969, www.nybooks.com/articles/1969/02/27/a-special-supplement-reflections-on-violence/.

Augustine. *City of God.* Translated by Henry Bettenson, Penguin, 2003.

Awwād, Tawfīq Yūsuf. *al-Raghīf* [The Loaf of Bread]. 1939. *al-Mu'allafāt al-Kāmila,* Maktaba Lubnān, 1987, pp. 210–32.

Babel, Isaac. Red Cavalry *and Other Stories.* W. W. Norton, 2003.

Baetens, Jan, and Hugo Frey. *The Graphic Novel: An Introduction.* Cambridge UP, 2015.

Bagnold, Enid. *Diary without Dates.* Heinemann, 1918.

Ballobar, Conde de. *Jerusalem in World War I: The Palestine Diary of a European Diplomat.* I. B. Tauris, 2011.

Barbusse, Henri. *Le feu: Journal d'une escouade*. 1916. Edited by Pierre Paraf, Flammarion, 1965.

———. *Under Fire: The Story of a Squad*. Translated by Robin Buss, Penguin, 2004.

Barham, Peter. *Forgotten Lunatics of the Great War*. Yale UP, 2004.

Barker, Pat. *Another World*. Penguin, 1999.

———. "Going Home Again: An Interview with Pat Barker." Interview by Donna Perry. *The Literary Review*, vol. 34, no. 2, 1991, pp. 235–44.

———*Regeneration*. Penguin, 1991.

Barnes, Djuna. *Nightwood*. New Directions, 1937.

Barry, John. *The Great Influenza*. Penguin, 2005.

Barry, Sebastian. *A Long Long Way*. Penguin, 2006.

———. "Reading Guide: *A Long Long Way*." *Penguin Random House*, www.penguinrandomhouse.com/books/288975/a-long-long-way-by-sebastian-barry/9780143035091/readers-guide/.

———. "'Really All Danger': An Interview with Sebastian Barry." Interview by Maria Kurdi, *New Hibernia Review*, vol. 8, no. 1, Spring 2004, pp. 41–53.

Bataille, Henry. *La divine tragédie*. Bibliothèque-Charpentier, 1916.

The Battle of the Somme. 1916. Edited by Charles Urban, cinematography by Geoffrey Malins and John B. McDowell, Imperial War Museum, 1987.

Baxter, Archibald. *We Will Not Cease: The Autobiography of a Conscientious Objector*. 1939. 2nd ed. Caxton Press, 1968.

Baym, Nina. "Melodramas of Beset Manhood: How Theories of American Fiction Exclude Women Authors." *Locating American Studies*, edited by Lucy Maddox, Johns Hopkins UP, 1999, pp. 215–34.

Beckett, Samuel. "Dante . . . Bruno; Vico . . . Joyce." *Our Exagmination round His Factification for Incamination of Work in Progress*, New Directions, 1962, pp. 3–22.

Beckmann, Max. *Die Nacht*. 1919. Kunstsammlung Nordrhein-Westfalen, Düsseldorf.

Beiner, Guy. "Making Sense of Memory: Coming to Terms with Conceptualisations of Historical Remembrance." *Remembering 1916: The Easter Rising, the Somme and the Politics of Memory in Ireland*, edited by Richard S. Grayson and Fearghal McGarry, Cambridge UP, 2016, pp. 13–23.

Bentley, E. C. *Trent's Last Case*. 1913. *Project Gutenberg*, 5 Jan. 2015, www.gutenberg.org/ebooks/2568.

Benz automobile advertisement. *Koelnische Zeitung*, 19 July 1916, p. 3.

Bertrand, Adrien. *The Call of the Soil*. Translated by J. Lewis May, John Lane, 1919.

Beynon, Francis Marion. *Aleta Day*. 1919. Broadview Press, 2000.

Bhabha, Homi. *The Location of Culture*. Routledge, 1994.

Bird, Will R. *And We Go On*. 1930. Introduction and afterword by David Williams. McGill-Queen's UP, 2014.

———. *Ghosts Have Warm Hands*. Clarke, Irwin, 1968.

Bland, Lucy, and Laura Doan. *Sexology Uncensored: The Documents of Sexual Science*. U of Chicago P, 1998.

Bluemel, Kristin. "Casualty of War, Casualty of Empire: Mulk Raj Anand in England." *New Readings in the Literature of British India, 1780–1947*, edited by Shafquat Towheed, Ibidem, 2007, pp. 301–26.

———. *Intermodernism: Literary Culture in Mid-Twentieth Century Britain*. Edinburgh UP, 2009.

Blunden, Edmund. *Undertones of War*. 1928. U of Chicago P, 2007.

Bond, Brian. *The Unquiet Western Front: Britain's Role in Literature and History*. Cambridge UP, 2002.

Bone, Muirhead. *The Battle of the Somme*. 1916. Malvern, p. 25.

———. *Road Liable to Be Shelled*. 1916. Malvern, p. 27.

———. *The Western Front: Drawings by Muirhead Bone*. 2 vols., Doubleday, Page, 1917.

Borden, Mary. *The Forbidden Zone*. 1929. Hesperus, 2008.

Bourke, Joanna. *An Intimate History of Killing: Face to Face Killing in Twentieth-Century Warfare*. Basic Books, 2000.

Boxwell, David A. "The Follies of War: Cross-Dressing and Popular Theatre on the British Front Lines, 1914–18." *Modernism/Modernity*, vol. 9, no.1, 2002, pp. 1–20.

Boyd, Thomas. *Through the Wheat*. 1923. Edited by Matthew J. Bruccoli, Southern Illinois UP, 1978. Lost American Fiction.

Boyden, Joseph. *Three Day Road*. Penguin, 2005.

Bradford, Richard, editor. *Life Writing: Essays on Autobiography, Biography and Literature*. Palgrave Macmillan, 2009.

Brannigan, John. *Pat Barker*. Manchester UP, 2005.

Brennan, Christopher. "Irish to English." Wallace-Crabbe and Pierce, p. 39

Brenner, Hildegard. "Die Republikaner beugen sich dem Wort der Obrigkeit." *"Das war ein Vorspiel nur . . .": Bücherverbrennung, Deutschland 1933: Voraussetzungen und Folgen*, Akademie der Kuenste, 1983, pp. 65–80.

Bristow, Nancy K. *American Pandemic: The Lost Worlds of the 1918 Influenza Pandemic*. Oxford UP, 2012.

Brittain, Vera. *Chronicle of Youth: Vera Brittain's War Diary, 1913–1917*. Edited by Alan Bishop, Victor Gollancz, 1981.

———. *Testament of Experience*. Virago, 1980.

———. *Testament of Youth: An Autobiographical Study of the Years 1900–1925*. 1933. Penguin, 1994.

Brock, Peter. *Against the Draft: Essays on Conscientious Objection from the Radical Reformation to the Second World War*. U of Toronto P, 2006.

Brontë, Charlotte. *Villette*. Edited by Helen M. Cooper, Penguin, 2004.

Brooke, Rupert. "The Soldier." *The Poetical Works*, edited by G. Keynes, rev. ed., Faber and Faber, 1974, p. 23.

Brooker, Peter, and Andrew Thacker, editors. *Geographies of Modernism*. Routledge, 2005.

Brooks, Max. *The Harlem Hellfighters*. Illustrated by Caanan White, Broadway Books, 2014.

Brown, Lloyd. *The Story of Maps*. 1949. Dover Publications, 1979.

Buck, Claire. "British Women's Writing of the Great War." Sherry, *Cambridge Companion*, pp. 85–112.

———. *Conceiving Strangeness in British First World War Writing*. Palgrave Macmillan, 2015.

Bulkeley, H. J. *Four War Plays for School Children:* Scarlet Fever, The Scouts, The Hospital Hut, Home! Routledge, 1917.

Bunbury, Henry Shirley. "Arouse Jamaica." *Daily Gleaner*, 8 Oct. 1915, p. 13.

———. "A Chant for Our Contingent." *Daily Gleaner*, 16 Oct. 1915, p. 13.

Burke, Edmund. *A Philosophical Enquiry into the Origin of our Ideas of the Sublime and Beautiful*. Edited by James T. Boulton, U of Notre Dame P, 1968.

Butler, Judith. *Frames of War: When Is Life Grievable?* Verso, 2010.

Byerly, Carol R. *Fever of War: The Influenza Epidemic in the U.S. Army during World War I*. New York UP, 2005.

Byrnes, Heidi, et al., editors. *Realizing Advanced Foreign Language Writing Development in Collegiate Education: Curricular Design, Pedagogy, Assessment*. Spec. issue of *The Modern Language Journal*, vol. 94, 2010, pp. i–vi, 1–235.

Byron, May. *The Peek-a-Boos in War Time*. Illustrated by Chloë Preston, Henry Frowde and Hodder and Stoughton, 1916.

Cameron, D. Y. *The Battlefield of Ypres*. 1919. Malvern, p. 99.

Campbell, James. "Combat Gnosticism: The Ideology of First World War Poetry Criticism." *New Literary History*, vol. 30, no. 1, 1999, pp. 203–15.

Campbell, William Wilfred. "Our Dead." W. Campbell, *Selected Poetry*, p. 149.

———. *Selected Poetry and Essays*. Edited by Laurel Boone, Wilfred Laurier Press, 1987.

———. "The Summons." W. Campbell, *Selected Poetry*, pp. 197–98.

Canfield, Dorothy. "A Little Kansas Leaven." *Home Fires in France*, Henry Holt and Company, 1918, pp. 132–72.

Cardinal, Agnès. "Women and the Language of War in France." *Women and World War I: The Written Response*, edited by Dorothy Goldman, Macmillan, 1993, pp. 150–68.

Cardinal, Agnès, et al., editors. *Women's Writing on the First World War*. Oxford UP, 2003.

Caruth, Cathy. *Unclaimed Experience: Trauma, Narrative, and History*. Johns Hopkins UP, 1996.

Casimir, Jon. "Secret Life of Matilda." *Sydney Morning Herald*, 19 Apr. 2002.

Castle, Terry, editor. *The Literature of Lesbianism: A Historical Anthology from Ariosto to Stonewall*. Columbia UP, 2003.

Cather, Willa. *One of Ours*. 1922. Vintage, 1991.

Ceadel, Martin. *Pacifism in Britain, 1914–1945: The Defining of a Faith*. Clarendon, 1980.

Chabon, Michael. *Maps and Legends: Reading and Writing along the Borderlines*. Fourth Estate, 2010.

Chandan, Amarjit. *How They Suffered: World War One and Its Impact on Punjabis*. Academy of the Punjab in North America, apnaorg.com/articles/amarjit/1998.

Child, Philip. *God's Sparrows*. 1937. McClelland and Stewart, 1978.

Childers, Erskine. *The Riddle of the Sands*. 1903. *Project Gutenberg*, 1 Oct. 2000, www.gutenberg.org/ebooks/2360.

Chomsky, Aviva. *West Indian Workers in the United Fruit Company in Costa Rica, 1870–1940*. Louisiana State UP, 1996.

Clampin, David. "Commercial Advertising as Propaganda in World War One." *The British Library: World War One*, www.bl.uk/world-war-one/articles/commercial-advertising-as-propaganda.

Clark, Christopher. *The Sleepwalkers: How Europe Went to War in 1914*. Harper, 2013.

Clark, Greg "The Symbol." *My Grandfather's War*, edited by William D. Mathieson, Macmillan, 1981, pp. 320–21. Originally published in *Weekend Magazine*, Nov. 1967.

Clarke, Thomas J., et al. "Proclamation of the Provisional Government of the Irish Republic." 1916. *Irish Historical Documents since 1800*, edited by Alan O'Day and John Stevenson, Gill and Macmillan, 1992, pp. 160–61.

Clausewitz, Carl von. *On War*. 1832. Translated by J. J. Graham, 1874. *Project Gutenberg*, central.gutenberg.org/articles/on_war.

Cobley, Evelyn. *Representing War*. U of Toronto P, 1993.

Cohen, Debra Rae. *Remapping the Home Front: Locating Citizenship in British Women's Great War Fiction*. Northeastern UP, 2002.

Cole, Sarah. *At the Violet Hour: Modernism and Violence in England and Ireland*. Oxford UP, 2012.

———. *Modernism, Male Friendship, and the First World War*. Cambridge UP, 2003.

Colette. *Mitsou, ou comment l'esprit vient aux filles*. 1919. *Internet Archive*, 30 Mar. 2011, archive.org/details/mitsououcommentl00cole.

Colgate's Ribbon Dental Cream. Advertisement. *The Youth's Companion*, 10 Oct. 1918, p. 525. Layson and Scanlan.

Collins, Geneviève. "Writers and the War." *The Great War and the French People*, edited by Jean-Jacques Becker, Berg, 1993, pp. 161–77.

"Comme Jolie Souvenir de la Guerre." *L'écho de Paris* 27 June 1915, p. 3.

Condini, Ned, editor and translator. *An Anthology of Modern Italian Poetry: In English Translation, with Italian Text*. MLA, 2009.

Connor, Ralph. "Canada's Word." *Princess Mary's Gift Book*. Authorized Canadian ed., Hodder and Stoughton, 1914, p. 22.

Conrad, Joseph. *The Shadow-Line*. Edited by J. H. Stape et al., Cambridge UP, 2013.

Cook, Tim. *Shock Troops: Canadians Fighting the Great War, 1917–1918*. Vol. 2, Penguin, 2008.

"Correspondence of the Military Intelligence Division Relating to 'Negro Subversion,' 1917–1941." National Archives Trust Fund Board, National Archives and Records Administration, 1987. M1440.

Cotter, Joseph. "A Sonnet to Negro Soldiers." *Crisis*, June 1918, p. 64. The Modernist Journals Project, library.brown.edu/cds/mjp/render.php?view=mjp_object&id=crisiscollection.

Cream of Wheat. Advertisement. *The Youth's Companion*, 27 Sept. 1917, p. 540. Layson and Scanlan.

Crosby, Alfred. *America's Forgotten Pandemic: The Influenza of 1918*. Cambridge UP, 1989.

Cross, Tim. *The Lost Voices of World War I*. U of Iowa P, 1988.

Crouthamel, Jason. *The Great War and German Memory: Society, Politics and Psychological Trauma, 1914–1945.* U of Exeter P, 2009.

Culleton, Claire. *Working Class Culture, Women, and Britain, 1914–1921.* Palgrave Macmillan, 2000.

Culpin, Millais. *Psychoneuroses of War and Peace.* Cambridge UP, 1920.

Dangerfield, George. *The Strange Death of Liberal England: 1910–1914.* Putnam, 1935.

Danielson, Susan, and Ann Marie Fallon. *Community-Based Learning and the Work of Literature.* Anker Publishing, 2007.

Darrow, Margaret H. *French Women and the First World War: War Stories of the Home Front.* Berg, 2000.

Das, Santanu. "Ardour and Anxiety: Politics and Literature in the Indian Homefront." Liebau et al., pp. 29–53.

———. "Experiences of Colonial Troops." *British Library,* http://www.bl.uk/world-war-one/articles/colonial-troops.{14}

———. "Indian Sepoy Experience in Europe, 1914–1918: Archive, Language and Feeling." *Twentieth Century British History,* vol. 25, no. 3, Aug. 2014, pp. 391–417.

———. "'Indian Sisters! . . . Send Your Husbands, Brothers, Sons': India, Women and the First World War." *The Women's Movement in Wartime: International Perspectives, 1914–1919,* edited by Alison S. Fell and Ingrid Sharp, Palgrave Macmillan, 2007, pp. 18–35.

———. *Indian Troops in Europe, 1914–1918.* Mapin, 2015.

———, editor. *Race, Empire, and First World War Writing.* Cambridge UP, 2011.

———. "Reframing Life / War 'Writing': Objects, Letters, and Songs of Indian Soldiers, 1914–1918." *Writing War, Writing Lives,* edited by Kate McLoughlin et al., *Textual Practice,* vol. 29, no. 7, Dec. 2015, 1266–87.

———. "Sensing the Indian Sepoy in the First World War." *Comparative Critical Studies,* vol. 9, 2012, pp. 7–18.

———. *Touch and Intimacy in First World War Literature.* Cambridge UP, 2005.

———. "Writing Empire, Fighting War: India, Great Britain, and the First World War." *India in Britain: South Asian Networks and Connections, 1858–1950,* edited by Susheila Nasta, Palgrave Macmillan, 2013, pp. 28–45.

Davis, Richard Harding. "The Man Who Had Everything." *Lost Road,* Charles Scribner's Sons, 1916, pp. 308–30.

———. *With the French in France and Salonika.* Charles Scribner's Sons, 1916.

Davis, Ryan A. *The Spanish Flu: Narrative and Cultural Identity in Spain.* Palgrave Macmillan, 2013.

Dayfield Body Shield. Advertisement. *Daily Mail,* 9 Feb. 1916, p. 2.

de Ambris, Alceste, and F. T. Marinetti. "Fascist Manifesto, 1919." *Conservapedia,* 18 July 2016, www.conservapedia.com/Fascist_Manifesto,_1919.

Defenders of the Empire: A Postcard Painting Book. Father Tuck's Patriotic Series, c. 1914.

Deist, Wilhelm. *Militaer und Innenpolitik im Weltkrieg, 1914–1918.* Droste, 1970.

De Lisser, Rose. "The Appeal." *Daily Gleaner,* 26 Oct. 1915, p. 6.

Dellamora, Richard. *Radclyffe Hall: A Life in the Writing.* U of Pennsylvania P, 2011.

Dendooven, Dominiek, and Piet Chilens, editors. *World War I: Five Continents in Flanders*. Lannoo, 2008.

de Paor, Liam. *On the Easter Proclamation and Other Declarations*. Four Courts, 1997.

Derrida, Jacques. *Monolinguism of the Other; or, The Prosthesis of Origin*. Translated by Patrick Mensah, Stanford UP, 1998.

Deslandes, Paul R. *Oxbridge Men: British Masculinity and the Undergraduate Experience, 1850–1920*. Indiana UP, 2005.

Detaille, Édouard. *Le rêve*. *Musée D'Orsay*, www.musee-orsay.fr/en/collections/works-in-focus/painting/commentaire_id/the-dream-7166.html?cHash=cac405db3e.

de Zoete, Matthew. "Remembrance Day." *Bottom of the World*, Shiprecords, 2008.

Dix, Otto. *Der Kreig*. 1924. Museum of Modern Art, New York. 159.1934.1–50.

———. *Die Skatspieler*. 1920. National Gallery of Art, Washington DC.

Doan, Laura. *Disturbing Practices: History, Sexuality, and Women's Experience of Modern War*. U of Chicago P, 2013.

Doenitz, Karl. *Die Fahrten der Breslau*. Ullstein, 1917.

Donaldson, Walter. *How 'Ya Gonna Keep 'Em Down on the Farm (after They've Seen Paree?)*. Waterson, Berlin, and Snyder, 1919.

Dorgelès, Roland. *Wooden Crosses*. G. P. Putnam and Sons, 1921.

Dos Passos, John. *Three Soldiers*. George H. Doran, 1921.

Douanne, G. Poster. *Library of Congress*, www.wdl.org/fr/item/361/.

Doughty, Charles M. *Travels in Arabia Deserta*. 2 vols. Dover, 1967.

Douglas, Keith. "Desert Flowers." *Collected Poems*, edited by John Waller et al., Faber and Faber, 1966, 129.

Dowling, Linda. *Hellenism and Homosexuality in Victorian Oxford*. Cornell UP, 1994.

Dowling, Martin. *Traditional Music and Irish Society: Historical Perspectives*. Ashgate, 2014.

Doyle, Laura, and Laura Winkiel, editors. *Geomodernisms: Race, Modernism, and Modernity*. Indiana UP, 2005.

"Dramatic Gossip: The Call for Khaki." *Referee*, 24 June 1917, p. 2.

Du Bois, W. E. B. "Close Ranks." *The Crisis*, vol. 16, no. 3, July 1918, p. 111. The Modernist Journals Project, library.brown.edu/cds/mjp/render.php?id=1292948438561750&view=mjp_object.

———. "Returning Soldiers." *The Crisis*, vol. 18, no. 1, May 1919, pp. 13–14. The Modernist Journals Project, library.brown.edu/cds/mjp/render.php?id=1292948438561750&view=mjp_object.

Duhamel, Georges. *Civilisation, 1914–1917*. Mercure de France, 1918.

———. *La vie des martyrs, 1914–1916*. Mercure de France, 1917.

Duhamelet, Geneviève. *Les inépousées*. Albin Michel, 1918.

Dyer, Geoff. *The Missing of the Somme*. Penguin, 1995.

Eberwein, Robert. *The Hollywood War Film*. Wiley-Blackwell, 2010.

Edelman, Lee. *No Future: Queer Theory and the Death Drive*. Duke UP, 2004.

Eder, M. D. *War-Shock: The Psycho-neuroses in War Psychology and Treatment*. William Heinemann, 1917. *Internet Archive*, 27 Feb. 2012, archive.org/details/39002022350160.med.yale.edu.

Edney, Matthew H. *Mapping an Empire: The Geographical Construction of British India, 1765–1843.* U of Chicago P, 1997.

Einhaus, Ann-Marie. *The Short Story and the First World War.* Cambridge UP, 2013.

Eksteins, Modris. *Rites of Spring: The Great War and the Birth of the Modern Age.* Doubleday, 1989.

Eliot, T. S. *Collected Poems, 1909–1962.* 1963. Harcourt Brace and Company, 1991.

Ellsworth-Jones, Will. *We Will Not Fight: The Untold Story of the First World War's Conscientious Objectors.* Aurum, 2007.

Elshtain, Jean Bethke, editor. *Just War Theory.* New York UP, 1992.

———. "Reflections on War and Political Discourse: Realism, Just War, and Feminism in a Nuclear Age." *Political Theory*, vol. 13, no. 1, February, 1985, pp. 39–57. *JSTOR*, www.jstor.org/stable/191629.

Emecheta, Buchi. *The Slave Girl.* George Braziller, 1980.

Emmert, Scott D., and Steven Trout. *World War I in American Fiction: An Anthology of Short Stories.* Kent State UP, 2014.

Enloe, Cynthia. *Does Khaki Become You? The Militarization of Women's Lives.* Pandora Press, 1988.

Fanning, Patricia J. *Influenza and Inequality: One Town's Tragic Response to the 1918 Influenza.*U of Massachusetts P, 2010.

Fansa, Mamoun, and Detlef Hoffmann, editors. *Lawrence von Arabien: Genese eines Mythos.* Philipp von Zabern, 2010.

Farrell, Keith, director. *A Terrible Beauty.* Tile Films, 2012.

Fauset, Jessie Redmon. *There Is Confusion.* 1928. Northeastern UP, 1989.

Fell, Alison S. "Nursing the Other: The Representation of Colonial Troops in French and British First World War Nursing Memoirs." Das, *Race*, pp. 158–74.

Fengler, Maria. "No Way Back to Tipperary: Re-imagining the Great War in Sebastian Barry's *A Long Long Way.*" *Re-imagining the First World War: New Perspectives in Anglophone Literature and Culture*, edited by Anna Branach-Kallas and Nelly Strehlau, Cambridge Scholars, 2015, pp. 209–21.

Ferenczi, Sandor, et al. *Psycho-analysis and the War Neuroses.* The International Psycho-analytic Press, 1921. *Internet Archive*, archive.org/details/Psycho-analysisAndTheWarNeuroses.

Ferguson, Niall. *The Pity of War.* Penguin, 1999.

Field, Frank. *British and French Writers of the First World War: Comparative Studies in Cultural History.* Cambridge UP, 1991.

Filipović, Zlata, and Melanie Challenger, editors. *Stolen Voices: Young People's War Diaries from World War I to Iraq.* Penguin Books, 2006.

Finnan, Joseph P. *John Redmond and Irish Unity, 1912–1918.* Syracuse UP, 2004.

First World War: A Global View. The National Archives, livelb.nationalarchives.gov.uk/first-world-war/a-global-view/.

Fisher, Jane Elizabeth. *Envisioning Disease, Gender, and War: Women's Narratives of the 1918 Influenza Pandemic.* Palgrave Macmillan, 2012.

Fisher, Susan R. *Boys and Girls in No Man's Land: English-Canadian Children and the First World War.* U of Toronto P, 2011.

Fitzgerald, F. Scott. *This Side of Paradise.* 1920. *Novels and Stories, 1920–1922*, edited by Jackson Bryer, American Library, 2000, pp. 1–252.

Fletcher, C. R .L., and Rudyard Kipling. *A School History of England*. Clarendon, 1911.

Ford, Ford Madox. "Arms and the Mind / War and the Mind." *War Prose*, edited by Max Saunders, Carcanet Press, 1999, pp. 36–48.

———. *No Enemy: A Tale of Reconstruction*. Edited by Paul Skinner, Carcanet Press, 2002.

———. *No More Parades*. 1925. Edited by Joseph Wiesenfarth, Carcanet Press, 2011.

———. *Parade's End*. 1924–28. Vintage, 2012.

The Ford Motor Co. and Taylorism in the 1920s. Directed by Elizabeth Cornell. *Critical Commons*, http://www.criticalcommons.org/Members/ecornell1/clips/ford-and-taylor-in-the-1920s-part-one-1.mp4/view.

Forman, S. E. "The Watch Tower." *St. Nicholas*, vol. 42, no. 2, Sept. 1915, pp. 963–68.

Forster, E. M. "Mohammed El Adl's Book." *Alexandria: A History and a Guide [and] Pharos and Pharillon*, edited by Miriam Allott, Andre Deutsch, 2004, pp. 322–46.

Forstmann, Walther. *Mit U39 auf Jagd im Mittelmeer*. Ullstein, 1917.

Forter, Greg. *Gender, Race, and Mourning in American Modernism*. Cambridge UP, 2011.

Forty, Simon, editor. *World War I: A Visual Encyclopedia*. PRC Publishing, 2002.

Foster, Roy. " 'Something of Us Will Remain': Sebastian Barry and Irish History." *Out of History: Essays on the Writings of Sebastian Barry*, edited by Christina Hunt Mahony, Catholic U of America P, 2006, pp. 183–97, 255–56.

Foucault, Michel. *Discipline and Punish*. Vintage Books, 1977.

Franchot, Annie Wood. *War Babies*. Illustrated by Mary Louise Davis, William R. Jenkins, 1914.

Frank, Joseph. "Spatial Form in Modern Literature." *The Idea of Spatial Form*, Rutgers UP, 1991, pp. 31–66.

Frankel, Jonathan. "Symposium: The Jews and the European Crisis, 1914–21." *The Jews and the European Crisis, 1914–1921*, edited by Frankel, Oxford UP, 1988, pp. 3–144.

Franks, Claudia Stillman. *Beyond the Well of Loneliness: The Fiction of Radclyffe Hall*. Avebury, 1982.

Franz Sauer Regenmäntel. *Koelnische Zeitung*, 5 June 1916, p. 3.

Freedman, Ariela. "Dorothy Sayers and the Case of the Shell-Shocked Detective." *Partial Answers: Journal of Literature and the History of Ideas*, vol. 8, no. 2, 2010, pp. 365–87. *Project MUSE*, muse.jhu.edu/article/382606/pdf.

Freud, Sigmund. *Beyond the Pleasure Principle*. 1920. *The Standard Edition of the Complete Psychological Works of Sigmund Freud*, translated by James Strachey, vol. 18, The Hogarth Press, 1955, pp. 5–64.

———. "Introduction to *Psycho-analysis and the War Neuroses*." 1919. *The Standard Edition of the Complete Psychological Works of Sigmund Freud*, translated by James Strachey, vol. 17. Hogarth Press, 1955, pp. 206–15.

Friedman, Susan Stanford. "Planetarity: Musing Modernist Studies." *Modernism/Modernity*, vol. 17, no. 3, 2010, pp. 471–99.

Frisby, H. G. F. Document Archives, box 01/48/1. Imperial War Museum, London.

Frith, Simon. *Performing Rights: Evaluating Popular Music.* Oxford UP, 1996.

Fuenfzig Jahre Ullstein, 1877–1927. Ullstein, 1927.

Fussell, Paul. *The Great War and Modern Memory.* Oxford UP, 1975.

Galway, Elizabeth A. "Competing Representations of Boy Soldiers in First World War Children's Literature." *Children in Armed Conflicts*, special issue of *Peace Review: A Journal of Social Justice*, vol. 24, no. 3, Sept. 2012, pp. 298–304.

Gamages. Advertisement. *Daily Mail*, 4 Apr. 1916, p. 1.

Garvey, Marcus. Letter to Booker T. Washington. 12 Apr. 1915. Hill 1: 116–17.

———. Letter to Lewis Harcourt. Hill 11: 76–77.

———. "Liberty Hall Dedicated at Great Mass Meeting." Hill 1: 472. Originally published in *Negro World*, 2 Aug. 1919, p. 1.

George, W. L. "The War of Liberation." *English Review*, vol. 23, Dec. 1916, pp. 510–24.

Gibney, John. *A History of the East Rising in Fifty Objects.* Mercier, 2016.

Gilbert, Martin. *The Battle of the Somme: The Heroism and Horror of War.* McClelland and Stewart, 2006.

———. *The First World War.* HarperCollins, 1994.

Gilbert, Sandra M., and Susan Gubar. *No Man's Land: The Place of the Woman Writer in the Twentieth Century.* 3 vols., Yale UP, 1988.

Gilkes Romero, Juliet. *At the Gates of Gaza.* Oberon, 2015.

Gill, Douglas, and Gloden Dallas. "Mutiny at Etaples Base in 1917." *Past and Present*, vol. 69, Nov. 1975, pp. 88–112. *JSTOR*, www.jstor.org/stable/i226595.

Gold Diggers of 1933. Directed by Mervyn LeRoy, Warner Bros., 1933.

Gosling, George Campbell. "Lloyd George's Ministry Men." *World War I Centenary: Continuations and Beginnings*, U of Oxford, ww1centenary.oucs.ox.ac.uk/body-and-mind/lloyd-georges-ministry-men/.

Gough, Paul. "Commemoration of War." *The Ashgate Research Companion to Heritage and Identity*, edited by Brian Graham and Peter Howard, Ashgate, 2008, pp. 215–29.

Goulding, Edmund. *God Save the King.* 1914. *British Literature of World War I.* Edited by Andrew Maunder and Angela K. Smith, vol. 5, Pickering and Chatto, 2011, pp. 1–20.

Goya, Francisco. *Los desastres de la guerra.* 1810–20. Metropolitan Museum of Art, New York.

Grabein, Paul. *Im Auto durch Feindesland.* Ullstein, 1916.

Grabolle, Harro. *Verdun and the Somme.* Akademiai Kiado, 2004.

Gramsci, Antonio. *Selections from the Prison Notebooks.* 1971. Edited and translated by Quentin Hoare and Geoffrey Nowell Smith, International Publishers, 2003.

Grannum, Guy. *Tracing Your Caribbean Ancestors: A National Archives Guide.* A and C Black, 2012.

Grant, R. G. *World War I: The Definitive Visual History: From Sarajevo to Versailles.* DK, 2014.

Graves, Robert. *Good-bye to All That.* 1929. Introduction by Paul Fussell, Anchor, 1998.

Grayzel, Susan. *Women's Identities at War: Gender, Motherhood, and Politics in Britain and France during the First World War*. North Carolina UP, 1999.
Grenfell, Julian. *Anthem for Doomed Youth: Twelve Soldier Poets of the First World War*. Edited by Jon Stallworthy, Constable, 2002.
Grierson, Lee. "The Work of Film in the Age of Fordist Mechanization." *Cinema Journal*, vol. 51, no. 3, Spring 2012, pp. 25–51.
Groch-Begley, Hannah. "World War One's Forgotten Female Shell-Shock Victims." *The Atlantic*, 8 Sept. 2014, www.theatlantic.com/health/archive/2014/09/world-war-ones-forgotten-female-shell-shock-victims/378995/.
Grosz, George. *Republican Automatons*. 1920. Museum of Modern Art, New York.
———. *Street Scene*. 1925. Metropolitan Museum of Art, New York.
Groves, Edith Lelean. *The Making of Canada's Flag (A Patriotic Play)*. William Briggs, 1916.
———. *The Wooing of Miss Canada*. McClelland, Goodchild and Stewart, 1917.
Gurney, Ivor. "Strange Hells." *Poetry by Heart*, www.poetrybyheart.org.uk/poems/strange-hells/.
Gygi, Fabio. "Shattered Experiences—Recycled Relics: Strategies of Representation and the Legacy of the Great War." *Matters of Conflict: Material Culture, Memory and the First World War*, edited by Nicholas J. Saunders, Routledge, 2004, pp. 72–89.
Halberstam, Judith. *Female Masculinity*. Duke UP, 1998.
Hall, Donald E., and Annamarie Jagose, editors. *The Routledge Queer Studies Reader*. Routledge, 2012.
Hall, Radclyffe. *Miss Ogilvy Finds Herself*. William Heinemann, 1934.
Hameiri, Avigdor. *The Great Madness*. Translated by Jacob Freedman, Vantage Press, 1952.
Hamilton, Cicely. *William: An Englishman*. 1919. Persephone Books, 1999.
Hämmerle, Christa. *Heimat/Front: Geschlechtergeschichte/n des Ersten Weltkriegs in Österreich-Ungarn*. Böhlau Verlag, 2014.
Hämmerle, Christa, et al., editors. *Gender and the First World War*. Palgrave, 2014.
Hammond, Michael. *The Big Show: British Cinema Culture in the Great War, 1914–1918*. Exeter UP, 2006.
Hanna, Abdallah. "The First World War according to the Memories of 'Commoners' in the Bilād al-Shām." Liebau et al., pp. 29–53.
Harding, George Matthews. *Cleaning Out Boche Machine Gun Nest*. 1917–18. Smithsonian Institution. AF*25740.
Harris, John. *The Somme: Death of a Generation*. 1966. White Lion, 1975.
Harrison, Charles Yale. *Generals Die in Bed*. 1930. Annick Press, 2002.
Harrods Weekly Price List. *The Harrods Archive*, 23–28 July 1917.
Harshav, Benjamin, editor and translator. *American Yiddish Poetry: A Bilingual Anthology*. U of California P, 1986.
Harte, Liam. *Reading the Contemporary Irish Novel, 1987–2007*. Wiley Blackwell, 2014.
Harvey, David. *The Condition of Postmodernity*. Blackwell, 1990.

Harvie, Robert. *The King's Uniform: Eighteen Addresses to Children*. H. R. Allenson, 1915.
Hayes, Clair W. *The Boy Allies with Haig in Flanders; or, The Fighting Canadians of Vimy Ridge*. A. L. Burt, 1918.
Haytock, Jennifer. *At Home, at War: Domesticity and World War I in American Literature*. Ohio State UP, 2003.
Heaney, Seamus. "In Memoriam Francis Ledwidge." *Selected Poems, 1966–1987*, Noonday Press, 1991, pp. 144–45.
———. "The Interesting Case of Nero, Chekhov's Cognac and a Knocker." *The Government of the Tongue*, Faber and Faber, 1988, pp. xi–xxiii.
Hegglund, Jon. *World Views: Metageographies of Modernist Fiction*. Oxford UP, 2012.
Hellé, André, illustrator. *French Toys*. L'Avenir Féminin, 1915.
Heller, Monica, editor. *Codeswitching: Anthropological and Linguistic Perspectives*. Mouton de Gruyter, 1988.
Hemingway, Ernest. *A Farewell to Arms*. 1929. Simon and Schuster, 1995.
———. *In Our Time*. 1925. Simon and Schuster, 1996.
Herman, Judith. *Trauma and Recovery*. Basic Books, 1997.
Higgins, Michael D. "President Higgins: Openness to Perspectives of Others Must Be at Heart of Remembering." *The Irish Times*, 1 July 2016, www.irishtimes.com/news/ireland/irish-news/president-higgins-openness-to-others-must-be-at-heart-of-remembering-1.2705750.
Higonnet, Margaret R., editor. "Glossary of French Terms." Higonnet, *Nurses*, pp. xxxix–xli.
———, editor. *Lines of Fire: Women Writers of World War One*. Plume, 1999.
———, editor. *Nurses at the Front: Writing the Wounds of the Great War*. Northeastern UP, 2001.
———. "Women in the Forbidden Zone: War, Women, and Death." *Death and Representation*, edited by Sarah Goodwin and Elisabeth Bronfen, Johns Hopkins UP, 1993, pp.192–212.
Higonnet, Margaret R., and Patrice L.-R. Higonnet. "The Double Helix." *Behind the Lines: Gender and the Two World Wars*, edited by M. Higonnet et al., Yale UP, 1987, pp. 31–50.
Hill, Robert A., editor. *The Marcus Garvey and Universal Negro Improvement Association Papers*, vol. 1, U of California P, 1983.
———, editor. *The Marcus Garvey and Universal Negro Improvement Association Papers*. Vol. 11, Duke UP, 2011.
Hitler, Adolf. *Mein Kampf*. Franz Eher, 1925.
Hochschild, Adam. *To End All Wars: A Story of Loyalty and Rebellion, 1914–1918*. Houghton Mifflin, 2011.
Hoecker, Paul Oskar. *An der Spitze meiner Kompagnie*. Ullstein, 1914.
"Homage à Foch." *La dépeche de Lille*, 24 May 1936. Clipping in Archives Municipales de Lille, box no. 3 M 62.
"Home Front, *N*." *Oxford English Dictionary*, www.oed.com.colorado.idm.oclc.org/view/Entry/282874?redirectedFrom=home+front#eid.
Homer. *The Odyssey*. Translated by Robert Fitzgerald, Farrar, Strauss, and Giroux, 1998.

Honigsbaum, Mark. *Living with Enza: The Forgotten Story of Britain and the Great Flu Pandemic of 1918.* Palgrave Macmillan, 2009.

Hope, Ascott R. *The School of Arms: Stories of Boy Soldiers and Sailors.* E. P. Dutton, c. 1915.

Horgan, John. *The End of War.* McSweeney's, 2014.

Houlbrook, Matt. *Queer London: Perils and Pleasures in the Sexual Metropolis, 1918–57.* U of Chicago P, 2005.

Hourani, Albert. *Arabic Thought in the Liberal Age, 1789–1939.* Cambridge UP, 1989.

Howarth, William L. "Some Principles of Autobiography." *New Literary History*, vol. 5, no. 2, Winter 1974, pp. 363–81.

Howe, Glenford D. *Race, War and Nationalism: A Social History of West Indians in the First World War.* Ian Randle, 2002.

Hubel, Theresa. "A Mutiny of Silence: Swarnakumari Devi's Sati." *Ariel*, vol. 41, no. 3, 2011, pp. 167–90.

Hueffer, Ford Madox, and Violet Hunt. *Zeppelin Nights.* John Lane, 1916.

Hueppauf, Bernd. "Literature." *1914–1918 Online: International Encyclopedia of the First World War*, www.1914-1918-online.net/.

Hughes, Ted. "National Ghost." 1965. *Winter Pollen: Occasional Prose*, edited by William Scammell, Faber and Faber, 1994, pp. 70–72.

Hulme, T. E. *Further Speculations.* U of Minnesota P, 1955.

Hunt, Nigel. *Memory, War and Trauma.* Cambridge UP, 2010.

Hynes, Samuel. *A War Imagined: The First World War and English Culture.* Atheneum, 1991.

"In England Now." *Bystander*, 10 Mar. 1915, p. 327.

Islam, Kazi Nazrul. "The Rebel." *Kazi Nazrul Islam: A New Anthology*, Bangla Academy, 1990, pp. 20–25.

J'accuse. Directed by Abel Gance. 1919. Lobster Films, 2008.

Jack, George Morton. *The Indians Army on the Western Front, 1914–1915.* Cambridge UP, 2014.

Jagose, Annamarie. *Queer Theory: An Introduction.* New York UP, 1996.

James, C. L. R. *The Black Jacobins.* 1938. Alison and Busby, 1980.

James, Pearl. "History and Masculinity in F. Scott Fitzgerald's *This Side of Paradise.*" *Modern Fiction Studies*, vol. 51, no. 1, 2005, pp. 1–33.

———. *The New Death: American Modernism and World War I.* U of Virginia P, 2013.

———, editor. *Picture This: World War I Posters and Visual Culture.* U of Nebraska P, 2010.

James, William. "The Moral Equivalent of War." 1910. *Constitution Society*, www.constitution.org/wj/meow.htm.

Japrisot, Sébastien. *A Very Long Engagement.* 1991. Translated by Linda Coverdale, Picador, 2004.

Jeffery, Keith. *Ireland and the Great War.* Cambridge UP, 2000.

Jenkins, Elinor. "Dulce et Decorum?" Reilly, p. 57.

Johnson, Fenton. "War Profiles." *Crisis*, June 1918, p. 65.

Johnston, Wayne. *The Custodian of Paradise*, W. W. Norton, 2006.

Jones, David. *In Parenthesis.* Faber and Faber, 1937.

Jones, Heather. "Imperial Captivities: Colonial Prisoners of War in Germany and the Ottoman Empire, 1914–1918." Das, *Race*, pp. 175–93.

Jones, Nigel. *The War Walk: A Journey along the Western Front.* 1983. Cassell, 2004.

Jouve, Pierre Jean. *Danse des morts.* Action Sociale, 1917.

———. *Poème contre le grand crime.* Demain, 1916.

———. *Vous êtes des hommes.* La Nouvelle Revue Française, 1915.

Joyce, James. *Finnegans Wake.* Wordsworth Classics, 2012.

Judge, Jack, and Harry Williams. "It's a Long Way to Tipperary." 1912. *When This Bloody War Is Over: Soldiers' Songs of the First World War*, compiled by Max Arthur, Piatkus, 2001, pp. 27–28.

Jünger, Ernst. *In Stahlgewittern: Aus dem Tagebuch eines Stoßtruppführers.* 1920. E. S. Mittler und Sohn, 1925.

———. *Storm of Steel.* Translated by Michael Hoffmann, Penguin, 2004.

Kahn, Elizabeth. "Art from the Front: Death Imagined and the Neglected Majority." *Art History*, vol. 8, no. 2, June 1985, pp. 192–208.

Kant, Immanuel. *Critique of Judgment.* Translated by J. H. Bernard, Hafner, 1951.

Kaplan, Laurie. "Deformities of the Great War: The Narratives of Mary Borden and Helen Zenna Smith." *Women and Language*, vol. 27, no. 2, 2004, pp. 35–43. *MLA International Bibliography*, www.ebscohost.com/academic/mla-international-bibliography.

Keegan, John. *The First World War.* Vintage Books, 2000.

Keene, Jennifer D. *Doughboys, the Great War, and the Remaking of America.* Johns Hopkins UP, 2001.

———. "Images of Racial Pride: African American Propaganda Posters in the First World War." James, *Picture*, pp. 206–40.

Kelly, Jean, editor. *Love Letters from the Front.* Marino Press, 2000.

Kendall, Tim. *Modern English War Poetry.* Oxford UP, 2006.

———, editor. *The Oxford Handbook of British and Irish War Poetry.* Oxford UP, 2007.

———, editor. *Poetry of the First World War: An Anthology.* Oxford UP, 2013.

Keneally, Thomas. *The Daughters of Mars.* Sceptre, 2012.

Khoury, Dina Rizk. "Ambiguities of the Modern: The Great War in the Memoirs and Poetry of the Iraqis." Liebau et al., pp. 29–53.

Kipling, Rudyard. "Big Steamers." *Poetry Lovers Page*, www.poetryloverspage.com/poets/kipling/big_steamers.html.

———. *The Eyes of Asia.* Doubleday, 1918.

———. "The Gardener." *War Stories and Poems*, edited by Andrew Rutherford, Oxford UP, 2009, pp. 310–20.

Kirchner, Ernst Ludwig. *Self-Portrait as a Soldier.* 1915. Allen Memorial Art Museum, Oberlin College.

Klaeber, Kurt. *Der Krieg: Das Erste Volksbuch vom grossen Krieg.* Internationaler Arbeiter-Verlag, 1929.

Klausner, Joseph. *Saul Tchernichowsky.* Hebrew University of Jerusalem, 1947.

Klay, Phil, "After War, a Failure of the Imagination." *New York Times*, 8 Feb. 2014, www.nytimes.com/2014/02/09/opinion/sunday/after-war-a-failure-of-the-imagination.html?_r=0.

Klein, Holger, editor. *The First World War in Fiction.* Macmillan, 1976.

Kolata, Gina. *Flu: The Story of the Great Influenza Pandemic of 1918 and the Search for the Virus That Caused It.* Touchstone, 2001.

Koller, Christian. "The Recruitment of Colonial Troops in Africa and Asia and Their Deployment in Europe during the First World War." *Immigrants and Minorities*, vol. 26, no. 1–2, 2008, pp. 111–33.

Kramer, Alan. *Dynamic of Destruction.* Oxford UP, 2007.

"Kriegsliteratur." *Der Grosse Herder.* Herder, 1933.

Kubrick, Stanley, director. *Paths of Glory.* United Artists, 1957.

LaCapra, Dominick. *Writing History, Writing Trauma.* Johns Hopkins UP, 2001.

La Motte, Ellen. *The Backwash of War: The Human Wreckage of the Battlefield As Witnessed by an American Hospital Nurse.* 1916. Project Gutenberg, www.gutenberg.org/files/26884/26884-h/26884-h.htm.

———. "Heroes." Higonnet, *Nurses*, pp. 5–11.

Lange, Britta. "South Asian Soldiers and German Academics." Ahuja, Liebau, and Roy, pp. 148–84.

Lange, Karl. *Marneschlacht und deutsche Oeffentlichkeit, 1914–1939: Eine verdraengte Niederlage und ihre Folgen.* Bertelsmann Universitaetsverlag, 1974.

Laqueur, Thomas W. "The Names of the Great War." *The Work of the Dead: A Cultural History of Mortal Remains*, Princeton UP, 2015, pp. 447–88, 662–69.

Larès, Maurice. *T. E. Lawrence, la France et les Français.* Publications de la Sorbonne, 1980.

Lawrence, T. E. *Seven Pillars of Wisdom.* Harmondsworth: Penguin, 1983.

———. *Seven Pillars of Wisdom: A Triumph: The Complete 1922 Text.* Edited by Jeremy Wilson, Castle Hill Press, 1997.

Lawrence of Arabia. Directed by David Lean, Columbia Pictures, 1962.

Lawson, Henry. "England Yet." Wallace-Crabbe and Pierce, p. 44.

Layson, Hana, and Patricia Scanlan. *World War I in U.S. Popular Culture.* Newberry Library, dcc.newberry.org/collections/world-war-i-in-us-popular-culture.

Ledwidge, Francis. "After Court Martial." Ledwidge, *Complete Poems*, p. 196.

———. "The Call to Ireland." Ledwidge, *Complete Poems*, p. 136.

———. *The Complete Poems.* Edited by Liam O'Mera, Goldsmith Press, 1997.

———. "The Irish in Gallipoli." Ledwidge, *Complete Poems*, p. 240.

Lee, Hermione. *Body Parts: Essays on Life Writing.* Random House, 2008.

Leed, Eric. *No Man's Land: Combat and Identity in World War I.* Cambridge UP, 1979.

Leese, Peter. *Shell Shock: Traumatic Neurosis and the British Soldiers of the First World War.* Palgrave Macmillan, 2002.

Lefebvre, Henri. *La production de l'espace.* Éditions Anthropos, 1974.

———. *The Production of Space.* Translated by Donald Nicholson-Smith, Blackwell, 1991.

Leopold, Elisabeth, et al., editors. *Trotzdem Kunst! Österreich, 1914–1918.* Christian Brandstätter Verlag, 2014.

Lerner, Paul. *Hysterical Men: War, Psychiatry, and the Politics of Trauma in Germany, 1890–1930.* Cornell UP, 2003.

Lessing, Gotthold Ephraim. *Laocoön: An Essay upon the Limits of Painting and Poetry.* Johns Hopkins UP, 1984.

Let England Shake: Seamus Murphy Meets the Audience. *Iceland Chronicles*, 25 Sept. 2011, icelandchronicles.com/2011/09/riff-2011-day-3-let-england-shake-seamus-murphy-meets-audience/.

Lewis, Wyndham. *Blasting and Bombardiering*. U of California P, 1967.

Leys, Ruth. *Trauma: A Genealogy*. U of Chicago P, 2000.

Liebau, Heike, et al., editors. *The World in World Wars: Experiences and Perspectives for Africa and Asia*. Brill, 2010.

Limon, John. *Writing after War: American War Fiction from Realism to Postmodernism*. Oxford UP, 1994.

Lind, Francis T. *The Letters of Mayo Lind*. Creative Book, 2001.

Linge, Ken, and Pam Linge. "Missing." *Missing but Not Forgotten: Men of the Thiepval Memorial, Somme*, Pen and Sword, 2015, pp. 8–173.

———. *Thiepval: The Panel of the Missing*. Thiepval Visitor Centre, Thiepval, France, 2004.

Lithinés du Dr. Gustin. Advertisement. *L'écho de Paris*, 5 July 1915, p. 3.

———. Advertisement. *L'écho de Paris*, 9 Aug. 1915, p. 3.

Liulevcius, Vejas. *War Land on the Eastern Front: Culture, National Identity and German Occupation in World War I*. Cambridge UP, 2005.

Lloyd, David. *Battlefield Tourism: Pilgrimage and the Commemoration of the Great War in Britain, Australia and Canada, 1919–1939*. Berg, 1998.

Locke, Alain. *The New Negro*. 1925. Touchstone Books, 1999.

Loew, Camila. "Miss Represented: Women at War, Propaganda vs. Autobiographical Writing." *(Mis)Representations: Intersections of Culture and Power*, edited by Fernando Galván Bern et al., Peter Lang, 2003, pp. 123–33.

Longinus. *On Great Writing (On the Sublime)*. Translated by G. M. A. Grube, Hackett, 1991.

Longley, Edna. *The Living Stream: Literature and Revisionism in Ireland*. Bloodaxe, 1994.

Löschnigg, Martin. "'. . . the Novelist's Responsibility to the Past': History, Myth, and the Narratives of Crisis in Pat Barker's *Regeneration* Trilogy, 1991–1995." *Zeitschrift für Anglistik und Amerikanistik*, vol. 47, no. 3, 1999, pp. 214–28.

Loughran, Tracey. "Shell Shock, Trauma, and the First World War: The Making of a Diagnosis and Its Histories." *Journal of the History of Medicine and Allied Sciences*, vol. 67, no. 1, 2012, pp. 94–119. *OUP Academic*, doi.org/10.1093/jhmas/jrq052.

Lubow, Arthur. *The Reporter Who Would Be King: A Biography of Richard Harding Davis*. Charles Scribner's Sons, 1992.

Lucas, E. V. *Swollen-Headed William: Painful Stories and Funny Pictures (After the German!)*. Illustrated by Geo. Morrow, 4th ed., Musson, 1914.

Lunn, Joe. "France's Legacy to Demba Mboup? A Senegalese Griot and His Descendants Remember His Military Service during the First World War." Das, *Race*, pp. 108–24.

———. "Kande Kamara Speaks: An Oral History of the West African Experience in France, 1914–18." *Africa and the First World War*, edited by Melvin Page, Macmillan, 1987, pp. 28–53.

———. "Male Identity and Martial Codes of Honor: A Comparison of the War Memoirs of Robert Graves, Ernst Jünger, and Kande Kamara." *Journal of Military History*, vol. 69, no. 3, July 2005, pp. 713–55.

———. *Memoirs of the Malestrom: A Senegalese Oral History of the First World War.* Heinemann, 1999.

Lussu, Emilio. *Sardinian Brigade.* Translated by Marion Rawson, Prion, 2000.

Macaulay, Thomas. "Minute on Education." 1835. Frances W. Pritchett's Web site, www.columbia.edu/itc/mealac/pritchett/00generallinks/macaulay/txt_minute_education_1835.html.

Macdonald, Lyn. "The Somme Front." *English Literature of the Great War Revisited: Proceedings of the Symposium on the British Literature of the First World War, University of Picardy, 1986*, edited by Michel Roucoux, Presses de l'U. F.R. Clerc, 1989, pp. 143–58.

Mack, John. *A Prince of Our Disorder: The Life of T. E. Lawrence.* Weidenfeld and Nicolson, 1976.

MacKenzie, John M. "Lakes, Rivers and Oceans: Technology, Ethnicity and the Shipping of Empire in the Late Nineteenth Century." *Maritime Empires: British Imperial Maritime Trade in the Nineteenth Century*, edited by David Killingray et al., Boydell and Brewer, 2004, pp. 111–27.

Mackintosh's Toffee. Advertisement. *Telegraph*, 9 Jan. 1917, p. 1.

Mahfouz, Naguib. *The Palace Walk.* Translated by William Maynard Hutchins and Olive E. Kenny, Anchor-Doubleday, 1991.

Major, Kevin. *No Man's Land.* Doubleday, 1995.

Malherbe, Henry. *The Flame That Is France.* Translated by Van Wyck Brooks, Century, 1918.

Malouf, David. *Fly Away Peter.* Chatto and Windus, 1982.

Malvern, Sue. *Modern Art, Britain and the Great War: Witnessing, Testimony and Remembrance.* Yale UP, 2004.

Mann, Susan, editor. *The War Diary of Clare Gass, 1915–1918.* McGill-Queen's UP, 2000.

Manning, Frederic. *Her Privates We.* P. Davis, 1929.

Mansfield, Katherine. *Selected Stories.* Edited by Vincent O'Sullivan, W. W. Norton, 2005.

Manzi, Angelo. Message about the undergraduate seminar Literature of World War I. Received by Margaret Higonnet, 5 May 2015.

March, William. *Company K.* 1933. Edited by Philip D. Beidler, U of Alabama P, 1989.

Marcus, Jane. "Afterword: Corpus/Corps/Corpse: Writing the Body in/at War." *Not So Quiet . . . : Stepdaughters of War*, by Helen Zenna Smith, Feminist Press, 1989, pp. 241–93.

Marcus, Sharon. "Queer Theory for Everyone: A Review Essay." *Signs: Journal of Women in Culture and Society*, vol. 31, no. 1, 2005, 191–218.

Marinetti, F. T. "Founding and Manifesto of Futurism." Translated by James Joll, Pantheon Books, 1960, pp. 139–40.

Markish, Peretz. "The Heap." *Against the Apocalypse: Responses to Catastrophe in Modern Jewish Culture*, by David Roskies, Syracuse UP, 1984, 98–101.

Markovits, Claude. "Indian Soldiers' Experiences in France during World War I." Liebau et al., pp. 29–53.

Marsland, Elizabeth. *The Nation's Cause: French, English, and German Poetry of the First World War.* Routledge, 1991.

Martin, J. R. "Genre and Language Learning: A Social Semiotic Perspective." *Linguistics and Education: An International Research Journal*, vol. 20, no .1, 2009, pp. 10–21.

Martinet, Marcel. *Les temps maudits*. Union Générale d'Éditions, 1975.

Matthews, Harley. "True Patriot." Wallace-Crabbe and Pierce, pp. 49–59.

Maunder, Andrew, editor. *British Literature of World War I: An Anthology*. Vol 5, Pickering and Chatto, 2011.

Maxim, Hiram, et al. "Overcoming Curricular Bifurcation: A Departmental Approach to Curriculum Reform." *Die Unterrichtspraxis*, vol. 46, no. 1, Spring 2013, pp. 1–26.

Mayran, Camille. *The Story of Gotton Connixloo*. Translated by Van Wyck Brooks, E. P. Dutton, 1920.

McCarthy, Mark. *Ireland's 1916 Rising: Explorations of History-Making, Commemoration and Heritage in Modern Times*. Ashgate, 2012.

McCormack, John, performer. "It's a Long Way to Tipperary." By Jack Judge and Harry Williams / 1914. *First World War.com: A Multimedia History of World War One*, edited by Michael Duffy, www.firstworldwar.com/audio/itsalongway totipperary.htm.

McCutcheon, John T. Introduction. *The Deserter*, by Richard Harding Davis, Charles Scribner's Sons, 1917, pp. v–xvi.

McKay, Claude. *Home to Harlem*. 1928. Northeastern UP, 1987.

———. "The Soldier's Return." *World War I in American Fiction: An Anthology of Short Stories*, edited by Scott D. Emmert and Steven Trout, Ohio State UP, 2014, pp. 190–94.

McLoughlin, Noah. "Code Use and Identity in *La Grande Illusion* and *Xala*." *Glottopol: Revue de sociolinguistique en ligne*, vol. 12, 2008, pp. 123–34.

McNulty, Eugene. "Incommensurate Histories: The Remaindered Irish Bodies of the Great War." *Conflict, Nationhood and Corporeality in Modern Literature: Bodies-at-War*, edited by Petra Rau, Palgrave Macmillan, 2010, pp. 64–82.

Mead, Margaret. "Warfare Is Only an Invention—Not a Biological Necessity." *Asia*, vol. 40, no. 1 8, August, 1940, pp. 402–05.

Mencken, H. L. "Portrait of an American Citizen." *Willa Cather: The Contemporary Reviews*, edited by Margaret Anne O'Connor, Cambridge UP, 2001, pp. 141–43.

Michelin Guides to the Battle-fields, 1914–1918: The Somme. Vol. 1, G. H. Smith and Son.

Middlebrook, Martin. *The First Day on the Somme, 1 July 1916*. 1971. Penguin, 1984.

Mignola, Mike, et al. *Baltimore: The Plague Ships*. Dark Horse, 2011.

Miller, Elizabeth, editor. *Arms and the Newfoundlander*. Harry Cuff, 1994.

Mills, Pat, and Joe Colquhoun. *Charley's War: 2 June 1916–1 August 1916*. Titan Books, 2004.

Mir, Farina. *The Social Space of Language: Vernacular Culture in British Colonial Punjab*. U of California P, 2010.

Missing of the Somme. Historial de la Grande Guerre, 2012.

Missoffe, Mathieu, and Charlie Adlard. *Curse of the Wendigo*. Dynamite Publishing, 2012.

Mitchell, W. J. T. *Iconology: Image, Text, Ideology.* U of Chicago P, 1987.
Mjagkij, Nina. *Loyalty in Time of Trial: The African-American Experience during World War I.* Rowman and Littlefield, 2011.
Montague, C. E. *Disenchantment.* 1922. Chatto and Windus, 1929.
Montale, Eugenio. *Collected Poems: 1920–1954.* Translated by Jonathan Galassi, revised edition, Farrar, Straus, and Giroux, 2012.
———. "Distant, I was with you when your father." Montale, *Collected Poems,* pp. 194–95.
———. "Valmorbia, Flowering Clouds of Plants." Montale, *Collected Poems,* pp. 56–57.
"Le monument au Foch." *Le reveil du nord,* 17 Nov. 1935. Clipping in Archives Municipales de Lille, box no. 3 M 62.
"Le monument du marechal Foch." *L'œuvre,* 24 Oct. 1935. Clipping in Archives Municipales de Lille, box no. 3 M 62.
Moore, Christopher. *Trench Fever: An Intimate Story of the First World War.* Abacus, 1999.
Morel, E. D. *Truth and the War.* National Labour Press, 1916.
Morgan, Harry. "When the Germans Took Jamaica." *Jamaica Times,* 7 Nov. 1914, p. 28, and 14 Nov. 1914, pp. 4, 29.
Morrison, Rob, and Charlie Adlard. *White Death.* AIT Planet Lar, 2002.
Morrison, Toni. *Sula.* Knopf, 1973.
Morrow, John H. *The Great War: An Imperial History.* Routledge, 2004.
Morsey, Konrad. *T. E. Lawrence und der arabische Aufstand, 1916–18.* Biblio-Verlag, 1976.
Mosse, George L. *Fallen Soldiers: Reshaping the Memory of the World Wars.* Oxford UP, 1990.
Mousa, Suleiman. *T. E. Lawrence: An Arab View.* Translated by Albert Boutros, Oxford UP, 1966.
Mueller, Hans-Harold. *Der Krieg und die Schriftsteller.* Metzler, 1986.
Mullen, John. "Propaganda and Dissent in British Popular Song during the Great War." *Textes et contextes,* vol. 6, 2011, revuesshs.u-bourgogne.fr/textes&contextes/document.php?id=1478.
Mussolini, Benito. "The Doctrine of Fascism." Translated by Jane Soames. *The Living Age,* Living Age, 1933, pp. 235–44.
Myers, Charles S. "A Contribution to the Study of Shell Shock." *Lancet,* 13 Feb. 1915, pp. 316–20.
———. *Shell Shock in France, 1914–1918.* Cambridge UP, 1940.
Nash, John. *Oppy Wood.* 1918–19 / oil on canvas. Imperial War Museum, London. Malvern, p. 100.
Nash, Paul. *Landscape—Year of Our Lord, 1917.* 1918 / pen and ink / National Gallery of Canada, Ottawa. Malvern, p. 65.
———. *The Menin Road.* 1918–19 / oil on canvas. Imperial War Museum, London. Malvern, p. 95.
———. *Ruin: Sunset.* 1917–18 / pastel. Imperial War Museum, London. Malvern, p. 66.
———. *Sunrise: Inverness Copse.* 1918 / pastel. Imperial War Museum, London. Malvern, p. 32.

———. *We Are Making a New World.* 1917–18 / oil on canvas. Imperial War Museum, London. Malvern, p. 20.

Natter, Wolfgang. *Literature at War. Representing the Time of Greatness" in Germany, 1914–1940.* Yale UP, 1999.

Neiberg, Michael. *The Military Atlas of World War I.* Chartwell Books, 2014.

———. "What Students Need to Know about World War I." *Foreign Policy Research Institute*, vol. 13, no. 19, Aug. 2008, files.eric.ed.gov/fulltext/ED505421.pdf.

Nelson, Robert. *Solider Newspapers of the First World War.* Cambridge UP, 2011.

Nestlé: La ration du soldat. Advertisement. *L'écho de Paris*, 14 Apr. 1915, p. 2.

Nevinson, C. R. W. *After a Push.* 1917 / oil on canvas / Imperial War Museum, London. Malvern, p. 61.

———. *Flooded Trench on the Yser.* 1915 / oil on canvas. Malvern, p. 7.

———. *La Mitrailleuse.* 1915 / oil on canvas. Tate, London.

———. *Marching Men.* 1916 / drawing. Imperial War Museum, London.

———. *Paths of Glory.* 1917 / oil on canvas. Imperial War Museum, London.

———. *The Roads of France.* 1917–18 / oil on canvas / Canadian War Museum, Ottawa. Malvern, pp. 56–57.

Nicholson, G. W. L. *Canadian Expeditionary Force, 1914–1919: Official History of the Canadian Army in the First World War.* 2nd rev. ed., R. Duhamel, Queen's Printer, 1964.

Nicolson, Juliet. *The Great Silence.* Grove, 2011.

1916 Necrology 485. Glasnevin Trust, www.glasnevintrust.ie/visit-glasnevin/news/1916-list/.

The 1918–1919 Influenza Pandemic in the United States. Public Health Reports, vol. 125, supplement 3, Apr. 2010, pp. 1–144. *JSTOR*, www.jstor.org/stable/i40070055.

Noailles, Anna de. *Les forces éternelles.* Fayard, 1920.

Noakes, Vivien. *Voices of Silence: The Alternative Book of First World War Poetry.* History Press, 2006.

Norris, Margot. *Writing War in the Twentieth Century.* U of Virginia P, 2000.

Nunnery, Katie. "Language in *Across the Black Waters.*" 18 Nov. 2014. Graduate seminar paper.

O'Brien, Tim. *The Things They Carried.* 1990. Houghton Mifflin Harcourt, 2011.

Omissi, David. "Europe through Indian Eyes." *English Historical Review*, vol. 122, no. 496, 2007, pp. 371–96.

———. *Indian Voices of the Great War: Soldiers' Letters, 1914–1918.* Macmillan, 1999.

Opdycke, Sandra. *The Flu Epidemic of 1918: America's Experience in the Global Health Crisis.* Routledge, 2014. Critical Moments in Health Ser.

Orr, Emily. "A Recruit from the Slums." *Scars upon My Heart: Women's Poetry and Verse of the First World War*, edited by Catherine W. Reilly, Virago, 1981, p. 87.

Orton, George W. *Bob Hunt in Canada.* Whitman Publishing, 1916.

Orwell, George. *All Art Is Propaganda: Critical Essays by George Orwell.* Edited by George Packer, Houghton Mifflin Harcourt, 2008.

Ouditt, Sharon. *Fighting Forces, Writing Women: Identity and Ideology in the First World War.* Routledge, 1994.

Owen, Harold, and John Bell, editors. *Wilfred Owen: Collected Letters.* Oxford UP, 1967.

Owen, Wilfred. "Disabled." Owen, *Wilfred Owen*, p. 175.

———. "Dulce et Decorum Est." Owen, *Wilfred Owen*, p. 140.

———. Letter to Susan Owen. 19 Jan. 1917. Owen and Bell, pp. 428–29.

———. *Wilfred Owen: The Complete Poems and Fragments.* Edited by Jon Stallworthy, Chatto and Windus, 1983.

Paget, Stephen. *Essays for Boys and Girls: A First Guide toward the Study of the War.* Macmillan, 1916.

Palmer, Roy. *"What a Lovely War!": British Soldiers' Songs.* Michael Joseph, 1990.

Palmer, Svetlana, and Sarah Wallis, editors. *Intimate Voices from the First World War.* HarperCollins, 2003.

Le panorama. Mémorial 1815, www.waterloo1815.be/index.php?page=le-panorama.

Paris, Michael. *Over the Top: The Great War and Juvenile Literature in Britain.* Praeger, 2004.

Pearse, Padraic. "The Coming Revolution" 1913. *The Coming Revolution: Political Writings of Patrick Pearse*, Phoenix Press, 1916, pp. 89–100. *MostBooks*, www.mostbooks.download/the-coming-revolution-political-writings-of-patr-1.html.

——— "Graveside Oration." 1915. *The Coming Revolution: Political Writings of Patrick Pearse*, Phoenix Press, 1916, pp. 133–38. *MostBooks*, www.mostbooks.download/the-coming-revolution-political-writings-of-patr-1.html.

Pennell, Catriona. "Popular History and Myth-Making: The Role and Responsibility of First World War Historians in the Centenary Commemorations, 2014–2018." *Historically Speaking*, vol. 13, no. 5, Nov. 2012, pp. 11–14.

Peters, Ada, and Ethel Peters. *War Poems.* Union Publishing, 1919. West Virginia Humanities Council / West Virginia Campus Compact's Campus-Community LINK Project, www.thebookofwarpoems.

"Petition to King George V by Kingston UNIA." Oct. 1935. National Archives, London. CO318/418/4/71062.

"Petition to Secretary of State for the Colonies." 5 Oct. 1935. National Archives, London. CO318/418/4/71062.

Petrone, Karen. *The Great War and Russian Memory.* U of Indiana P, 2011.

Phillips, Howard, and David Killingray. *The Spanish Influenza Pandemic of 1918–19: New Perspectives.* Routledge, 2003.

Phillips, William Raglan. "De War Time Solo." *Jamaica Times*, 12 Dec. 1914, p. 9.

———. "Victoria First Gran-Pickney: How Him Turn Out Bad." *Jamaica Times*, 12 Dec. 1914, p. 9.

Phosferine: Tonic Medicine. Advertisement. *Telegraph*, 5 July 1917, p. 4.

Pichel, Beatriz. "Photography, Masculinity and the Body during the First World War in France." The First World War in a Gendered Perspective Conference, U of Vienna, 30 Sept. 2011.

Pier, Arthur Standwood. *The Son Decides: The Story of a Young German-American.* Houghton Mifflin, 1918.

Plueschow, Gunther. *Die Abenteur des Fliegers von Tsingtau.* Ullstein, 1916.

Pope, Daniel. "The Advertising Industry and World War I." *The Public Historian*, vol. 2, no. 3, 1980, pp. 4–25.

Porter, Katherine Anne. *Pale Horse, Pale Rider*. Houghton Mifflin Harcourt, 1990.
Pound, Ezra. "Homage to Sextus Propertius." 1926. *Personae: Collected Shorter Poems of Ezra Pound*, edited by Lea Baechler and A. Walton Litz, rev. ed., New Directions, 1990, pp. 203–24.
Princess Mary's Gift Book. Authorized Canadian ed. Hodder and Stoughton, 1914.
Proctor, Tammy. *Female Intelligence: Women and Espionage in the First World War*. New York UP, 2003.
Prosser, Jay. *Second Skins: The Body Narratives of Transsexuality*. Columbia UP, 1998.
Prost, Antoine. "Les monuments aux morts." *Les lieux de mémoire*, edited by Pierre Nora, vol. 2, Gallimard, 1986, pp. 307–30.
———. "Verdun." *Les lieux de mémoire*, edited by Pierre Nora, vol. 3, Gallimard, 1997, pp. 376–401.
PU. *RIFF 2011—Let England Shake: Seamus Murphy Meets the Audience. Iceland Chronicles*, 25 Sept. 2011, icelandchronicles.com/2011/09/riff-2011-day-3-let-england-shake-seamus-murphy-meets-audience/.
Ramsey, Paul. "The Just War according to St. Augustine." Elshtain, *Just War*, pp. 8–22.
Rauchensteiner, Manfried, editor. "*An Meine Völker!" Der Erste Weltkrieg, 1914–1918*. Amalthea, 2014.
Rawlinson, Mark. *Pat Barker*. Palgrave Macmillan, 2010.
Rechter, David. *The Jews of Vienna and the First World War*. Littman Library of Jewish Civilization, 2000.
Redcam, Tom. "To Britain's Nameless Heroes." *Jamaica Times*, 12 Sept. 1914, p. 1.
Reilly, Catherine. *The Virago Book of Women's War Poetry and Verse*. Virago, 1997.
Reinharz, Jehuda, and Yaacov Shavit. *Glorious, Accursed Europe*. Brandeis UP, 2010. Tauber Institute Series for the Study of European Jewry.
Remarque, Erich Maria. *All Quiet on the Western Front*. 1929. Translated by A. W. Wheen, Ballantine, 1982.
———. *Im Westen nichts Neues*. 1929. Kiepenhauer und Witsch, 1998.
Renoir, Jean. *La grande illusion* [Grand Illusion]. 1937. Criterion, 1999.
Report of the War Office Committee of Enquiry into "Shell-Shock." London, 1922.
Reynès-Monlaur, Marie. *Les autels morts*. Plon-Nourrit, 1917.
———. *La fin de Claude*. Plon-Nourrit, 1918.
———. *Les paroles secrètes*. Plon-Nourrit, 1915.
Reynolds, Kimberley. "'A Prostitution Alike of Matter and Spirit': Anti-war Discourses in Children's Literature and Childhood Culture before and during World War I." *Children's Literature in Education*, vol. 44, 2013, pp. 120–39.
Richards, Donald Ray. *The German Bestseller in the Twentieth Century: A Complete Bibliography and Analysis, 1915–1940*. Herbert Lang, 1968.
Richthofen, Manfred Freiherr von. *Der rote Kampfflieger*. Ullstein, 1917.
Ringuet. *Thirty Acres*. Translated by Felix Walter and Dorothea Walter, Macmillan, 1940.
Rivers, W. H. R. *Instinct and the Unconscious*. Cambridge UP, 1922.
———. "The Repression of War Experience." 1918. *The Return of the Soldier*, edited by Bernard Schweizer and Charles Thorne, Broadview Press, 2010, pp. 193–212.
Roberts, Charles G. D. *The Collected Poems of Sir Charles G. D. Roberts*. Edited by Desmond Pacey, Wombat, 1985.

Roberts, David. *We Are the Dead: Poems and Paintings from the Great War, 1914–1918.* Helion, 2014.
Roberts, Mary Louise. *Civilization without Sexes: Reconstructing Gender in Postwar France, 1917–1927.* Chicago UP, 1994.
Robinett, Jane. "The Narrative Shape of Traumatic Experience." *Literature and Medicine*, vol. 26, no. 2, 2007, pp. 290–311. *Project MUSE*, muse.jhu.edu/article/242731.
Robson, Stuart. *The First World War.* Longman, 1988.
Rolland, Romain. *Au-dessus de la mêlée.* Ollendorff, 1919.
Rolls, S. C. *Steel Chariots in the Desert.* Leonaur, 2005.
Roskies, David. "The Pogrom Poem and the Literature of Destruction." *Notre Dame English Journal*, vol. 11, no. 2, 1979, www.jstor.org/stable/40062456?seq=4.
Ross, Derek. "The Theatre." *Herald*, 22 May 1915, p. 11.
Russell, Bertrand. *Justice in War-Time.* 1916. Spokesman, 2005.
Ruthven, K. K. *A Guide to Ezra Pound's* Personae, *1926.* U of California P, 1969.
Sacco, Joe. *The Great War: July 1, 1916: The First Day of the Battle of the Somme: An Illustrated Panorama.* Norton, 2013.
Sáenz, José de la Luz. *The World War I Diary of José de la Luz Sáenz.* Edited and translated by Emilio Zamora, Texas A&M P, 2014.
Saint-Amour, Paul K. *Tense Future: Modernism, Total War, Encyclopedic Form.* Oxford UP, 2015.
Sammons, Jeffrey T., and John H. Morrow. *Harlem's Rattlers and the Great War: The Undaunted 369th Regiment and the African American Quest for Equality.* U of Kansas P, 2014.
Sargent, John Singer. *The Interior of a Hospital Tent.* 1918. *Imperial War Museum, London*, www.iwm.org.uk/collections/item/object/23728.
Sassoon, Siegfried. "Aftermath." Sassoon, *War Poems*, p. 91.
———. "Base Details." Sassoon, *War Poems*, p. 48.
———. "Finished with the War: A Soldier's Declaration." Graves, p. 260.
———. "Glory of Women." Sassoon, *War Poems*, p. 57.
———. *Memoirs of an Infantry Officer.* 1930. Faber and Faber, 2000.
———. *The Memoirs of George Sherston.* Literary Guild of America, 1937.
———. *The War Poems of Siegfried Sassoon.* William Heinemann, 1919.
Saunders, Max. *Self Impression: Life-Writing, Autobiografiction, and the Forms of Modern Literature.* Oxford UP, 2010.
Sauret, Henriette. *Les forces détournées, 1914–1917.* Les Forgerons, 1918.
La Sauvegarde: Gas Mask. Advertisement. *L'écho de Paris*, 27 June 1915, p. 3.
Sayers, Dorothy. *Whose Body?* 1923. Dover Publications, 2009.
Scarry, Elaine. *The Body in Pain: The Making and Unmaking of the World.* Oxford UP, 1985.
Schaller, Charlotte. *At War!* Great Richards, 1917.
Schneider, Mark Robert. *"We Return Fighting": The Civil Rights Movement in the Jazz Age.* Northeastern UP. 2002.
Schwarz, Wilhelm. *War and the Mind of Germany.* Peter Lang, 1975.
Scranton, Roy. "The Trauma Hero: From Wilfred Owen to *Redeployment* and *American Sniper*." *Los Angeles Review of Books*, 25 Jan. 2015, lareviewofbooks.org/article/trauma-hero-wilfred-owen-redeployment-american-sniper/#!.
Sebald, W. G. *The Emigrants.* Translated by Michael Hulse, Harvill, 1996.

Sedgwick, Eve Kosofsky. *Tendencies*. Duke UP, 1993.

Self, Will. *Umbrella*. Grove, 2013.

Selzer, Mark. "Wound Culture: Trauma in the Pathological Public Sphere." *October*, Spring 1997, pp. 3–26.

Service, Robert W. *Rhymes of a Red Cross Man*. Barse and Hopkins, 1916.

Shannon, Brent. *The Cut of His Coat: Men, Dress, and Consumer Culture in Britain, 1860–1914*. Ohio UP, 2006.

Sheffield, G. D. [Gary]. "'Oh! What a Futile War': Representations of the Western Front in Modern British Media and Popular Culture." *War, Culture and the Media: Representations of the Military in Twentieth-Century Britain*, edited by Ian Stewart and Susan L. Carruthers, Flicks Books, 1996, 54–74.

———. "A Once in a Century Opportunity? Some Personal Reflections on the Centenary of the First World War." *Voices of War and Peace*, www.voicesofwarandpeace.org/wp-content/uploads/2014/11/Personal-Reflections-by-Gary-Sheffield.pdf.

Shelton, Matthew. "Identity, Epigrams, Epithets, and Obscene Renderings in Mulk Raj Anand's *Across the Black Waters*." 18 Nov. 2014. Graduate Seminar paper.

Shephard, Ben. *A War of Nerves: Soldiers and Psychiatrists in the Twentieth Century*. Harvard UP, 2001.

Shepherd, William Gunn. "The Scar That Tripled." *Metropolitan*, July 1917, pp. 7+.

Sherman, Daniel J. *The Construction of Memory in Interwar France*. U of Chicago P, 1999.

Sherry, Vincent, editor. *The Cambridge Companion to the Literature of the First World War*. Cambridge UP, 2005.

———. *The Great War and the Language of Modernism*. Oxford UP, 2003.

Shirley, Edward. "How We Caught the Spy." *The Jolly Book for Boys and Girls*, edited by Shirley, Thomas Nelson and Sons, c. 1916, pp. 9–29.

Shoebridge, Tim. *First World War by the Numbers*. New Zealand History, 10 Oct. 2016, nzhistory.govt.nz/war/first-world-war-by-numbers.

Shoulder Arms. Performance by Charles Chaplin, First National Pictures, 1918.

Showalter, Elaine. *The Female Malady: Women, Madness, and English Culture, 1830–1980*. Pantheon, 1985.

Silkin, Jon. *The Penguin Book of First World War Poetry*. Rev. ed., Penguin Books, 1996.

Sillitoe, Alan. *Raw Material*. Charles Scribner's Sons, 1972.

Sinclair, May. *Tree of Heaven*. Macmillan, 1917.

Smith, Alison. "All Quiet on the Filmic Front? Codeswitching and the Representation of Multilingual Europe in *La grande illusion* (Jean Renoir, 1937) and *Joyeux Noël* (Christian Carion, 2005)." *Journal of Romance Studies*, vol. 10, no. 2, 2010, pp. 37–52.

Smith, G. Elliot, and T. H. Pear. *Shell Shock and Its Lessons*. 2nd ed., Longmans Green, 1918. *Internet Archive*, 17 Feb . 2009, archive.org/details/shellshockandit00peargoog.

Smith, Helen Zenna (Evadne Price). *Not So Quiet . . . : Stepdaughters of War*. 1930. Feminist Press, 1989.

Smith, Laurajane. *Uses of Heritage*. Routledge, 2006.

Smith, Leonard V. *The Embattled Self: French Soldiers' Testimony of the Great War*. Cornell UP, 2007.

Smith, Richard. "'Heaven Grant You Strength to Fight the Battle for Your Race'": Nationalism, Pan-Africanism, and the First World War in Modern Memory." Das, *Race*, pp. 265–82.

———. *Jamaican Volunteers in the First World War: Race, Masculinity and the Development of National Consciousness*. Manchester UP, 2004.

———. "TV documentary, Post-colonial Melancholia, and the Representation of West Indian Volunteers in the British Great War Memory." *The Great War in Post-memory Literature and Film*, edited by Martin Löschnigg and Marzena Sokolowska-Paryz, De Gruyter, 2014.

Smith, Sidonie, and Julia Watson. *Reading Autobiography: A Guide for Interpreting Life Narratives*. U of Minnesota P, 2010.

Smythe, Carroll F., editor. *Mother Goose's Garden: The New National Literature for Children*. F. and H. McLean, c.1918.

Solzhenitsyn, Aleksandr. *August 1914: The Red Wheel, Knot I*. Translated by H. T. Willetts, Farrar, Straus, and Giroux, 1989.

Sommer, Doris. *Bilingual Aesthetics: A New Sentimental Education*. Duke UP, 2004.

Southard, E. E. *Shell-Shock and Other Neuropsychiatric Problems Presented in Five Hundred and Eight-Nine Case Histories*. W. M. Leonard, 1919. *Internet Archive*, 14 May 2007, archive.org/details/shellshockothern00soutuoft.

Spencer, Stanley. *Unveiling Cookham War Memorial*. 1922 / oil on canvas. Malvern, p. 163.

Spiegelman, Art. *In the Shadow of No Towers*. Pantheon, 2004.

———. *Maus*. Pantheon, 1987.

Stamp, Gavin. *The Memorial to the Missing of the Somme*. Profile, 2007.

Steiner, Wendy. *The Colors of Rhetoric: Problems in the Relation between Modern Literature and Painting*. U of Chicago P, 1982.

Stevenson, David. *Cataclysm: The First World War as Political Tragedy*. Basic Books, 2004.

Strang, Herbert. *Great Britain and the War: A Book for Boys and Girls*. Henry Frowde / Hodder and Stoughton, 1916.

Strychacz, Thomas F. *Hemingway's Theaters of Masculinity*. Louisiana State UP, 2003.

Stryker, Susan. "Transgender Feminism: Queering the Woman Question." *Third Wave Feminism: A Critical Exploration*, edited by Stacy Gillis et al., Palgrave, 2004, pp. 59–70.

Supplement 3: The 1918–1919 Influenza Pandemic in the United States. Public Health Reports (1974–), vol. 125, Apr. 2010, pp. 1–144. JSTOR, www.jstor.org/stable/i40070055.

Svarnakumari Devi (Mrs. Ghosal). "Mutiny (A True Story)." 1919. Higonnet, *Lines*, pp. 384–89.

Tabachnick, Stephen. *T. E. Lawrence*. Rev. ed., Twayne, 1997.

Tagore, Rabindranath. "Crossing." *Indian Ink: Being Splashes from Various Pens in Aid of the Imperial Indian War Fund*, Thacker and Spink, 1915, 34.

———. *Nationalism*. 1917. Penguin, 2010.

———. "The Oarsmen." *The English Writings of Rabindranath Tagore*, edited by Sisir Das, vol. 1, Sahitya Academy, 1999.

Tal, Kali. *Worlds of Hurt: Reading the Literatures of Trauma*. Cambridge UP, 1996.

Tardi, Jacques. *Adèle et la Bête*. Casterman, 1976.
———. *Le der des ders*. Casterman, 1999.
———. *It Was the War of the Trenches*. Translated by Kim Thompson, Fantagraphics, 2010.
———. *Momies en folie*. Casterman, 1978.
Tardi, Jacques, and Didier Daeninckx. *Varlot Soldat*. L'Association, 1999.
Taubenberger, Jeffery K., and David M. Morens. "1918 Influenza: The Mother of All Pandemics." *CDC Emerging Infectious Diseases*, vol. 12, no. 1, Jan. 2006. *Centers for Disease Control and Prevention*, doi:10.3201/eid1201.050979.
Taylor, Martin, editor. *Lads: Love Poetry of the Trenches*. Duckworth, 1998.
"Taylorism on ABC World Report." Narrated by Peter Jennings, ABC Television, 27 Oct. 2007. *YouTube*, 28 Oct. 2011, www.youtube.com/watch?v=slfFJXVAepE.
Tchernichowsky, Saul. "From the Melodies of the Time." Translated by Glenda Abramson. *Hebrew Writing of the First World War*, by Abramson, Vallentine Mitchell, 2008, pp. 115–17.
Theweleit, Klaus. *Women, Floods, Bodies, History*. Translated by Chris Turner, U of Minnesota P, 1987. Vol. 1 of *Male Fantasies*.
———. *Male Bodies: Psychoanalyzing the White Terror*. Translated by Chris Turner, U of Minnesota P, 1987. Vol. 2 of *Male Fantasies*.
Thomas, Edward. "Roads." *Last Poems*. Selwyn and Blount, 1918, pp. 74–76.
Thomas, Gregory M. *Treating the Trauma of the Great War: Soldiers, Civilians, and Psychiatry in France, 1914–1940*. Louisiana State UP, 2009.
Thomas, Lowell. *With Lawrence in Arabia*. Garden City Publishing, 1924.
Thomson, Alistair. *Anzac Memories: Living with the Legend*. 1994. New ed., Monash UP, 2013.
Thompson, Gordon V., and William Davis. *When We Wind Up the Watch on the Rhine*. Thompson Publishing Company, 1917.
Thursfield, Amanda. "Pat Barker." *British Council: Literature*, British Council Arts Group, literature.britishcouncil.org/writer/pat-barker.
Titre Goldfilled: Bague Tricolore. Advertisement. *L'écho de Paris*, 25 Apr. 1915, p. 3.
Trakl, Georg. "Grodek." Translated by John Hollander. *War Poems*, edited by Hollander, Knopf, 1999, p. 160.
Travers, Tim. *Leadership in the Trenches*. Macmillan, 2000.
Trout, Steven. *Memorial Fictions: Willa Cather and the First World War*. U of Nebraska P, 2002.
Tuchman, Barbara. *The Guns of August*. 1962. Ballantine, 1990.
Tylee, Claire, editor. *War Plays by Women*. Routledge, 1999.
Ungaretti, Giuseppe. "I Am a Presence." Condini, pp. 200–01.
———. "Once upon a Time." Condini, pp. 198–99.
———. "San Martino del Carso." Condini, pp. 202–03.
———. "Vanity." *A Major Selection of the Poetry of Giuseppe Ungaretti*. Translated by Diego Bastianutti, Exile Editions, 1994, pp. 120–21.
"Les vandales du Square Jussieu." *L'enchainee*, 25 Oct. 1935. Archives Municipales de Lille, box no. 3 M 62.
Vandercook, Margaret. *The Red Cross Girls in Belgium*. John C. Winston, 1916.
Vandermeulen, David. *Fritz Haber*. 4 vols. Delcourt, 2005–14.

Varley, Fred. *For What?* c. 1918 / Canadian War Museum, Ottawa. Malvern, p. 138.
Vernon, Alex. "War, Gender, and Ernest Hemingway." *Hemingway Review*, vol. 22, no. 1, 2002, pp. 36–57.
Viebeg, Clara. *Töchter der Hekuba: Ein Roman aus unserer Zeit*. 1917. *Internet Archive*, 5 Feb. 2015, archive.org/details/bub_gb_aX85AAAAMAAJ.
Vildrac, Charles. *Chants du désespéré*. Gallimard, 1920.
Virilio, Paul. *The Administration of Fear*. Translated by Ames Hodges, MIT P, 2012.
Vogel, Bruno. *Es lebe der Krieg! Ein Brief*. 4th ed., Klaus Gruhl, 1978.
Voigt, Ellen Bryant. *Kyrie*. W. W. Norton, 1995.
Vonnegut, Kurt. *Bluebeard*. Delacorte, 1987.
Wallace-Crabbe, Chris, and Peter Pierce, editors. *Clubbing of the Gunfire: A Hundred and One Australian War Poems*. Melbourne UP, 1984.
Walter, George, editor. *The Penguin Book of First World War Poetry*. Penguin, 2004.
Walzer, Michael. *Just and Unjust Wars*. 1977. 3rd ed., Basic Books, 2000.
"War Comments." *Bystander*, 7 Oct. 1914, p. 2.
Waterman, David. *Pat Barker and the Mediation of Social Reality*. Cambria, 2009.
Weber, Fritz. *Alpenkrieg*. Kolitsch, 1928.
Weeks, Jeffrey. "Que[e]rying the Modern Homosexual." *Journal of British Studies*, vol. 51, no. 3, 2012, pp. 523–39.
———. *Sexuality*. Routledge, 2003.
We Heard the Bells: The Influenza of 1918. U.S. Department of Health and Human Services, 2010.
Wehner, Josef Magnus. *Langemarck: Ein Vermaechtnis*. Langen-Mueller, 1932.
Weir, Peter, director. *Gallipoli*. Associated R and R, 1981.
Weisbord, Robert G. "British West Indian Reaction to the Italian-Ethiopian War: An Episode in Pan-Africanism." *Caribbean Studies*, vol. 10, no. 1, 1970, pp. 34–41.
Weisstein, Ulrich. "Literature and the Visual Arts." *Interrelations of Literature*, edited by Jean-Pierre Barricelli and Joseph Gibaldi, MLA, 1982, pp. 251–77.
Wells, H. G. *Mr. Britling Sees It Through*. Cassell, 1916. *Project Gutenberg*, www.gutenberg.org/ebooks/14060.
West, Rebecca. *The Return of the Soldier*. 1918. Penguin, 1998.
Whalan, Mark. *The Great War and the Culture of the New Negro*. U of Florida P, 2008.
Whatsoever a Man Soweth. 1917. Directed by Joseph Best, *BFI Screenonline*, www.screenonline.org.uk/film/id/1358391/index.html.
Whitehead, Anne. *Trauma Fiction*. Edinburgh UP, 2004.
Whitworth, Geoffrey. *The Child's ABC of the War*. Illustrated by Stanley North, George Allen and Unwin, 1914.
Widdowson, Peter. *On Thomas Hardy: Late Essays and Earlier*. Palgrave Macmillan, 1998.
Willetts, Karl. Interview by Peter Grant. 29 May 2014.
Williams, Chad. *Torchbearers of Democracy: African American Soldiers in the World War I Era*. U of North Carolina P, 2010.
Williams, David. "Film and the Mechanization of Time in the Myth of the Great War Canon." *English Studies in Canada*, vol. 41, nos. 2–3, June–Sept. 2015, pp. 165–90.

———. "Spectres of Time: Seeing Ghosts in Will Bird's Memoirs and Abel Gance's *J'accuse*." *Canadian Literature*, vol. 219, Winter 2013, pp. 113–30.

Williams, R. James. *A to Z in the Puff-Puff.* Dean's Rag Books, c. 1914.

Wilson, Jeremy. *Lawrence of Arabia: The Authorized Biography of T. E. Lawrence.* Athenaeum, 1990.

Wilson, Ross J. *Cultural Heritage of the Great War in Britain.* Ashgate, 2013.

Winter, Jay, editor. *The Legacy of the Great War: Ninety Years On.* U of Missouri P, 2009.

———. "Pilgrimage and Tourism on the Somme." *Missing*, pp. 184–91.

———. "Shell-shock and the Cultural History of the Great War." *Journal of Contemporary History*, vol. 35, no. 1, 2000, pp. 7–11. *JSTOR*, www.jstor.org/stable/261177?seq=1#page_scan_tab_contents.

———. *Sites of Memory, Sites of Mourning.* Cambridge UP, 1995.

Wollaeger, Mark. *Modernism, Media, and Propaganda.* Princeton UP, 2006.

A Woman in Berlin: Eight Weeks in the Conquered City. Translated by Philip Boehm, Picador, 2005.

"Women and Patriotism." *The Girl's Own Paper and Woman's Magazine*, vol. 36, no. 1, 1915, p. 36.

Woolf, Virginia. *Essays.* Edited by Andrew McNeillie and Stuart N. Clarke, 6 vols., Harcourt, 1988–2011.

———. *Jacob's Room.* 1922. Harcourt Brace, 1990.

———. *Mrs. Dalloway.* 1925. Harcourt Brace, 1992.

———. *On Being Ill.* Paris Press, 2012.

———. *Three Guineas.* Harcourt Brace, 1938.

———. *To the Lighthouse.* 1927. Harcourt Brace, 1991.

"World War One Remembered across the Commonwealth." BBC 1, 4 Aug. 2014.

Worth, Paul W., and Jim Cartwright, compilers. *John McCormack: A Comprehensive Discography.* Greenwood, 1986.

Yealland, Lewis R. *Hysterical Disorders of Warfare.* Macmillan, 1918.

Yeats, W. B. *The Collected Poems of W. B. Yeats.* Edited by Richard J. Finneran, Scribner, 1996.

———. "Easter 1916." Yeats, *Collected Poems*, pp. 180–82.

———. Introduction. *The Oxford Book of Modern Verse, 1892–1935*, 1936, edited by Yeats, Oxford UP, 1966, pp. v–xlv.

———. "An Irish Airman Foresees His Death." Yeats, *Collected Poems*, p. 135.

———. "On Being Asked for a War Poem." Yeats, *Collected Poems*, pp. 155–56.

Yelvington, Kelvin A. "The War in Ethiopia and Trinidad, 1935–1936." *The Colonial Caribbean in Transition: Essays on Post-emancipation Social and Cultural History*, edited by Bridget Brereton and Kelvin A. Yelvington, UP of Florida, 1999, pp. 189–225.

Yoe, Craig, editor. *The Great Anti-war Cartoons.* Fantagraphics, 2009.

Yver, Colette. *Mirabelle of Pampeluna.* Translated by Lucy Humphrey Smith, Charles Scribner's Sons, 1919.

Index

Abdullah I, king of Jordan, 141
Abitisindo, 35
Ackroyd, Matthew, 287
Acton, Mary, 320
Adams, Bryan, 285
Adlard, Charlie, 279, 280, 281
Agnon, Samuel Joseph, 121–22
Ahern, Dermot, 276n15
Ahuja, Ravi, 129
Airy, Anna, 218
Akhmatova, Anna, 57
Aldington, Richard, 135, 229, 263
Al-Hakim, Tawfiq, 144, 146, 149n3
Allatini, Rose (A. T. Fitzroy), 167, 181
Allen, Hervey, 79
Allenby, Edmund, 71, 140, 142
Amadi, Elechi, 198–99, 200n8
Amatt, W. G., 202
Anand, Lal Chand, 134–35
Anand, Mulk Raj, 9, 31, 61, 69–71, 72, 72 (nn 4, 11), 73 (nn 13, 15), 133, 134–36
Angell, Norman, 19
Angray, Kanhoji, 69
Annaud, Jean-Jacques, 68–69, 70, 72n9
Ansky, S., 120, 121
Anzaldúa, Gloria, 65
Apollinaire, Guillaume, 20, 57, 112–13
Appleby, Eric, 236, 237
Arcos, René, 115
Arendt, Hannah, 17, 27n1
Aristophanes, 141
Asche, Oscar, 230
Astley, Virginia, 287
Aston, Peter, 91
Auden, W. H., 60
Augustine, 17, 27n2
Awwad, Tawfiq Yusuf, 144, 146–48

Babel, Isaac, 122
Babinski, Joseph, 156
Baetens, Jan, 12, 283
Baez, Joan, 286
Bagnold, Enid, 38
Bairnsfather, Bruce, 162
Ball, Hugo, 57
Balla, Giacomo, 172
Ballobar, Conde de, 149n1
Barbara (Monique Andrée Serf), 286
Barbusse, Henri, 3, 8, 66, 71, 104, 115–17, 117n1, 162, 187, 288, 317, 319
Barham, Peter, 158
Barker, Pat, 12, 61, 126, 156–57, 158, 180, 182–83, 265, 266, 267, 268–70, 274, 275n2
Barnes, Djuna, 173–75
Barrie, J. M., 233–34
Barry, John, 194, 200n9
Barry, Sebastian, 199, 265, 266, 267, 271–74, 276 (nn 11, 15)
Bass, John, 259
Bataille, Henry, 113
Baxter, Archibald, 167
Baym, Nina, 83
Beckett, Samuel, 55
Beckmann, Max, 213
Beiner, Guy, 275n2
Bentley, E. C., 19
Bergonzi, Bernard, 35
Bertrand, Adrien, 111
Bettignies, Louise de, 251, 253–54, 256n
Beumelburg, Werner, 103
Beynon, Francis Marion, 21
Bhabha, Homi, 133
Biggs, Herman, 194
Binyon, Laurence, 134
Bird, Will R., 248
Blanche, Jacques-Émile, 176n3
Bland, Lucy, 179
Blondell, Joan, 4
Bloem, Walter, 104
Bluemel, Kristin, 10, 70, 72n4, 73n16
Blunck, Hans Friedrich, 103
Blunden, Edmund, 38, 42, 54, 127, 138, 139, 140, 186–87, 188, 189, 191n5, 235, 239, 317, 318, 319
Boccioni, Umberto, 172
Bogle, Eric, 285, 287
Bolt, Robert, 143
Bonaparte, Napoleon, 242, 247, 321

Bond, Brian, 57
Bone, Muirhead, 57, 320, 321
Bonikowski, Wyatt, 7
Booth, Allyson, 49n1
Borden, Mary, 10, 82, 83, 84, 159, 162, 237, 238
Borden, Robert, 95
Bourke, Joanna, 57
Boutry, Edgar, 254
Boxwell, David A., 183
Boyd, Thomas, 79
Boyden, Joseph, 95, 275n1
Bradford, Richard, 124n2
Brandon, John, 229, 232
Brangwyn, Frank, 215
Brannigan, John, 270
Brassens, Georges, 286
Braybon, Gail, 8
Brel, Jacques, 286
Brennan, Christopher, 97
Brenner, Hildegard, 103
Briggs, Marlene, 12
Bristow, Nancy K., 195, 200n6
Brittain, Vera, 6, 54, 60, 61, 127, 162, 163–64, 235, 239, 295
Brock, Peter, 166
Brocklesby, Bert, 167
Brontë, Charlotte, 72n2
Brooke, Rupert, 57, 77, 78, 232
Brooker, Peter, 191n1
Brooks, Max, 279
Brown, Lloyd, 192n6
Buck, Claire, 7, 9, 21, 38, 39n5, 136n3
Buffton, Deborah D., 12
Bulkeley, H. J., 224
Bunbury, Henry Shirley, 87
Burke, Edmund, 319
Butler, Judith, 26, 239, 240
Byerly, Carol R., 195
Byrnes, Heidi, 308, 314n1
Byron, May, 224

Cameron, D. Y., 321
Campbell, James, 3, 41
Campbell, William Wilfred, 94–95
Canfield, Dorothy, 81–82
Carco, Francis, 23
Cardinal, Agnès, 6, 34
Carossa, Hans, 103
Carpenter, Edward, 181
Carrá, Carlo, 172
Cartwright, Jim, 271
Caruth, Cathy, 154, 157, 159, 193
Casement, Roger, 91
Casimir, Jon, 286
Castle, Terry, 182
Cather, Willa, 58, 75, 76, 77–78, 81, 83, 195
Ceadel, Martin, 166
Chabon, Michael, 283
Chandan, Amarjit, 132
Challenger, Melanie, 236
Chaplin, Charlie, 76–77
Child, Philip, 96
Childers, Erskine, 19
Chilens, Piet, 136n1
Chilton, Charles, 229
Chomsky, Aviva, 86
Clampin, David, 207
Clark, Christopher, 20
Clark, Greg, 94, 97
Clarke, Thomas J., 271, 272, 273
Clausewitz, Carl, 17, 18
Cloutier, Stephen, 9
Cobley, Evelyn, 84n3
Cohen, Debra Rae, 20, 126
Cole, Sarah, 17–18, 25–26, 49n1, 179
Colette, 6
Collins, Geneviève, 111
Collins, Judy, 286
Collins, Sewell, 234n4
Collins, Shirley, 286, 289n2
Colquhoun, Joe, 282
Conrad, Joseph, 319–20
Cook, Tim, 246
Cornell, Elizabeth, 243
Cotter, Joseph, Jr., 90
Coverdale, Linda, 275n1
Crosby, Alfred, 200n1
Cross, Tim, 20, 34
Crouthamel, Jason, 158
Croxall, Brian, 297
Culleton, Claire, 36
Culpin, Millais, 158
Cummings, E. E., 34, 57

Dallas, Gloden, 164, 168n1
Daly, Victor, 37
Dangerfield, George, 43
Danielson, Susan, 307n1
Darrow, Margaret H., 254

Das, Santanu, 8, 22, 28, 29, 30, 31–32, 33–34, 36, 37, 38, 38n2, 49n2, 53, 59, 72n12, 126, 132, 136n3, 137 (nn 4, 6–7), 180
David, William, 74
Davies, George Llewelyn, 233
Davis, Richard Harding, 258–63
Davis, Ryan A., 200n6de Ambris, Alceste, 170
Davis, William, 74
Deer, Patrick, 11
Deist, Wilhelm, 104
Delacroix, Eugène, 216
de Lisser, Rose, 87
Dellamora, Richard, 182
Dendooven, Dominiek, 136n1
de Paor, Liam, 276n12
Derrida, Jacques, 72n5
Deslandes, Paul R., 182
Desrouseaux, Alexandre, 255
Desruelles, Félix-Alexandre, 251
Detaille, Édouard, 247–48
Deuchar, Maude, 232–33
Devi, Mokkhada, 130
Dexter, Mary, 72n3
de Zoete, Matthew, 285
Dix, Beulah, 234n4
Dix, Otto, 217, 314n5
Djemal Pasha, Ahmad, 147
Doan, Laura, 7, 24, 179
Doenitz, Karl, 104
Donaldson, Walter, 75
Dorgelès, Roland, 115
Dos Passos, John, 34, 58, 79
Douanne, G. 27n6
Doughty, Charles M., 141
Douglas, Keith, 52
Dowling, Linda, 182
Dowling, Martin, 271
Dowson, Ernest, 141
Doyle, Laura, 191n1
Drouin, Jeffrey, 12
Du Bois, W. E. B, 58, 78
Duhamel, Georges, 115
Duhamelet, Geneviève, 114
Dumoulin, Louis, 278
Dunbar-Nelson, Alice, 234n4
Dyer, Geoff, 268
Dylan, Bob, 285

Earle, David M., 264n2
Eberwein, Robert, 245
Edelman, Lee, 179
Eder, M. D., 158
Edeson, Arthur, 245
Edney, Matthew H., 190, 192n8
Egger-Lienz, Albin, 314nn4–5
Einhaus, Anne-Marie, 257
Eksteins, Modris, 42, 84n3, 171, 176n3
El-Adl, Mohammed, 39n5
Eliot, T. S., 4, 25, 41, 44, 46–47, 57, 134, 295
Ellis, Havelock, 179
Ellis, Walter, 230
Ellsworth-Jones, Will, 167
Elshtain, Jean Bethke, 24, 27n2
Emecheta, Buchi, 198, 199, 200n8
Emerson, Robert, 287
Emmett, Robert, 91
Enloe, Cynthia, 6, 11

Fallon, Ann Marie, 307n1
Fasih, Memed, 236–37
Fanning, Patricia J., 200n6
Fansa, Mamoun, 139
Farrell, Keith, 276n14
Fauset, Jessie, 22, 37
Feisal, Emir, 139, 140, 141, 142
Fell, Alison, 37
Fengler, Maria, 273
Ferenczi, Sándor, 157
Ferré, Leo, 286
Ferguson, Niall, 56, 57,
Fernald, Anne E., 5, 7
Field, Frank, 34
Filipović, Zlata, 236
Finnan, Joseph P., 276n13
Fish (Derek William Dick), 285
Fisher, Jane Elizabeth, 9, 12, 80, 200n8
Fisher, Susan R., 227
Fitzgerald, F. Scott, 75, 76–77, 78
Flanders, Michael, 286
Foch, Ferdinand, 251, 254–56
Ford, Ford Madox, 21, 54, 159, 188, 190, 317, 318–19, 320,
Ford, Henry, 243
Forster, E. M., 39n5
Forstmann, Walther, 105
Forter, Greg, 84n1
Forty, Simon, 29
Foster, Roy, 274
Foucault, Michel, 17, 27n1
Franchot, Annie Wood, 226

Frank, Joseph, 320
Frankel, Jonathan, 119
Franks, Claudia Stillman, 182
Franz Josef I, 173, 310, 311, 315n9
Franz Ferdinand, 20, 173
Freedman, Ariela, 158
Fresnay, Pierre, 72n8
Freud, Sigmund, 26, 157
Frey, Hugo, 12, 283
Friedman, Susan Stanford, 191n1
Frisby, H. G., 189, 190
Frith, Simon, 287
Fussell, Paul, 4, 22, 41–42, 49, 54, 55, 58, 66, 84n3, 126, 189, 218, 317, 318, 319

Gal, Susan, 72n1
Galás, Diamanda, 288
Galassi, Jonathan, 319
Galway, Elizabeth A., 10
Gance, Abel, 247–48
Gandhi, Mahatma Mohandas, 131, 132
Garnett, David, 167
Garvey, Marcus, 87, 88, 90
Gass, Clare, 236
George V, 91
Géricault, Théodore, 216
Ghosh, Amitav, 137n7
Gibney, John, 276n12
Gilbert, Martin, 119, 269, 275n5
Gilbert, Sandra M., 84n1
Gilkes Romero, Juliet, 91
Gill, Douglas, 164, 167n1
Gillies, Harold, 216
Golden, Christopher, 281
Goldman, Dorothy, 34
Gough, Herbert, 71
Gough, Paul, 268
Goulding, Edmund, 231–32
Gosling, George Campbell, 3
Goya, Francisco, 217
Grabein, Paul, 105
Grabolle, Harro, 34, 35
Gramsci, Antonio, 93
Grannum, Guy, 89
Grant, Duncan, 167
Grant, Peter, 12
Grant, R. G., 164
Grant, William Wellington Wellwood, 91
Gray, Norah Neilson, 218
Grayzel, Susan, 232
Greenberg, Uri Zvi, 123
Greene, Graham, 24
Gregory, Augusta, 100
Gregory, Robert, 100
Grenfell, Julian, 189, 190
Grierson, Lee, 243
Grimm, Hans, 103
Groch-Begley, Hannah, 160
Grosz, George, 214, 217
Groves, Edith Lelean, 224, 226
Gubar, Susan, 84n1
Gurney, Ivor, 3, 4, 233, 303
Gygi, Fabio, 213, 215

Haggard, H. Rider, 281
Hainisch, Marianne, 311–12
Halberstam, Judith, 182
Hale, Edward Everett, 262
Hall, Donald E., 184n1
Hall, Radclyffe, 182
Hameiri, Avigdor, 120
Hamilton, Cecily, 23
Hämmerle, Christa, 24, 310, 315n9
Hammond, Michael, 243
Hankey, Donald, 60
Hanna, Abdallah, 36
Harcourt, Lewis, 87, 88
Harding, George Matthews, 213
Harding, Mike, 285
Hardy, Thomas, 231
Hare, Jimmy, 259
Harris, John, 268
Harrison, Charles Yale, 95, 244–47
Harshav, Benjamin, 123
Hart, Tim, 286
Harte, Liam, 274
Harvey, David, 191n3
Harvey, PJ, 286, 288–89
Harvie, Robert, 225
Harwood, H. M., 234n4
Hattaway, Judith, 34
Hayes, Clair, 224
Haytock, Jennifer, 84n1
Heaney, Seamus, 100, 239
Hegglund, Jon, 191n1
Heller, Monica, 72 (nn 1, 7)
Helmers, Marguerite, 10
Hemingway, Ernest, 3, 54, 57, 58, 66, 67, 75, 82–84, 263
Herman, Judith, 154

Higgins, Michael D., 274
Higonnet, Margaret, 9, 34, 35, 159, 218, 236
Higonnet, Patrice, 236
Hilborn, Stan, 287
Hill, Robert A., 224
Hitler, Adolf, 107, 108, 170
Hochschild, Adam, 56, 167, 200n1, 278
Hoecker, Paul, 105
Hoffmann, Detlef, 139
Hoffmann, E. T. A., 21
Homer, 21
Honigsbaum, Mark, 200n6
Hope, Ascott, 226
Horgan, John, 26
Houlbrook, Matt, 182
Hourani, Albert, 149
Howard, Walter, 234n4
Howarth, William L., 141
Howe, Glenford D., 88
Hubel, Teresa, 72n10
Hueffer, Ford Madox. *See* Ford Madox Ford
Hueppauf, Bernd, 106
Hughes, Ted, 12, 268
Hulme, T. E., 188
Hulse, Michael, 275n1
Hunt, Nigel, 240
Hunt, Violet, 21
Hussein bin Ali, 140
Hutchcroft, Anthony, 287
Hynes, Samuel, 3, 42, 54, 55, 186, 275n2, 319

Islam, Kazi Nazrul, 131

Jacobson, John, 287
Jacquet, Eugene, 253
Jagose, Annamarie, 184n1
Jahan, Sultan Kaikhusrau, 35
James, C. L. R., 90
James, Henry, 176n3
James, Pearl, 7, 76, 295
James, William, 19
Janco, Marcel, 217
Japrisot, Sebastian, 12, 21, 275n1
Jeanne d'Arc (Joan of Arc), 70, 254
Jeffery, Keith, 29, 38n2, 266
Jenkins, Elinor, 57
Jesse, F. Tennyson, 234n4
John, Gwen, 232
Johnson, Fenton, 89–90
Johnston, Wayne, 96
Jones, David, 54, 187, 190
Jones, Heather, 37
Jones, John Paul, 321
Jones, Nigel, 268
Jouve, Pierre Jean, 115, 116
Joyce, James, 41, 42, 55
Joyet, Bernard, 285
Judge, Jack, 271
Jünger, Ernst, 8, 35, 55, 60, 61, 103, 127, 288, 314n6, 317, 318

Kahn, Elizabeth, 216
Kamara, Kande, 35–36
Kant, Immanuel, 319
Kaplan, Laurie, 159
Kaufmann, Fritz, 156
Keegan, John, 192n6, 266, 275n5
Keene, Jennifer D., 79, 295
Kelly, Jean, 236
Kendall, Tim, 9, 59
Keneally, Thomas, 275n1
Khoury, Dina Rizk, 36
Khvatov, Dennis, 287
Killingray, David, 193, 194, 195, 200n7
Kipling, Rudyard, 33, 60, 127, 134, 223, 232, 321
Kirchner, Ernst Ludwig, 217
Kitchener, Horatio Herbert, 272
Klausner, Joseph, 123
Klaeber, Kurt, 108
Klein, Holger, 34, 121
Klemm, Wilhelm, 57
Klay, Phil, 239
Kolata, Gina, 194
Koller, Christian, 30, 36, 38n2
Kollwitz, Käthe, 314n5
Krafft-Ebing, Richard von, 179
Kramer, Alan, 7–8
Kubrick, Stanley, 27n5

LaCapra, Dominick, 276n10
Ladd, Anna Coleman, 216
La Motte, Ellen, 67, 72n6
Lange, Karl, 109n3
Laqueur, Thomas W., 267
Larabee, Mark, 12
Larès, Maurice, 140
Lawrence, D. H., 41, 176n3

Lawrence, T. E., 138–43, 144, 284
Lawson, Henry, 97
Lean, David, 143
Ledwidge, Francis, 100–01
Lee, Hermione, 124n1
Leed, Eric, 156
Leese, Peter, 158
Lefebvre, Henri, 185, 191n3
Léger, Fernand, 218
Leighton, Roland, 235
Leivick, Halpern, 123
Lerner, Paul, 155, 156, 158
Lersch, Heinrich, 103
Lessing, Gotthold, 320
Lewis, Wyndham, 188
Leyeles, Aaron, 123
Leys, Ruth, 154
Limon, John, 84n1
Lincoln, Abraham, 20
Lind, Francis, 96
Linge, Ken, 267, 275n7
Linge, Pam, 267, 275n7
Little Tich (Harry Relph), 231
Littlewood, Joan, 229
Liulevcius, Vejas, 106
Lloyd, David, 250
Lloyd-George, David, 3
Longinus, 319
Locke, Alain, 86
Loew, Camilla, 205
Long, P. W., 37
Longley, Edna, 275n2
Löschnigg, Martin, 275n3
Loughran, Tracey, 154
Loy, Mina, 57
Lubow, Arthur, 259, 263
Lucas, E. V., 226
Lunn, Joe, 22, 31, 32, 35–36
Lussu, Emilio, 317, 318
Lutyens, Edwin, 267, 268
Lyon, Janet, 176n2

Macaulay, Thomas, 125
MacDermot, Thomas, 87
Macdonald, Lyn, 268
MacGill, Patrick, 60
Mack, John, 143
MacKenzie, John M., 223
Macleish, Archibald, 57
Mahfouz, Naguib, 144–46, 147, 149n2
Malherbe, Henry, 112
Major, Kevin, 96
Malleson, Miles, 233
Malory, Thomas, 141
Malouf, David, 98–99
Mandelstam, Osip, 57
Mann, Susan, 236
Manning, Frederic, 34, 97–98, 288
Mansfield, Katherine, 23, 34
Manzi, Angelo, 72n3
March, William, 75, 79
Marcus, Jane, 159
Marcus, Sharon, 180
Marinetti, F. T., 57, 170–72, 175
Markish, Peretz, 123
Markowits, Claude, 32
Marshall, Austin John, 289n2
Marshik, Celia, 10, 12
Marsland, Elizabeth, 34
Martin, Amaya, 9
Martin, J. R., 309
Martinet, Marcel, 115, 116
Matthews, Harley, 98
Maunder, Andrew, 12, 233
Maxim, Hiram H., 314n1
Maxim, Hiram S., 209
Maxwell, William, 197
May, Mabel, 218
Mayran, Camille, 114
Mboup, Demba, 22
McCarthy, Mark, 274
McCartney, Paul, 284
McCay, Winsor, 162
McCormack, John, 271
McCrae, John, 226, 287
McCutcheon , John, 259, 261, 262–63
McDonald, Country Joe, 287
McKay, Claude, 21, 78–79
McLary, Laura, 12
McLean, Don, 285
McLoughlin, Noah, 72n7
McNulty, Eugene, 274
Mead, Margaret, 26
Meinertzhagen, Richard, 142
Meloy, Colin, 288
Mencken, H. L., 80
Mew, Charlotte, 11, 305
Middlebrook, Martin, 275n5
Mignola, Mike, 281
Milestone, Lewis, 52, 58, 245

Miller, Gary, 286
Mills, C. Wright, 27n1
Mills, Pat, 282
Mir, Farina, 129
Missoffe, Mathieu, 281
Mitchell, W. J. T., 320
Mjagki, Nina, 29
Montague, C. E., 319, 320
Montale, Eugenio, 317, 318, 319
Moore, Alan, 281
Moore, Christopher, 268
Morel, E. D., 50n3
Morens, David M., 200nn1–2
Morgan, Harry, 87
Morgenstern, Christian, 108
Morpugo, Michael, 1
Morris, William, 141
Morrison, Rob, 279, 280
Morrison, Toni, 22
Morrow, John H., 29, 58
Morsey, Konrad, 140
Morsi, Mohamed, 146
Morton, Frederick, 230
Mosse, George, 53, 54–55, 60, 62
Mousa, Suleiman, 140
Mott, Frederick, 155
Mountain Horse, Mike, 127
Mubarak, Hosni, 146
Mueller, Hans-Harold, 106
Muenchhausen, Boerries von, 103
Mukherji (Mukherjee), Kalyan Kumar, 32, 130
Mullen, John, 230
Murphy, Seamus, 288–89
Mussolini, Benito, 170, 172, 175, 175n1, 255
Myers, Charles S., 154, 157

Naidu, Sarojini, 32, 35, 132–33
Nash, John, 321
Nash, Paul, 52, 57, 213, 214, 218, 321
Nasser, Gamel Abdel, 146
Natter, Wolfgang, 103, 104, 106
Neiberg, Michael, 18, 19, 21, 27n4
Nelson, Robert, 104
Nicholson, G. W. L., 246
Nevinson, C. R. W., 215, 320, 321
Nicholson-Smith, Donald, 191n3
Nicolson, Juliet, 27n7
Noakes, Vivien, 10
Noailles, Anna de, 113
Nora, Pierre, 33
Norris, John, 314n1
Norris, Margot, 8
Nunnery, Katie, 73n13

Oates, Laurence, 231
O'Brien, Amber, 241n2
O'Brien, Tim, 217–18
O'Neil, Kevin, 281
Omissi, David, 31, 32, 33, 61, 73n14, 128, 137n4
Opdycke, Sandra, 200n6
Oppenheim, Hermann, 155
Orlando, Vittorio, 170
Orr, Emily, 165
Orton, George, 226
Orwell, George, 219
O'Toole, Peter, 143
Ouditt, Sharon, 182, 233
Outka, Elizabeth, 7, 12
Owen, Susan, 243, 320
Owen, Wilfred, 3, 18, 51, 54, 57, 59, 77, 126, 127, 133, 135, 162, 163, 215–16, 219, 226, 229, 233, 235, 239, 243, 246, 287, 307, 320

Pabst, G. W, 58
Paget, Stephen, 223
Palmer, Roy, 59
Palmer, Svetlana, 236, 237
Paris, Michael, 227
Patch, Henry John, 270
Paterson, Andrew Barton "Banjo," 289n2
Pear, T. H., 158
Pearse, Pádraig (Patrick) H., 90, 272
Péguy, Charles, 20
Pennell, Catriona, 18
Pericles, 92, 111
Perloff, Marjorie, 176n1
Peters, Ada, 23
Peters, Ethel, 23
Petrone, Karen, 6
Phillips, Howard, 193, 194, 195, 200n7
Phillips, John, 231
Phillips, William Raglan, 87
Pichel, Beatriz, 6
Pier, Arthur Standwood, 226
Plueschow, Gunther, 104
Porter, Katherine Anne, 80, 82, 83, 196, 197

Pope, Daniel, 202
Pound, Ezra, 41, 44, 45–46, 57
Prior, Maddy, 286
Proctor, Tammy, 254
Prosser, Jay, 182
Prost, Antoine, 250
Proust, Marcel, 176n3
Propertius, Sextus, 50n4

Raemaekers, Louis, 162
Rahman, Abdul, 129
Rai, Jasbahadur, 130, 137n6
Ramsey, Paul, 27n2
Rawlinson, Mark, 276n9
Rawls, John, 45
Réal del Sarte, Maxime, 253
Rechter, David, 119
Redmond, John, 272, 276n13
Reilly, Catherine W., 59
Reinharz, Juhuda, 119
Remarque, Erich Maria, 3, 8, 52, 54, 66, 67, 95, 103, 106, 109, 116, 136, 159, 162, 163, 170, 188, 244, 245, 247, 310
Renn, Ludwig, 107, 108
Renoir, Jean, 8, 67–68, 72n8
Reynès-Monlaur, Marie, 114
Reynolds, Kimberley, 227
Richthofen, Manfred von, 104, 105
Ringuet (Philippe Panneton), 95
Rivers, W. H. R., 61, 156–58
Roberts, Charles G. D., 94
Roberts, David, 219
Roberts, Frederick, 70
Roberts, Mary Louise, 254
Robinett, Jane, 159
Robson, Stuart, 163
Rolland, Romain, 114–15
Rolls, S. C., 138, 139, 141
Roosevelt, Theodore, 259
Rosselson, Leon, 286
Rosenberg, Isaac, 52, 54, 59, 229, 239
Roskies, David, 124n3
Ross, Derek, 230–31
Rossa, O'Donovan, 90
Rossetti, Christina, 141
Rossetti, Dante Gabriel, 141
Roth, Joseph, 123
Russell, Bertrand, 166
Russner, Käthe, 236
Ruthven, K. K., 50n4
Ryshina-Pankova, Marianna, 308

Sáenz, José de la Luz, 38n4
Saint-Amour, Paul K., 19
Sacco, Joe, 275n5, 278–79, 280
Sacré, Sergerémy, 287
Sammons, Jeffrey T., 58
Sandburg, Carl, 57
Sarbadhikari, Sisir Prasad, 32, 130
Sargent, John Singer, 193, 200n3
Sassoon, Siegfried, 6, 38, 42, 54, 57, 59, 62, 95, 126, 127, 140, 157, 163, 165, 167, 182, 183, 189, 219, 229, 230, 239, 287, 305
Saunders, Max, 124n2
Sauret, Henriette, 115
Sayers, Dorothy, 158
Scarry, Elaine, 26, 239–40
Schaller, Charlotte, 226
Schiele, Egon, 314nn4–5
Schlieffen, Alfred von, 19, 26, 191–92n6
Schneider, Mark Robert, 84n2
Scholes, Robert, 264n2
Schwarz, Wilhelm, 8
Scott, Kathleen, 216
Scott, Robert Falcon, 231
Scranton, Roy, 59
Sebald, W. G., 275n1
Sedgwick, Eve Kosofky, 183
Selassie, Haile, 91
Self, Will, 165
Selzer, Mark, 218
Sen, Amartya, 125
Sen, "Jon," 125, 136n1
Service, Robert W., 95–96, 287
Shakespeare, William, 231, 317
Shamsie, Kamila, 136
Shannon, Brent, 202
Shavit, Yaacov, 119
Shaw, George Bernard, 230
Sheffield, Gary [G. D.], 55, 57
Shelton, Matthew, 71, 73n16
Shephard, Ben, 155
Shepherd, William G., 259, 261–62, 263
Sheriff, R. C., 229
Sherman, Daniel J., 250
Sherry, Vincent, 9, 11, 49n1, 84n3
Sherwood, Margaret, 60
Shirley, Edward, 224
Showalter, Elaine, 156

Silkin, Jon, 57, 125
Sillitoe, Alan, 268
Sinclair, May, 167
Singer, Isaac Bashevis, 123
Singh, Amar, 32
Singh, Santa, 129
Singh, Sohan, 129
Shoebridge, Tim, 29
Smith, Alison, 67, 72 (nn 1, 7)
Smith, G. Elliot, 158
Smith, Helen Zenna, 158, 162, 182
Smith, Laurajane, 265
Smith, Leonard V., 11
Smith, Richard, 9, 36, 88, 92
Smith, Sidonie, 239, 240
Smythe, Caroll, 226
Solzhenitsyn, Aleksandr, 275n1
Sommer, Doris, 68
Sontag, Susan, 26
Sorum, Eve, 7
Soulacroix, Thérèse, 38
Southard, E. E., 158
Spencer, Stanley, 321
Spiegelman, Art, 281–82
Spivak, Gyatri, 125, 130
Stamp, Gavin, 275n6
Stein, Gertrude, 67
Steiner, Wendy, 320
Stenbeck, Ben, 281
Stephen, Leslie, 47, 48
Strachey, Lytton, 167
Stramm, August, 57
Strang, Herbert, 223
Stravinsky, Igor, 176n3
Strychacz, Thomas F., 84n1
Stryker, Susan, 182
Styles, Leslie, 228–29
Svarnakumari Devi, 69, 132

Tabor, June, 284
Tagore, Rabindranath, 69, 132, 133–34
Tal, Kali, 239, 240
Tardi, Jacques, 280–81
Tate, Trudi, 49n1
Taubenberger, Jeffery K., 200nn1–2
Taylor, Barry, 287
Taylor, Martin, 197
Taymur, Mahmud, 145
Tchernichowsky, Shaul, 122–23
Tennyson, Alfred, 20, 133
Thacker, Andrew, 191n1
Theweleit, Klaus, 7, 53, 55
Thomas, Berte, 229, 232, 234n1
Thomas, Edward, 20, 214
Thomas, Gregory M., 155, 156, 158
Thomas, Lowell, 140
Thompson, Gordon V., 74
Thompson, Richard, 286
Thomson, Alistair, 269, 275n8
Thursfield, Amanda, 268
Thurston, Ernest Temple, 233
Tilley, Alexander, 287
Tonks, Henry, 216
Trakl, Georg, 57, 317, 319
Travers, Tim, 57
Trout, Steven, 84n1
Trulin, Léon, 252
Tsvetayeva, Marina, 57
Tuchman, Barbara, 19
Tylee, Claire, 234n4
Tynan, Katherine, 232
Tzara, Tristan, 57

Ungar, Gladys, 229
Ungaretti, Giuseppe, 317, 318, 319
Urban, Charles, 242, 245, 247

Vandercook, Margaret, 225
Vandermeulen, David, 279
Varley, Fred, 321
Vernon, Alex, 84n1
Vidor, King, 58
Viebeg, Clara, 6
Vildrac, Charles, 115
Virilio, Paul, 24, 25, 26
Vittorio Emanuel II, 173, 175
Vittorio Emanuel III, 175
Vogel, Bruno, 107–08
Voigt, Ellen Bryant, 197–98
Vonnegut, Kurt, 275n1

Waison, L. P., 91
Wallis, Sarah, 236, 237
Walzer, Michael, 26
Washington, Booker T., 87
Waterman, David, 270
Watson, Julia, 239, 240
Weber, Fritz, 314n6
Weber, Max, 27n1
Weeks, Jeffrey, 179, 180
Wehner, Josef Magnus, 103, 108–09
Weir, Peter, 21

Weisbord, Robert G., 91
Weisstein, Ulrich, 320
Weizmann, Chaim, 139
Wellington, Arthur Wellesley, duke of, 242
Wells, H. G., 181, 281
Wentworth, Marion Craig, 234n4
West, Rebecca, 6, 20, 54, 60, 160, 169, 317, 319
Whalan, Mark, 37, 84n2
White, Canaan, 279
Whitehead, Anne, 270
Whitman, Walt, 131
Whitworth, Geoffrey, 222
Widdowson, Peter, 263
Willets, H. T., 275n1
Willetts, Karl, 287, 288
Williams, Chad, 84n2
Williams, David, 12, 242, 248
Williams, Harry, 271
Williams, R. James, 222
Wilson, Jeremy, 140, 141
Wilson, Ross J., 265, 283n2
Wilson, Woodrow, 86, 174
Winkiel, Laura, 191n1
Winter, Jay, 11, 33, 34, 56, 84n3, 154, 267
Wollaeger, Mark, 10, 56
Wood, Francis Derwent, 216
Woolf, Virginia, 4, 25, 26, 41, 44, 47–49, 54, 61, 75, 134, 158, 160, 166, 196–97, 295, 296, 304, 307, 319
Woolley, C. Leonard, 139
Wortabet, Edla, 37
Worth, Paul W., 271
Wulfman, Clifford, 264n2

Yealland, Lewis, 156–57, 158
Yeats, W. B., 41, 59, 93, 99–100, 164–65
Yelvington, Kevin A., 91
Yoe, Craig, 162, 165
Young, Winifred, 159
Yver, Colette, 112

Zaghlul, Saad, 145
Zamora, Emilio, 38n4